SEVEN SEAS ENTERTAINMENT PRESENTS

Miss Kobayashi's Dragon Maid

vo

story and art by coolky

TRANSLATION
Jenny McKeon

ADAPTATION
Shanti Whitesides

LETTERING
Jennifer Skarupa

LOGO DESIGN
KC Fabellon

COVER DESIGN
Nicky Lim

PROOFREADING
Stephanie Cohen

PRODUCTION MANAGER
Lissa Pattillo

MANAGING EDITOR
Julie Davis

EDITOR-IN-CHIEF
Adam Arnold

PUBLISHER
Jason DeAngelis

MISS KOBAYASHI'S DRAGON MAID VOL. 8

First published in Japan in 2019 by Futabasha Publishers Ltd., Tokyo.
English version published by Seven Seas Entertainment.
Under license from Futabasha Publishers Ltd.

Seven Seas press and purchase enquiries can be sent to Marketing Manager Lianne Sentar at press@gomanga.com. Information regarding the distribution and purchase of digital editions is available from Digital Manager CK Russell at digital@gomanga.com.

ISBN: 978-1-626929-94-4

Printed in Canada

First Printing: July 2019

10 9 8 7 6 5 4 3 2 1

FOLLOW US ONLINE: ***www.sevenseasentertainment.com***

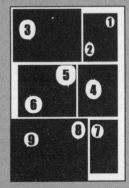

READING DIRECTIONS

This book reads from ***right to left***, Japanese style. If this is your first time reading manga, you start reading from the top right panel on each page and take it from there. If you get lost, just follow the numbered diagram here. It may seem backwards at first, but you'll get the hang of it! Have fun!!

1
2
3
4
5
6
7
8
9

Experience all that SEVEN SEAS has to offer!

Visit us online and follow us on Twitter!
SEVENSEASENTERTAINMENT.COM
TWITTER.COM/GOMANGA

Miss Kobayashi's DRAGON MAID

8

story & art by
coolkyousinnjya

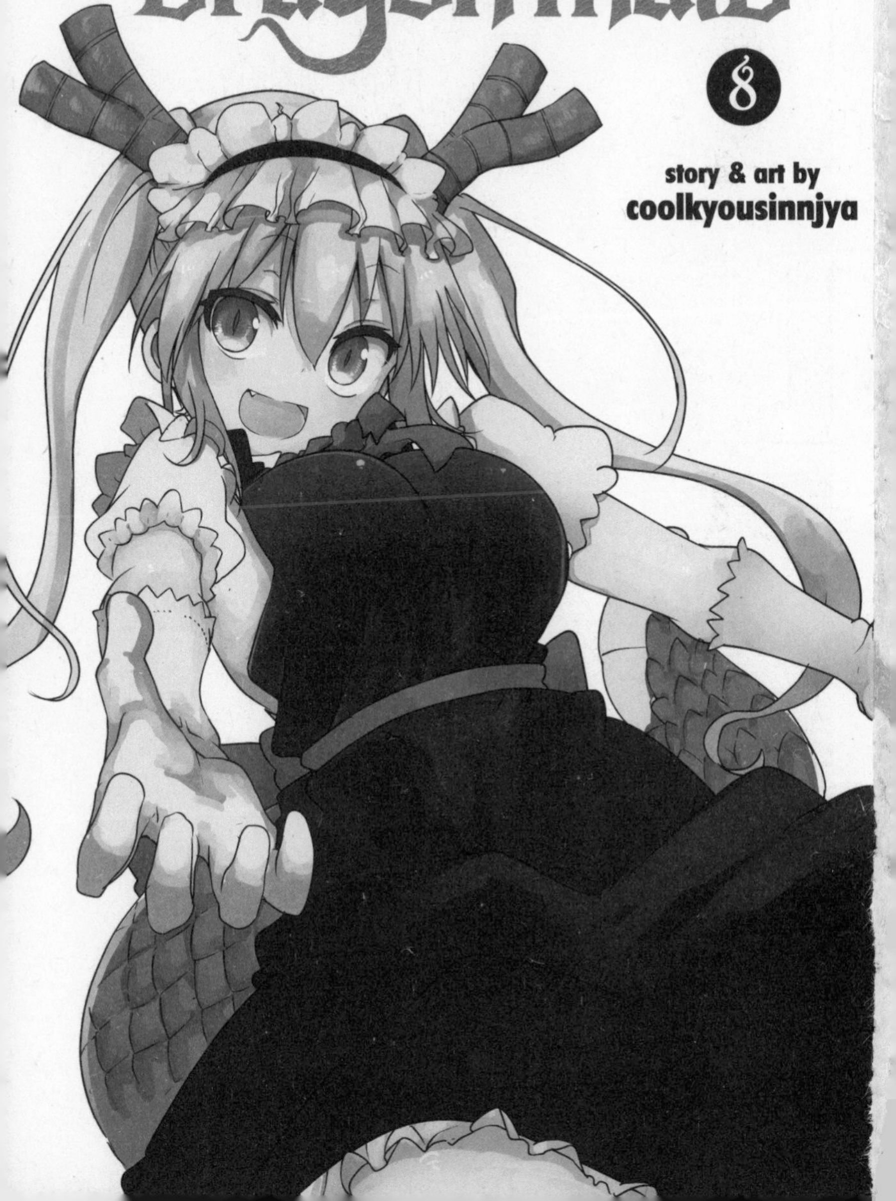

Miss Kobayashi's
Dragon Maid

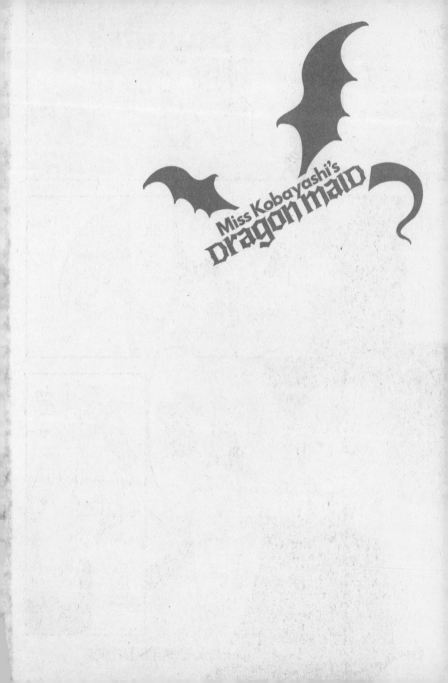

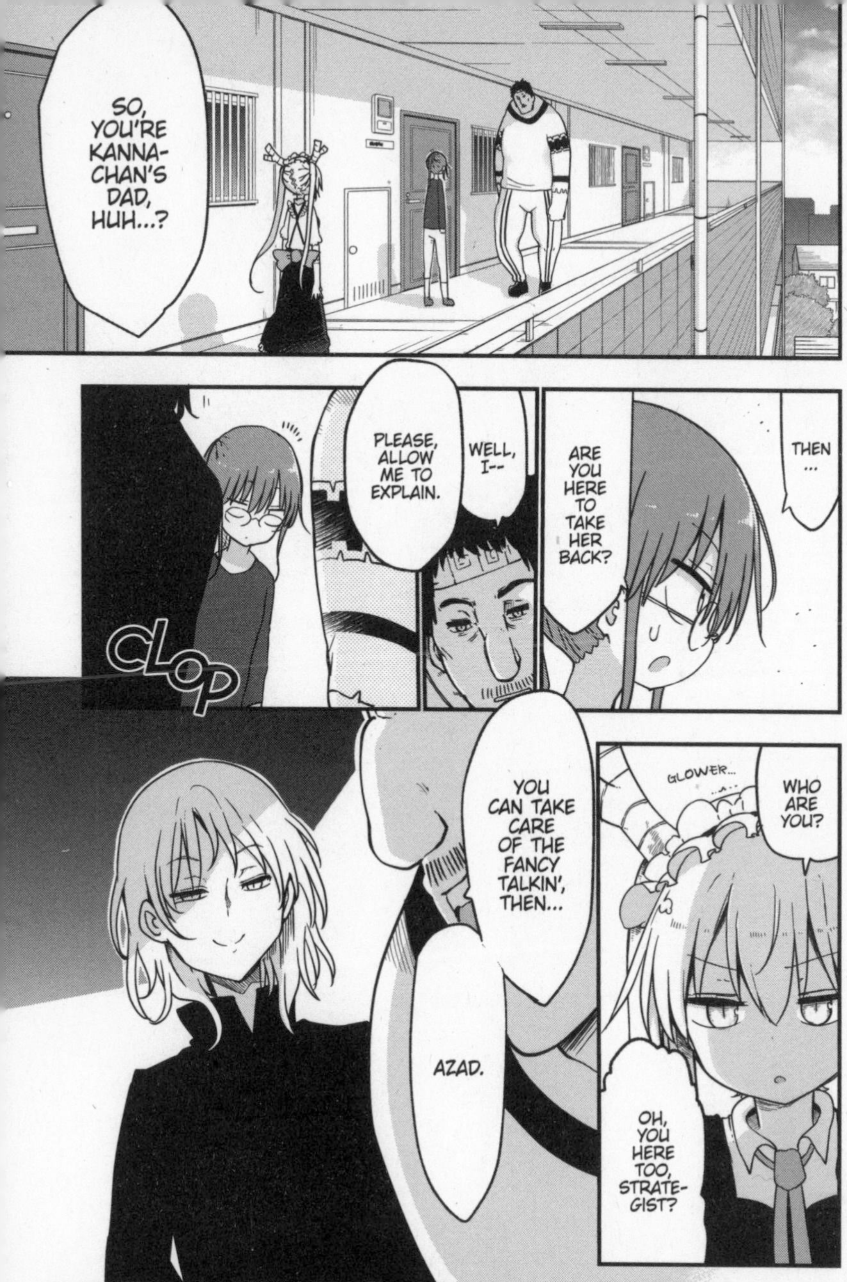
SO, YOU'RE KANNA-CHAN'S DAD, HUH...?
THEN ...
ARE YOU HERE TO TAKE HER BACK?
WELL, I--
PLEASE, ALLOW ME TO EXPLAIN.
CLOP
GLOWER...
WHO ARE YOU?
OH, YOU HERE TOO, STRATEGIST?
YOU CAN TAKE CARE OF THE FANCY TALKIN', THEN...
AZAD.

CHAPTER 69: KOBAYASHI AND KANNA'S FATHER

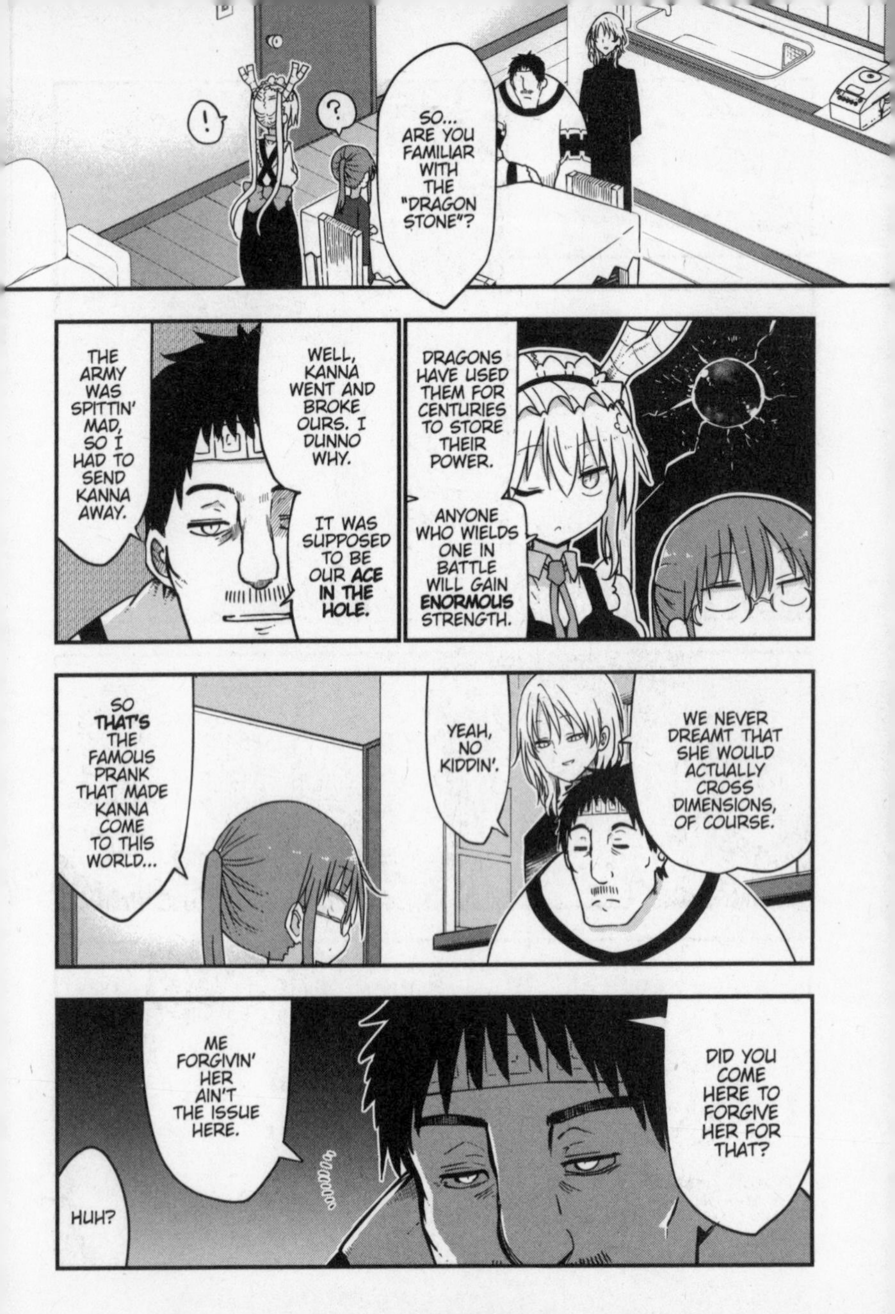
SO... ARE YOU FAMILIAR WITH THE "DRAGON STONE"?
?
!
DRAGONS HAVE USED THEM FOR CENTURIES TO STORE THEIR POWER.
ANYONE WHO WIELDS ONE IN BATTLE WILL GAIN **ENORMOUS** STRENGTH.
WELL, KANNA WENT AND BROKE OURS. I DUNNO WHY.
IT WAS SUPPOSED TO BE OUR **ACE IN THE HOLE.**
THE ARMY WAS SPITTIN' MAD, SO I HAD TO SEND KANNA AWAY.
WE NEVER DREAMT THAT SHE WOULD ACTUALLY CROSS DIMENSIONS, OF COURSE.
YEAH, NO KIDDIN'.
SO **THAT'S** THE FAMOUS PRANK THAT MADE KANNA COME TO THIS WORLD...
DID YOU COME HERE TO FORGIVE HER FOR THAT?
ME FORGIVIN' HER AIN'T THE ISSUE HERE.
HUH?

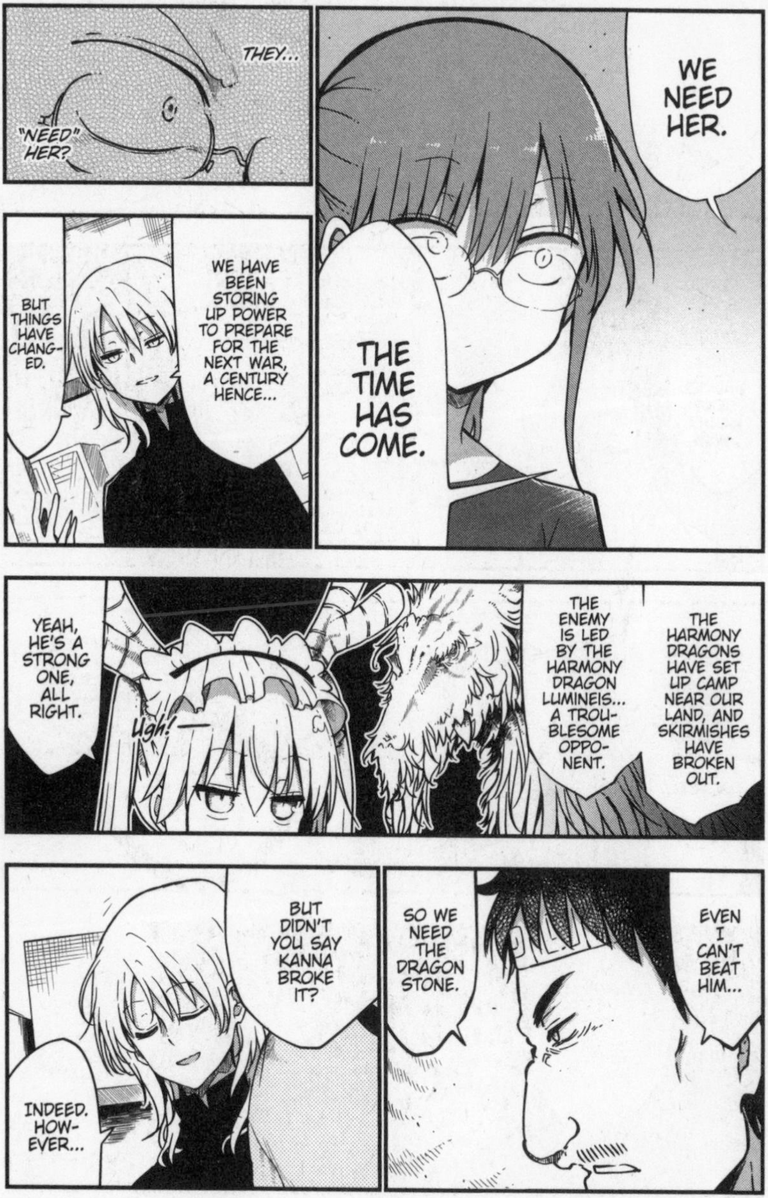
WE NEED HER.
THE TIME HAS COME.
THEY...
"NEED" HER?
WE HAVE BEEN STORING UP POWER TO PREPARE FOR THE NEXT WAR, A CENTURY HENCE...
BUT THINGS HAVE CHANG-ED.
THE HARMONY DRAGONS HAVE SET UP CAMP NEAR OUR LAND, AND SKIRMISHES HAVE BROKEN OUT.
THE ENEMY IS LED BY THE HARMONY DRAGON LUMINEIS... A TROU-BLESOME OPPO-NENT.
Ugh!
YEAH, HE'S A STRONG ONE, ALL RIGHT.
EVEN I CAN'T BEAT HIM...
SO WE NEED THE DRAGON STONE.
BUT DIDN'T YOU SAY KANNA BROKE IT?
INDEED. HOW-EVER...

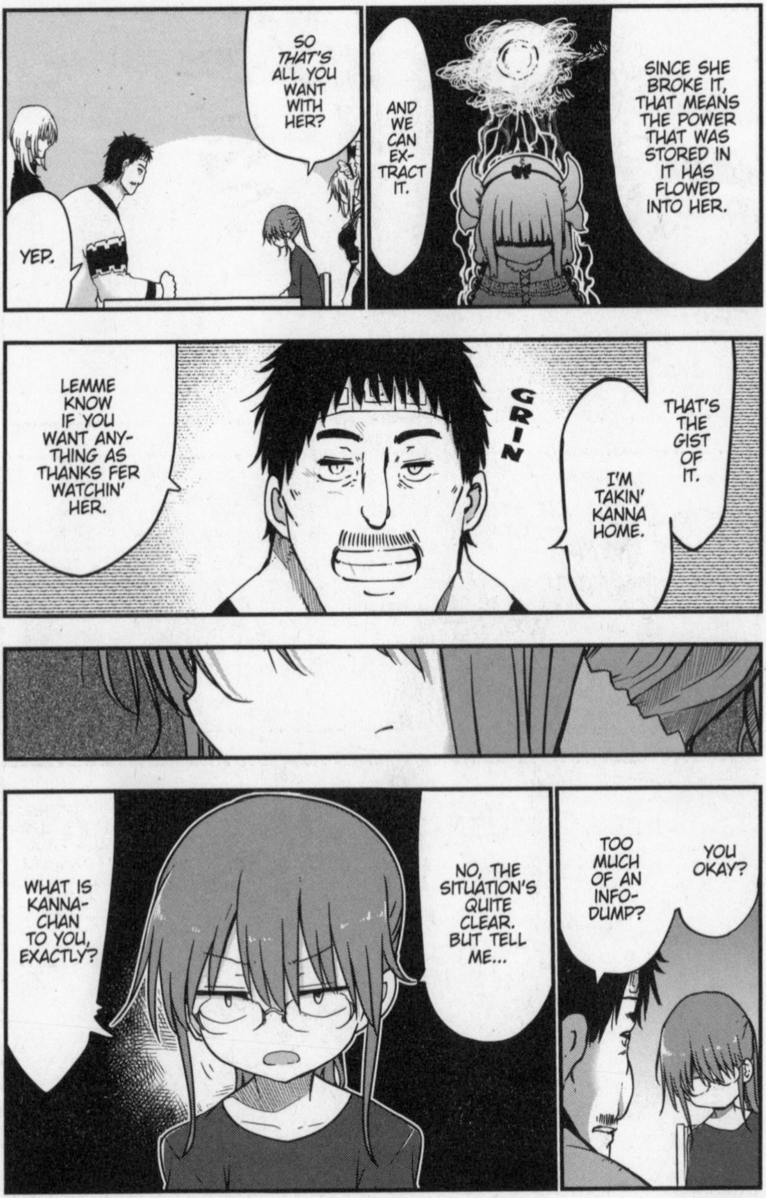
SINCE SHE BROKE IT, THAT MEANS THE POWER THAT WAS STORED IN IT HAS FLOWED INTO HER.
AND WE CAN EX-TRACT IT.
SO *THAT'S* ALL YOU WANT WITH HER?
YEP.
THAT'S THE GIST OF IT.
I'M TAKIN' KANNA HOME.
GRIN
LEMME KNOW IF YOU WANT ANY-THING AS THANKS FER WATCHIN' HER.
YOU OKAY?
TOO MUCH OF AN INFO-DUMP?
NO, THE SITUATION'S QUITE CLEAR. BUT TELL ME...
WHAT IS KANNA-CHAN TO YOU, EXACTLY?

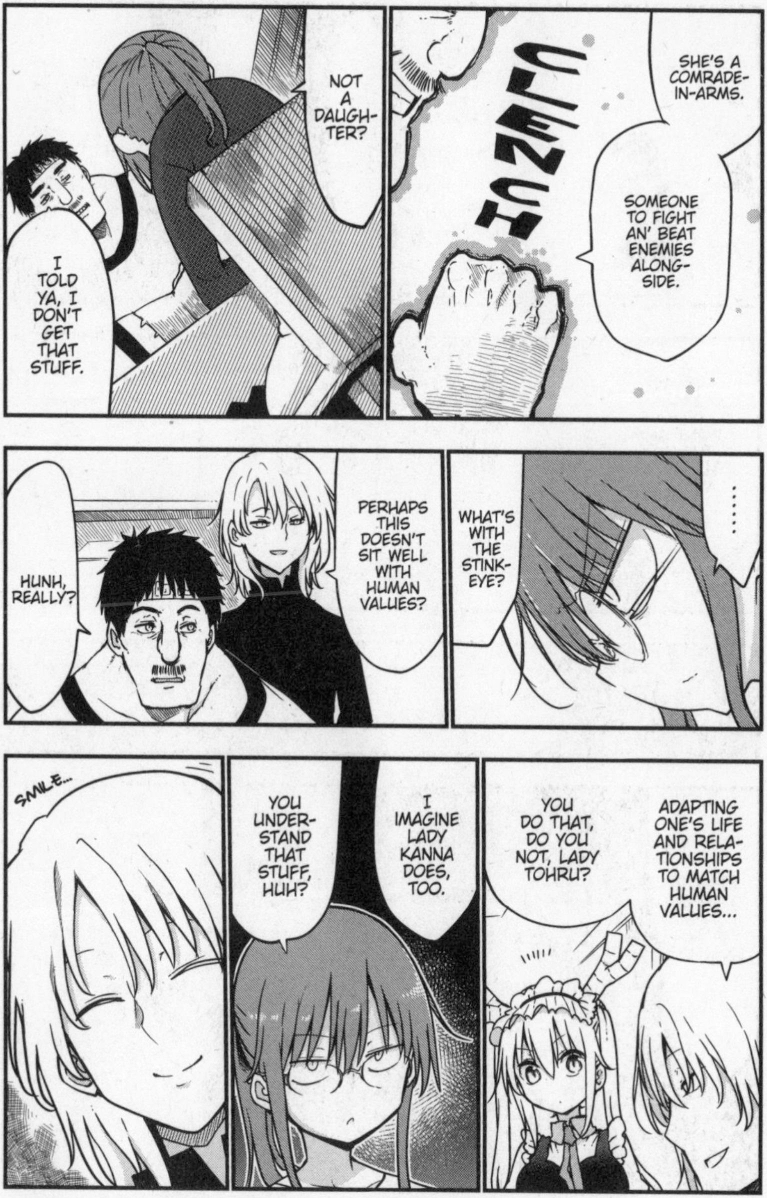
SHE'S A COMRADE-IN-ARMS.
SOMEONE TO FIGHT AN' BEAT ENEMIES ALONGSIDE.
CLENCH
NOT A DAUGHTER?
I TOLD YA, I DON'T GET THAT STUFF.
......
WHAT'S WITH THE STINK-EYE?
PERHAPS THIS DOESN'T SIT WELL WITH HUMAN VALUES?
HUNH, REALLY?
ADAPTING ONE'S LIFE AND RELATIONSHIPS TO MATCH HUMAN VALUES...
YOU DO THAT, DO YOU NOT, LADY TOHRU?
I IMAGINE LADY KANNA DOES, TOO.
YOU UNDERSTAND THAT STUFF, HUH?
SMILE...

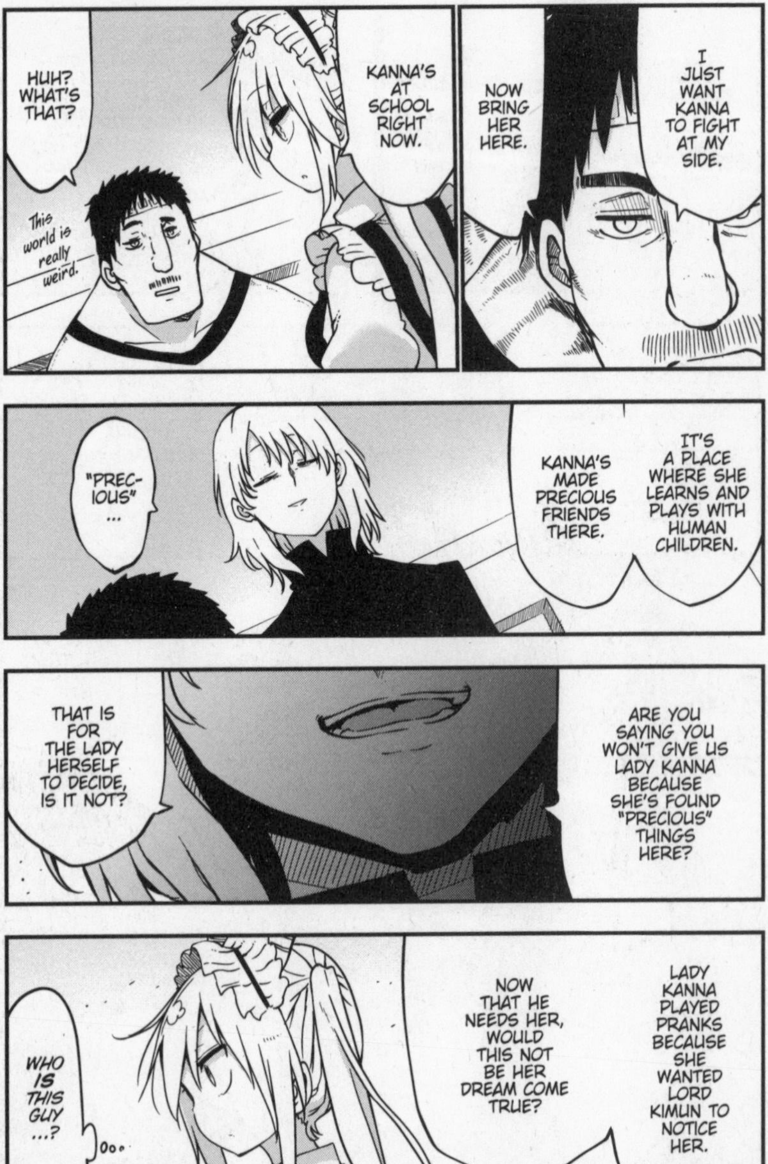
I JUST WANT KANNA TO FIGHT AT MY SIDE.
NOW BRING HER HERE.
KANNA'S AT SCHOOL RIGHT NOW.
HUH? WHAT'S THAT?
This world is really weird.
IT'S A PLACE WHERE SHE LEARNS AND PLAYS WITH HUMAN CHILDREN.
KANNA'S MADE PRECIOUS FRIENDS THERE.
"PREC-IOUS"...
ARE YOU SAYING YOU WON'T GIVE US LADY KANNA BECAUSE SHE'S FOUND "PRECIOUS" THINGS HERE?
THAT IS FOR THE LADY HERSELF TO DECIDE, IS IT NOT?
LADY KANNA PLAYED PRANKS BECAUSE SHE WANTED LORD KIMUN TO NOTICE HER.
NOW THAT HE NEEDS HER, WOULD THIS NOT BE HER DREAM COME TRUE?
WHO IS THIS GUY...?

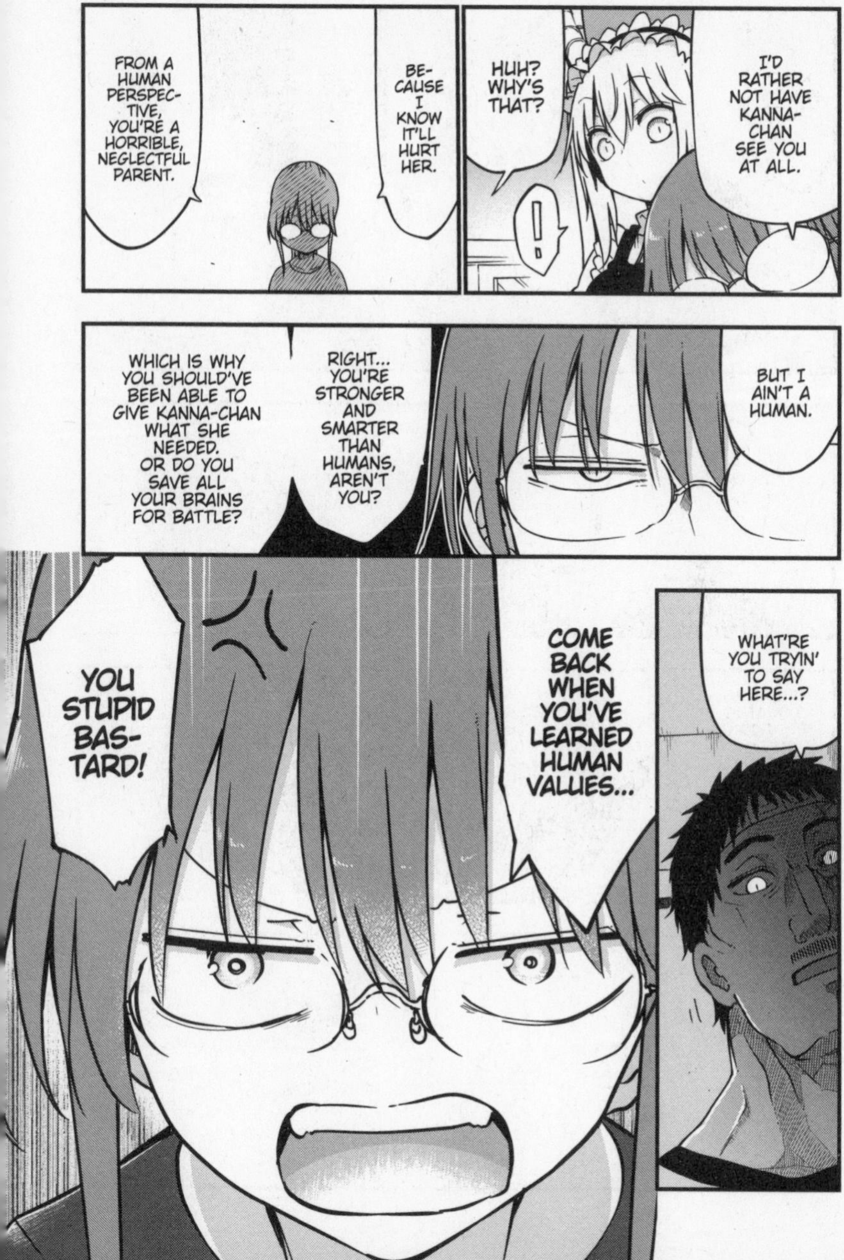
I'D RATHER NOT HAVE KANNA-CHAN SEE YOU AT ALL.
HUH? WHY'S THAT?
!
BE-CAUSE I KNOW IT'LL HURT HER.
FROM A HUMAN PERSPEC-TIVE, YOU'RE A HORRIBLE, NEGLECTFUL PARENT.
BUT I AIN'T A HUMAN.
RIGHT... YOU'RE STRONGER AND SMARTER THAN HUMANS, AREN'T YOU?
WHICH IS WHY YOU SHOULD'VE BEEN ABLE TO GIVE KANNA-CHAN WHAT SHE NEEDED. OR DO YOU SAVE ALL YOUR BRAINS FOR BATTLE?
WHAT'RE YOU TRYIN' TO SAY HERE...?
COME BACK WHEN YOU'VE LEARNED HUMAN VALUES...
YOU STUPID BAS-TARD!

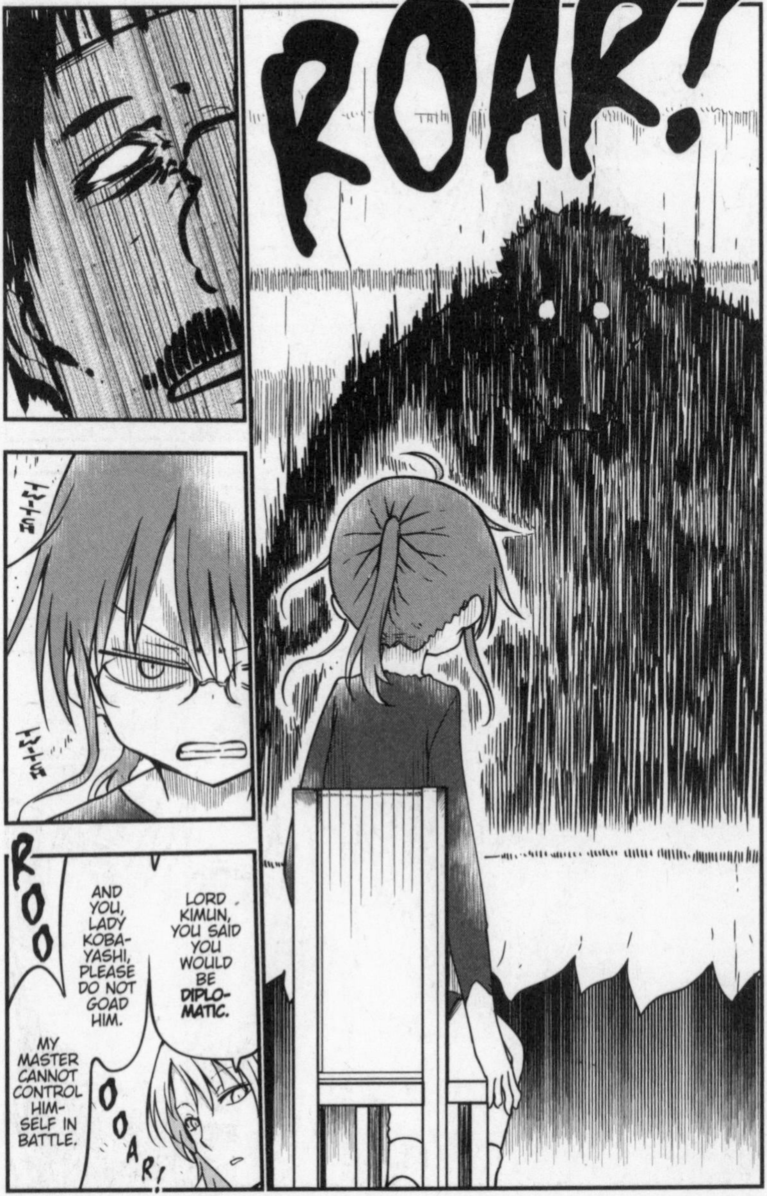
ROAR!
TWITCH
TWITCH
LORD KIMUN, YOU SAID YOU WOULD BE **DIPLOMATIC.**
AND YOU, LADY KOBAYASHI, PLEASE DO NOT GOAD HIM.
MY MASTER CANNOT CONTROL HIMSELF IN BATTLE.
ROOOOAR!

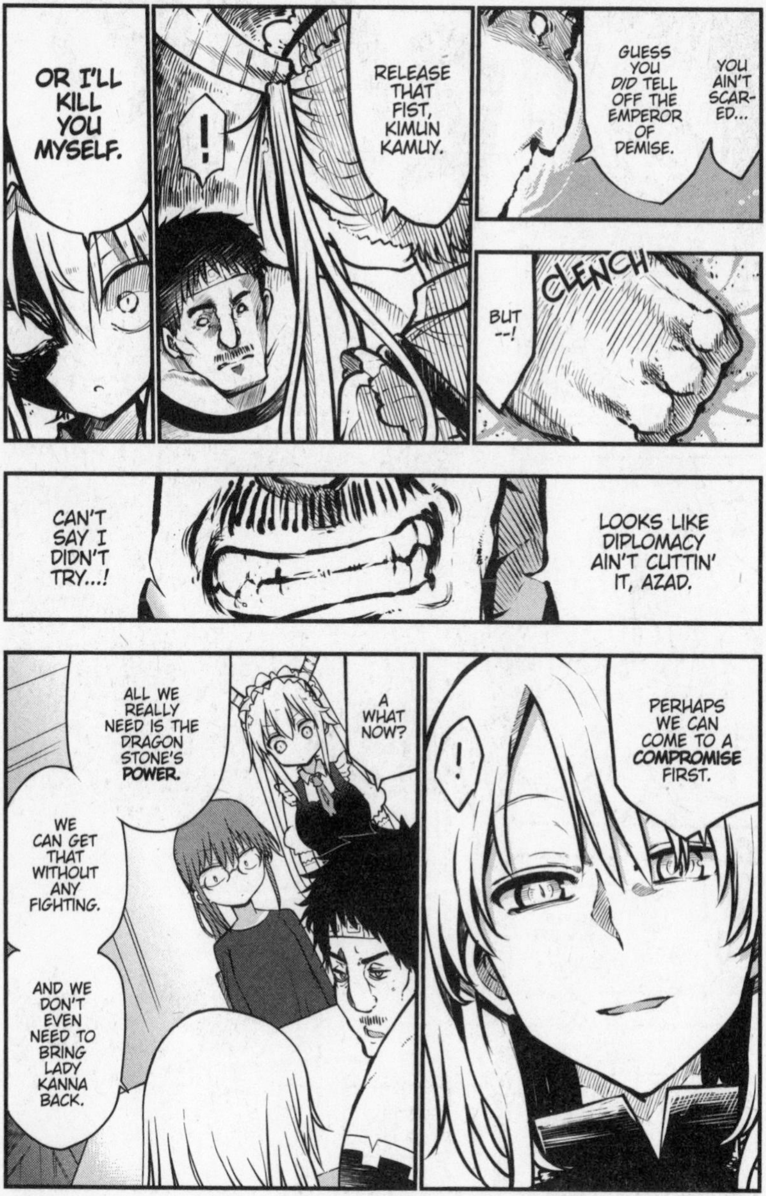
YOU AIN'T SCARED...
GUESS YOU *DID* TELL OFF THE EMPEROR OF DEMISE.
CLENCH
BUT --!
RELEASE THAT FIST, KIMUN KAMUY.
!
OR I'LL KILL YOU MYSELF.
LOOKS LIKE DIPLOMACY AIN'T CUTTIN' IT, AZAD.
CAN'T SAY I DIDN'T TRY...!
PERHAPS WE CAN COME TO A **COMPROMISE** FIRST.
!
A WHAT NOW?
ALL WE REALLY NEED IS THE DRAGON STONE'S **POWER.**
WE CAN GET THAT WITHOUT ANY FIGHTING.
AND WE DON'T EVEN NEED TO BRING LADY KANNA BACK.

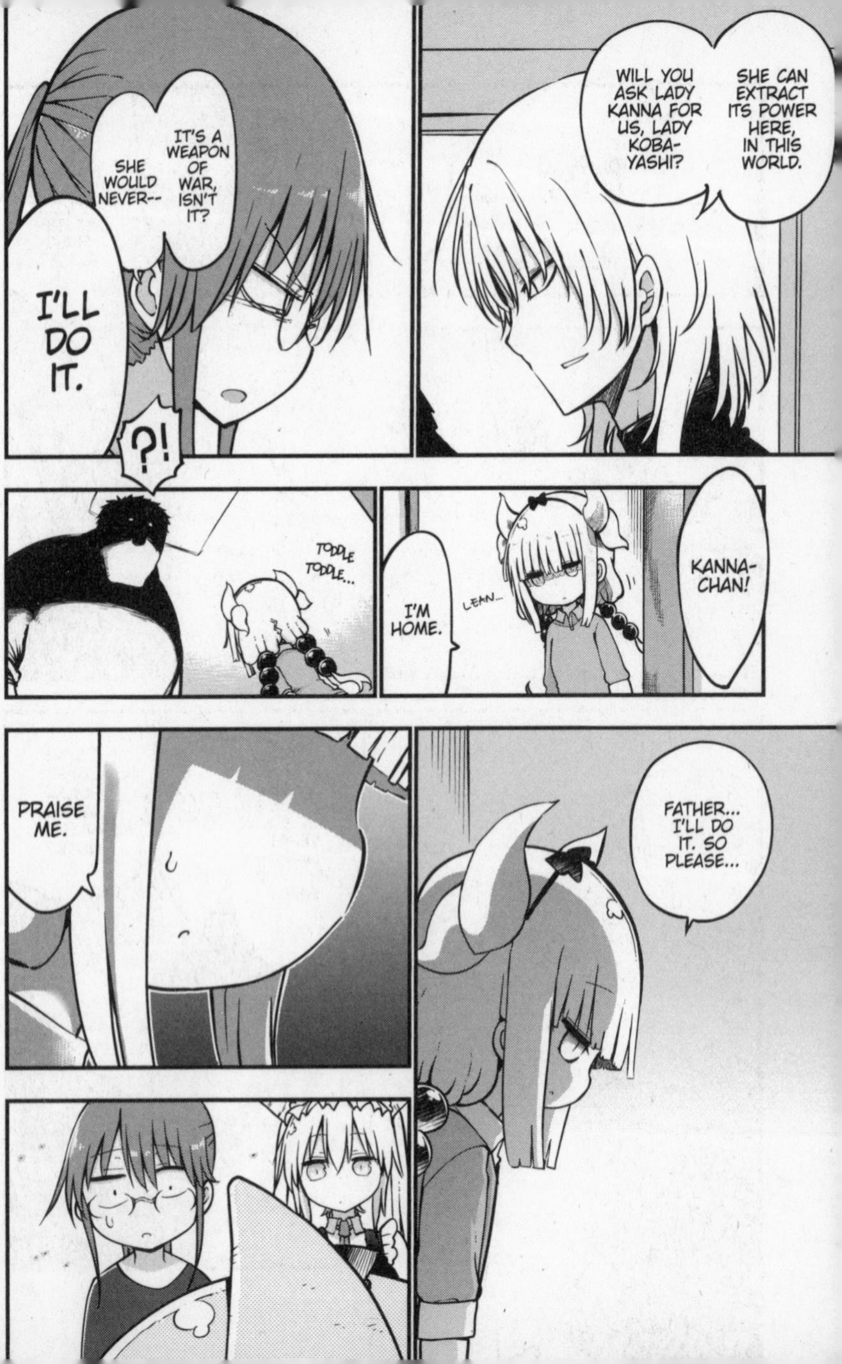
SHE CAN EXTRACT ITS POWER HERE, IN THIS WORLD.
WILL YOU ASK LADY KANNA FOR US, LADY KOBAYASHI?
IT'S A WEAPON OF WAR, ISN'T IT?
SHE WOULD NEVER--
I'LL DO IT.
?!
KANNA-CHAN!
LEAN...
I'M HOME.
TODDLE TODDLE...
FATHER... I'LL DO IT. SO PLEASE...
PRAISE ME.

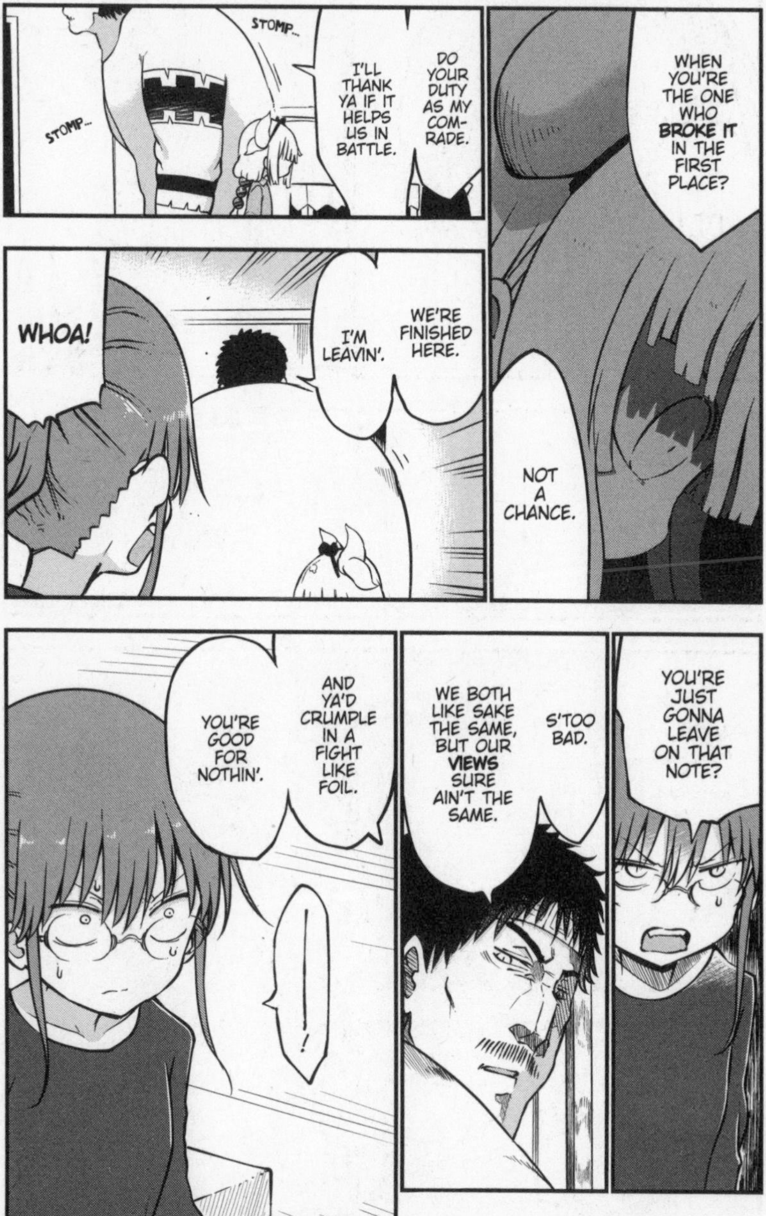
WHEN YOU'RE THE ONE WHO **BROKE IT** IN THE FIRST PLACE?
NOT A CHANCE.
DO YOUR DUTY AS MY COM-RADE.
I'LL THANK YA IF IT HELPS US IN BATTLE.
STOMP...
STOMP...
WE'RE FINISHED HERE.
I'M LEAVIN'.
WHOA!
YOU'RE JUST GONNA LEAVE ON THAT NOTE?
S'TOO BAD.
WE BOTH LIKE SAKE THE SAME, BUT OUR **VIEWS** SURE AIN'T THE SAME.
AND YA'D CRUMPLE IN A FIGHT LIKE FOIL.
YOU'RE GOOD FOR NOTHIN'.
!

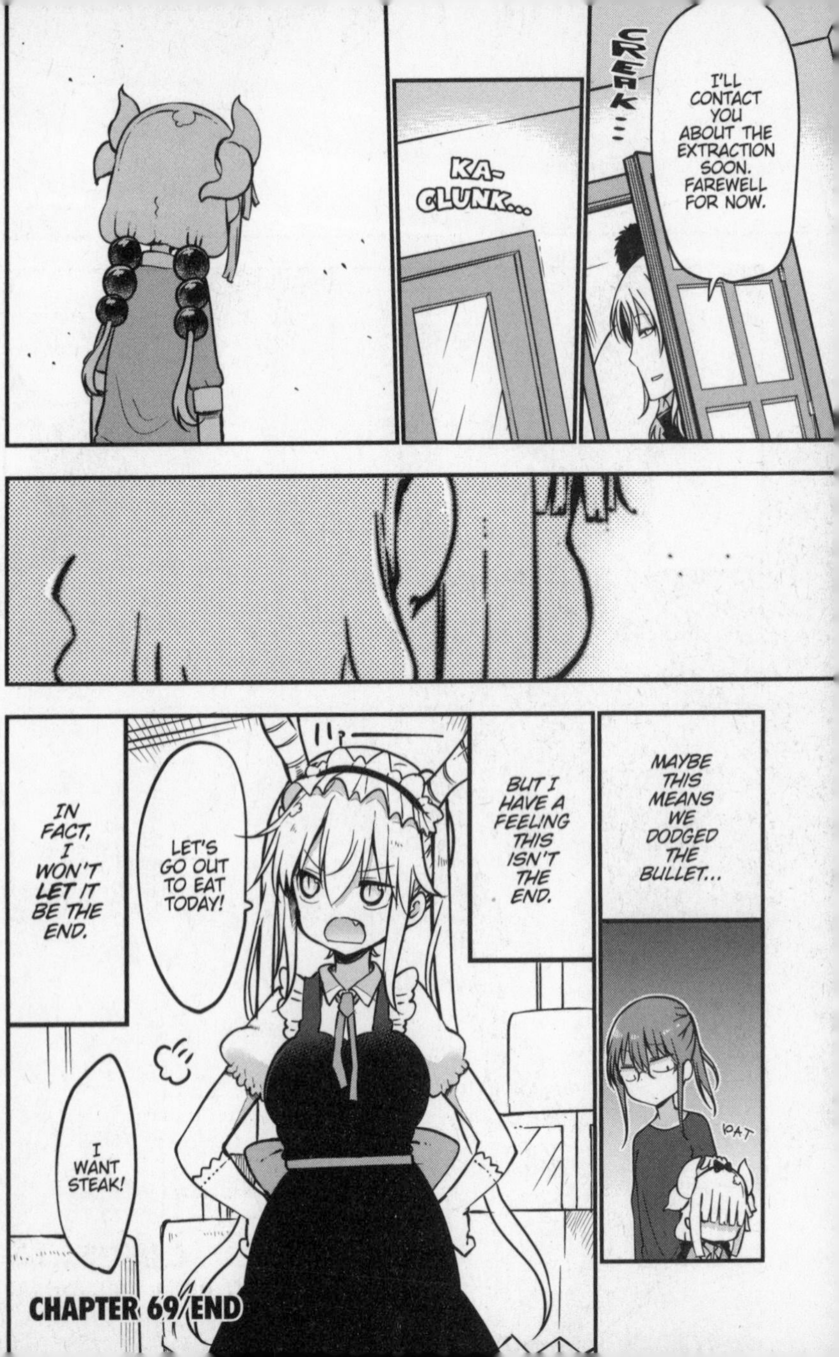
CREAK...
I'LL CONTACT YOU ABOUT THE EXTRACTION SOON. FAREWELL FOR NOW.
KA-CLUNK...
MAYBE THIS MEANS WE DODGED THE BULLET...
PAT
BUT I HAVE A FEELING THIS ISN'T THE END.
LET'S GO OUT TO EAT TODAY!
IN FACT, I WON'T LET IT BE THE END.
I WANT STEAK!
CHAPTER 69/END

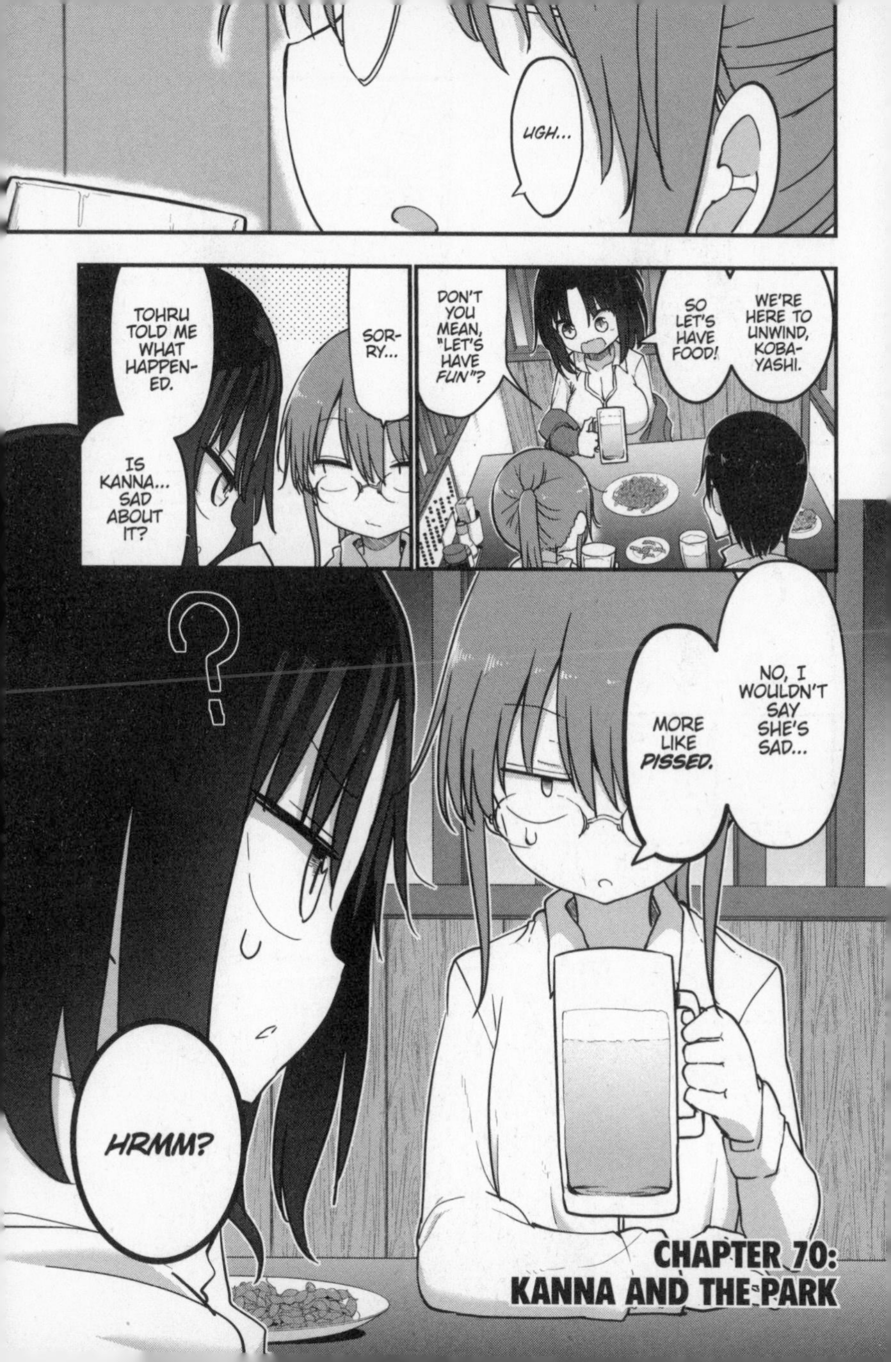
UGH...
WE'RE HERE TO UNWIND, KOBA-YASHI.
SO LET'S HAVE FOOD!
DON'T YOU MEAN, "LET'S HAVE FUN"?
SOR-RY...
TOHRU TOLD ME WHAT HAPPEN-ED.
IS KANNA... SAD ABOUT IT?
NO, I WOULDN'T SAY SHE'S SAD...
MORE LIKE PISSED.
?
HRMM?

CHAPTER 70: KANNA AND THE PARK

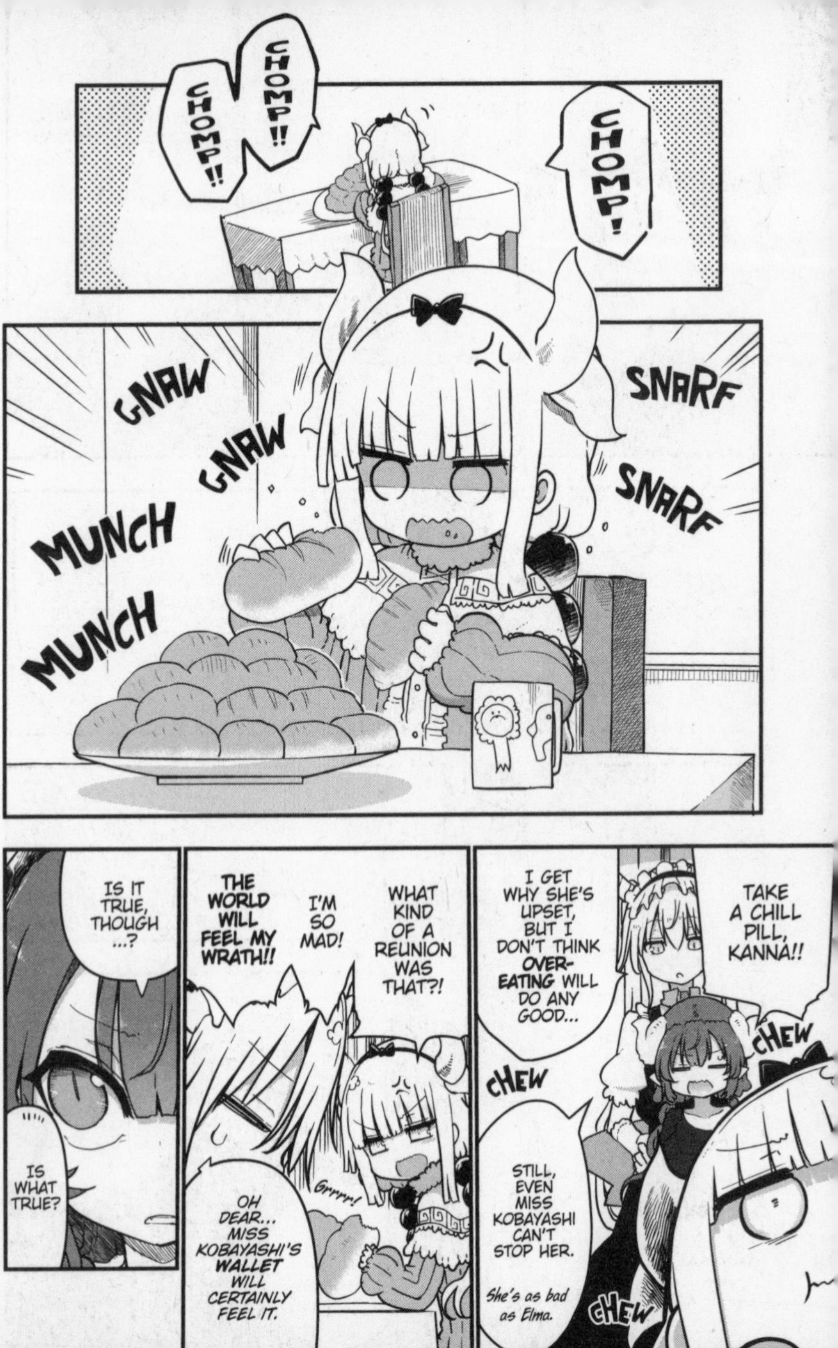
CHOMP!
CHOMP!! CHOMP!!
SNARF SNARF
GNAW GNAW
MUNCH MUNCH
TAKE A CHILL PILL, KANNA!!
I GET WHY SHE'S UPSET, BUT I DON'T THINK OVER-EATING WILL DO ANY GOOD...
CHEW CHEW
STILL, EVEN MISS KOBAYASHI CAN'T STOP HER.
She's as bad as Elma.
CHEW
WHAT KIND OF A REUNION WAS THAT?!
I'M SO MAD!
THE WORLD WILL FEEL MY WRATH!!
Grrrr!
OH DEAR... MISS KOBAYASHI'S WALLET WILL CERTAINLY FEEL IT.
IS IT TRUE, THOUGH ...?
IS WHAT TRUE?

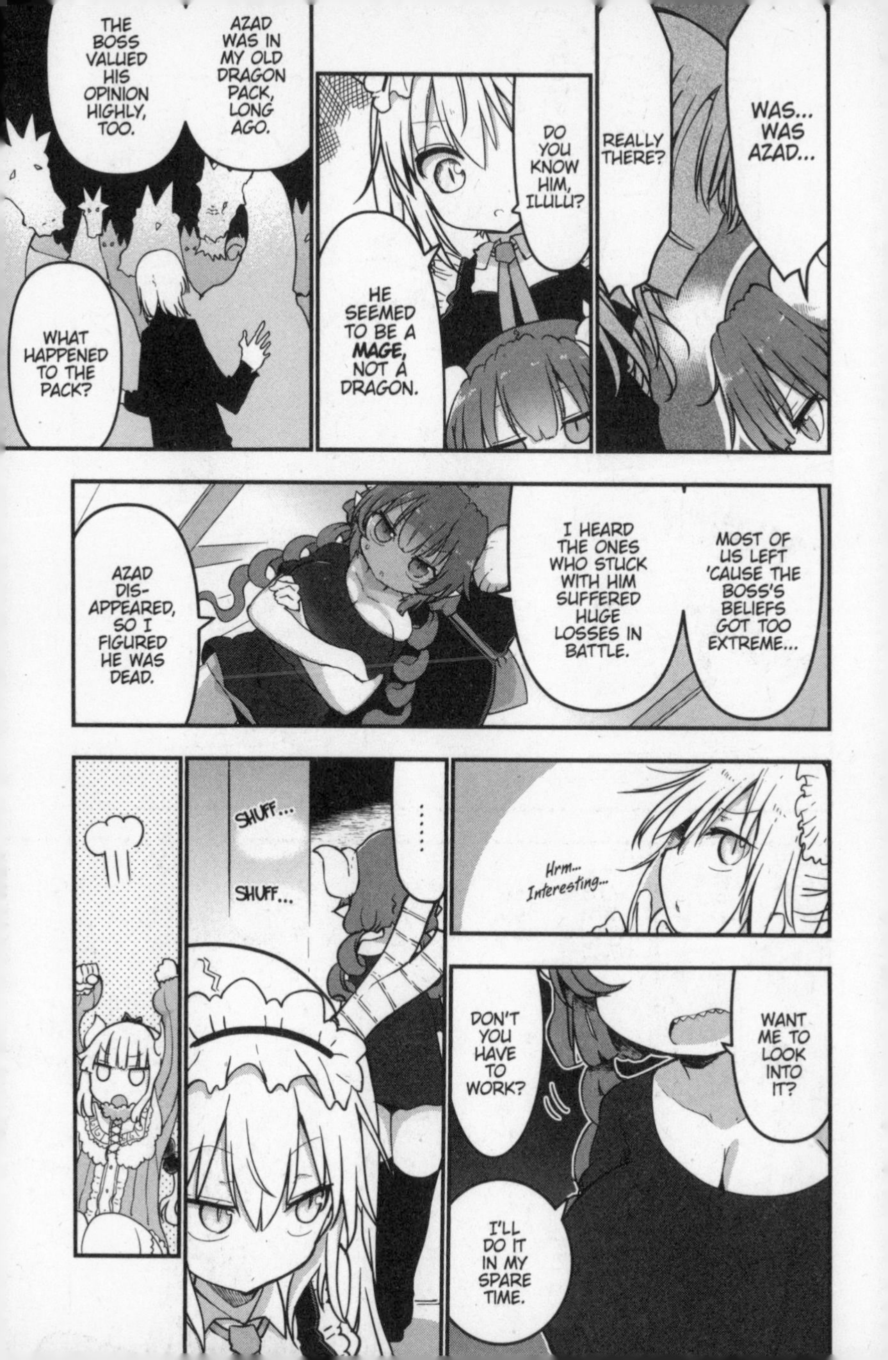
WAS... WAS AZAD...
REALLY THERE?
DO YOU KNOW HIM, ILULU?
HE SEEMED TO BE A **MAGE,** NOT A DRAGON.
AZAD WAS IN MY OLD DRAGON PACK, LONG AGO.
THE BOSS VALUED HIS OPINION HIGHLY, TOO.
WHAT HAPPENED TO THE PACK?
MOST OF US LEFT 'CAUSE THE BOSS'S BELIEFS GOT TOO EXTREME...
I HEARD THE ONES WHO STUCK WITH HIM SUFFERED HUGE LOSSES IN BATTLE.
AZAD DIS-APPEARED, SO I FIGURED HE WAS DEAD.
Hrm... Interesting...
WANT ME TO LOOK INTO IT?
DON'T YOU HAVE TO WORK?
I'LL DO IT IN MY SPARE TIME.
......
SHUFF...
SHUFF...

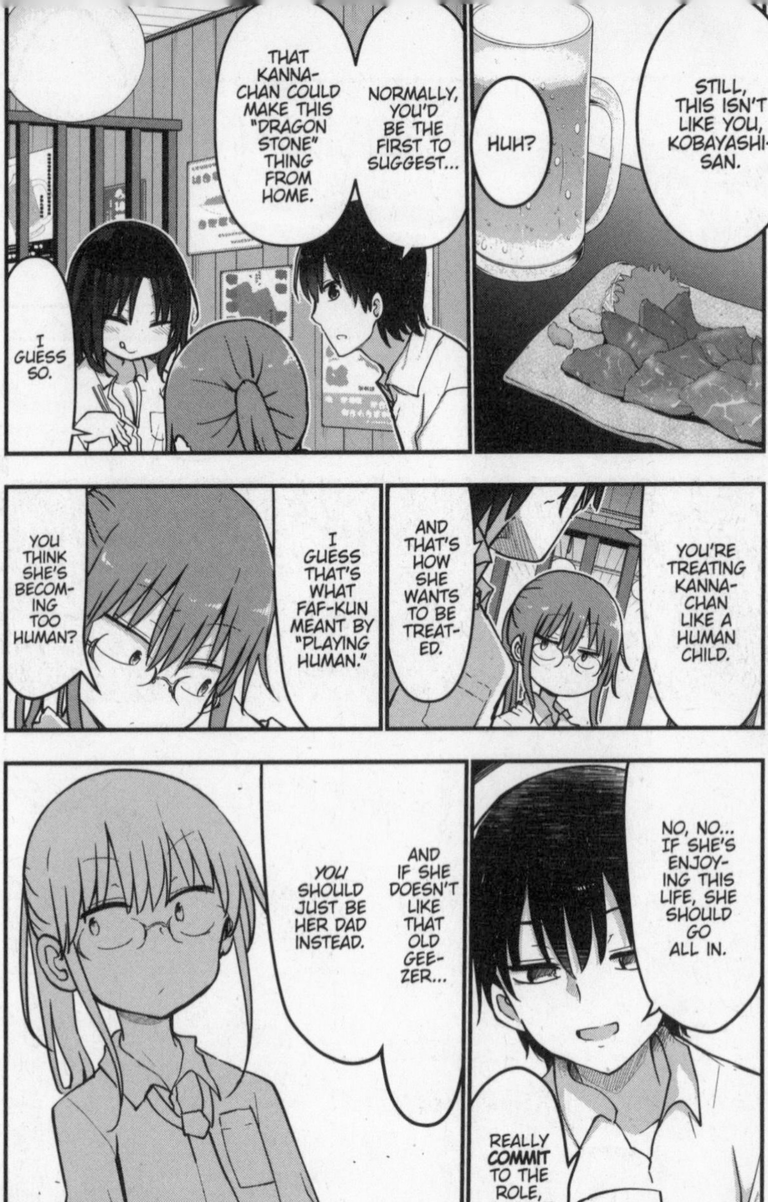
STILL, THIS ISN'T LIKE YOU, KOBAYASHI-SAN.
HUH?
NORMALLY, YOU'D BE THE FIRST TO SUGGEST...
THAT KANNA-CHAN COULD MAKE THIS "DRAGON STONE" THING FROM HOME.
I GUESS SO.
YOU'RE TREATING KANNA-CHAN LIKE A HUMAN CHILD.
AND THAT'S HOW SHE WANTS TO BE TREATED.
I GUESS THAT'S WHAT FAF-KUN MEANT BY "PLAYING HUMAN."
YOU THINK SHE'S BECOMING TOO HUMAN?
NO, NO... IF SHE'S ENJOYING THIS LIFE, SHE SHOULD GO ALL IN.
REALLY *COMMIT* TO THE ROLE, Y'KNOW?
AND IF SHE DOESN'T LIKE THAT OLD GEEZER...
YOU SHOULD JUST BE HER DAD INSTEAD.

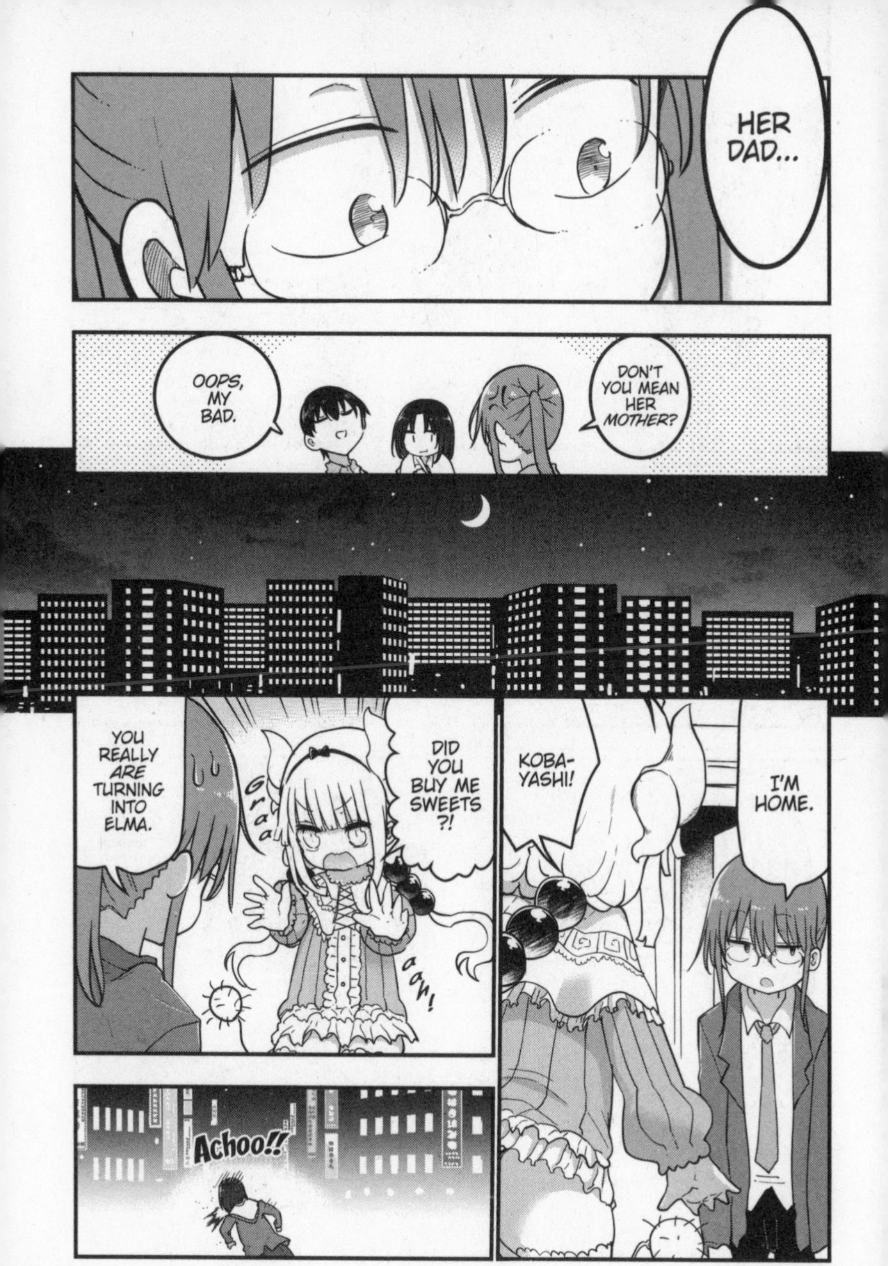
HER DAD...
DON'T YOU MEAN HER MOTHER?
OOPS, MY BAD.
I'M HOME.
KOBA-YASHI!
DID YOU BUY ME SWEETS?!
Graa
aah!
YOU REALLY ARE TURNING INTO ELMA.
Achoo!!

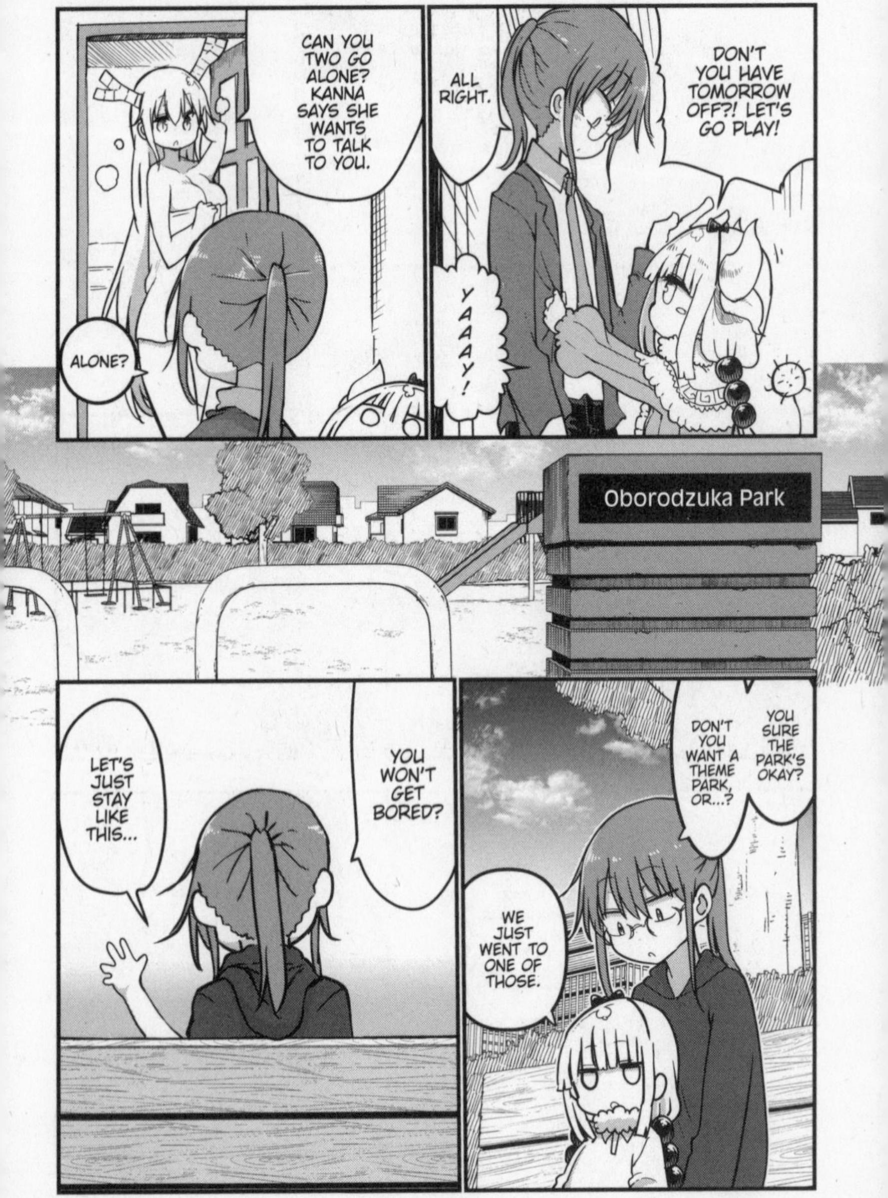

DON'T YOU HAVE TOMORROW OFF?! LET'S GO PLAY!
ALL RIGHT.
YAAAAY!
CAN YOU TWO GO ALONE? KANNA SAYS SHE WANTS TO TALK TO YOU.
ALONE?
Oborodzuka Park
YOU SURE THE PARK'S OKAY?
DON'T YOU WANT A THEME PARK, OR...?
WE JUST WENT TO ONE OF THOSE.
YOU WON'T GET BORED?
LET'S JUST STAY LIKE THIS...

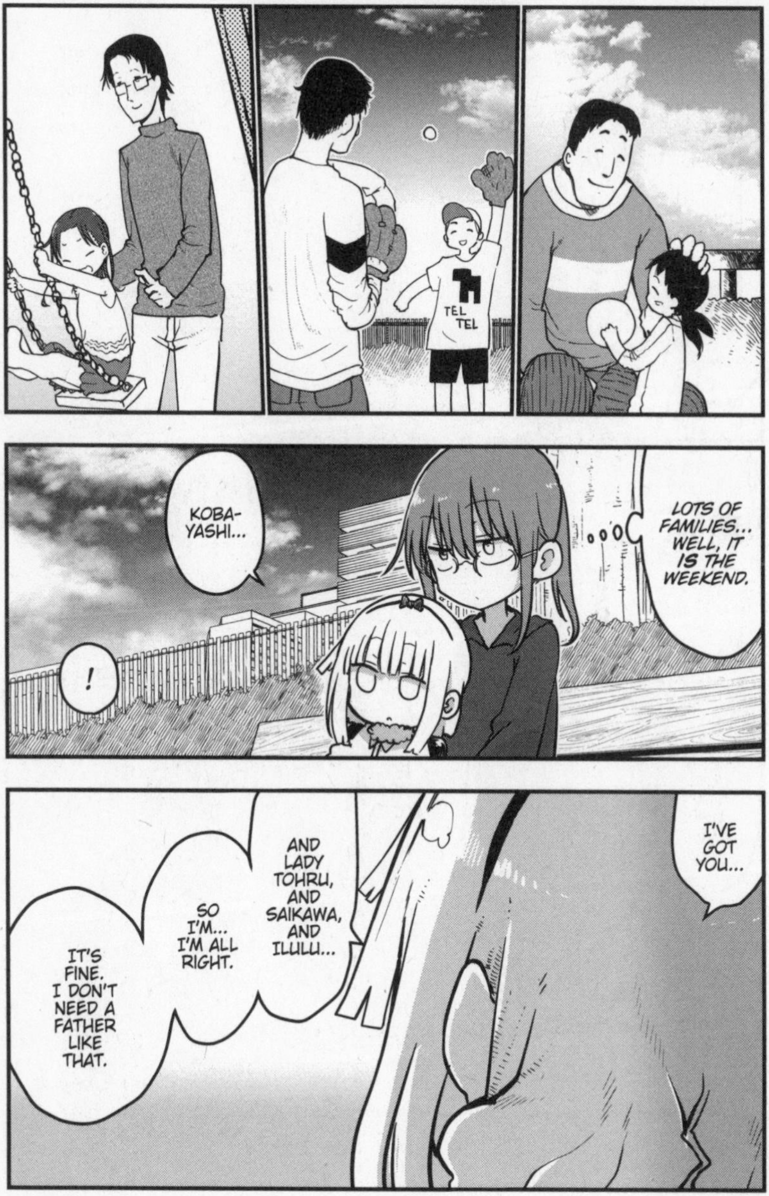
LOTS OF FAMILIES... WELL, IT *IS* THE WEEKEND.
KOBA-YASHI...
!
I'VE GOT YOU...
AND LADY TOHRU, AND SAIKAWA, AND ILULU...
SO I'M... I'M ALL RIGHT.
IT'S FINE. I DON'T NEED A FATHER LIKE THAT.

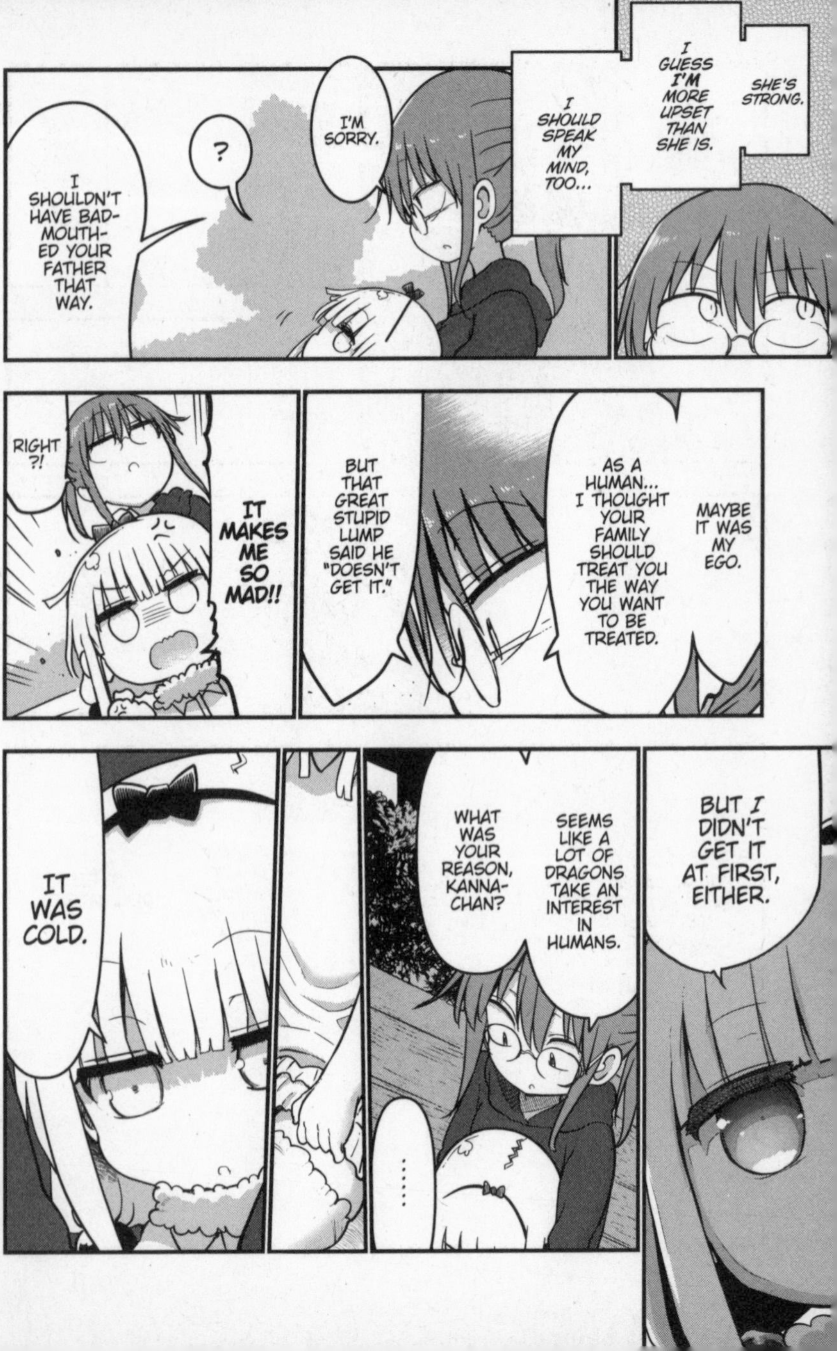
SHE'S STRONG.
I GUESS I'M MORE UPSET THAN SHE IS.
I SHOULD SPEAK MY MIND, TOO...
I'M SORRY.
?
I SHOULDN'T HAVE BAD-MOUTHED YOUR FATHER THAT WAY.
MAYBE IT WAS MY EGO.
AS A HUMAN... I THOUGHT YOUR FAMILY SHOULD TREAT YOU THE WAY YOU WANT TO BE TREATED.
BUT THAT GREAT STUPID LUMP SAID HE "DOESN'T GET IT."
IT MAKES ME SO MAD!!
RIGHT?!
BUT I DIDN'T GET IT AT FIRST, EITHER.
SEEMS LIKE A LOT OF DRAGONS TAKE AN INTEREST IN HUMANS.
WHAT WAS YOUR REASON, KANNA-CHAN?
......
IT WAS COLD.

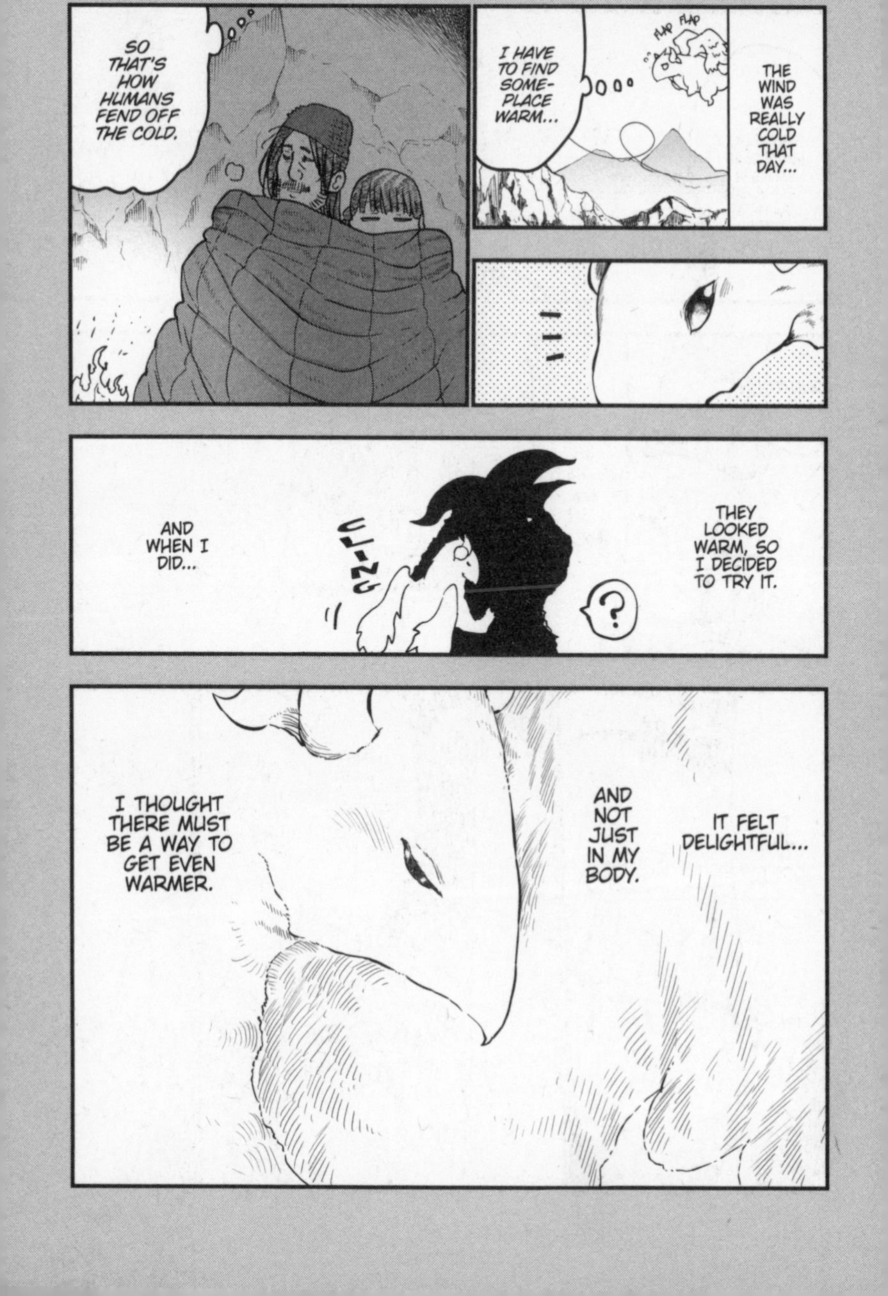
THE WIND WAS REALLY COLD THAT DAY...
FLAP FLAP
I HAVE TO FIND SOME-PLACE WARM...
...
SO THAT'S HOW HUMANS FEND OFF THE COLD.
THEY LOOKED WARM, SO I DECIDED TO TRY IT.
?
CLING
AND WHEN I DID...
IT FELT DELIGHTFUL...
AND NOT JUST IN MY BODY.
I THOUGHT THERE MUST BE A WAY TO GET EVEN WARMER.

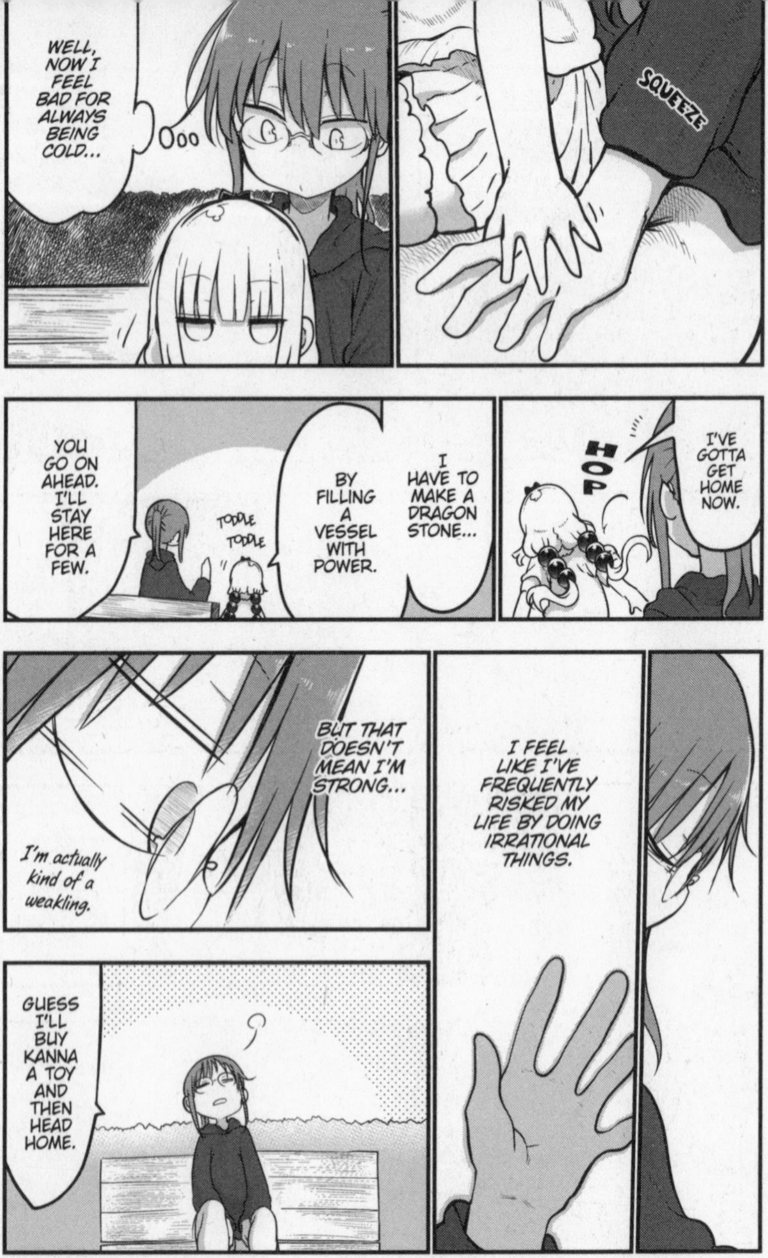
SQUEEZE
Ooo
WELL, NOW I FEEL BAD FOR ALWAYS BEING COLD...
HOP
I'VE GOTTA GET HOME NOW.
I HAVE TO MAKE A DRAGON STONE...
BY FILLING A VESSEL WITH POWER.
TODDLE TODDLE
YOU GO ON AHEAD. I'LL STAY HERE FOR A FEW.
I FEEL LIKE I'VE FREQUENTLY RISKED MY LIFE BY DOING IRRATIONAL THINGS.
BUT THAT DOESN'T MEAN I'M STRONG...
I'm actually kind of a weakling.
GUESS I'LL BUY KANNA A TOY AND THEN HEAD HOME.

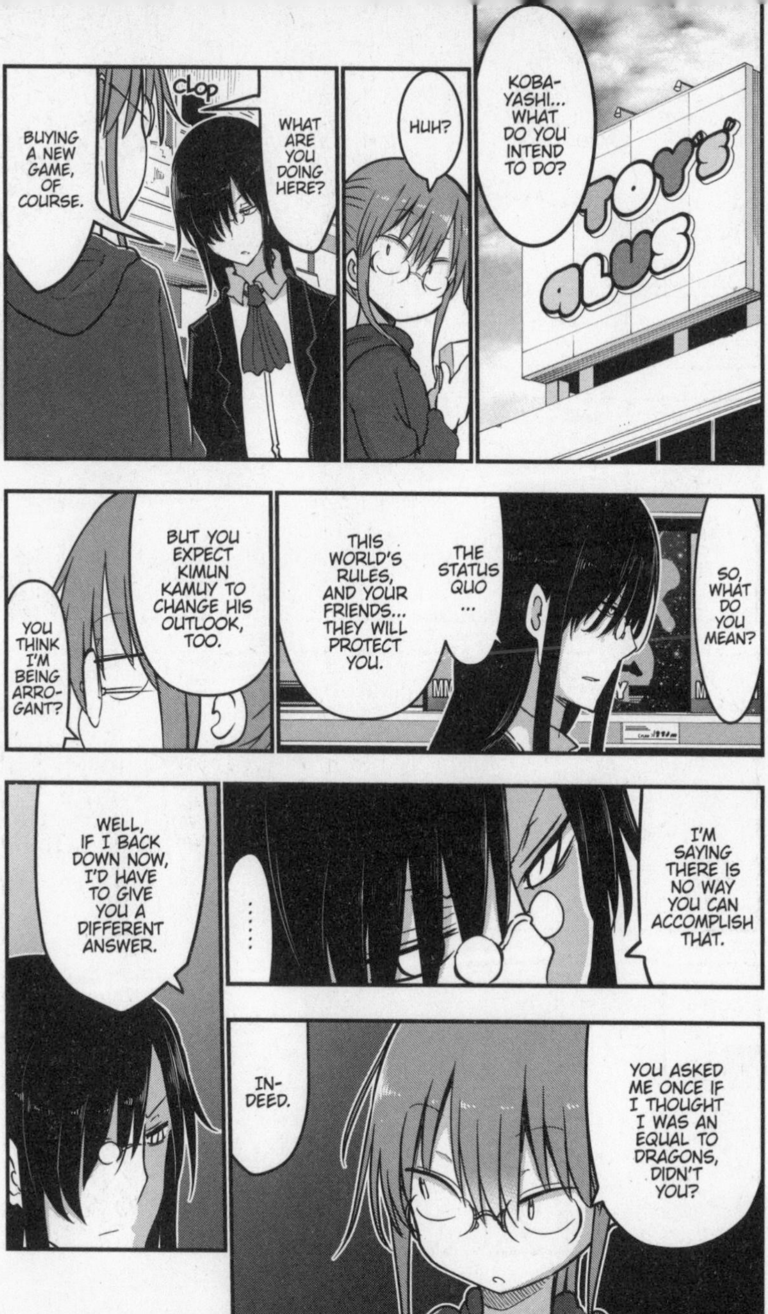
KOBA-YASHI... WHAT DO YOU INTEND TO DO?
TOY'S ALUS
HUH?
WHAT ARE YOU DOING HERE?
CLOP
BUYING A NEW GAME, OF COURSE.
SO, WHAT DO YOU MEAN?
THE STATUS QUO ...
THIS WORLD'S RULES, AND YOUR FRIENDS... THEY WILL PROTECT YOU.
BUT YOU EXPECT KIMUN KAMUY TO CHANGE HIS OUTLOOK, TOO.
YOU THINK I'M BEING ARRO-GANT?
I'M SAYING THERE IS NO WAY YOU CAN ACCOMPLISH THAT.
......
YOU ASKED ME ONCE IF I THOUGHT I WAS AN EQUAL TO DRAGONS, DIDN'T YOU?
IN-DEED.
WELL, IF I BACK DOWN NOW, I'D HAVE TO GIVE YOU A DIFFERENT ANSWER.

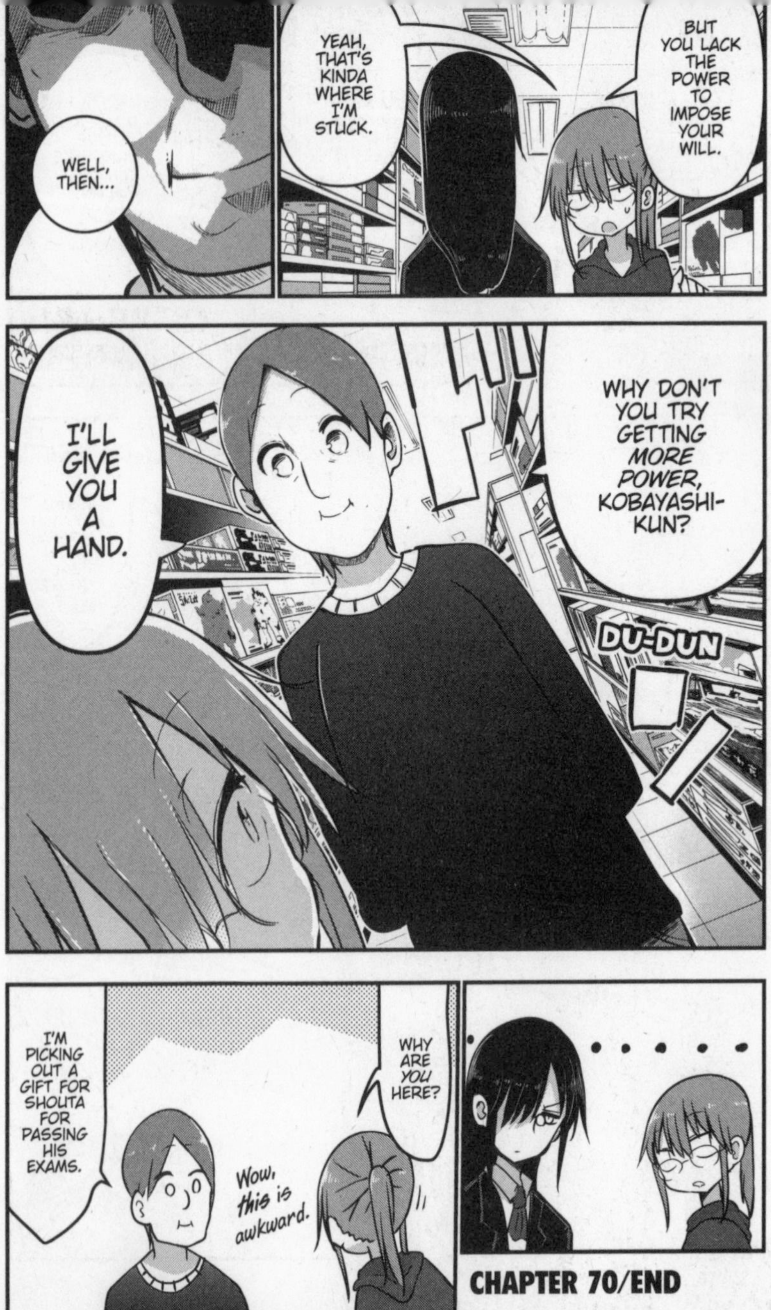
BUT YOU LACK THE POWER TO IMPOSE YOUR WILL.
YEAH, THAT'S KINDA WHERE I'M STUCK.
WELL, THEN...
WHY DON'T YOU TRY GETTING *MORE POWER,* KOBAYASHI-KUN?
I'LL GIVE YOU A HAND.
DU-DUN
......
WHY ARE *YOU* HERE?
I'M PICKING OUT A GIFT FOR SHOUTA FOR PASSING HIS EXAMS.
Wow, this is awkward.

CHAPTER 70/END

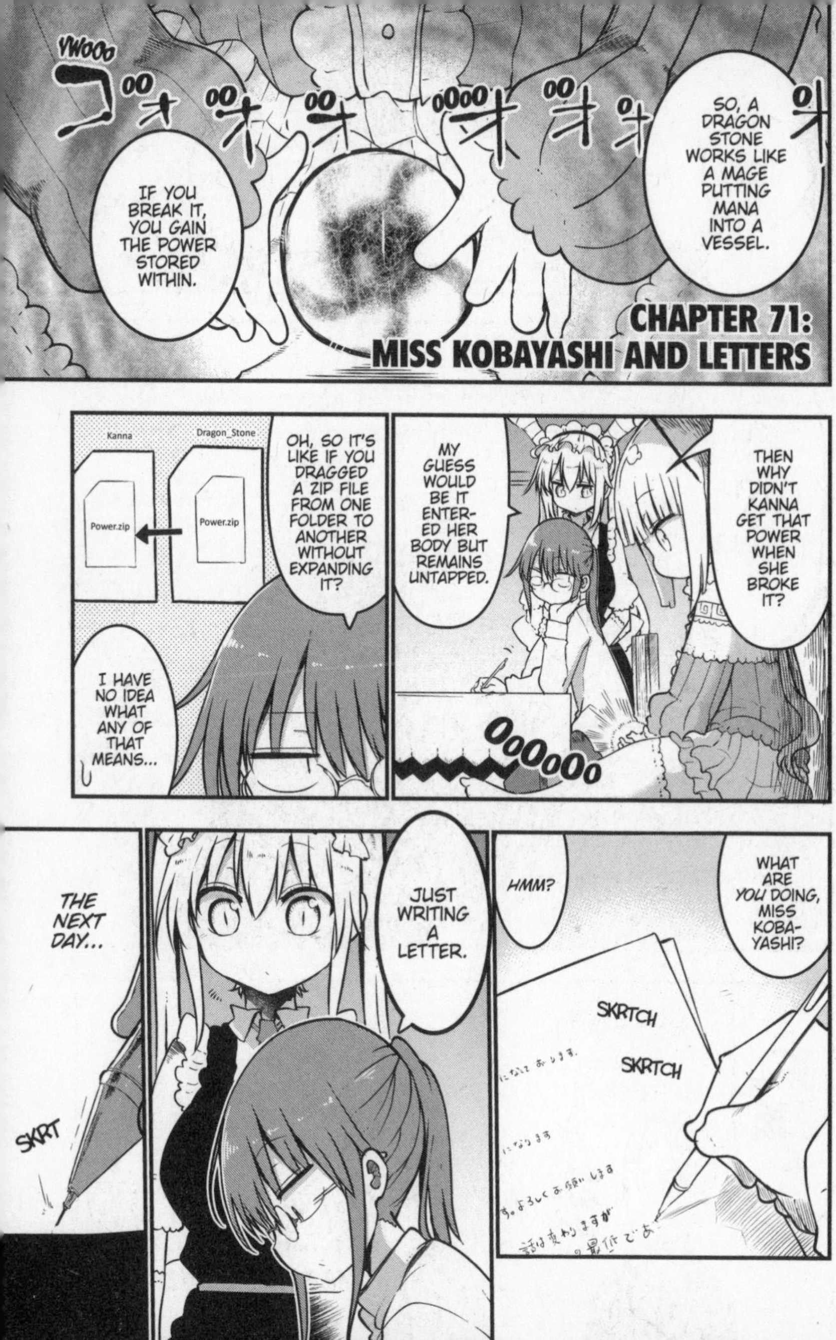
SO, A DRAGON STONE WORKS LIKE A MAGE PUTTING MANA INTO A VESSEL.
IF YOU BREAK IT, YOU GAIN THE POWER STORED WITHIN.
YWOOO
CHAPTER 71: MISS KOBAYASHI AND LETTERS
THEN WHY DIDN'T KANNA GET THAT POWER WHEN SHE BROKE IT?
MY GUESS WOULD BE IT ENTERED HER BODY BUT REMAINS UNTAPPED.
OOOOOO
OH, SO IT'S LIKE IF YOU DRAGGED A ZIP FILE FROM ONE FOLDER TO ANOTHER WITHOUT EXPANDING IT?
Dragon_Stone
Power.zip
Kanna
Power.zip
I HAVE NO IDEA WHAT ANY OF THAT MEANS...
WHAT ARE YOU DOING, MISS KOBAYASHI?
HMM?
SKRTCH
SKRTCH
JUST WRITING A LETTER.
THE NEXT DAY...
SKRT

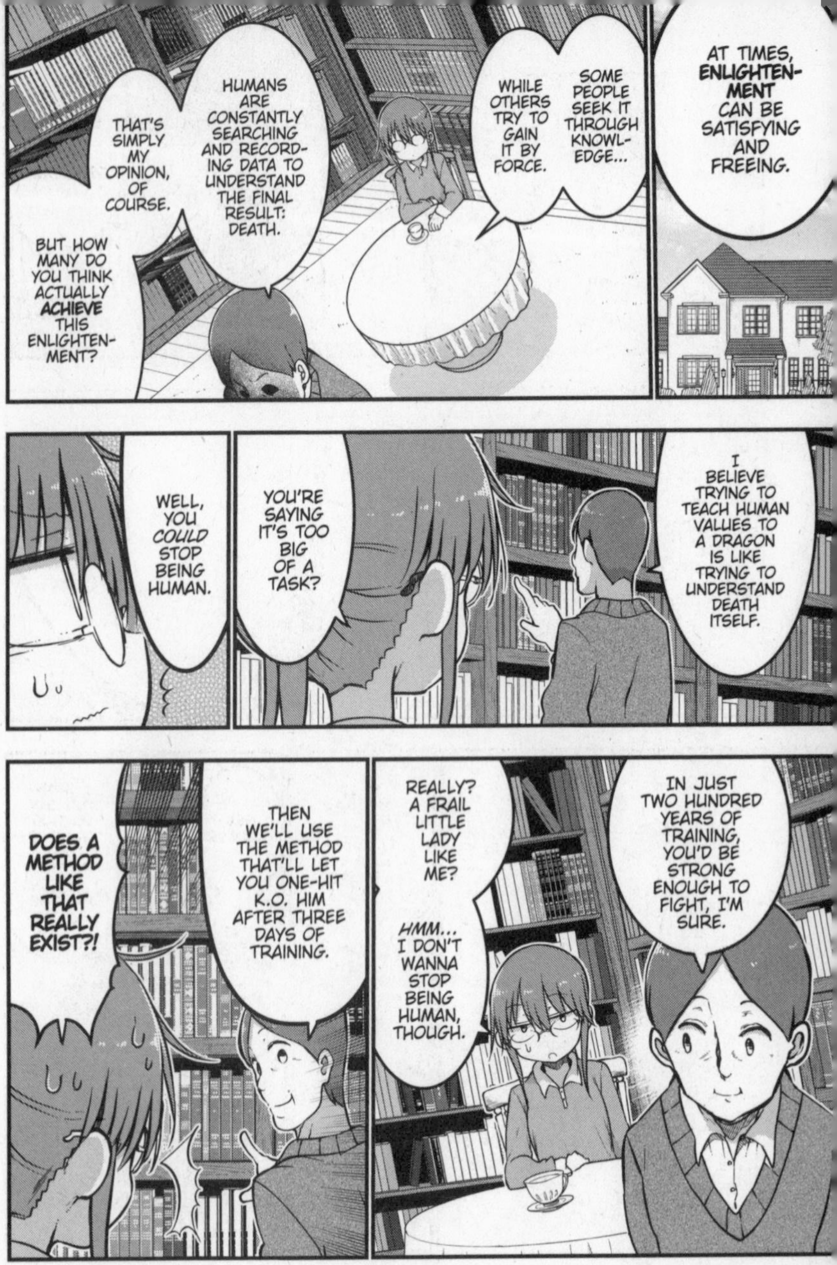
AT TIMES, ENLIGHTENMENT CAN BE SATISFYING AND FREEING.
SOME PEOPLE SEEK IT THROUGH KNOWLEDGE...
WHILE OTHERS TRY TO GAIN IT BY FORCE.
HUMANS ARE CONSTANTLY SEARCHING AND RECORDING DATA TO UNDERSTAND THE FINAL RESULT: DEATH.
THAT'S SIMPLY MY OPINION, OF COURSE.
BUT HOW MANY DO YOU THINK ACTUALLY ACHIEVE THIS ENLIGHTENMENT?
I BELIEVE TRYING TO TEACH HUMAN VALUES TO A DRAGON IS LIKE TRYING TO UNDERSTAND DEATH ITSELF.
YOU'RE SAYING IT'S TOO BIG OF A TASK?
WELL, YOU COULD STOP BEING HUMAN.
IN JUST TWO HUNDRED YEARS OF TRAINING, YOU'D BE STRONG ENOUGH TO FIGHT, I'M SURE.
REALLY? A FRAIL LITTLE LADY LIKE ME?
HMM... I DON'T WANNA STOP BEING HUMAN, THOUGH.
THEN WE'LL USE THE METHOD THAT'LL LET YOU ONE-HIT K.O. HIM AFTER THREE DAYS OF TRAINING.
DOES A METHOD LIKE THAT REALLY EXIST?!

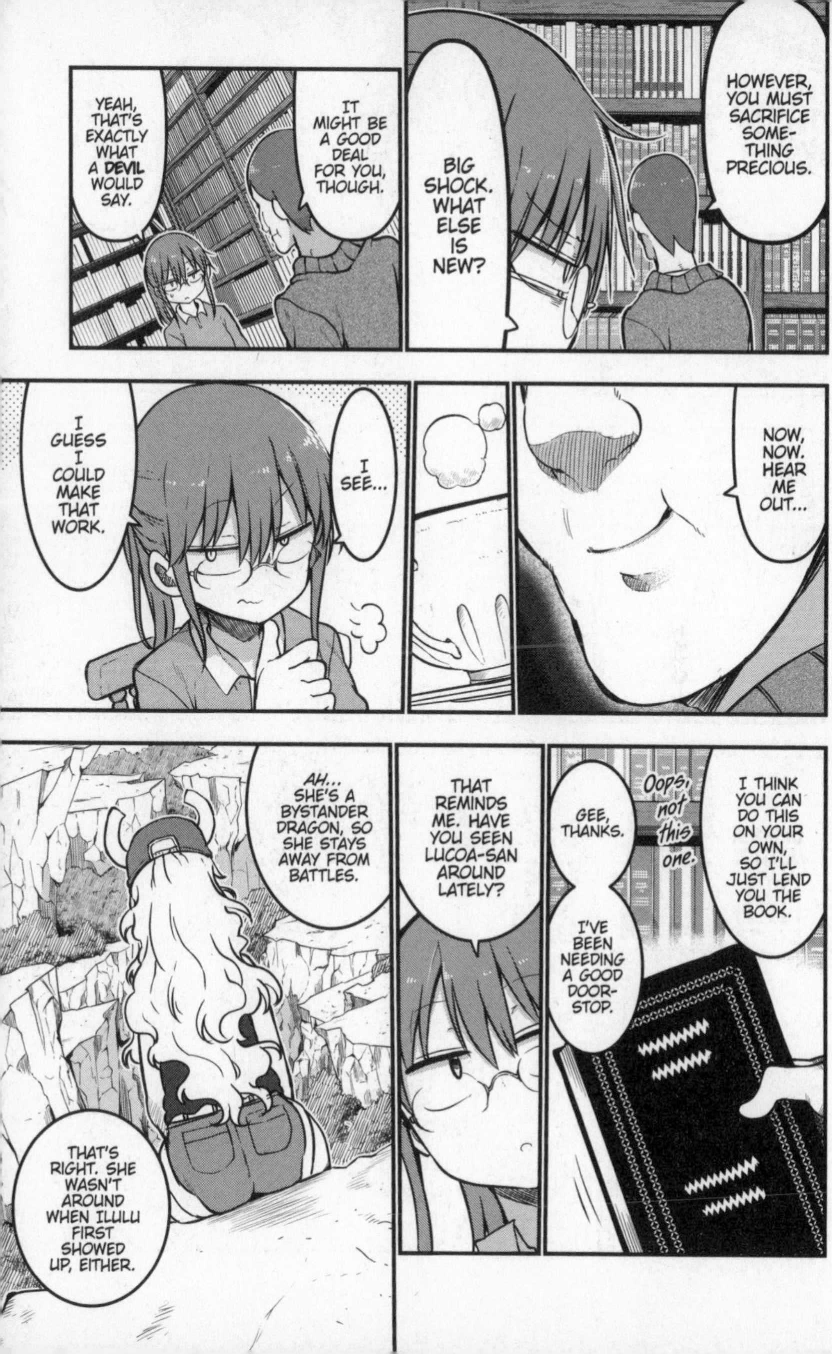
HOWEVER, YOU MUST SACRIFICE SOMETHING PRECIOUS.
BIG SHOCK. WHAT ELSE IS NEW?
IT MIGHT BE A GOOD DEAL FOR YOU, THOUGH.
YEAH, THAT'S EXACTLY WHAT A DEVIL WOULD SAY.
NOW, NOW. HEAR ME OUT...
I SEE...
I GUESS I COULD MAKE THAT WORK.
I THINK YOU CAN DO THIS ON YOUR OWN, SO I'LL JUST LEND YOU THE BOOK.
Oops, not this one.
GEE, THANKS.
I'VE BEEN NEEDING A GOOD DOORSTOP.
THAT REMINDS ME. HAVE YOU SEEN LUCOA-SAN AROUND LATELY?
AH... SHE'S A BYSTANDER DRAGON, SO SHE STAYS AWAY FROM BATTLES.
THAT'S RIGHT. SHE WASN'T AROUND WHEN ILULU FIRST SHOWED UP, EITHER.

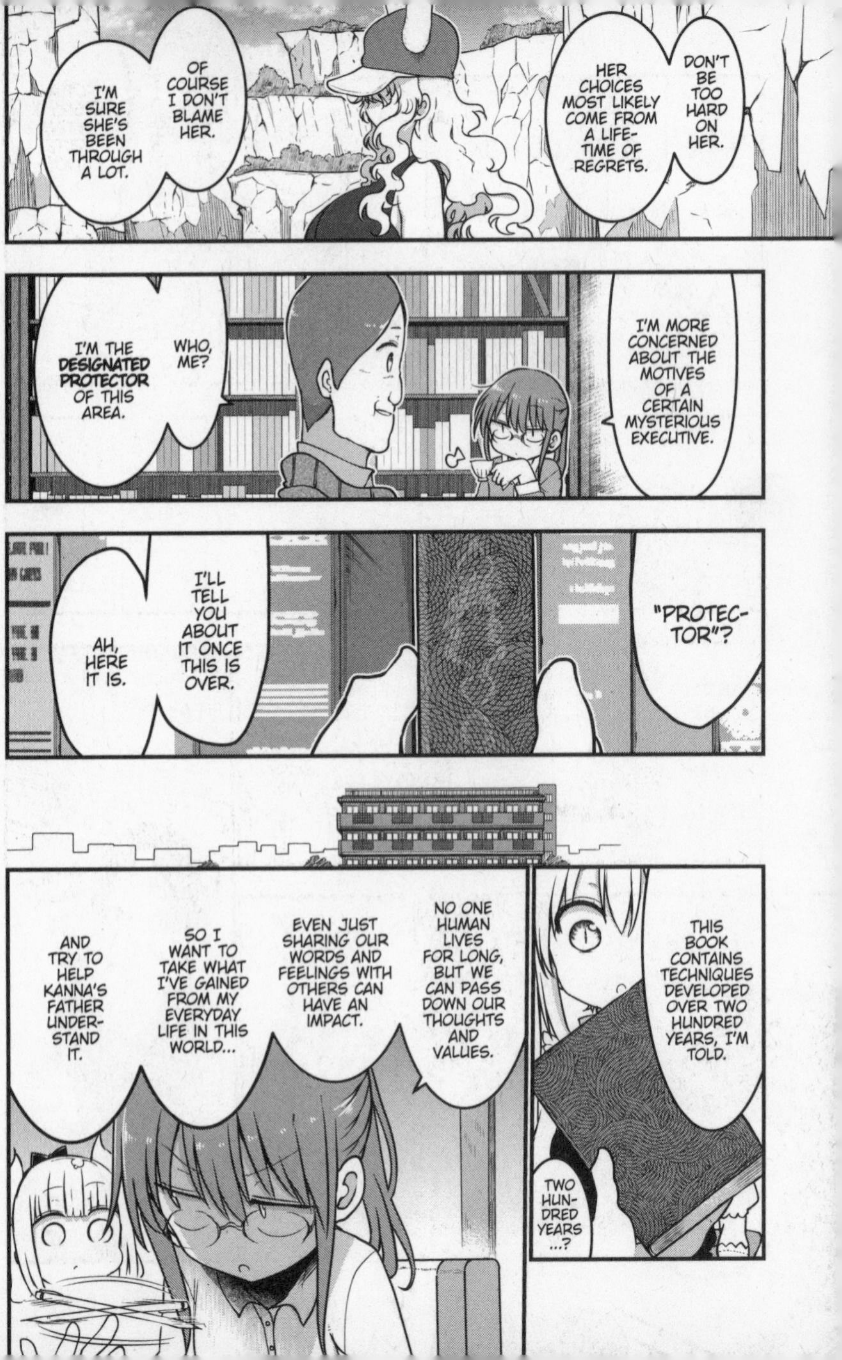
DON'T BE TOO HARD ON HER.
HER CHOICES MOST LIKELY COME FROM A LIFETIME OF REGRETS.
OF COURSE I DON'T BLAME HER.
I'M SURE SHE'S BEEN THROUGH A LOT.
I'M MORE CONCERNED ABOUT THE MOTIVES OF A CERTAIN MYSTERIOUS EXECUTIVE.
WHO, ME?
I'M THE **DESIGNATED PROTECTOR** OF THIS AREA.
"PROTECTOR"?
I'LL TELL YOU ABOUT IT ONCE THIS IS OVER.
AH, HERE IT IS.
THIS BOOK CONTAINS TECHNIQUES DEVELOPED OVER TWO HUNDRED YEARS, I'M TOLD.
TWO HUNDRED YEARS ...?
NO ONE HUMAN LIVES FOR LONG, BUT WE CAN PASS DOWN OUR THOUGHTS AND VALUES.
EVEN JUST SHARING OUR WORDS AND FEELINGS WITH OTHERS CAN HAVE AN IMPACT.
SO I WANT TO TAKE WHAT I'VE GAINED FROM MY EVERYDAY LIFE IN THIS WORLD...
AND TRY TO HELP KANNA'S FATHER UNDERSTAND IT.

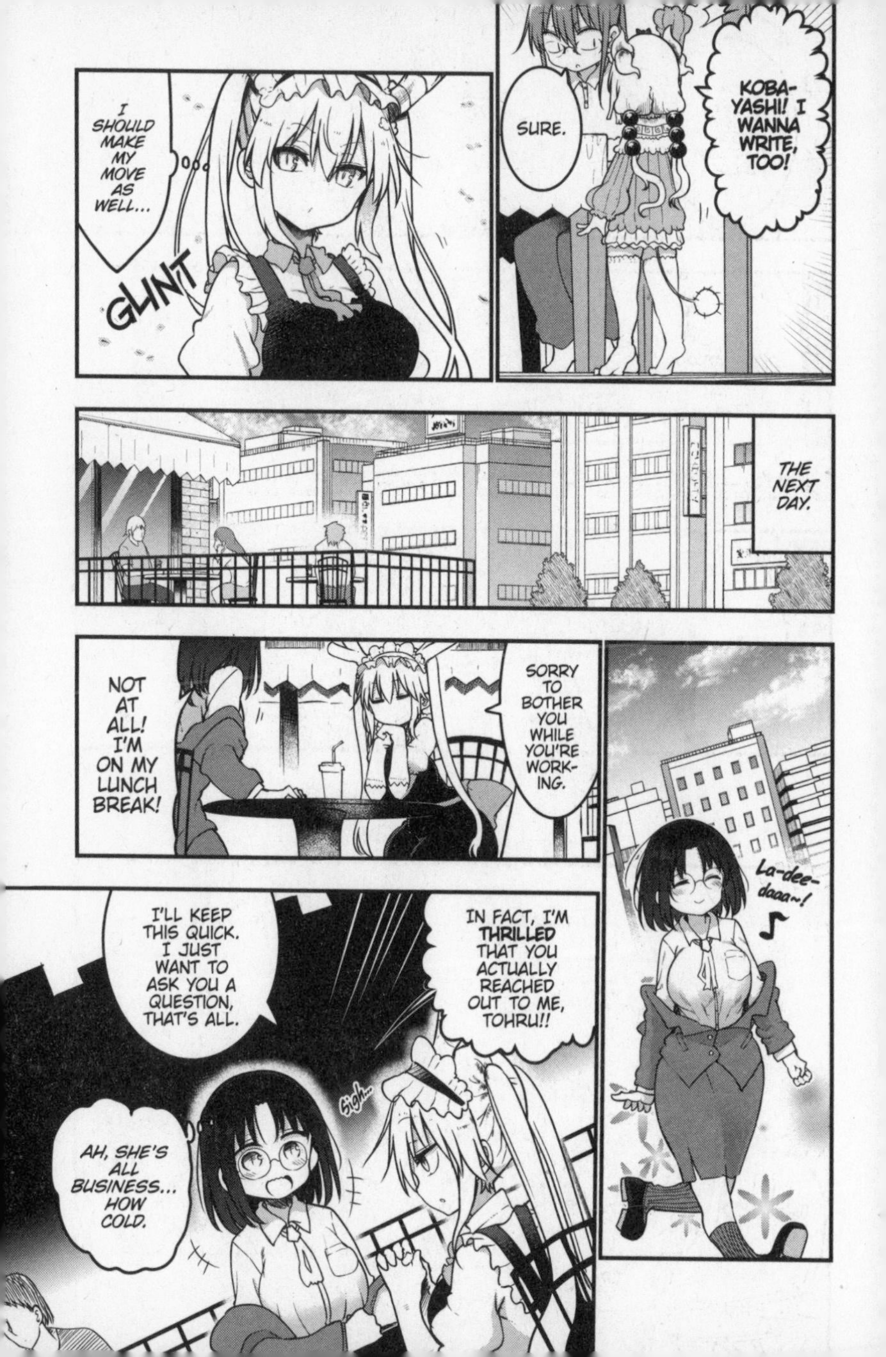
KOBA-YASHI! I WANNA WRITE, TOO!
SURE.
I SHOULD MAKE MY MOVE AS WELL...
GLINT
THE NEXT DAY.
La-dee-daaa~!
SORRY TO BOTHER YOU WHILE YOU'RE WORKING.
NOT AT ALL! I'M ON MY LUNCH BREAK!
IN FACT, I'M THRILLED THAT YOU ACTUALLY REACHED OUT TO ME, TOHRU!!
I'LL KEEP THIS QUICK. I JUST WANT TO ASK YOU A QUESTION, THAT'S ALL.
Sigh...
AH, SHE'S ALL BUSINESS... HOW COLD.

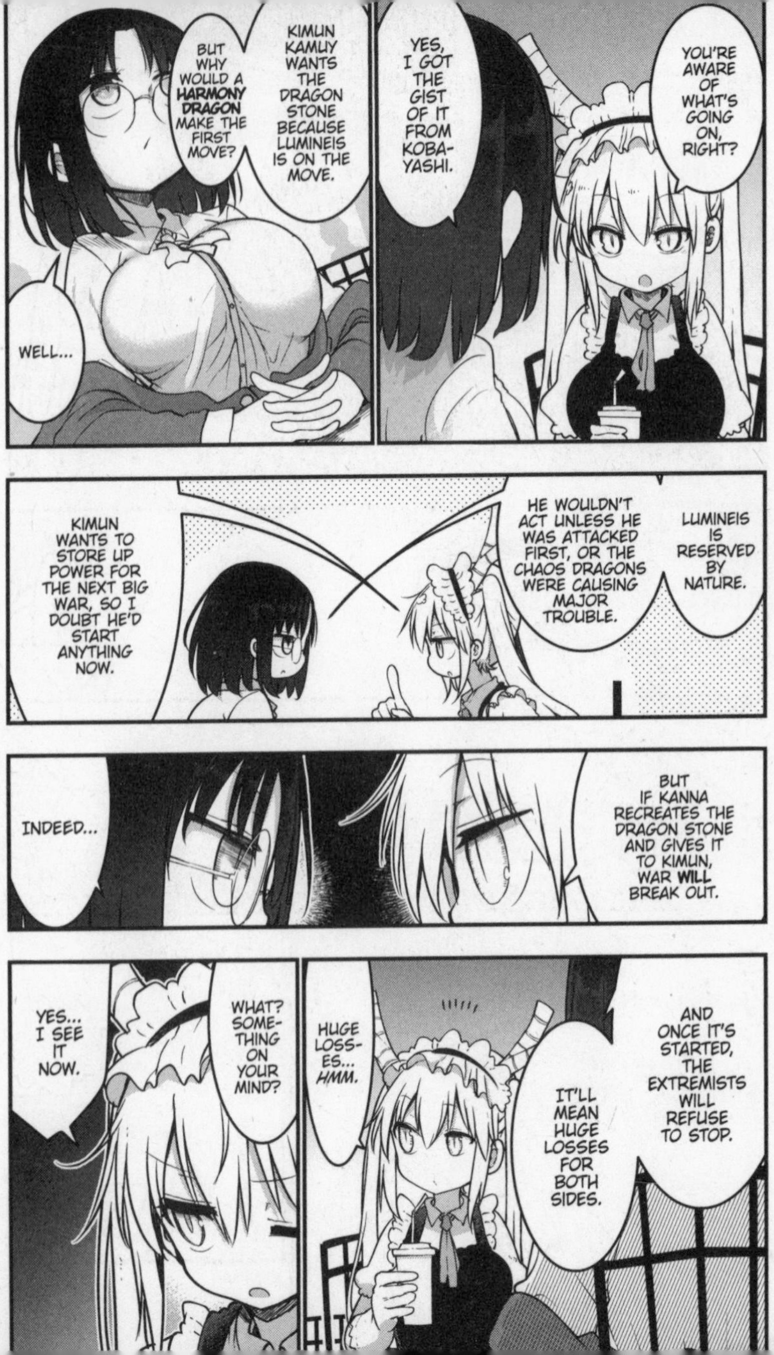
YOU'RE AWARE OF WHAT'S GOING ON, RIGHT?
YES, I GOT THE GIST OF IT FROM KOBA-YASHI.
KIMUN KAMUY WANTS THE DRAGON STONE BECAUSE LUMINEIS IS ON THE MOVE.
BUT WHY WOULD A **HARMONY DRAGON** MAKE THE FIRST MOVE?
WELL...
LUMINEIS IS RESERVED BY NATURE.
HE WOULDN'T ACT UNLESS HE WAS ATTACKED FIRST, OR THE CHAOS DRAGONS WERE CAUSING MAJOR TROUBLE.
KIMUN WANTS TO STORE UP POWER FOR THE NEXT BIG WAR, SO I DOUBT HE'D START ANYTHING NOW.
BUT IF KANNA RECREATES THE DRAGON STONE AND GIVES IT TO KIMUN, WAR **WILL** BREAK OUT.
INDEED...
AND ONCE IT'S STARTED, THE EXTREMISTS WILL REFUSE TO STOP.
IT'LL MEAN HUGE LOSSES FOR BOTH SIDES.
HUGE LOSS-ES... *HMM.*
WHAT? SOME-THING ON YOUR MIND?
YES... I SEE IT NOW.

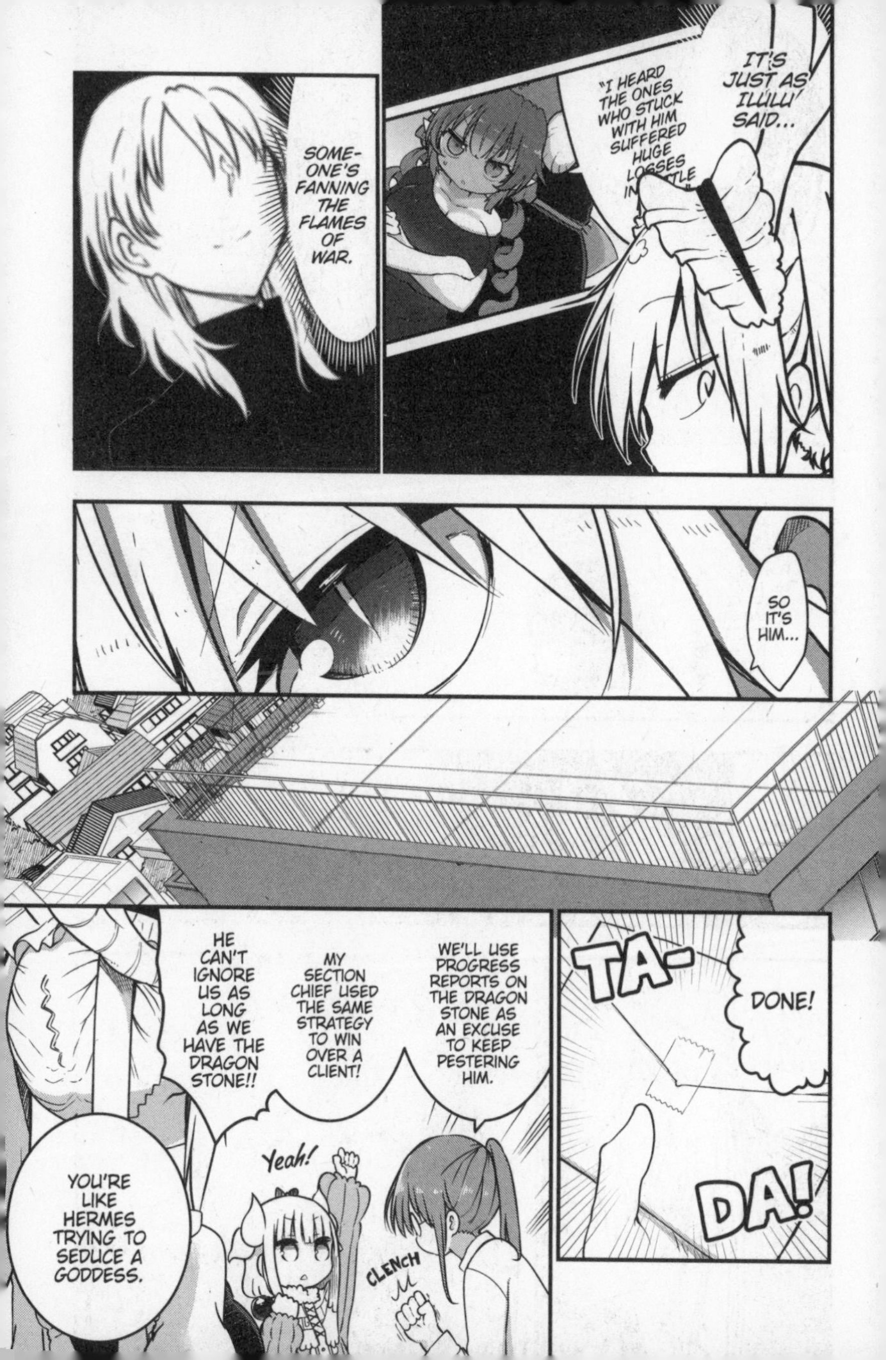
IT'S JUST AS ILULU SAID...
"I HEARD THE ONES WHO STUCK WITH HIM SUFFERED HUGE LOSSES IN
SOME-ONE'S FANNING THE FLAMES OF WAR.
SO IT'S HIM...
TA-
DONE!
DA!
WE'LL USE PROGRESS REPORTS ON THE DRAGON STONE AS AN EXCUSE TO KEEP PESTERING HIM.
MY SECTION CHIEF USED THE SAME STRATEGY TO WIN OVER A CLIENT!
HE CAN'T IGNORE US AS LONG AS WE HAVE THE DRAGON STONE!!
Yeah!
CLENCH
YOU'RE LIKE HERMES TRYING TO SEDUCE A GODDESS.

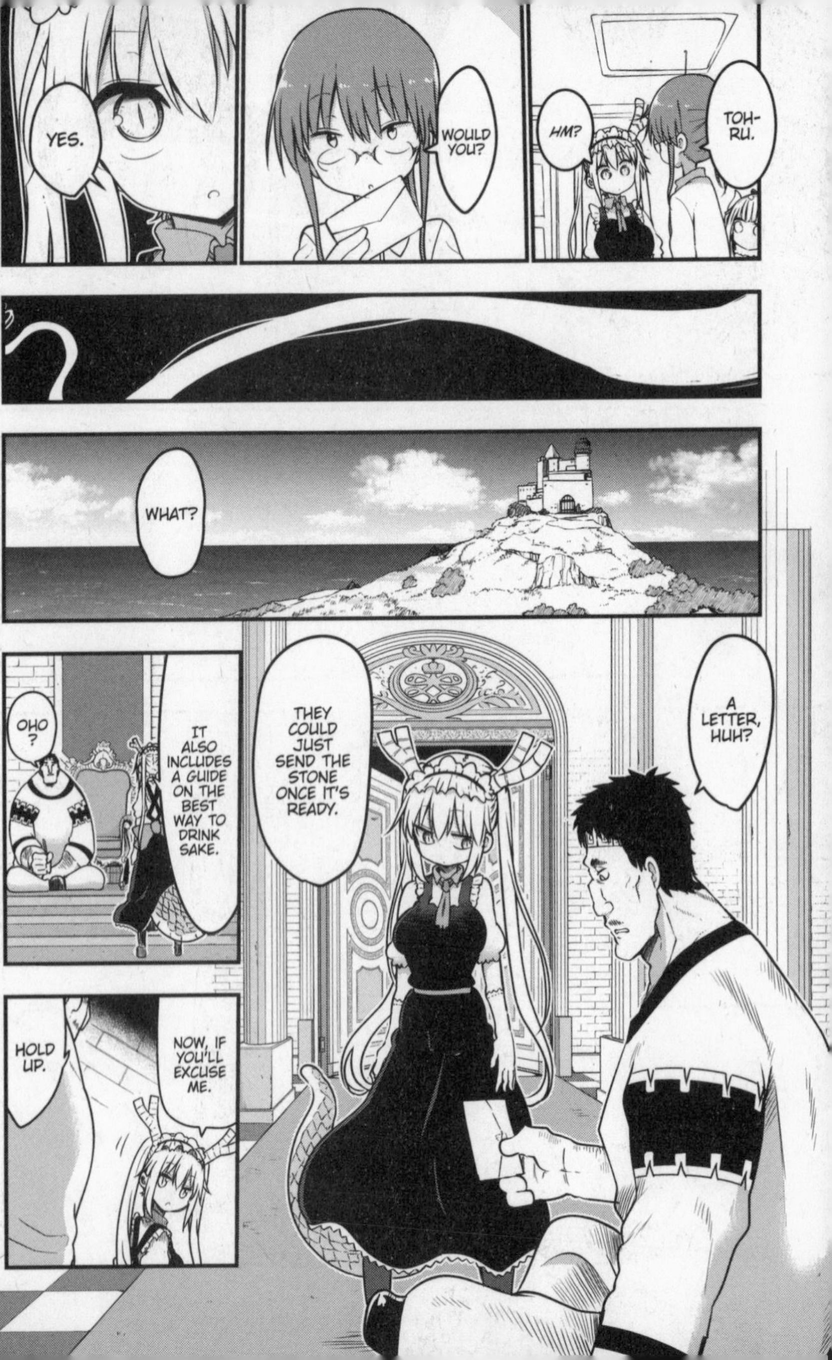
TOH-RU.
HM?
WOULD YOU?
YES.
WHAT?
A LETTER, HUH?
THEY COULD JUST SEND THE STONE ONCE IT'S READY.
IT ALSO INCLUDES A GUIDE ON THE BEST WAY TO DRINK SAKE.
OHO?
NOW, IF YOU'LL EXCUSE ME.
HOLD UP.

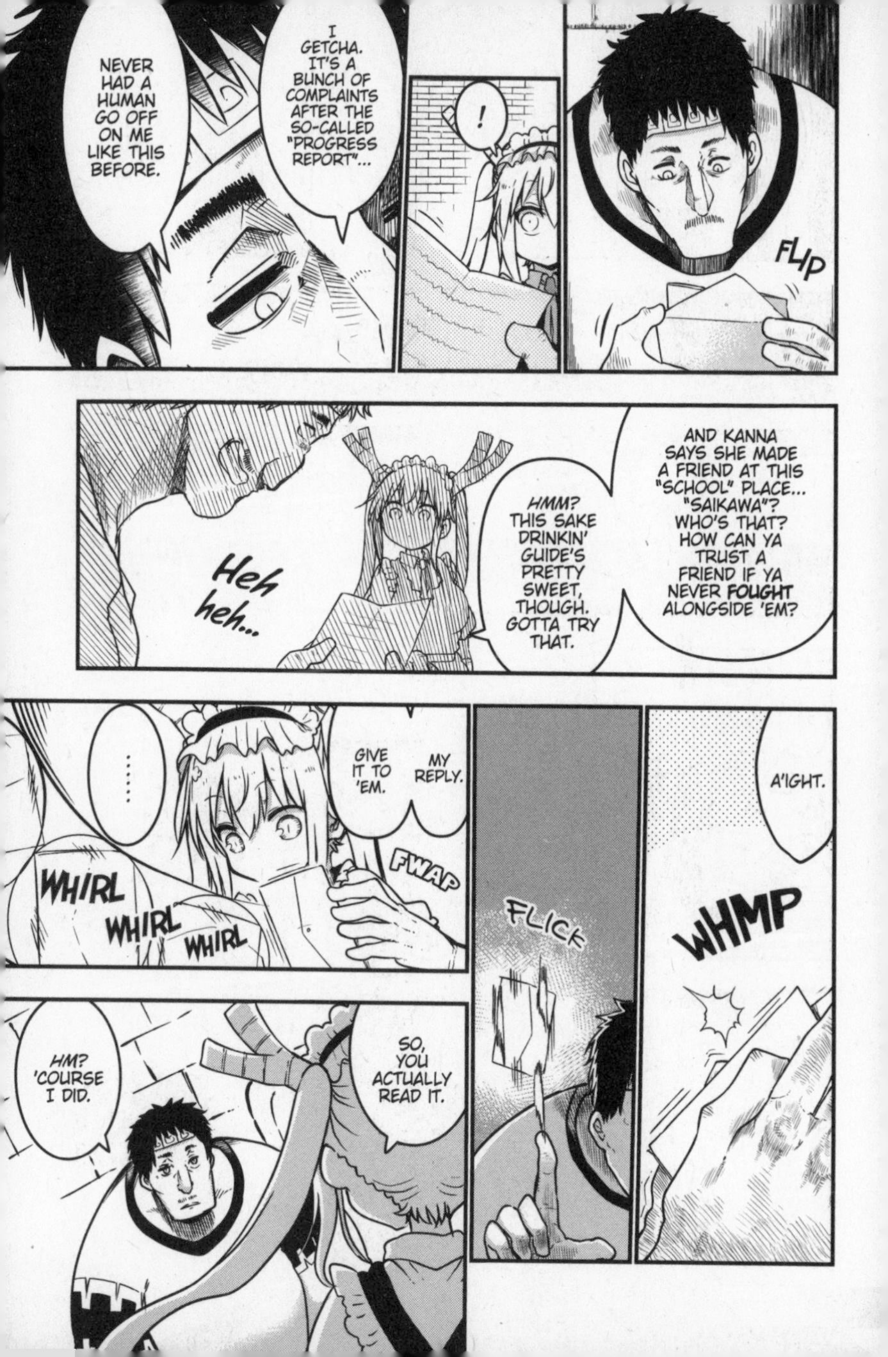
FLIP
!
I GETCHA. IT'S A BUNCH OF COMPLAINTS AFTER THE SO-CALLED "PROGRESS REPORT"...
NEVER HAD A HUMAN GO OFF ON ME LIKE THIS BEFORE.
AND KANNA SAYS SHE MADE A FRIEND AT THIS "SCHOOL" PLACE... "SAIKAWA"? WHO'S THAT? HOW CAN YA TRUST A FRIEND IF YA NEVER **FOUGHT** ALONGSIDE 'EM?
HMM? THIS SAKE DRINKIN' GUIDE'S PRETTY SWEET, THOUGH. GOTTA TRY THAT.
Heh heh...
A'IGHT.
WHMP
FLICK
MY REPLY.
GIVE IT TO 'EM.
FWAP
......
WHIRL
WHIRL
WHIRL
SO, YOU ACTUALLY READ IT.
HM? 'COURSE I DID.

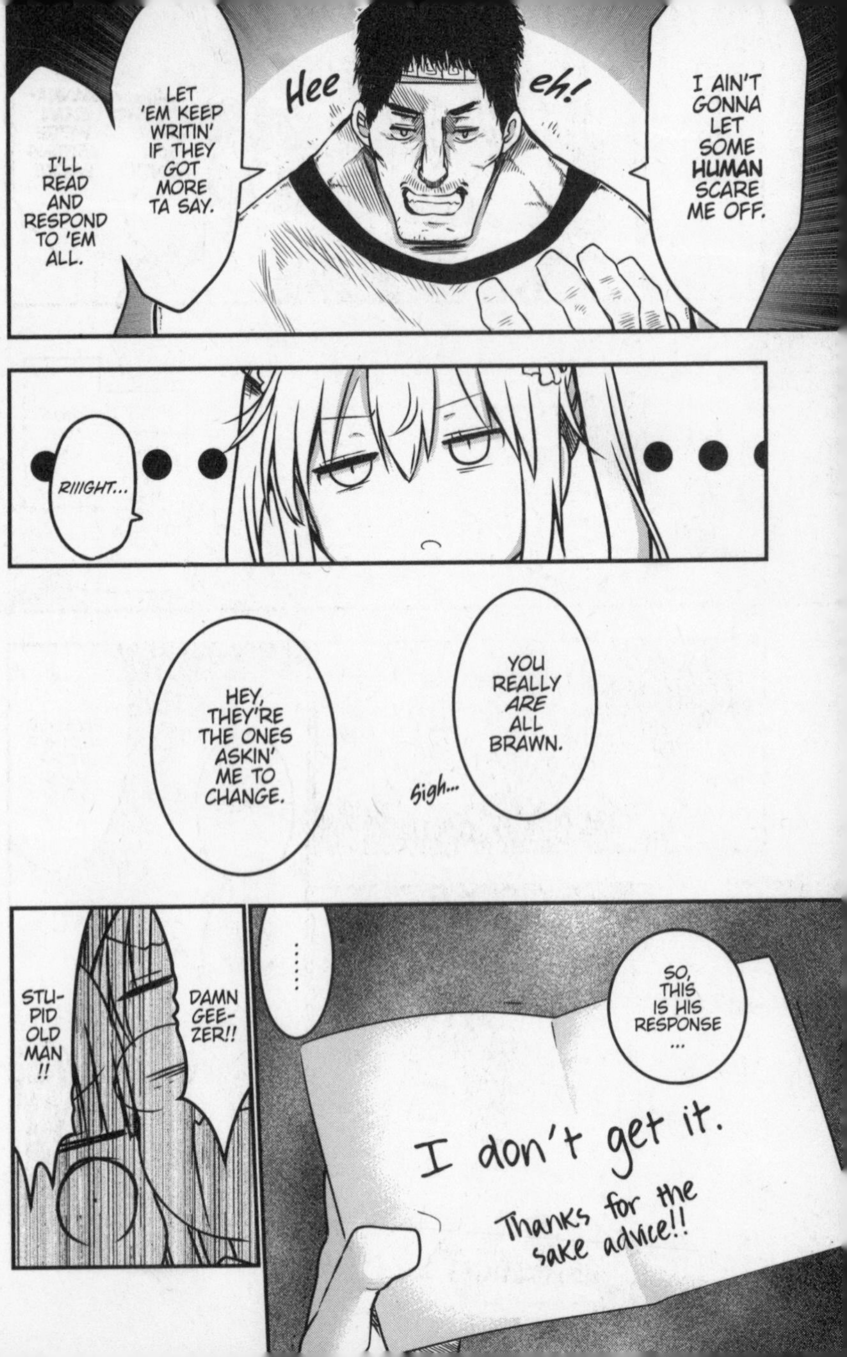
I AIN'T GONNA LET SOME HUMAN SCARE ME OFF.
Heeeh!
LET 'EM KEEP WRITIN' IF THEY GOT MORE TA SAY.
I'LL READ AND RESPOND TO 'EM ALL.
RIIIGHT...
YOU REALLY ARE ALL BRAWN.
Sigh...
HEY, THEY'RE THE ONES ASKIN' ME TO CHANGE.
SO, THIS IS HIS RESPONSE...
......
I don't get it.
Thanks for the sake advice!!
DAMN GEEZER!!
STUPID OLD MAN!!

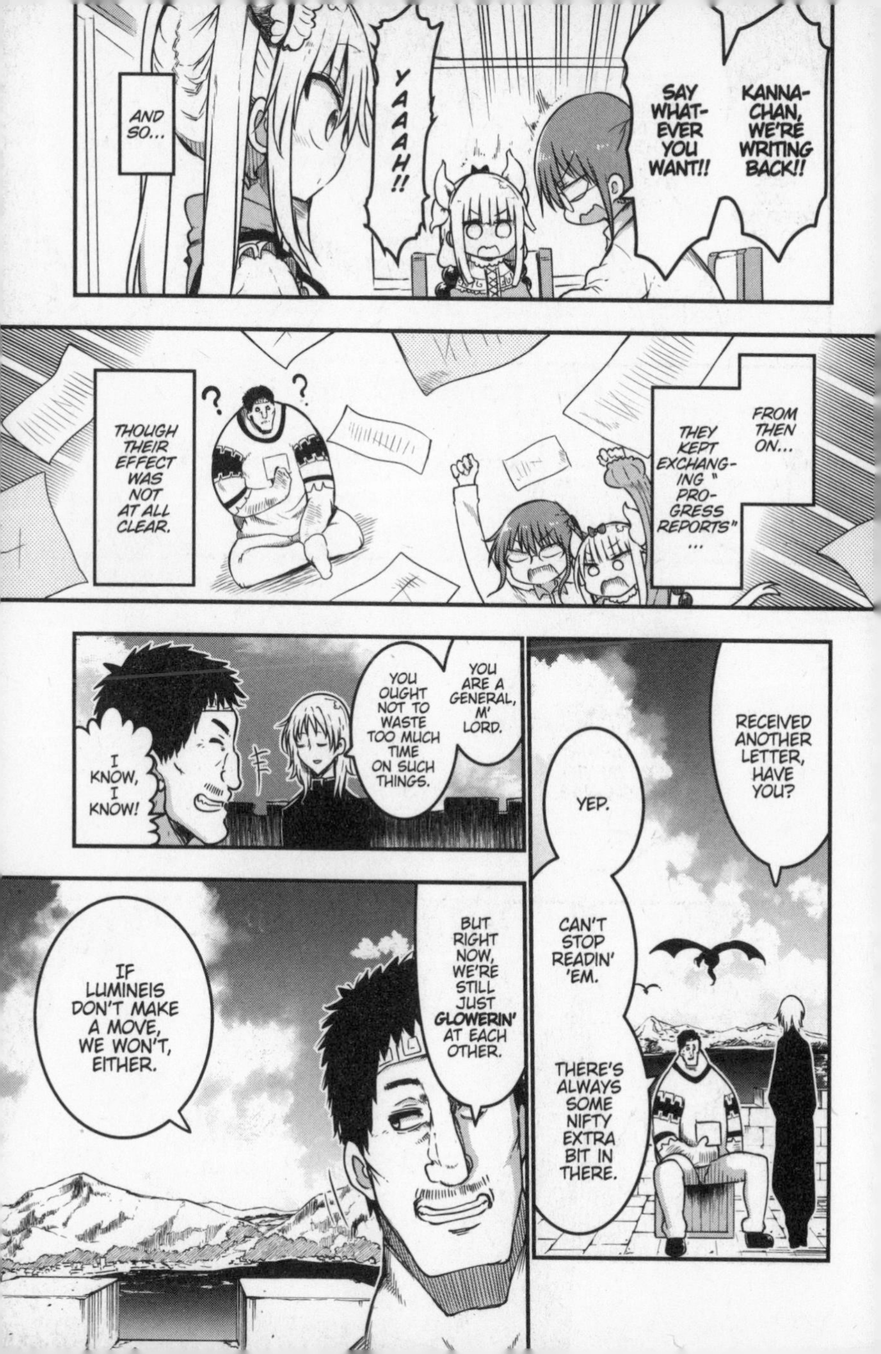
KANNA-CHAN, WE'RE WRITING BACK!!
SAY WHATEVER YOU WANT!!
YAAAAH!!
AND SO...
FROM THEN ON...
THEY KEPT EXCHANGING "PROGRESS REPORTS"...
THOUGH THEIR EFFECT WAS NOT AT ALL CLEAR.
RECEIVED ANOTHER LETTER, HAVE YOU?
YEP.
CAN'T STOP READIN' 'EM.
THERE'S ALWAYS SOME NIFTY EXTRA BIT IN THERE.
YOU ARE A GENERAL, M' LORD.
YOU OUGHT NOT TO WASTE TOO MUCH TIME ON SUCH THINGS.
I KNOW, I KNOW!
BUT RIGHT NOW, WE'RE STILL JUST **GLOWERIN'** AT EACH OTHER.
IF LUMINEIS DON'T MAKE A MOVE, WE WON'T, EITHER.

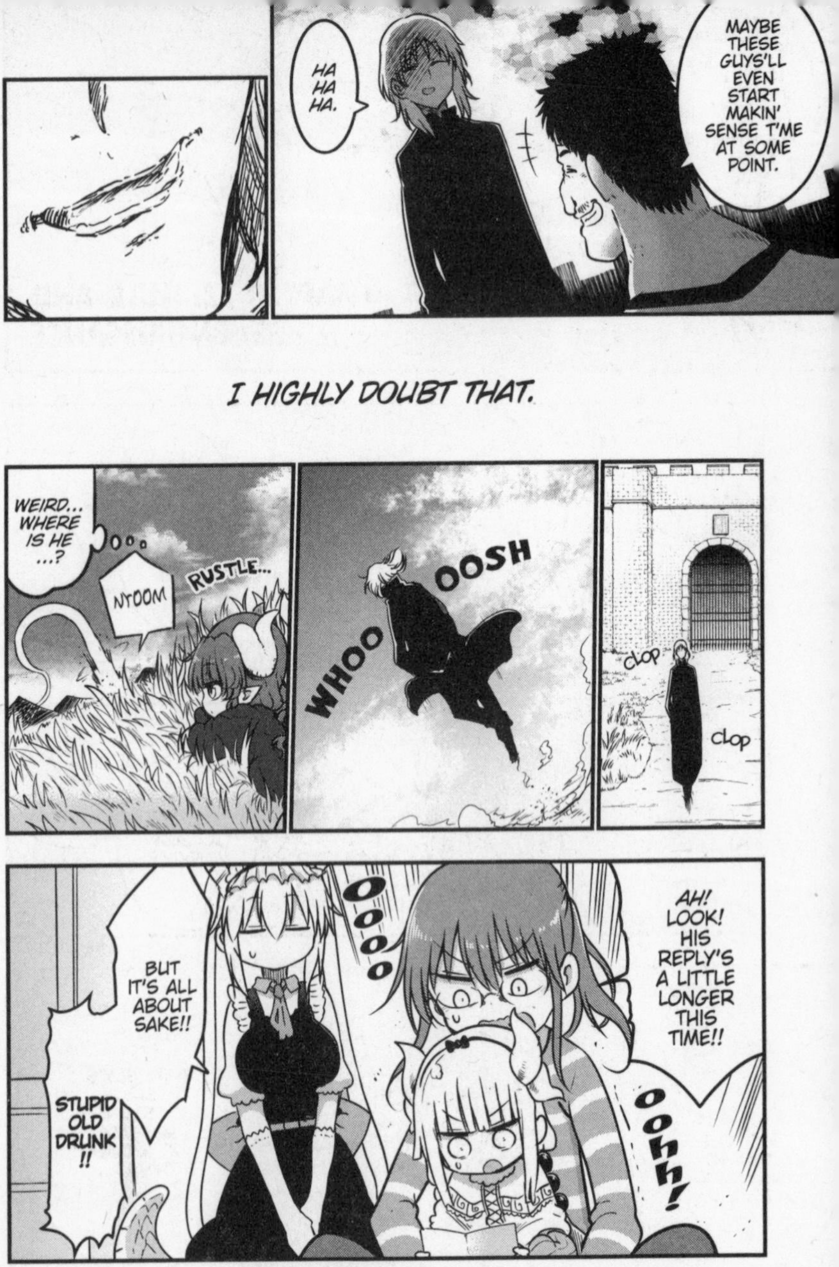
MAYBE THESE GUYS'LL EVEN START MAKIN' SENSE T'ME AT SOME POINT.
HA HA HA HA.
I HIGHLY DOUBT THAT.
CLOP
CLOP
WHOOOSH
WEIRD... WHERE IS HE ...?
RUSTLE...
NTOOM
AH! LOOK! HIS REPLY'S A LITTLE LONGER THIS TIME!!
OOOhh!
OOOOO
BUT IT'S ALL ABOUT SAKE!!
STUPID OLD DRUNK!!

CHAPTER 71/END

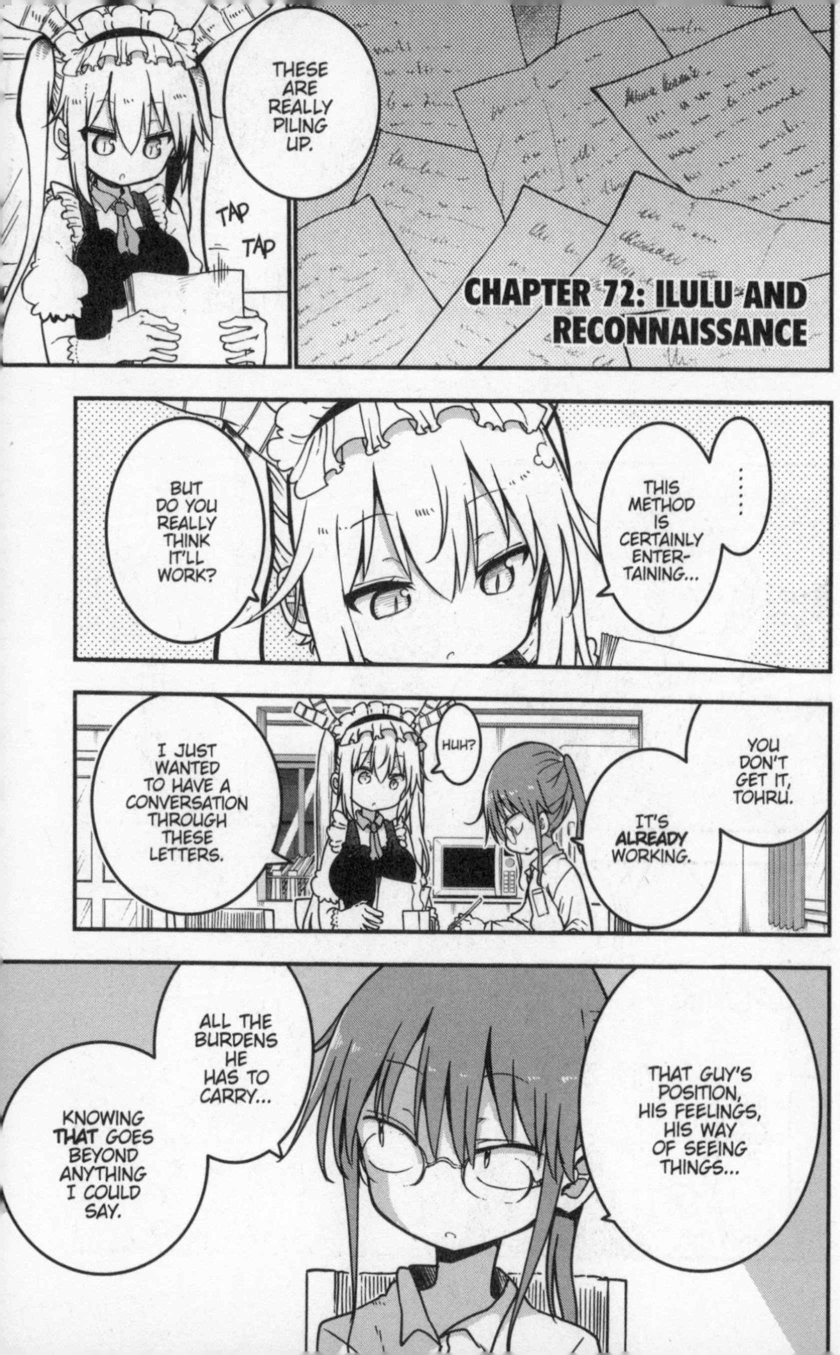
CHAPTER 72: ILULU AND RECONNAISSANCE
THESE ARE REALLY PILING UP.
TAP
TAP
......
THIS METHOD IS CERTAINLY ENTERTAINING...
BUT DO YOU REALLY THINK IT'LL WORK?
YOU DON'T GET IT, TOHRU.
IT'S ALREADY WORKING.
HUH?
I JUST WANTED TO HAVE A CONVERSATION THROUGH THESE LETTERS.
THAT GUY'S POSITION, HIS FEELINGS, HIS WAY OF SEEING THINGS...
ALL THE BURDENS HE HAS TO CARRY...
KNOWING THAT GOES BEYOND ANYTHING I COULD SAY.

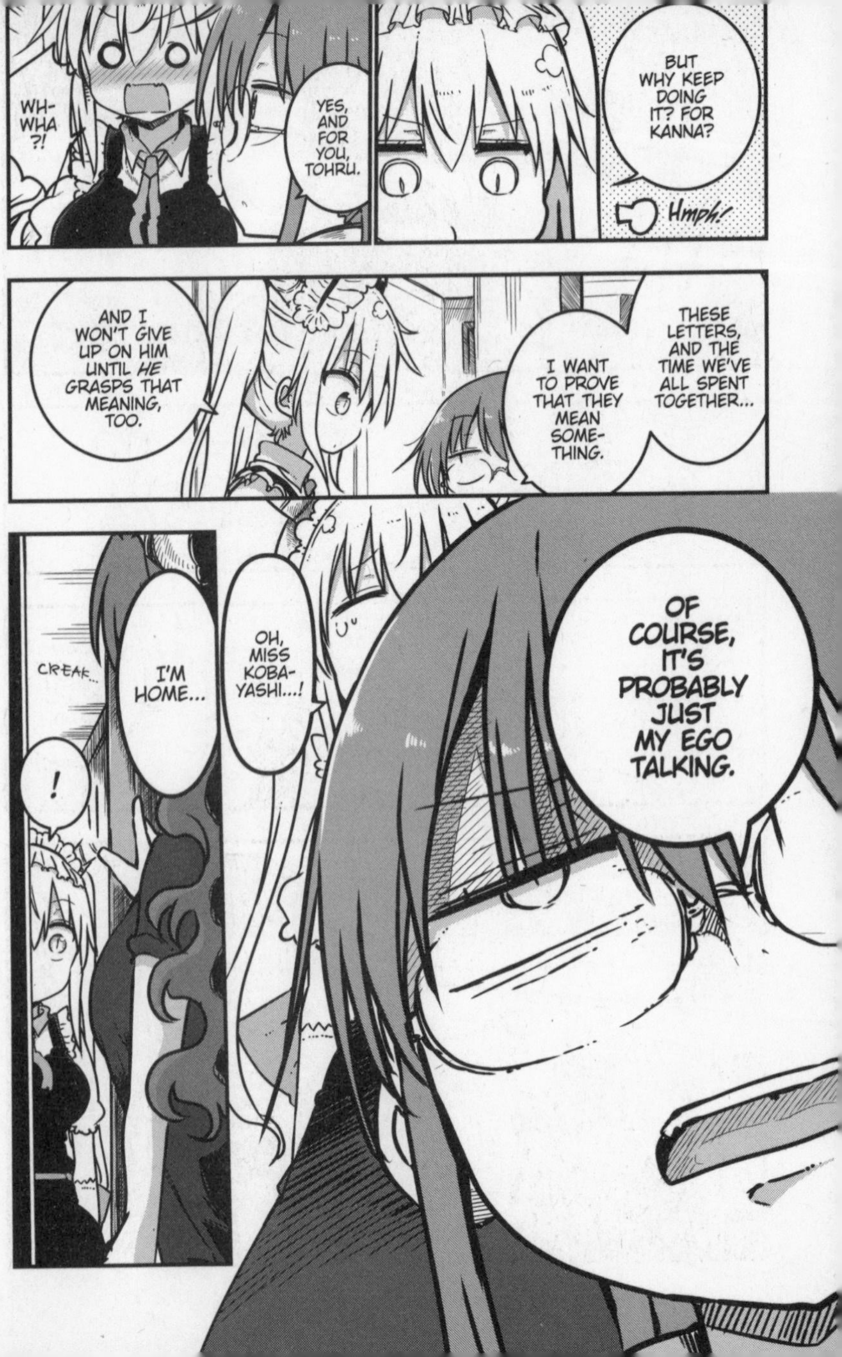
BUT WHY KEEP DOING IT? FOR KANNA?
Hmph!
YES, AND FOR YOU, TOHRU.
WH-WHA?!
THESE LETTERS, AND THE TIME WE'VE ALL SPENT TOGETHER...
I WANT TO PROVE THAT THEY MEAN SOMETHING.
AND I WON'T GIVE UP ON HIM UNTIL *HE* GRASPS THAT MEANING, TOO.
OF COURSE, IT'S PROBABLY JUST MY EGO TALKING.
OH, MISS KOBAYASHI...!
I'M HOME...
CREAK...
!

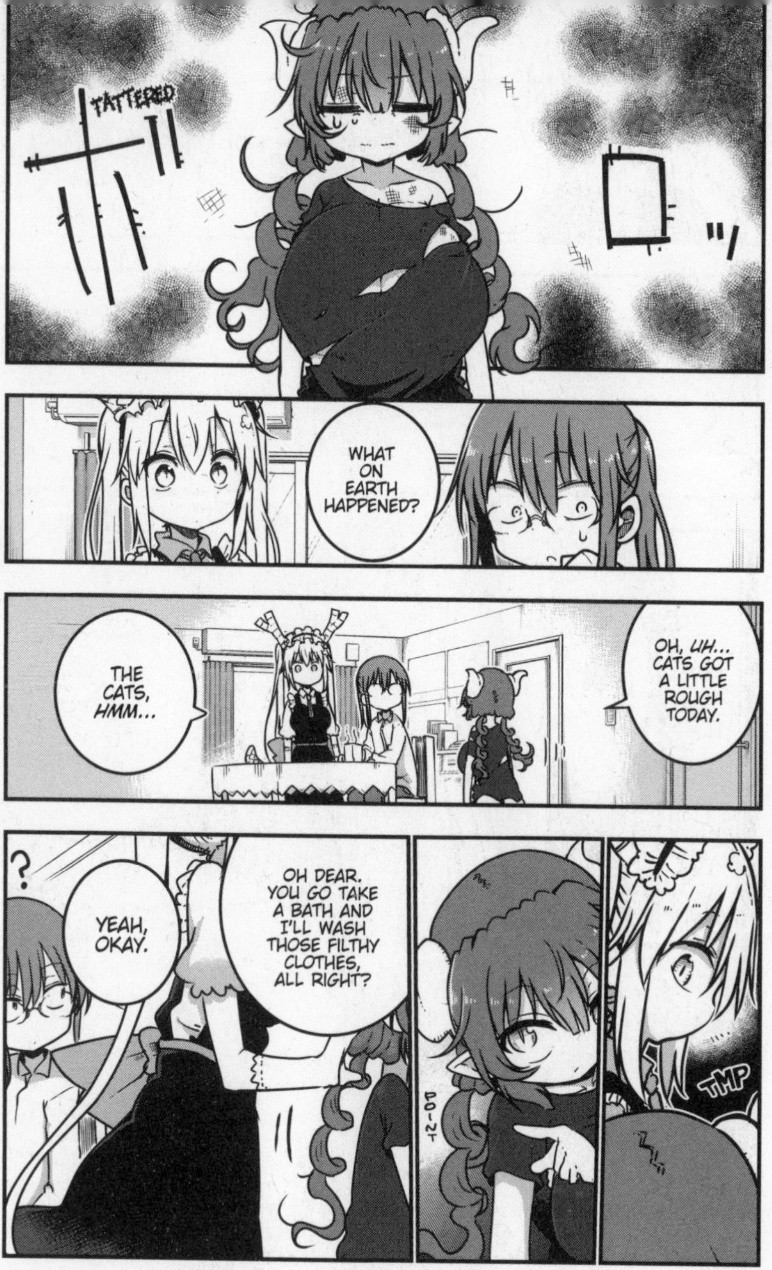
TATTERED
WHAT ON EARTH HAPPENED?
OH, UH... CATS GOT A LITTLE ROUGH TODAY.
THE CATS, HMM...
TMP
POINT
OH DEAR. YOU GO TAKE A BATH AND I'LL WASH THOSE FILTHY CLOTHES, ALL RIGHT?
YEAH, OKAY.

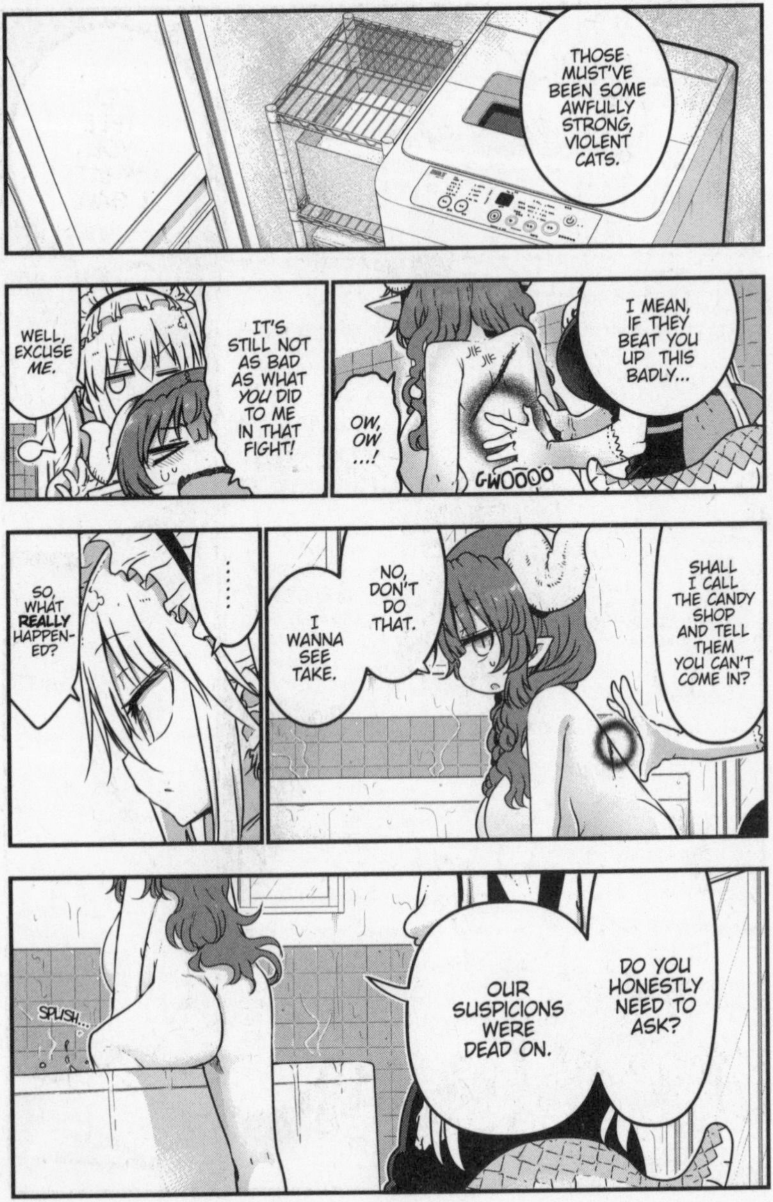
THOSE MUST'VE BEEN SOME AWFULLY STRONG, VIOLENT CATS.
I MEAN, IF THEY BEAT YOU UP THIS BADLY...
OW, OW ...!
GWOOOO
IT'S STILL NOT AS BAD AS WHAT *YOU* DID TO ME IN THAT FIGHT!
WELL, EXCUSE *ME*.
SHALL I CALL THE CANDY SHOP AND TELL THEM YOU CAN'T COME IN?
NO, DON'T DO THAT.
I WANNA SEE TAKE.
......
SO, WHAT **REALLY** HAPPENED?
DO YOU HONESTLY NEED TO ASK?
OUR SUSPICIONS WERE DEAD ON.
SPLISH...

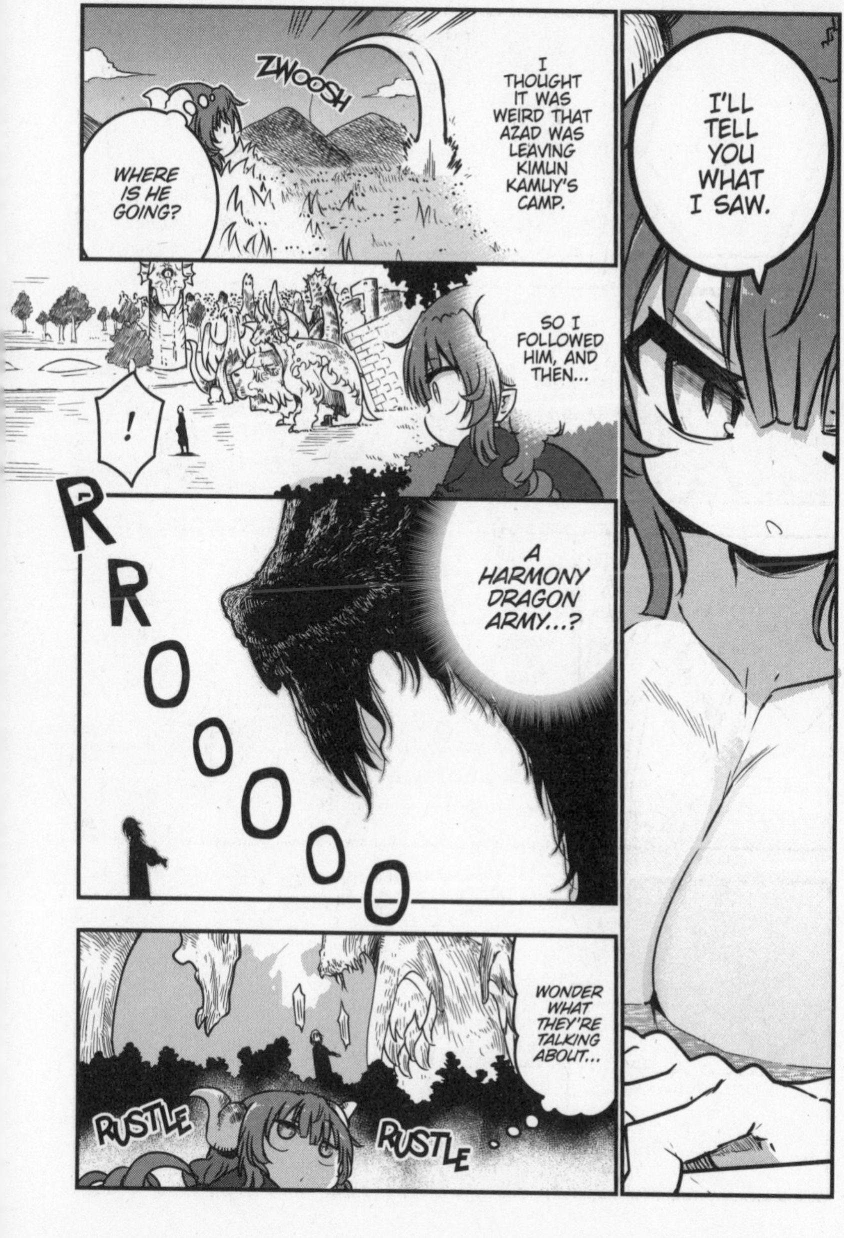
I'LL TELL YOU WHAT I SAW.
I THOUGHT IT WAS WEIRD THAT AZAD WAS LEAVING KIMUN KAMUY'S CAMP.
ZWOOSH
WHERE IS HE GOING?
SO I FOLLOWED HIM, AND THEN...
!
A HARMONY DRAGON ARMY...?
RRROOOOO
WONDER WHAT THEY'RE TALKING ABOUT...
RUSTLE
RUSTLE

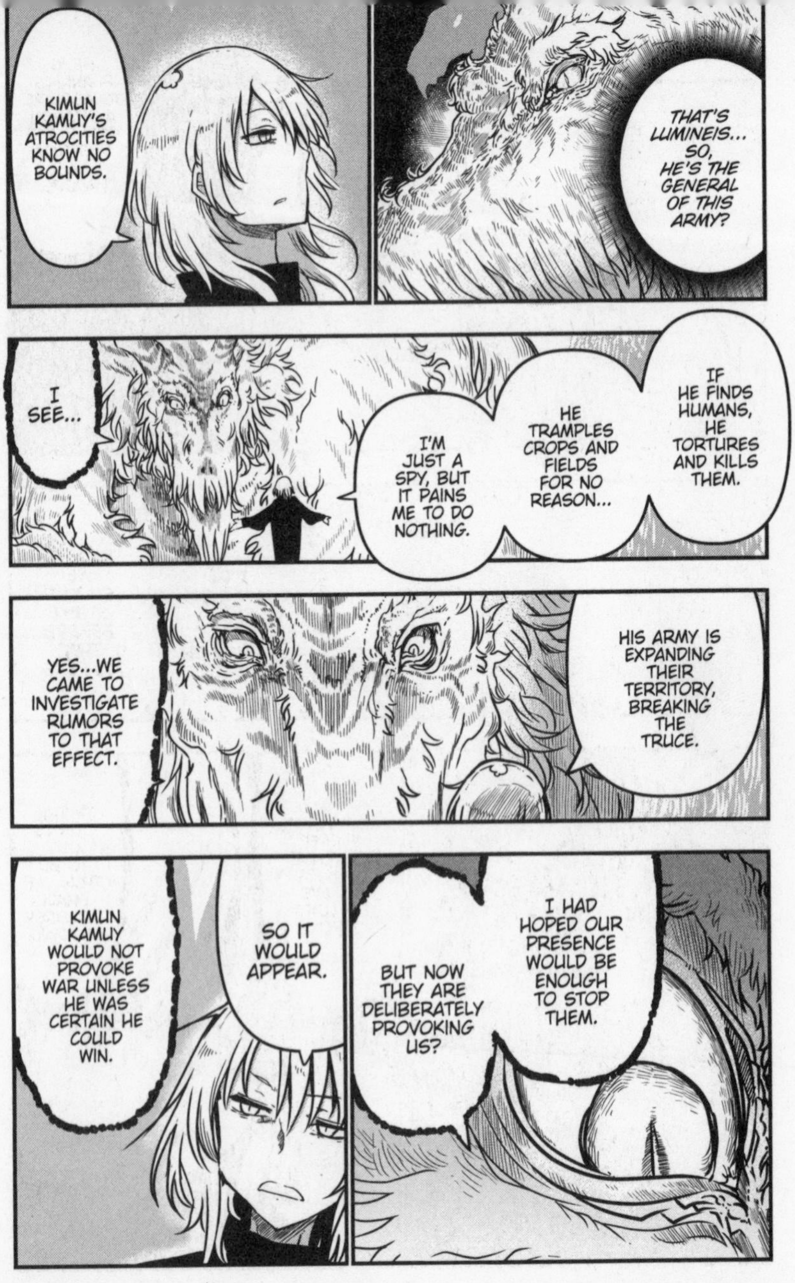
THAT'S LUMINEIS... SO, HE'S THE GENERAL OF THIS ARMY?
KIMUN KAMUY'S ATROCITIES KNOW NO BOUNDS.
IF HE FINDS HUMANS, HE TORTURES AND KILLS THEM.
HE TRAMPLES CROPS AND FIELDS FOR NO REASON...
I'M JUST A SPY, BUT IT PAINS ME TO DO NOTHING.
I SEE...
HIS ARMY IS EXPANDING THEIR TERRITORY, BREAKING THE TRUCE.
YES...WE CAME TO INVESTIGATE RUMORS TO THAT EFFECT.
I HAD HOPED OUR PRESENCE WOULD BE ENOUGH TO STOP THEM.
BUT NOW THEY ARE DELIBERATELY PROVOKING US?
SO IT WOULD APPEAR.
KIMUN KAMUY WOULD NOT PROVOKE WAR UNLESS HE WAS CERTAIN HE COULD WIN.

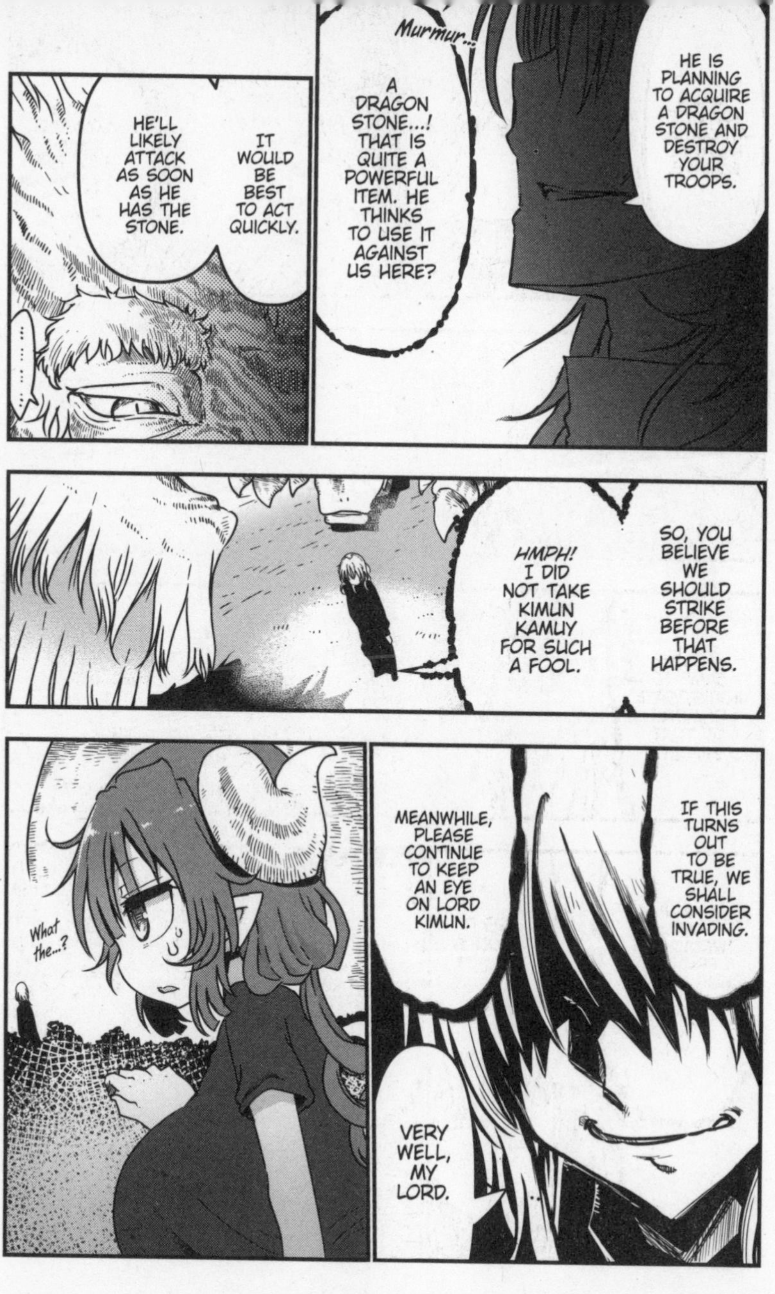
HE IS PLANNING TO ACQUIRE A DRAGON STONE AND DESTROY YOUR TROOPS.
Murmur...
A DRAGON STONE...! THAT IS QUITE A POWERFUL ITEM. HE THINKS TO USE IT AGAINST US HERE?
IT WOULD BE BEST TO ACT QUICKLY.
HE'LL LIKELY ATTACK AS SOON AS HE HAS THE STONE.
...
SO, YOU BELIEVE WE SHOULD STRIKE BEFORE THAT HAPPENS.
HMPH! I DID NOT TAKE KIMUN KAMUY FOR SUCH A FOOL.
IF THIS TURNS OUT TO BE TRUE, WE SHALL CONSIDER INVADING.
MEANWHILE, PLEASE CONTINUE TO KEEP AN EYE ON LORD KIMUN.
VERY WELL, MY LORD.
What the...?

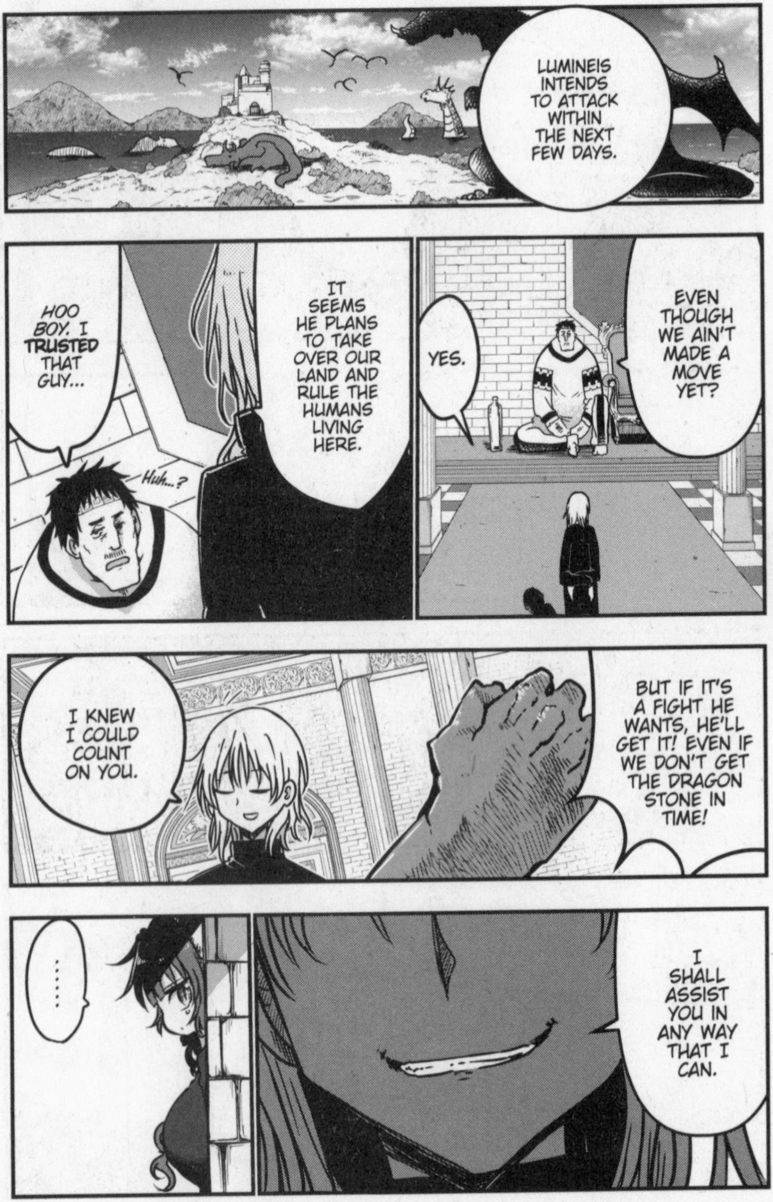
LUMINEIS INTENDS TO ATTACK WITHIN THE NEXT FEW DAYS.
EVEN THOUGH WE AIN'T MADE A MOVE YET?
YES.
IT SEEMS HE PLANS TO TAKE OVER OUR LAND AND RULE THE HUMANS LIVING HERE.
HOO BOY. I **TRUSTED** THAT GUY...
Huh...?
BUT IF IT'S A FIGHT HE WANTS, HE'LL GET IT! EVEN IF WE DON'T GET THE DRAGON STONE IN TIME!
I KNEW I COULD COUNT ON YOU.
I SHALL ASSIST YOU IN ANY WAY THAT I CAN.
......

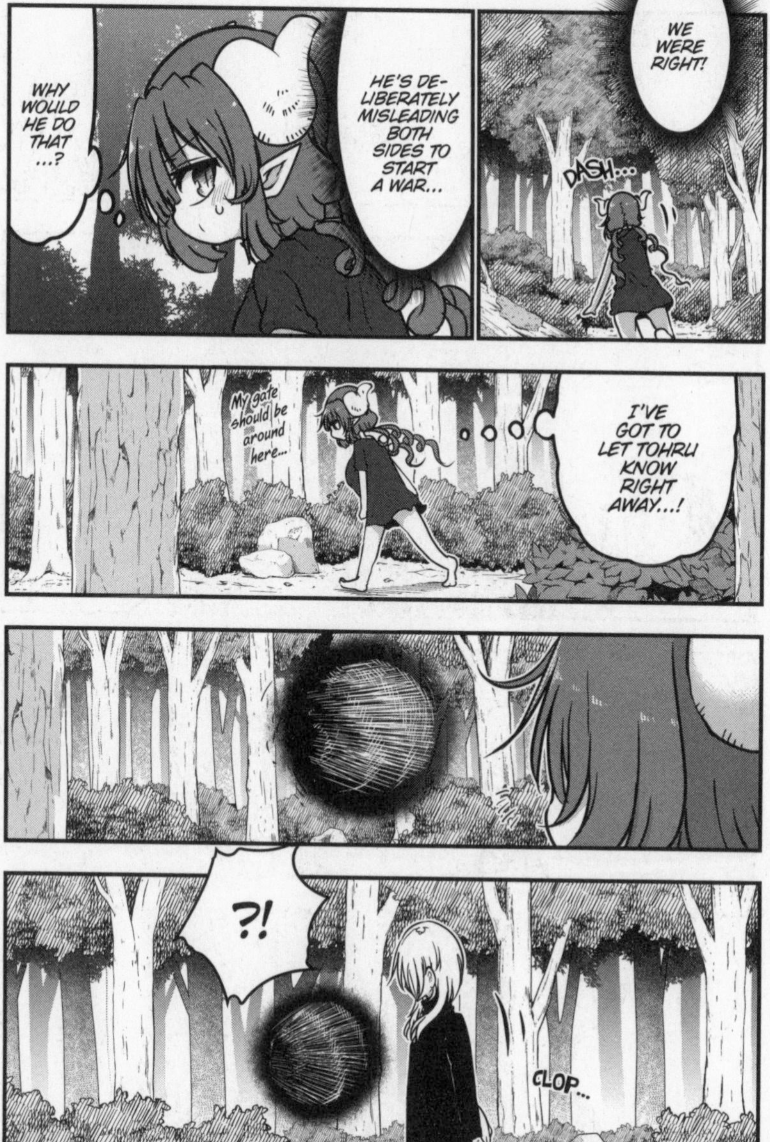

WE WERE RIGHT!
DASH...
HE'S DE-LIBERATELY MISLEADING BOTH SIDES TO START A WAR...
WHY WOULD HE DO THAT ...?
I'VE GOT TO LET TOHRU KNOW RIGHT AWAY...!
My gate should be around here...
?!
CLOP...

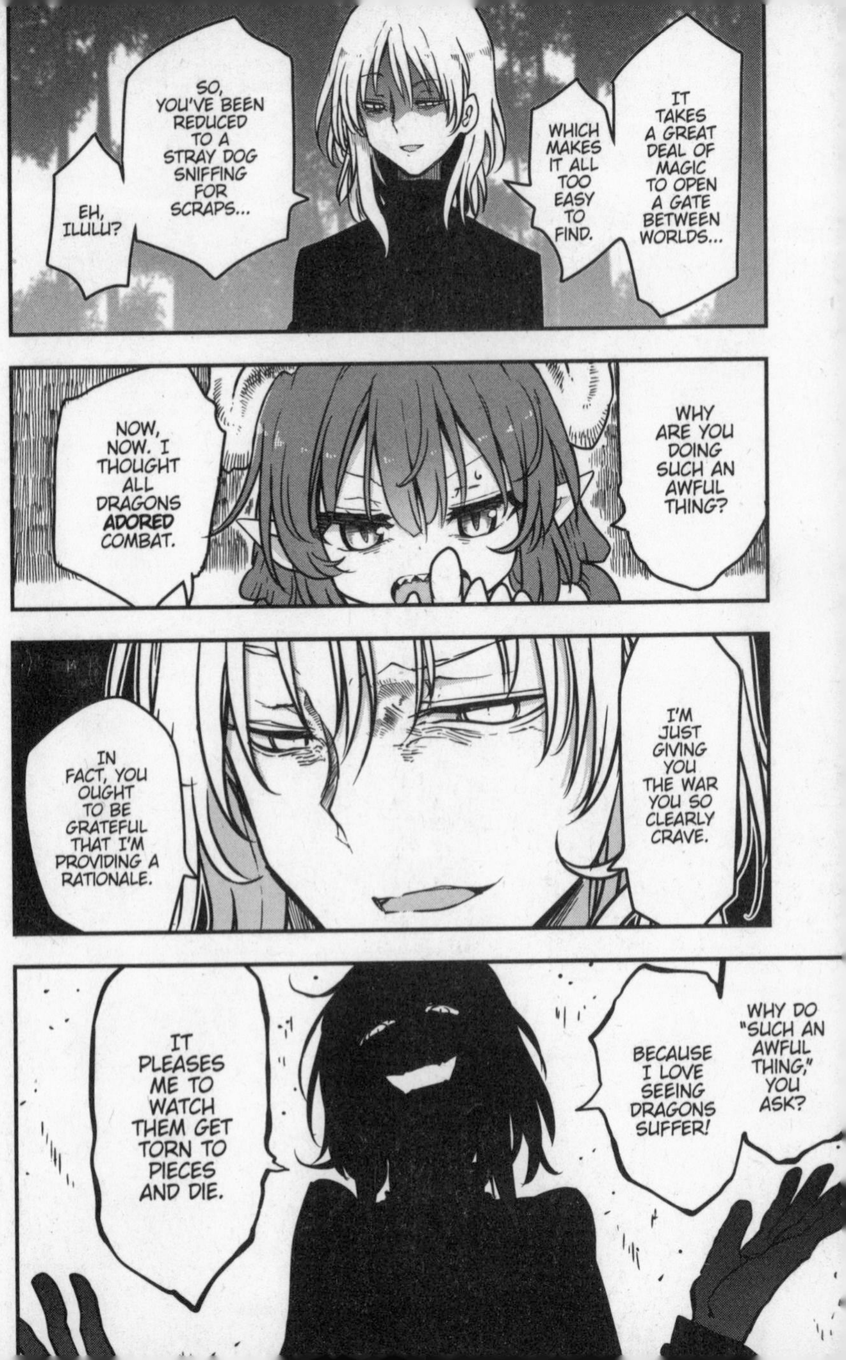
IT TAKES A GREAT DEAL OF MAGIC TO OPEN A GATE BETWEEN WORLDS...
WHICH MAKES IT ALL TOO EASY TO FIND.
SO, YOU'VE BEEN REDUCED TO A STRAY DOG SNIFFING FOR SCRAPS...
EH, ILULU?
WHY ARE YOU DOING SUCH AN AWFUL THING?
NOW, NOW. I THOUGHT ALL DRAGONS **ADORED** COMBAT.
I'M JUST GIVING YOU THE WAR YOU SO CLEARLY CRAVE.
IN FACT, YOU OUGHT TO BE GRATEFUL THAT I'M PROVIDING A RATIONALE.
WHY DO "SUCH AN AWFUL THING," YOU ASK?
BECAUSE I LOVE SEEING DRAGONS SUFFER!
IT PLEASES ME TO WATCH THEM GET TORN TO PIECES AND DIE.

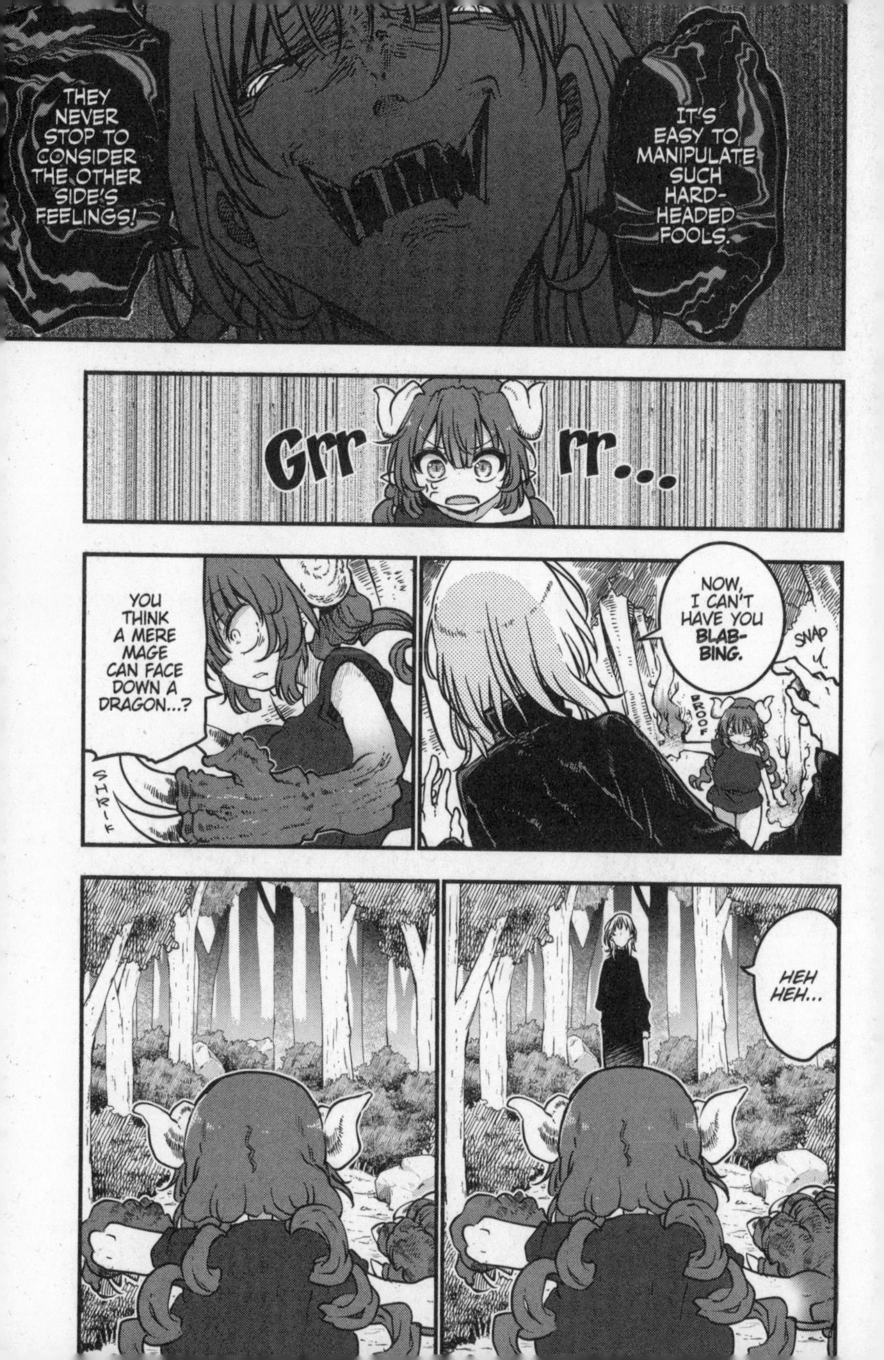
IT'S EASY TO MANIPULATE SUCH HARD-HEADED FOOLS.
THEY NEVER STOP TO CONSIDER THE OTHER SIDE'S FEELINGS!
Grrrr...
NOW, I CAN'T HAVE YOU BLABBING.
SNAP
BROOF
YOU THINK A MERE MAGE CAN FACE DOWN A DRAGON...?
SHRIK
HEH HEH...

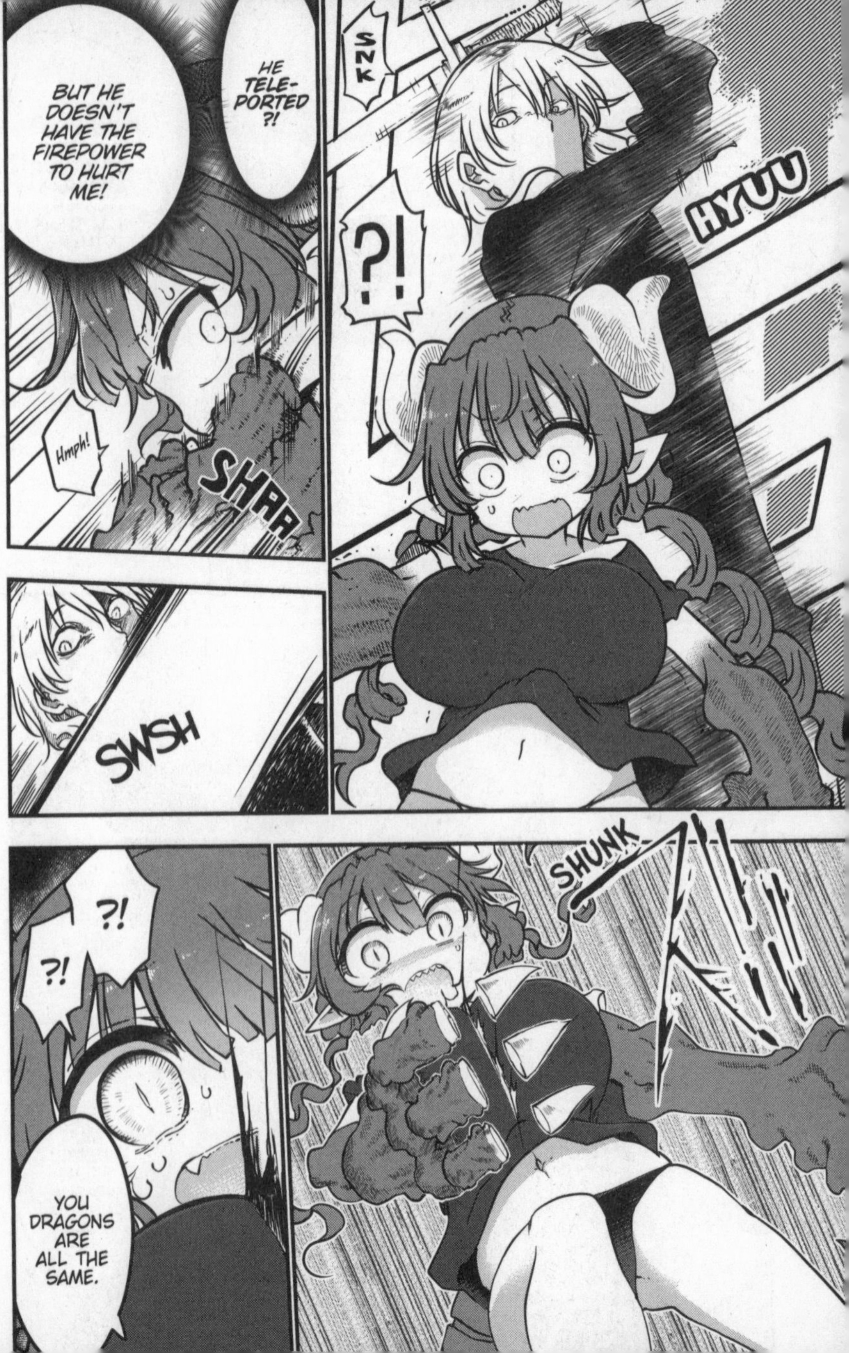
SNK
?!
HYUU
HE TELE-PORTED ?!
BUT HE DOESN'T HAVE THE FIREPOWER TO HURT ME!
Hmph!
SHAA
SWSH
SHUNK
?!
?!
YOU DRAGONS ARE ALL THE SAME.

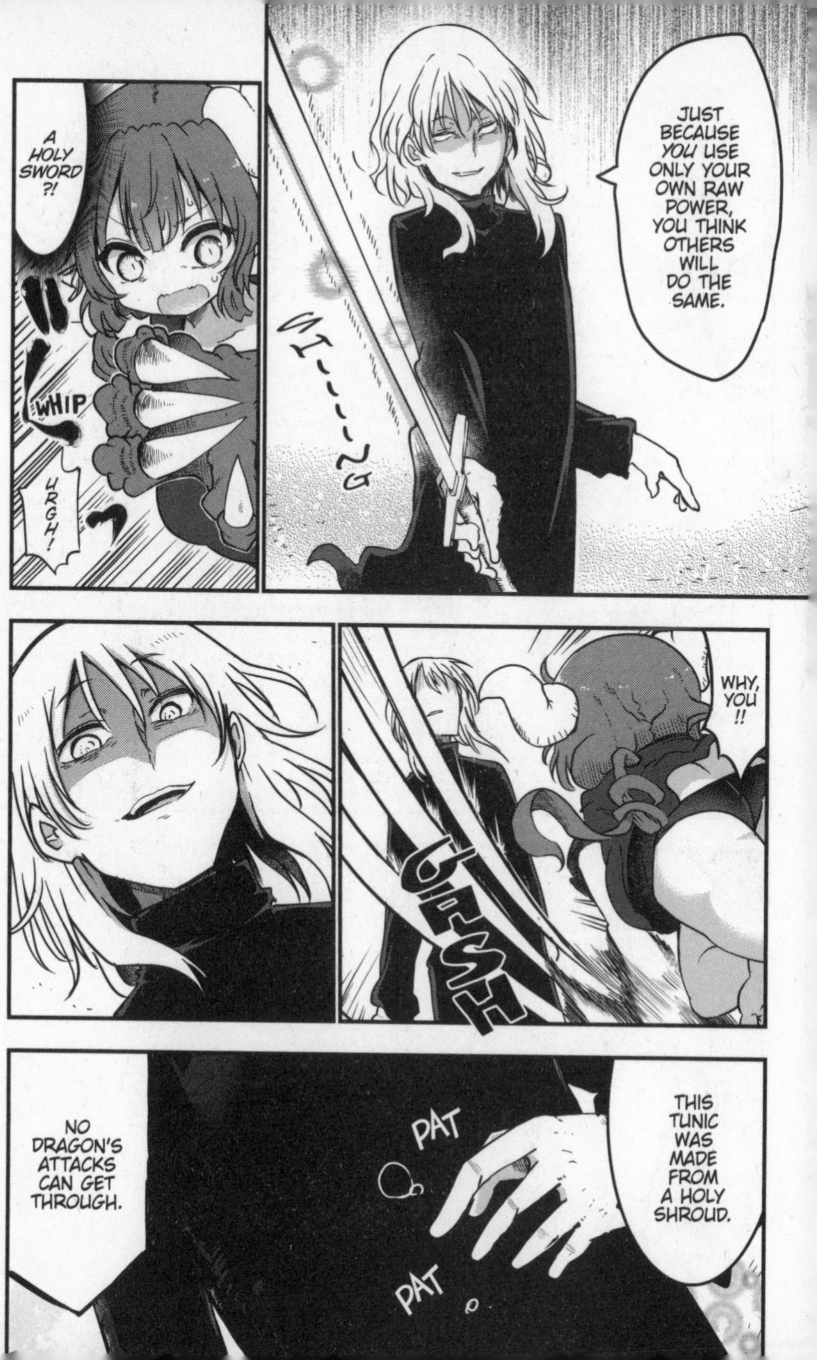
JUST BECAUSE YOU USE ONLY YOUR OWN RAW POWER, YOU THINK OTHERS WILL DO THE SAME.
A HOLY SWORD ?!
WHIP
URGH!
WHY, YOU !!
THIS TUNIC WAS MADE FROM A HOLY SHROUD.
PAT
PAT
NO DRAGON'S ATTACKS CAN GET THROUGH.

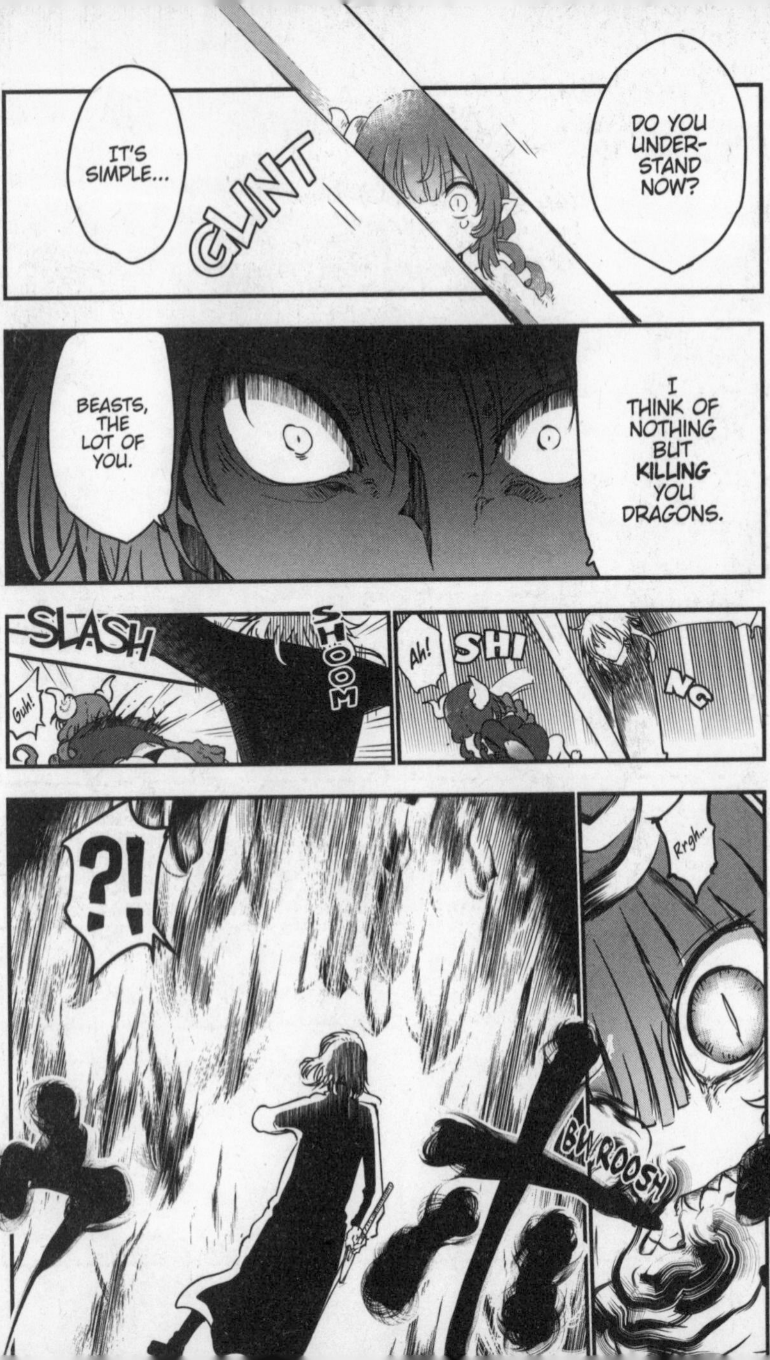
DO YOU UNDER-STAND NOW?
GLINT
IT'S SIMPLE...
I THINK OF NOTHING BUT KILLING YOU DRAGONS.
BEASTS, THE LOT OF YOU.
SHI NG
Ah!
SHOOM
SLASH
Guh!
Rrgh...
BWROOSH
?!

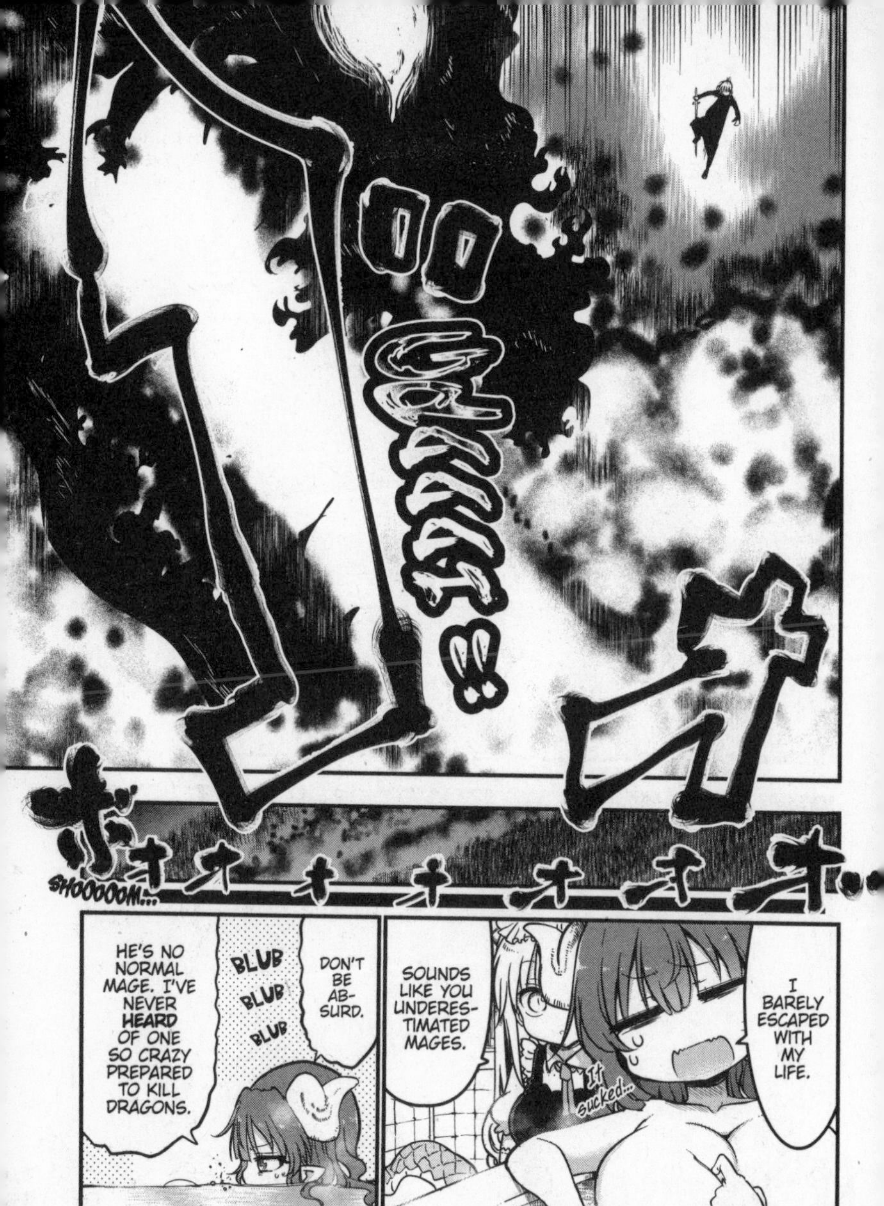
SHOOOOOM...
I BARELY ESCAPED WITH MY LIFE.
It sucked...
SOUNDS LIKE YOU UNDERESTIMATED MAGES.
DON'T BE ABSURD.
BLUB BLUB BLUB
HE'S NO NORMAL MAGE. I'VE NEVER **HEARD** OF ONE SO CRAZY PREPARED TO KILL DRAGONS.

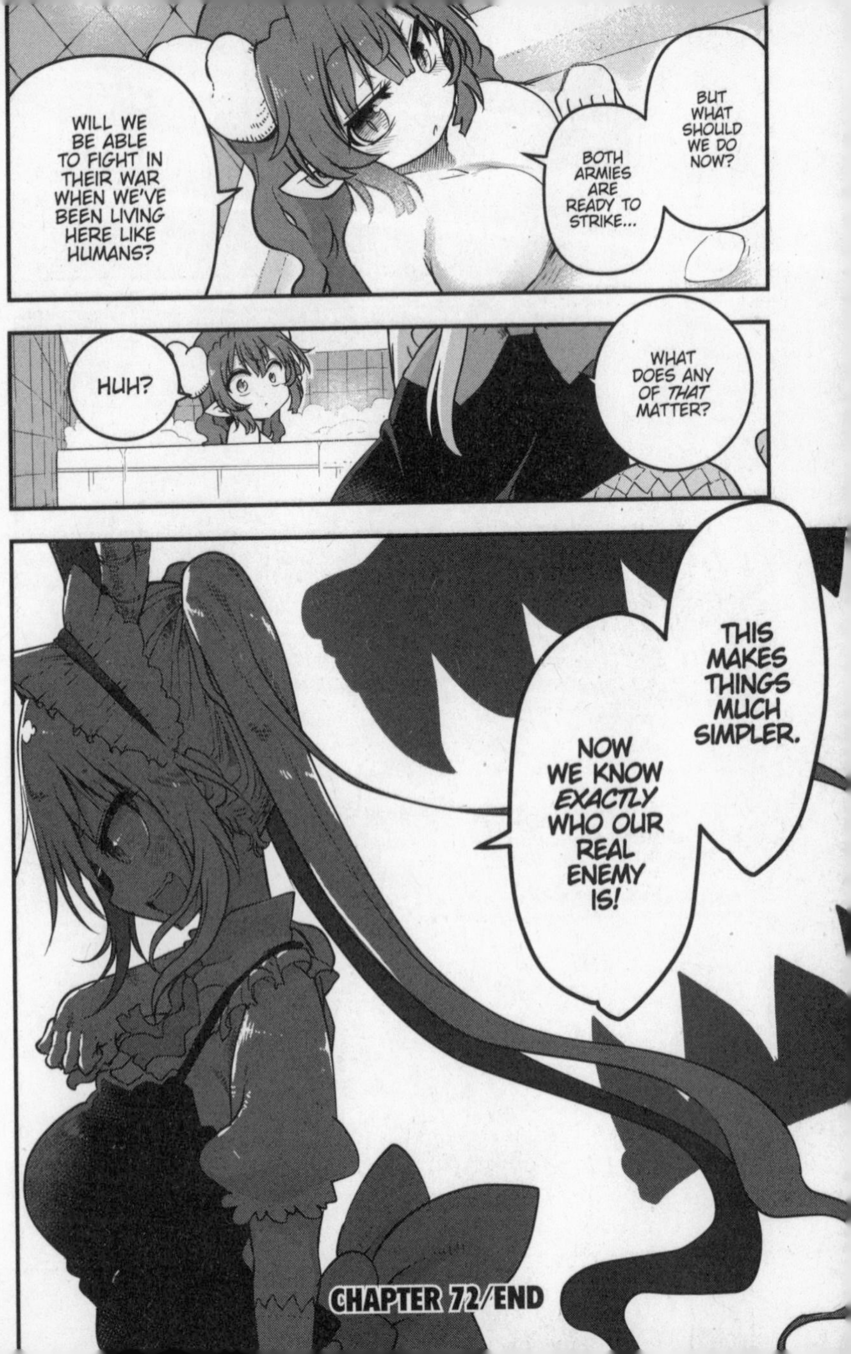
BUT WHAT SHOULD WE DO NOW?
BOTH ARMIES ARE READY TO STRIKE...
WILL WE BE ABLE TO FIGHT IN THEIR WAR WHEN WE'VE BEEN LIVING HERE LIKE HUMANS?
WHAT DOES ANY OF *THAT* MATTER?
HUH?
THIS MAKES THINGS MUCH SIMPLER.
NOW WE KNOW *EXACTLY* WHO OUR REAL ENEMY IS!
CHAPTER 72/END

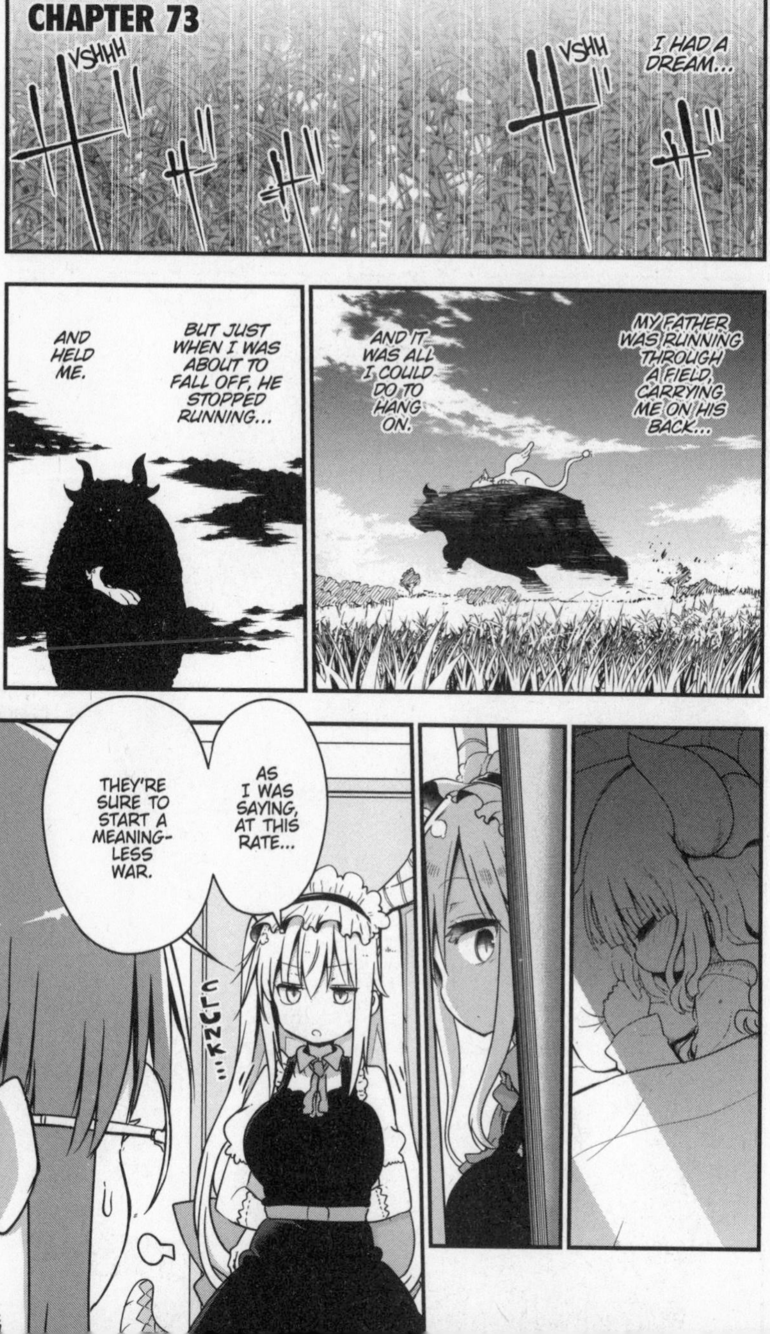
CHAPTER 73
I HAD A DREAM...
VSHH
VSHHH
MY FATHER WAS RUNNING THROUGH A FIELD, CARRYING ME ON HIS BACK...
AND IT WAS ALL I COULD DO TO HANG ON.
BUT JUST WHEN I WAS ABOUT TO FALL OFF, HE STOPPED RUNNING...
AND HELD ME.
AS I WAS SAYING, AT THIS RATE...
THEY'RE SURE TO START A MEANING-LESS WAR.
CLUNK...

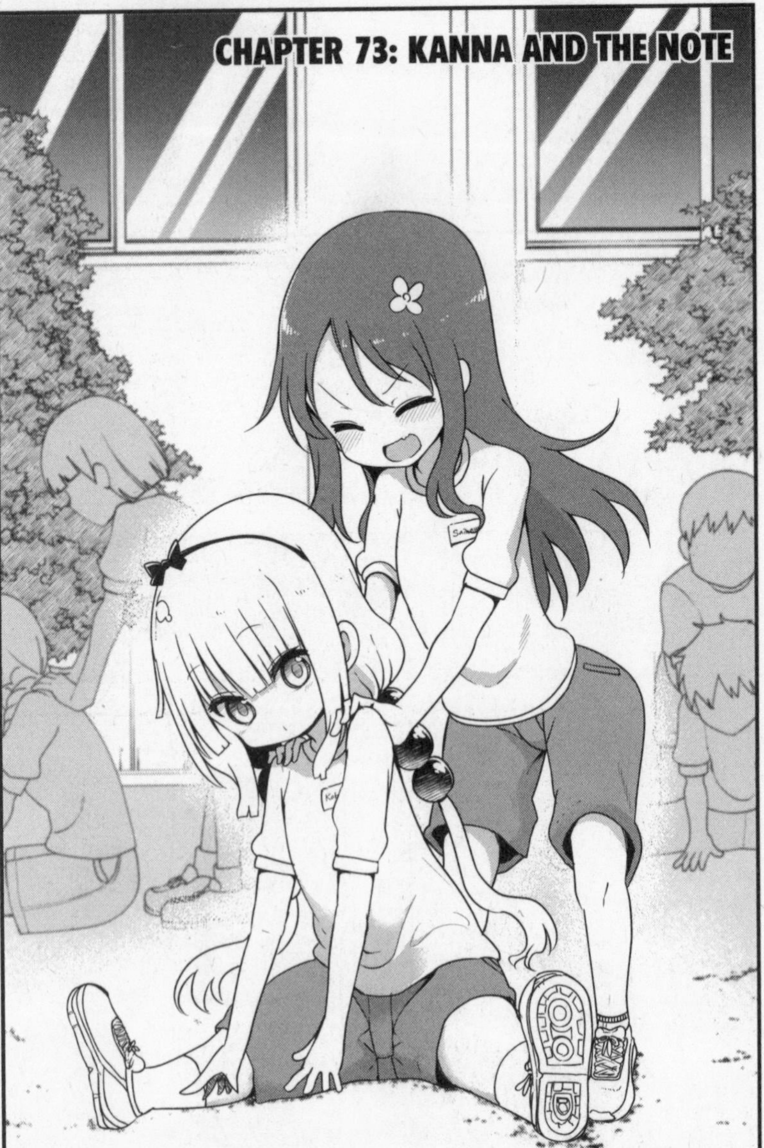
CHAPTER 73: KANNA AND THE NOTE

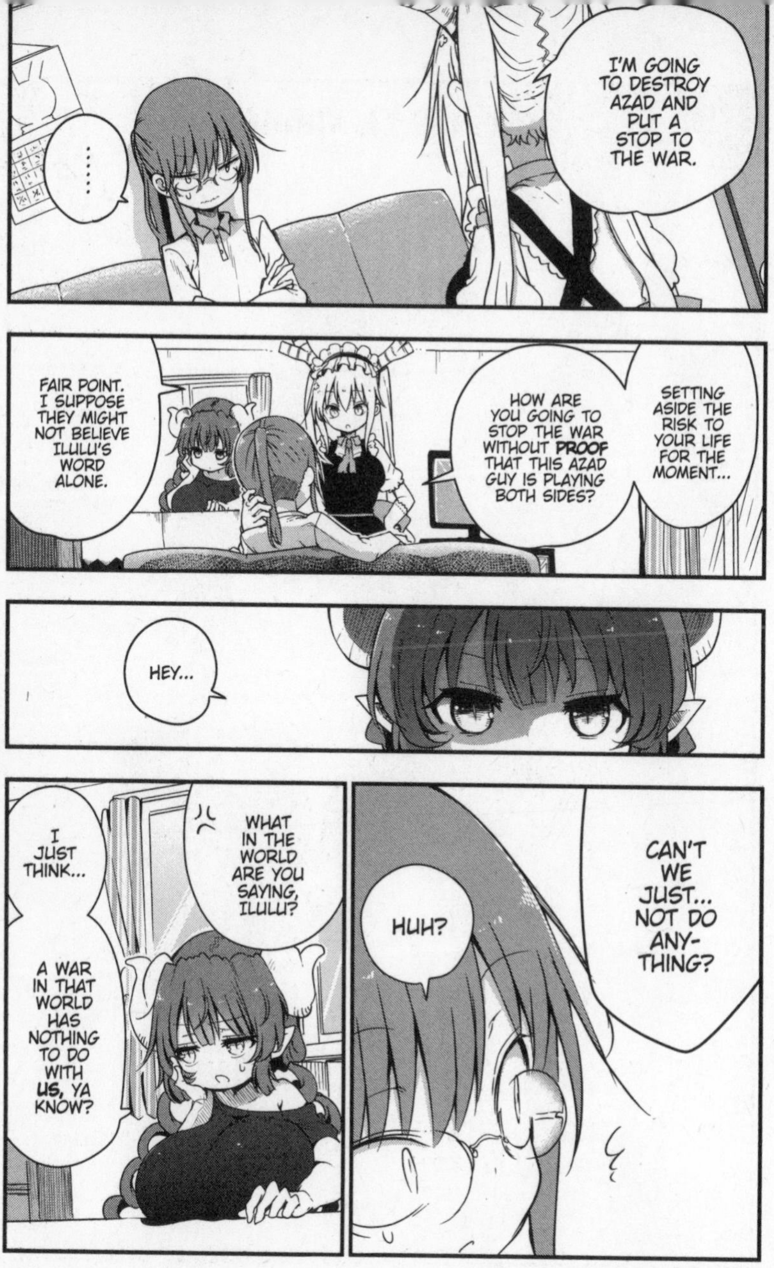
I'M GOING TO DESTROY AZAD AND PUT A STOP TO THE WAR.
......
SETTING ASIDE THE RISK TO YOUR LIFE FOR THE MOMENT...
HOW ARE YOU GOING TO STOP THE WAR WITHOUT **PROOF** THAT THIS AZAD GUY IS PLAYING BOTH SIDES?
FAIR POINT. I SUPPOSE THEY MIGHT NOT BELIEVE ILULU'S WORD ALONE.
HEY...
CAN'T WE JUST... NOT DO ANY-THING?
HUH?
WHAT IN THE WORLD ARE YOU SAYING, ILULU?
I JUST THINK...
A WAR IN THAT WORLD HAS NOTHING TO DO WITH **US**, YA KNOW?

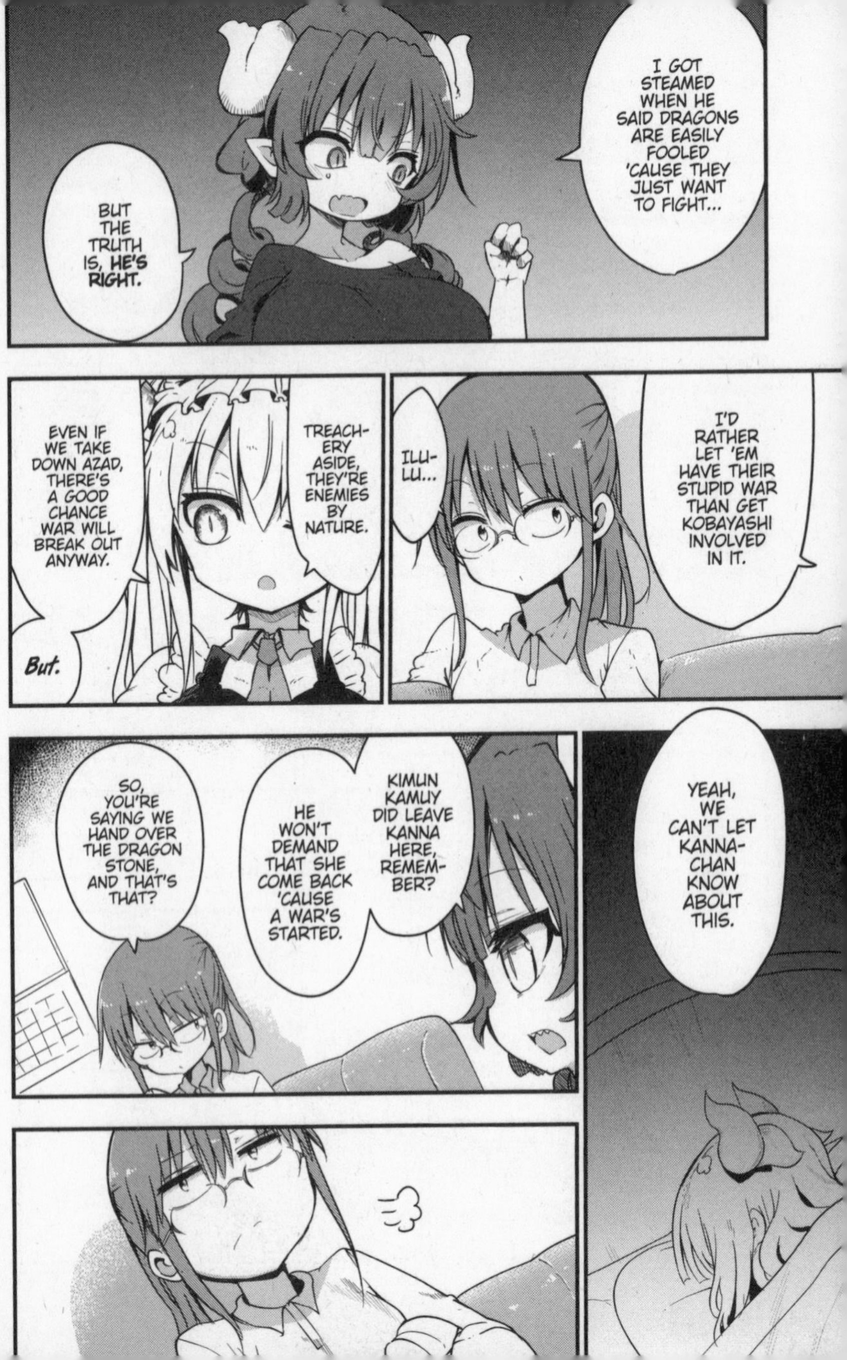
I GOT STEAMED WHEN HE SAID DRAGONS ARE EASILY FOOLED 'CAUSE THEY JUST WANT TO FIGHT...
BUT THE TRUTH IS, **HE'S RIGHT.**
I'D RATHER LET 'EM HAVE THEIR STUPID WAR THAN GET KOBAYASHI INVOLVED IN IT.
ILULU...
TREACHERY ASIDE, THEY'RE ENEMIES BY NATURE.
EVEN IF WE TAKE DOWN AZAD, THERE'S A GOOD CHANCE WAR WILL BREAK OUT ANYWAY.
But.
YEAH, WE CAN'T LET KANNA-CHAN KNOW ABOUT THIS.
KIMUN KAMUY DID LEAVE KANNA HERE, REMEMBER?
HE WON'T DEMAND THAT SHE COME BACK 'CAUSE A WAR'S STARTED.
SO, YOU'RE SAYING WE HAND OVER THE DRAGON STONE, AND THAT'S THAT?

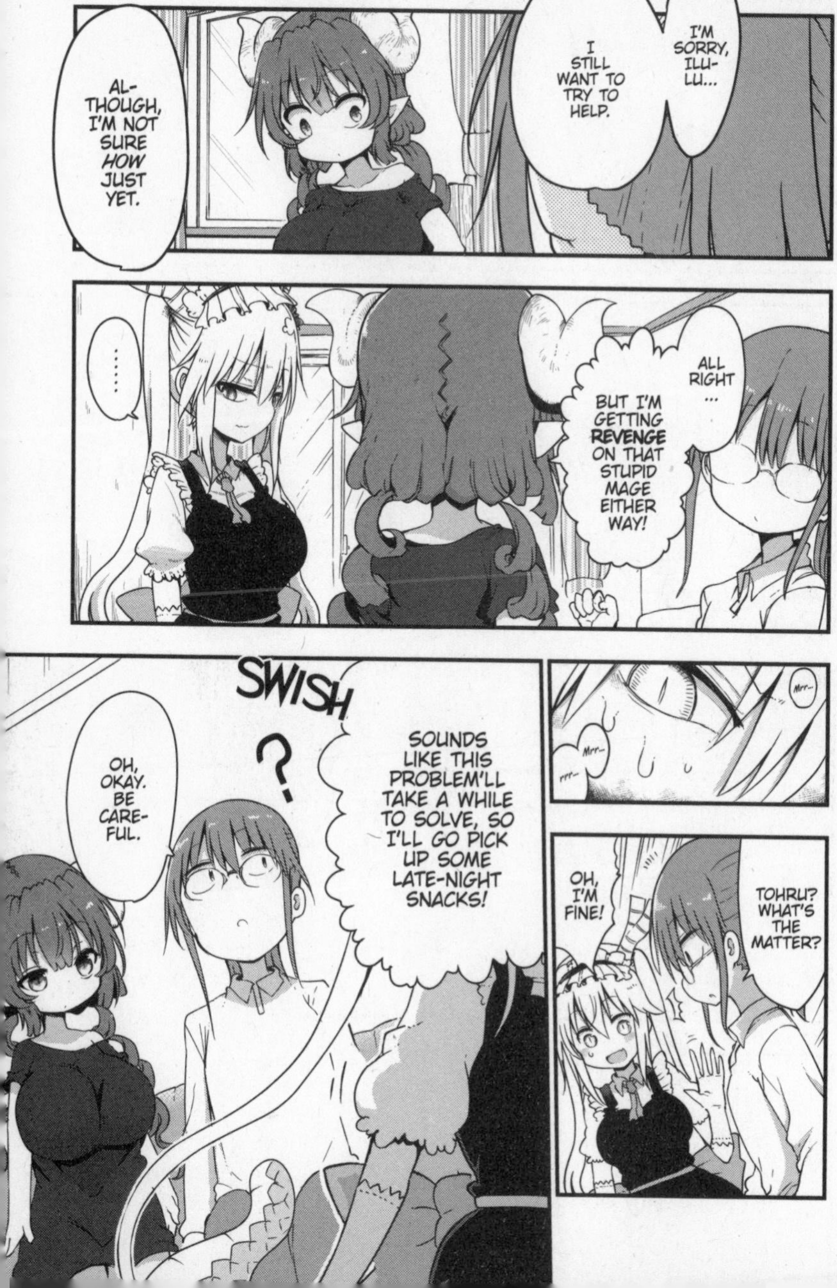
I'M SORRY, ILU-LU...
I STILL WANT TO TRY TO HELP.
AL-THOUGH, I'M NOT SURE *HOW* JUST YET.
ALL RIGHT...
BUT I'M GETTING **REVENGE** ON THAT STUPID MAGE EITHER WAY!
......
Mrr...
Mrr...
rrr...
TOHRU? WHAT'S THE MATTER?
OH, I'M FINE!
SWISH
SOUNDS LIKE THIS PROBLEM'LL TAKE A WHILE TO SOLVE, SO I'LL GO PICK UP SOME LATE-NIGHT SNACKS!
?
OH, OKAY. BE CARE-FUL.

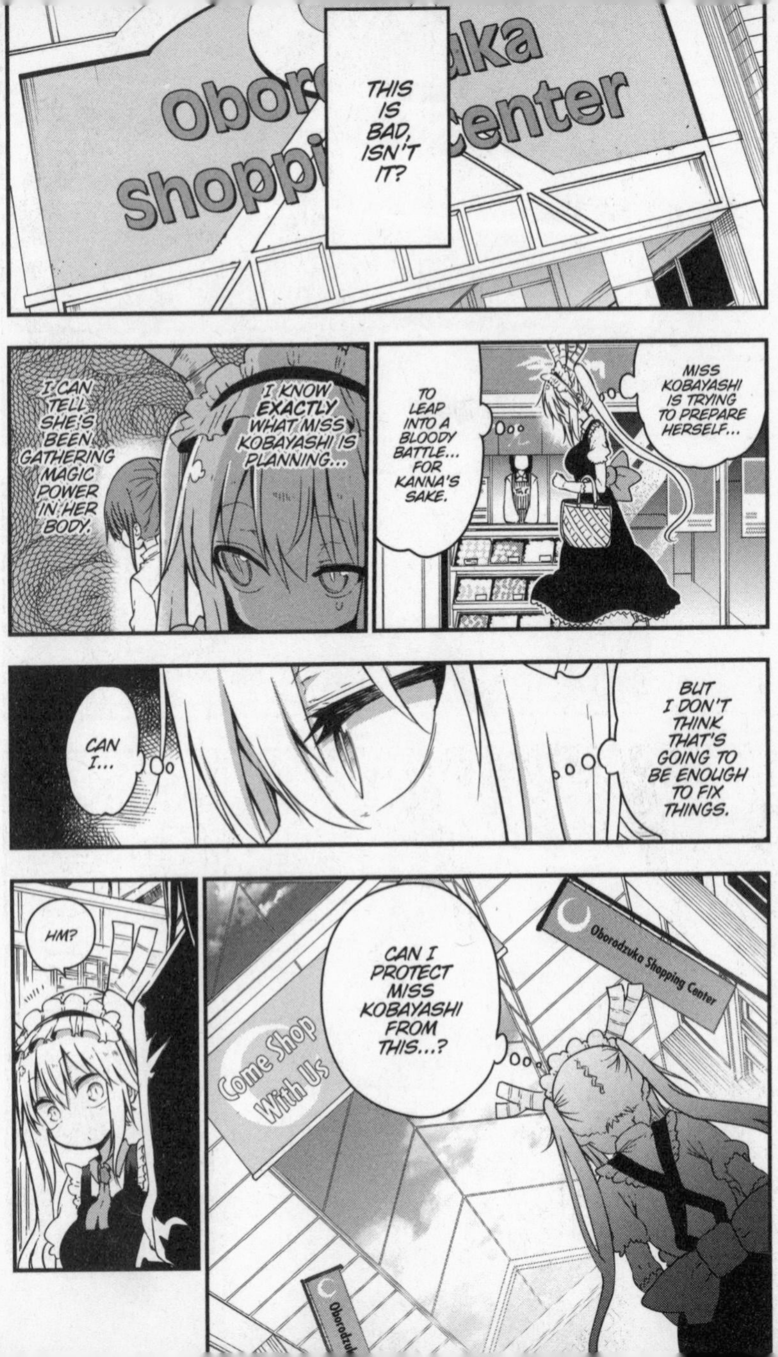
THIS IS BAD, ISN'T IT?
MISS KOBAYASHI IS TRYING TO PREPARE HERSELF...
TO LEAP INTO A BLOODY BATTLE... FOR KANNA'S SAKE.
I KNOW EXACTLY WHAT MISS KOBAYASHI IS PLANNING...
I CAN TELL SHE'S BEEN GATHERING MAGIC POWER IN HER BODY.
BUT I DON'T THINK THAT'S GOING TO BE ENOUGH TO FIX THINGS.
CAN I...
Oborodzuka Shopping Center
CAN I PROTECT MISS KOBAYASHI FROM THIS...?
Come Shop With Us
HM?

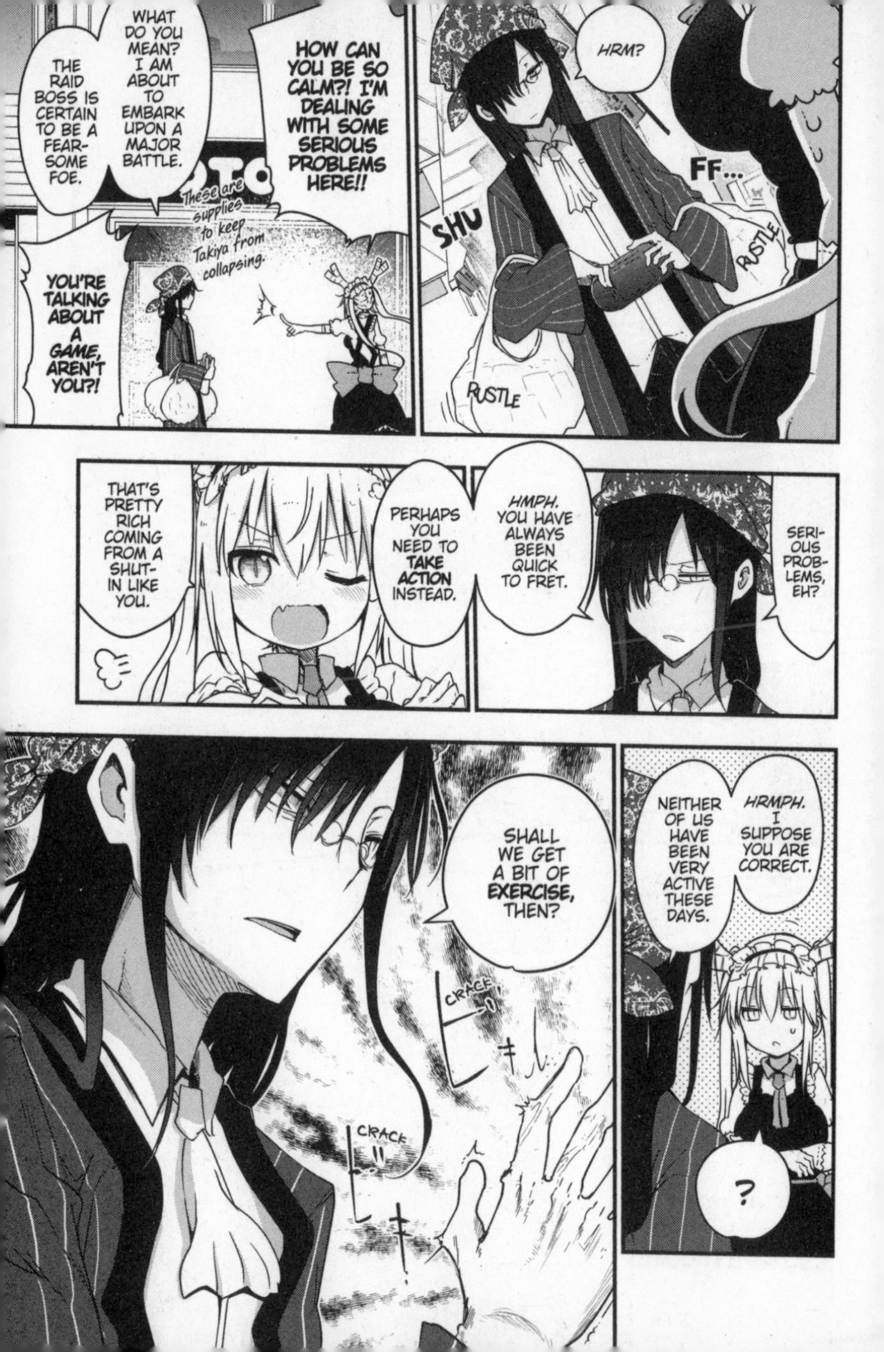
HRM?
FF...
SHU
RUSTLE
RUSTLE
HOW CAN YOU BE SO CALM?! I'M DEALING WITH SOME SERIOUS PROBLEMS HERE!!
WHAT DO YOU MEAN? I AM ABOUT TO EMBARK UPON A MAJOR BATTLE.
THE RAID BOSS IS CERTAIN TO BE A FEARSOME FOE.
These are supplies to keep Takiya from collapsing.
YOU'RE TALKING ABOUT A GAME, AREN'T YOU?!
SERIOUS PROBLEMS, EH?
HMPH. YOU HAVE ALWAYS BEEN QUICK TO FRET.
PERHAPS YOU NEED TO TAKE ACTION INSTEAD.
THAT'S PRETTY RICH COMING FROM A SHUT-IN LIKE YOU.
HRMPH. I SUPPOSE YOU ARE CORRECT.
NEITHER OF US HAVE BEEN VERY ACTIVE THESE DAYS.
?
SHALL WE GET A BIT OF EXERCISE, THEN?
CRACK!
CRACK!!

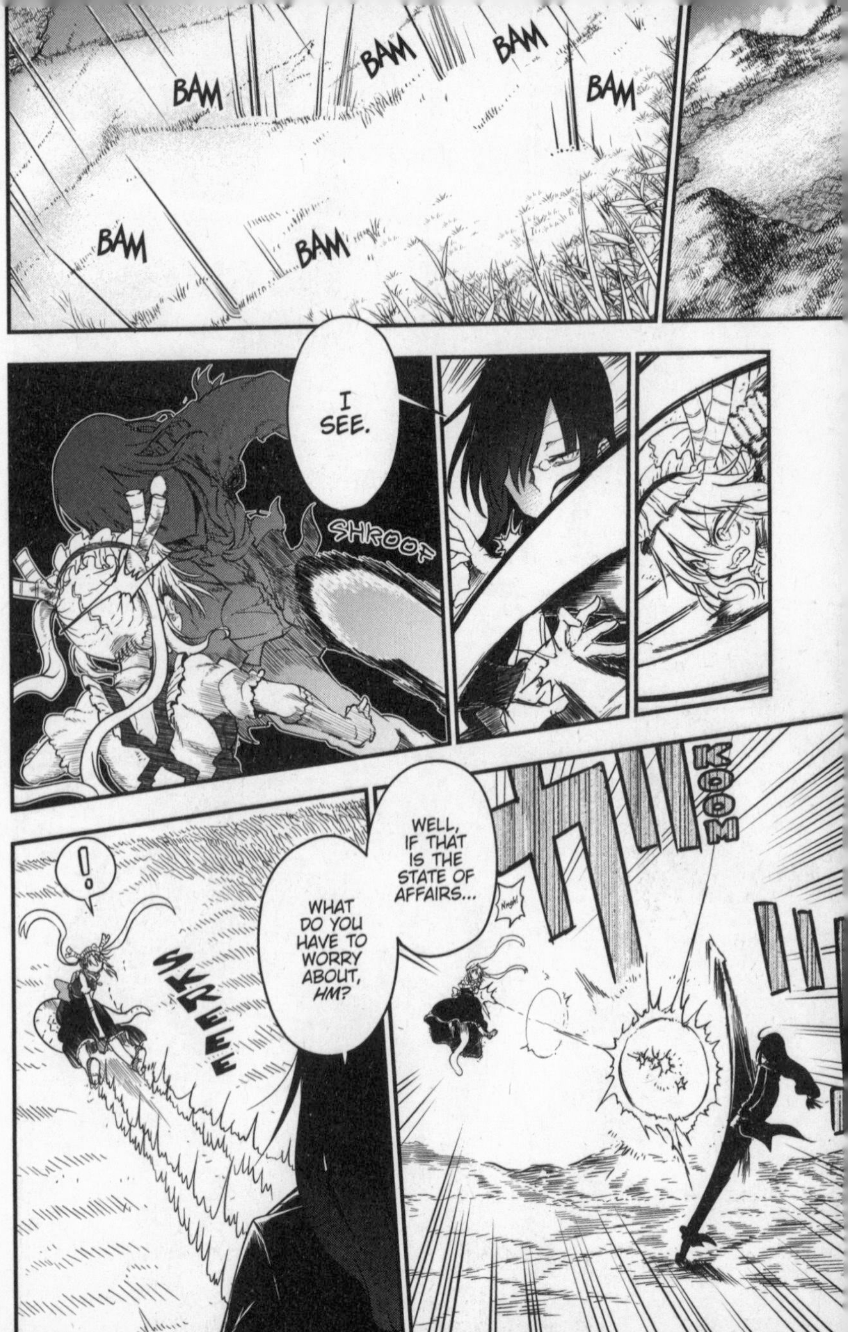
BAM
BAM
BAM
BAM
BAM
BAM
I SEE.
SHROOF
KOOM
WELL, IF THAT IS THE STATE OF AFFAIRS...
WHAT DO YOU HAVE TO WORRY ABOUT, HM?
Nngh!
SKREEE
!

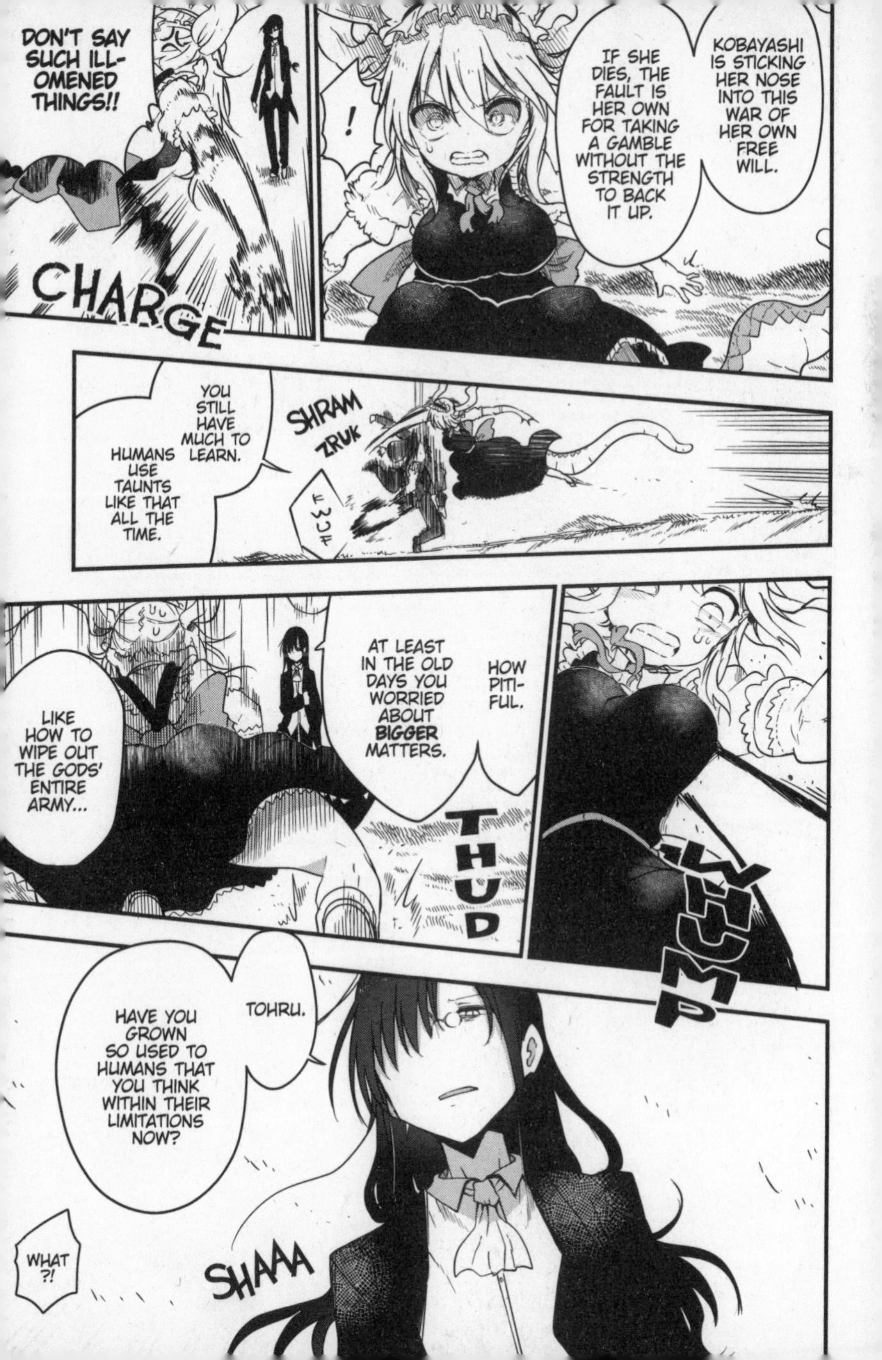
KOBAYASHI IS STICKING HER NOSE INTO THIS WAR OF HER OWN FREE WILL.
IF SHE DIES, THE FAULT IS HER OWN FOR TAKING A GAMBLE WITHOUT THE STRENGTH TO BACK IT UP.
!
DON'T SAY SUCH ILL-OMENED THINGS!!
CHARGE
SHRAM
ZRUK
FWUF
YOU STILL HAVE MUCH TO LEARN.
HUMANS USE TAUNTS LIKE THAT ALL THE TIME.
WHUMP
HOW PITI-FUL.
AT LEAST IN THE OLD DAYS YOU WORRIED ABOUT BIGGER MATTERS.
LIKE HOW TO WIPE OUT THE GODS' ENTIRE ARMY...
THUD
TOHRU.
HAVE YOU GROWN SO USED TO HUMANS THAT YOU THINK WITHIN THEIR LIMITATIONS NOW?
SHAAA
WHAT ?!

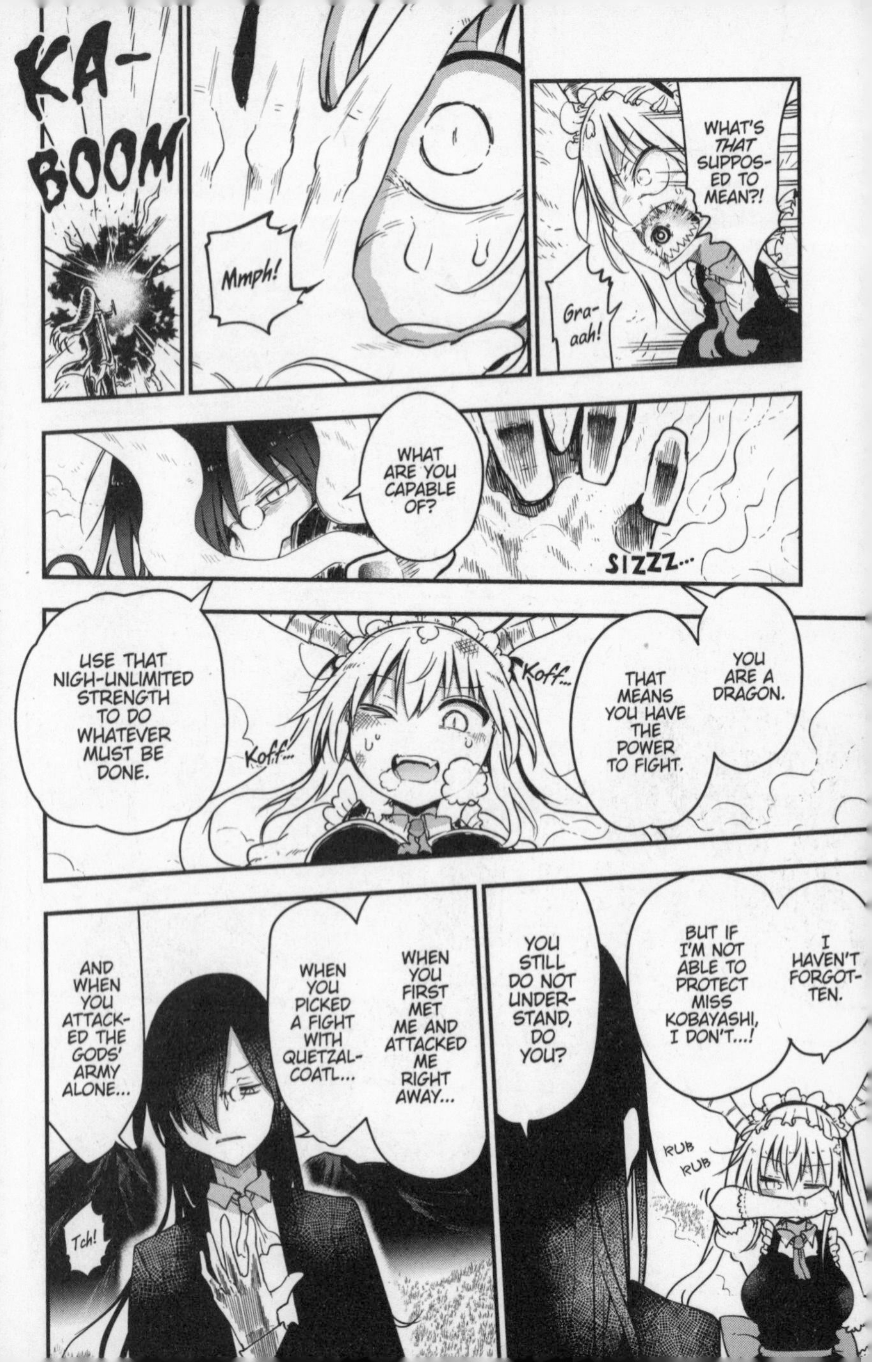
WHAT'S *THAT* SUPPOSED TO MEAN?!
Gra-aah!
Mmph!
KA-BOOM
WHAT ARE YOU CAPABLE OF?
SIZZZ...
YOU ARE A DRAGON.
THAT MEANS YOU HAVE THE POWER TO FIGHT.
Koff...
Koff...
USE THAT NIGH-UNLIMITED STRENGTH TO DO WHATEVER MUST BE DONE.
I HAVEN'T FORGOTTEN.
BUT IF I'M NOT ABLE TO PROTECT MISS KOBAYASHI, I DON'T...!
YOU STILL DO NOT UNDERSTAND, DO YOU?
RUB RUB
WHEN YOU FIRST MET ME AND ATTACKED ME RIGHT AWAY...
WHEN YOU PICKED A FIGHT WITH QUETZALCOATL...
AND WHEN YOU ATTACKED THE GODS' ARMY ALONE...
Tch!

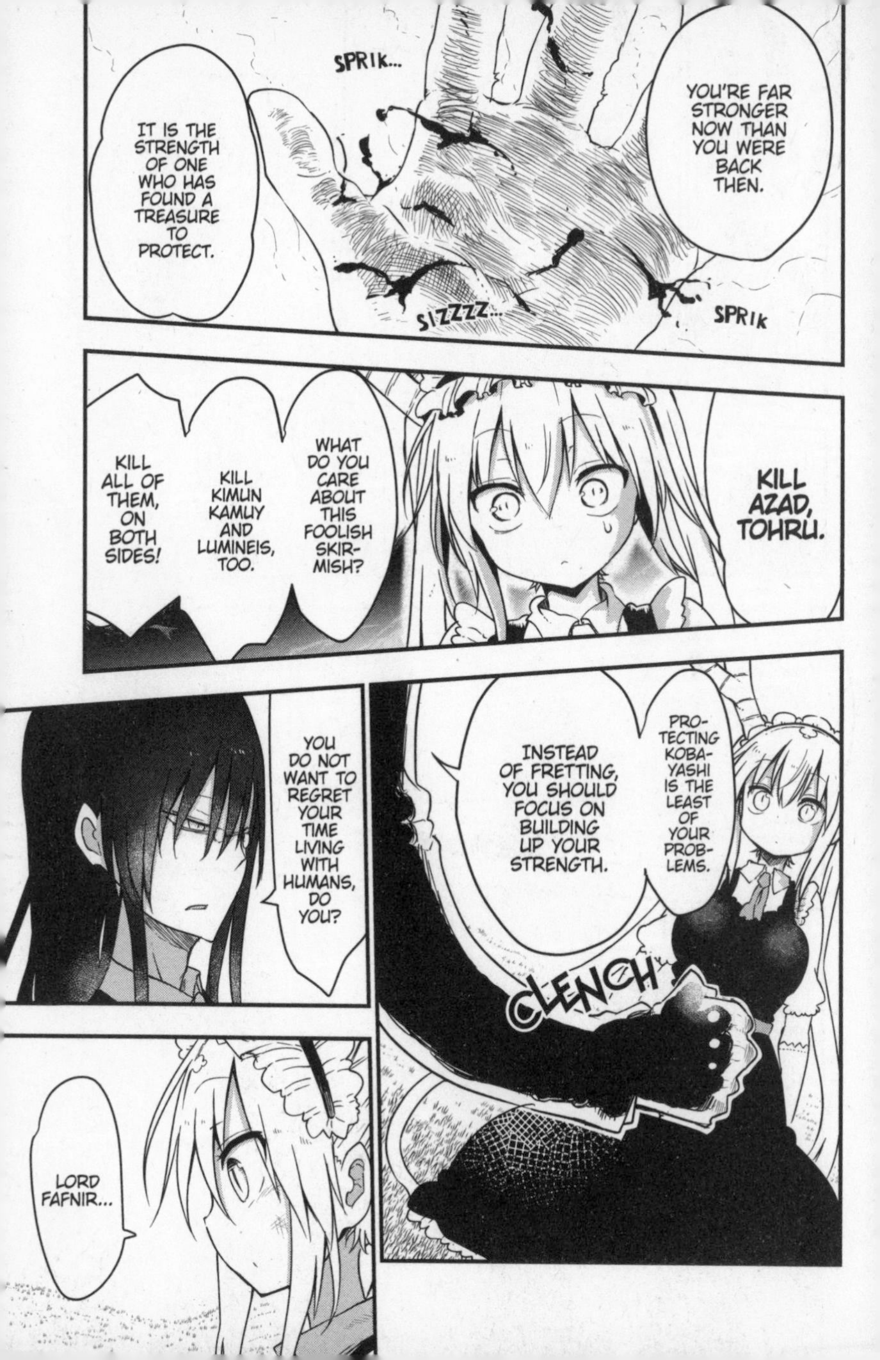
YOU'RE FAR STRONGER NOW THAN YOU WERE BACK THEN.
SPRIK...
IT IS THE STRENGTH OF ONE WHO HAS FOUND A TREASURE TO PROTECT.
SPRIK
SIZZZZ...
KILL AZAD, TOHRU.
WHAT DO YOU CARE ABOUT THIS FOOLISH SKIR-MISH?
KILL KIMUN KAMUY AND LUMINEIS, TOO.
KILL ALL OF THEM, ON BOTH SIDES!
PRO-TECTING KOBA-YASHI IS THE LEAST OF YOUR PROB-LEMS.
INSTEAD OF FRETTING, YOU SHOULD FOCUS ON BUILDING UP YOUR STRENGTH.
CLENCH
YOU DO NOT WANT TO REGRET YOUR TIME LIVING WITH HUMANS, DO YOU?
LORD FAFNIR...

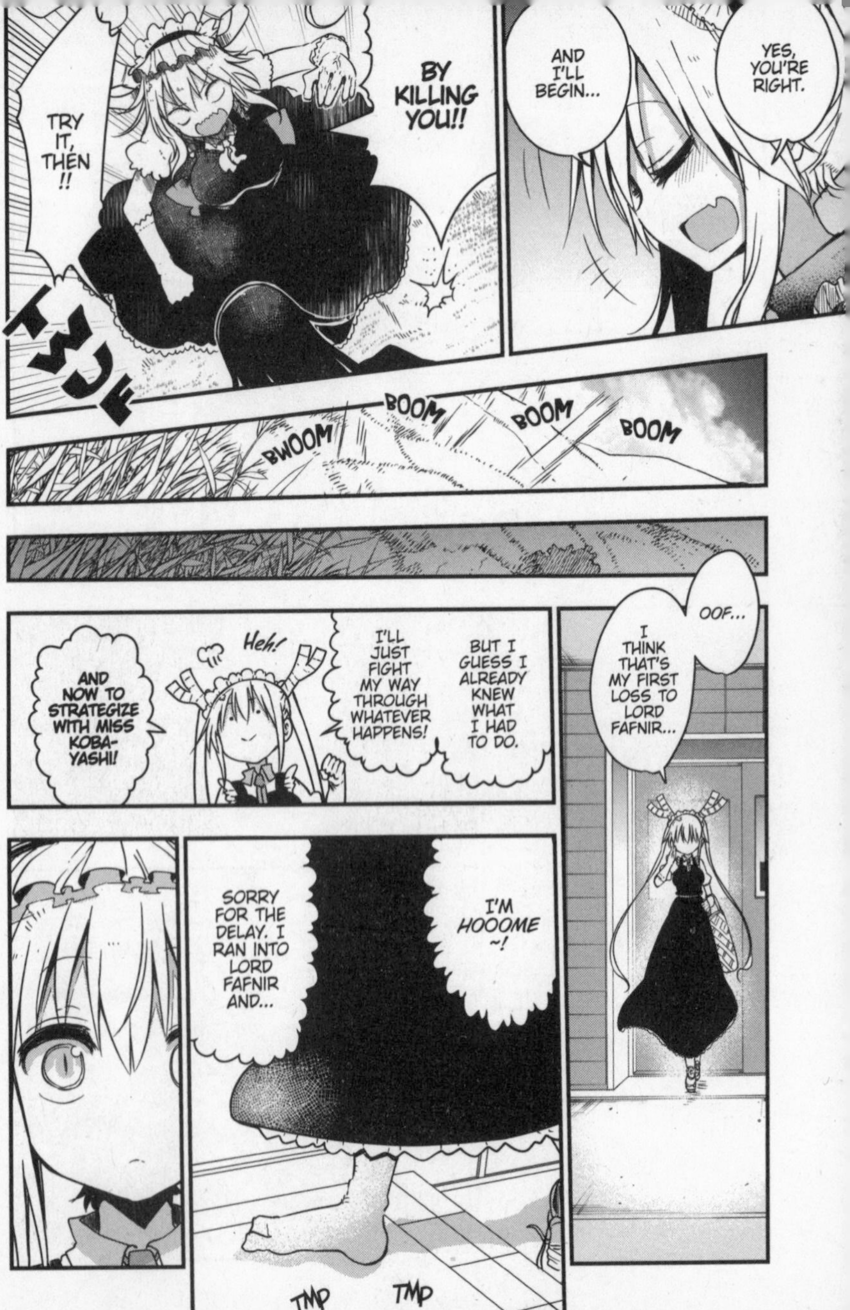
YES, YOU'RE RIGHT.
AND I'LL BEGIN...
BY KILLING YOU!!
TRY IT, THEN!!
FWUF
BOOM
BOOM
BOOM
BWOOM
OOF...
I THINK THAT'S MY FIRST LOSS TO LORD FAFNIR...
BUT I GUESS I ALREADY KNEW WHAT I HAD TO DO.
I'LL JUST FIGHT MY WAY THROUGH WHATEVER HAPPENS!
Heh!
AND NOW TO STRATEGIZE WITH MISS KOBA-YASHI!
I'M HOOOME ~!
SORRY FOR THE DELAY. I RAN INTO LORD FAFNIR AND...
TMP
TMP
...

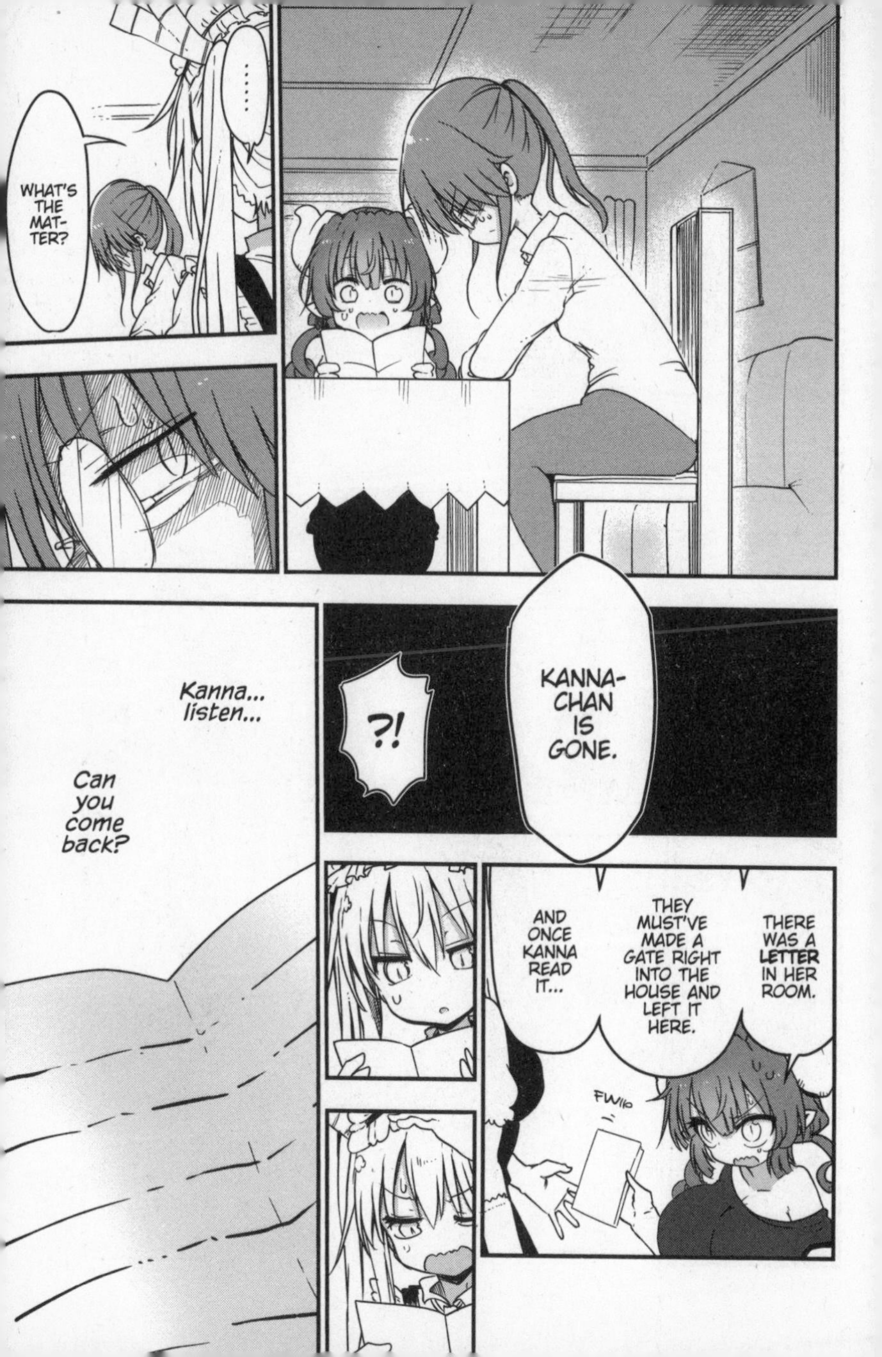
......
WHAT'S THE MATTER?
KANNA-CHAN IS GONE.
?!
THERE WAS A LETTER IN HER ROOM.
THEY MUST'VE MADE A GATE RIGHT INTO THE HOUSE AND LEFT IT HERE.
AND ONCE KANNA READ IT...
FWIP
Kanna... listen...
Can you come back?

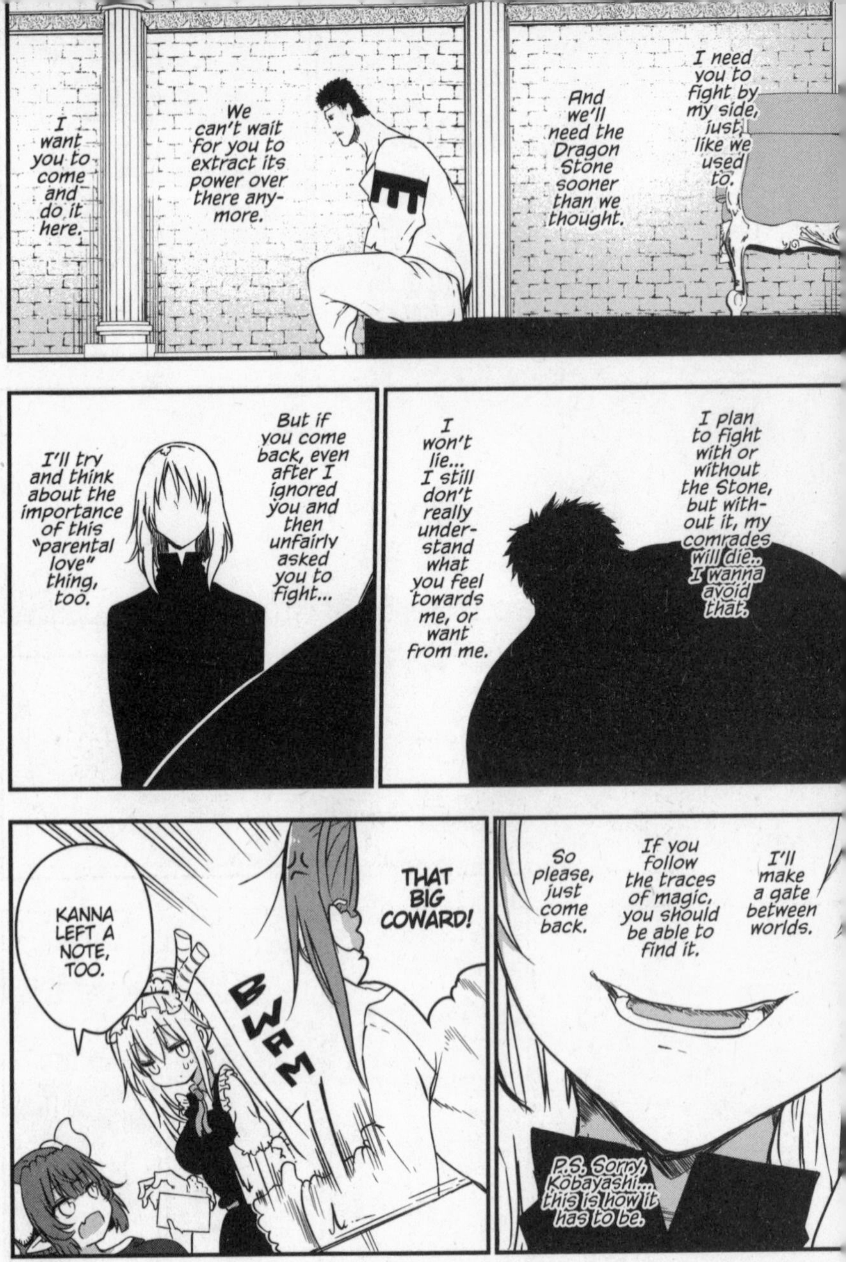
I need you to fight by my side, just, like we used to.
And we'll need the Dragon Stone sooner than we thought.
We can't wait for you to extract its power over there anymore.
I want you to come and do it here.
I plan to fight with or without the Stone, but without it, my comrades will die.. I wanna avoid that.
I won't lie... I still don't really understand what you feel towards me, or want from me.
But if you come back, even after I ignored you and then unfairly asked you to fight...
I'll try and think about the importance of this "parental love" thing, too.
I'll make a gate between worlds.
If you follow the traces of magic, you should be able to find it.
So please, just come back.
P.S. Sorry, Kobayashi... this is how it has to be.
THAT BIG COWARD!
BWAM
KANNA LEFT A NOTE, TOO.

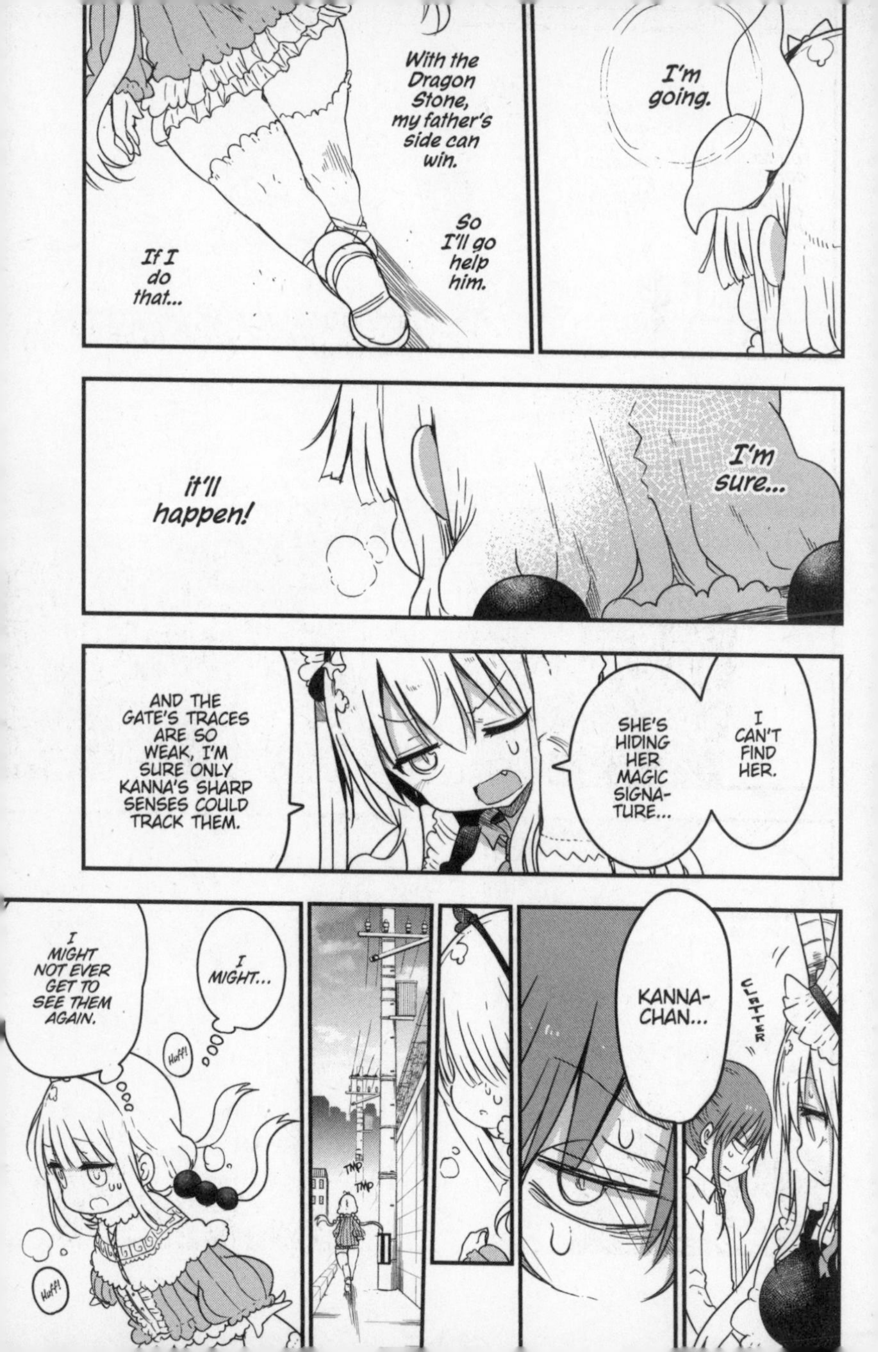

I'm going.
With the Dragon Stone, my father's side can win.
So I'll go help him.
If I do that...
I'm sure...
it'll happen!
I CAN'T FIND HER.
SHE'S HIDING HER MAGIC SIGNATURE...
AND THE GATE'S TRACES ARE SO WEAK, I'M SURE ONLY KANNA'S SHARP SENSES COULD TRACK THEM.
CLATTER
KANNA-CHAN...
TMP
TMP
I MIGHT...
I MIGHT NOT EVER GET TO SEE THEM AGAIN.
Huff!
Huff!

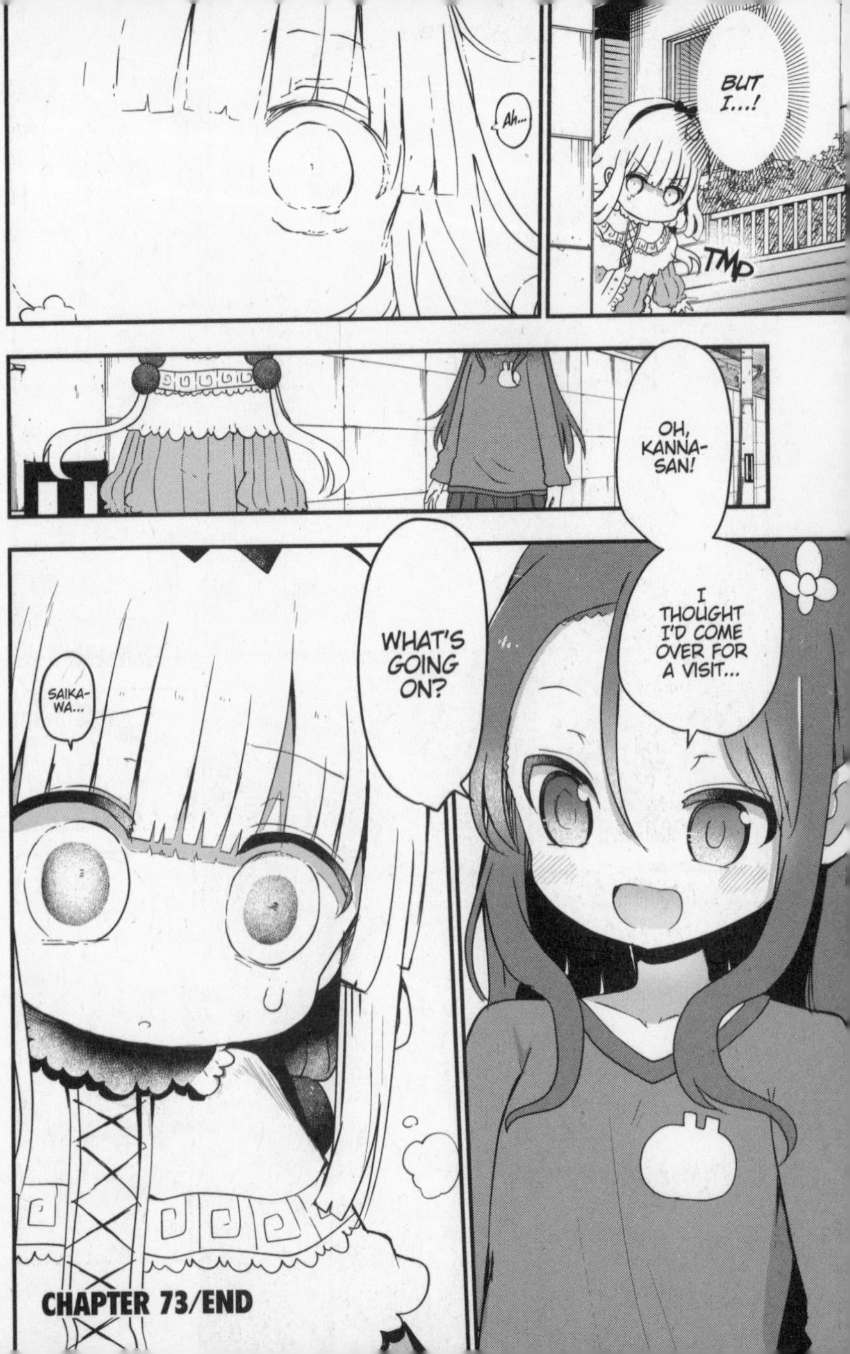
BUT I...!
TMP
Ah...
OH, KANNA-SAN!
I THOUGHT I'D COME OVER FOR A VISIT...
WHAT'S GOING ON?
SAIKA-WA...
CHAPTER 73/END

CHAPTER 74

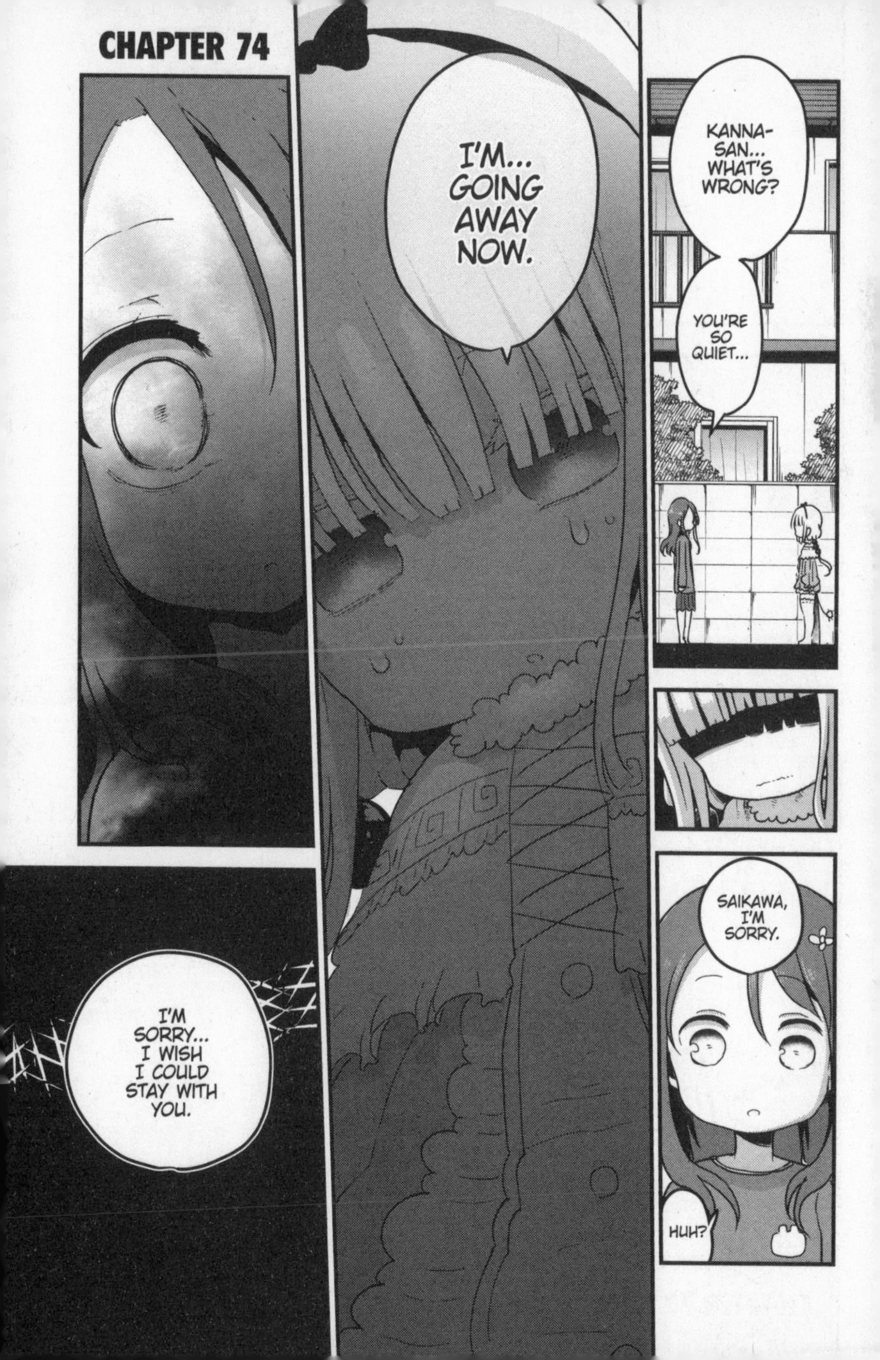
KANNA-SAN... WHAT'S WRONG?
YOU'RE SO QUIET...
SAIKAWA, I'M SORRY.
HUH?
I'M... GOING AWAY NOW.
I'M SORRY... I WISH I COULD STAY WITH YOU.

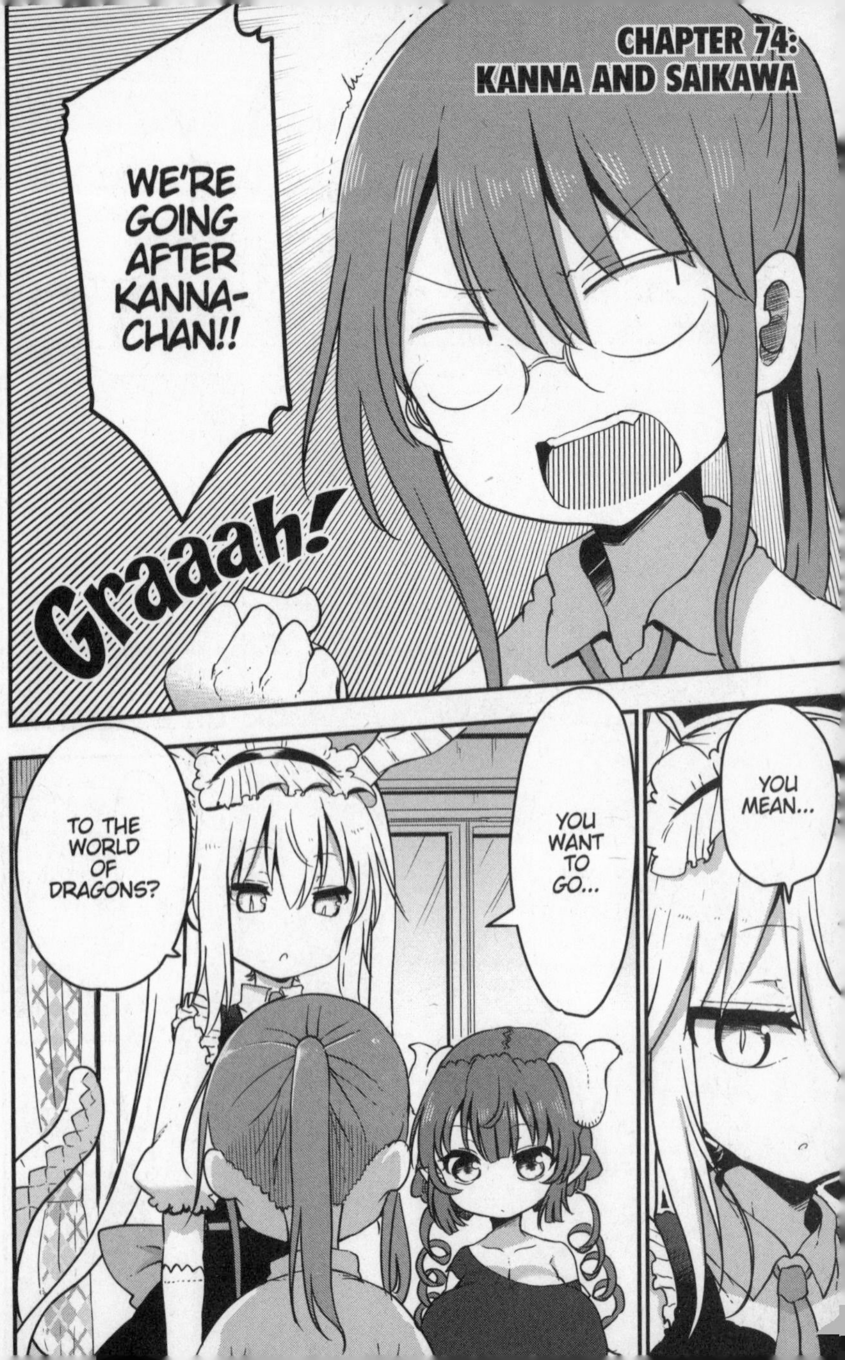
CHAPTER 74:
KANNA AND SAIKAWA
WE'RE GOING AFTER KANNA-CHAN!!
Graaah!
YOU MEAN...
YOU WANT TO GO...
TO THE WORLD OF DRAGONS?

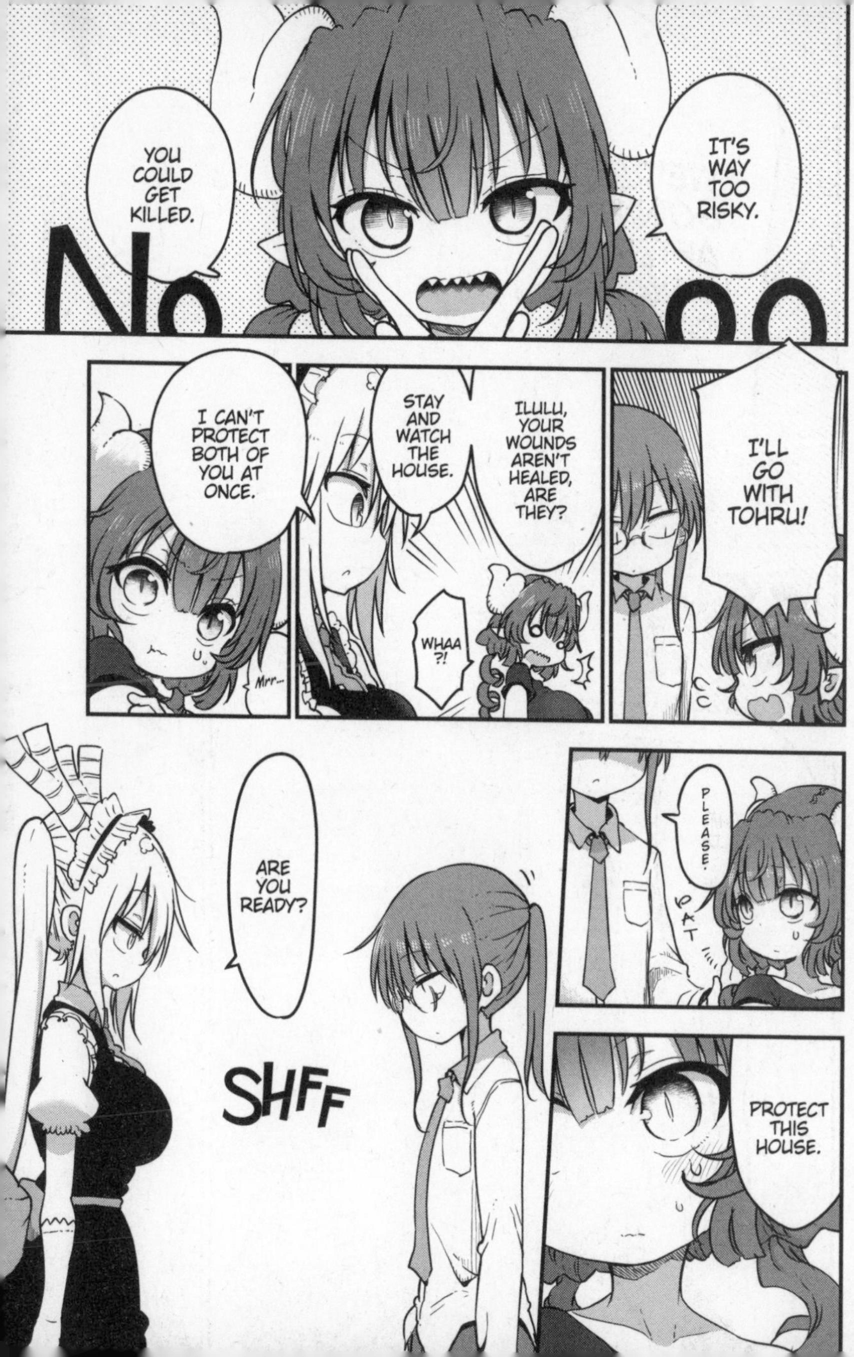
IT'S WAY TOO RISKY.
YOU COULD GET KILLED.
No
oo
I'LL GO WITH TOHRU!
ILULU, YOUR WOUNDS AREN'T HEALED, ARE THEY?
STAY AND WATCH THE HOUSE.
WHAA?!
I CAN'T PROTECT BOTH OF YOU AT ONCE.
Mrr...
PLEASE.
PAT
PROTECT THIS HOUSE.
ARE YOU READY?
SHFF

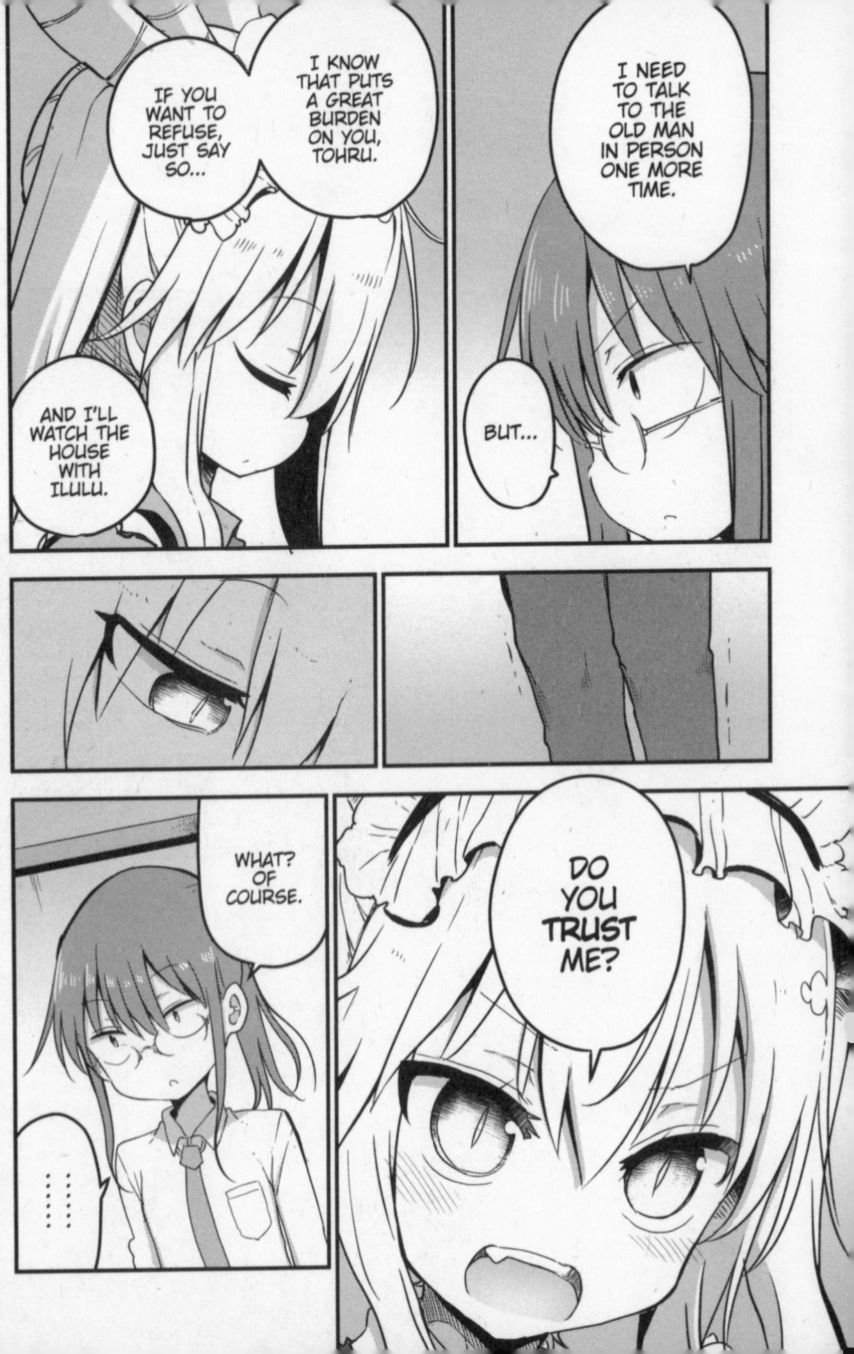
I NEED TO TALK TO THE OLD MAN IN PERSON ONE MORE TIME.
BUT...
I KNOW THAT PUTS A GREAT BURDEN ON YOU, TOHRU.
IF YOU WANT TO REFUSE, JUST SAY SO...
AND I'LL WATCH THE HOUSE WITH ILULU.
DO YOU TRUST ME?
WHAT? OF COURSE.
......

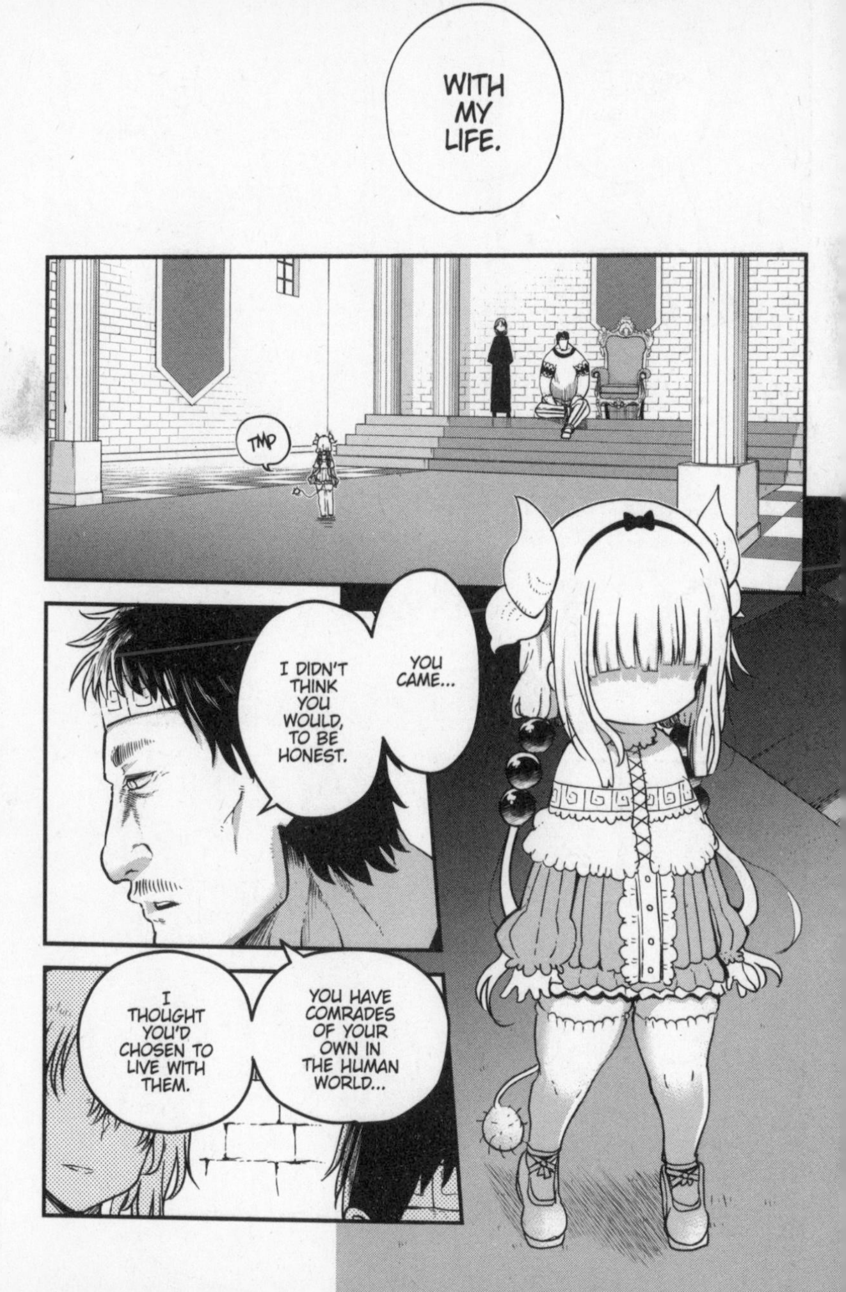
WITH MY LIFE.
TMP
YOU CAME...
I DIDN'T THINK YOU WOULD, TO BE HONEST.
YOU HAVE COMRADES OF YOUR OWN IN THE HUMAN WORLD...
I THOUGHT YOU'D CHOSEN TO LIVE WITH THEM.

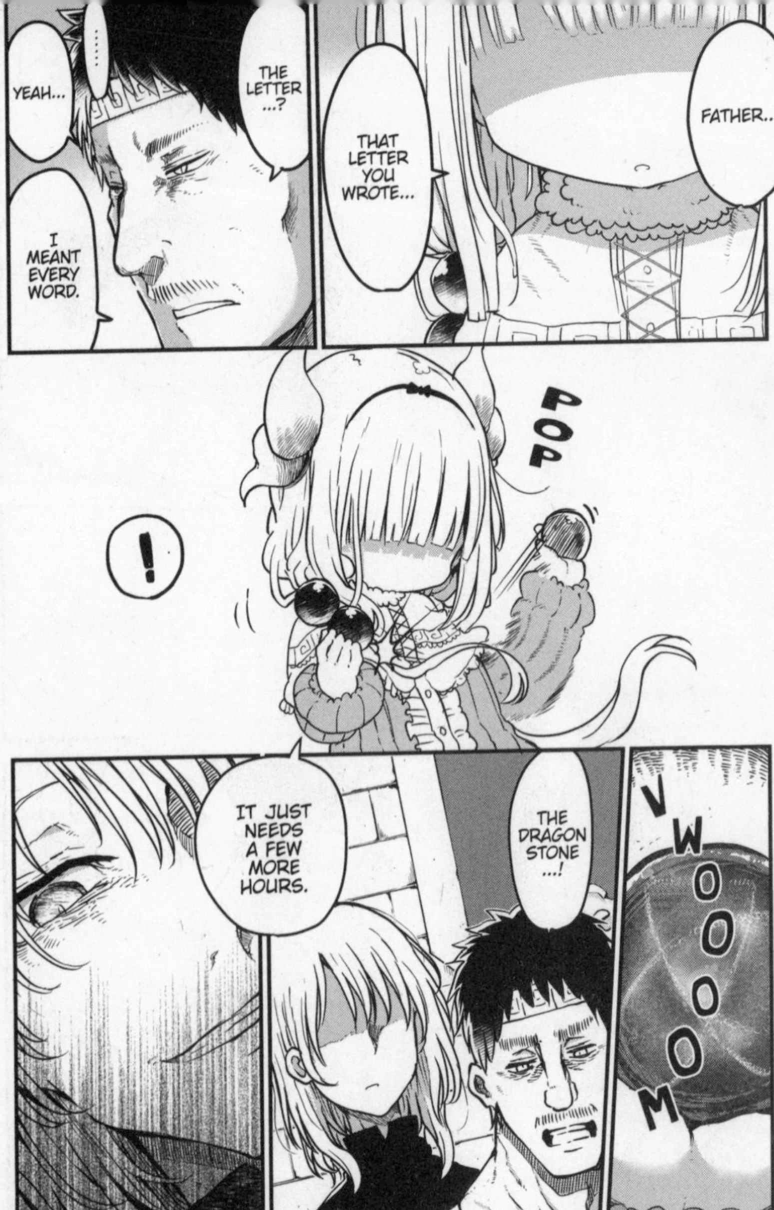
FATHER...
THAT LETTER YOU WROTE...
THE LETTER ...?
......
YEAH...
I MEANT EVERY WORD.
POP
!
VWOOOOM
THE DRAGON STONE ...!
IT JUST NEEDS A FEW MORE HOURS.

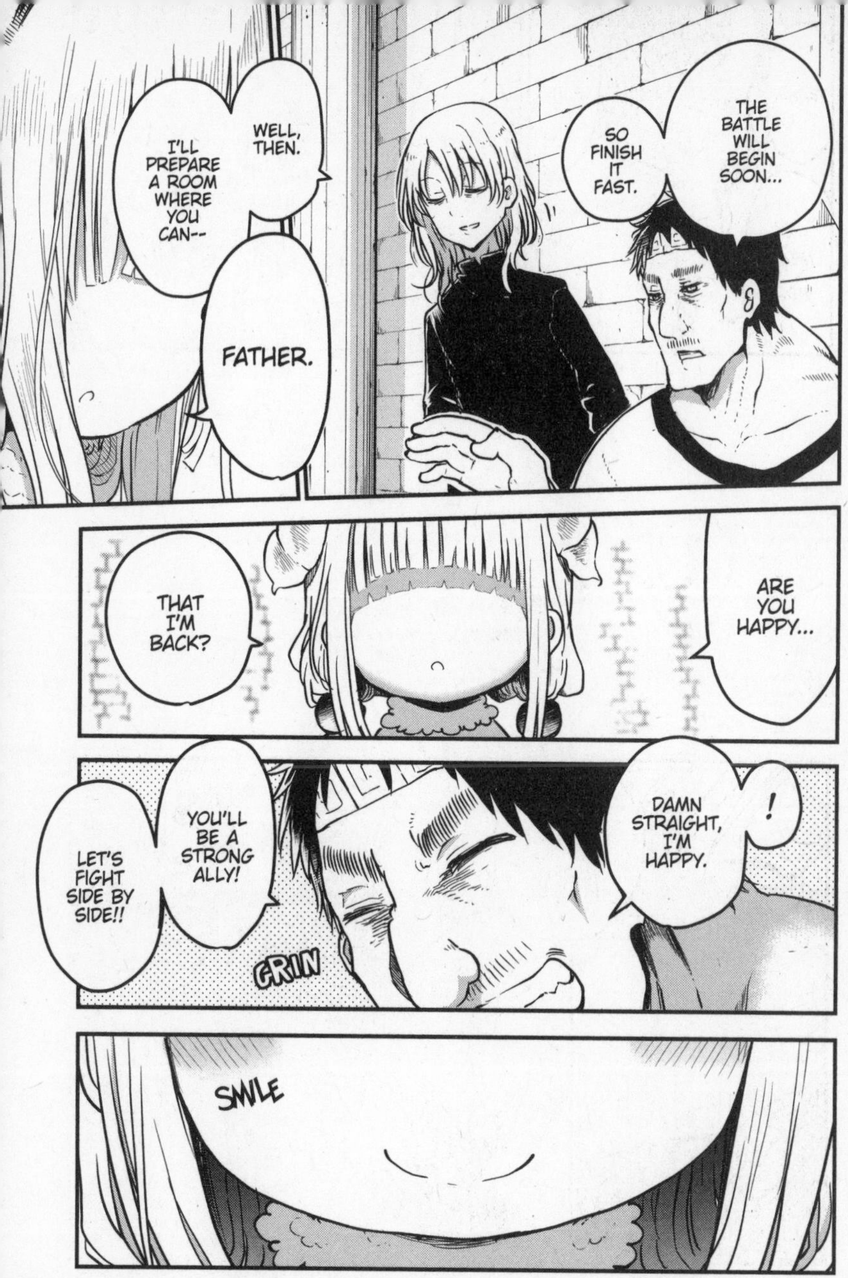
THE BATTLE WILL BEGIN SOON...
SO FINISH IT FAST.
WELL, THEN.
I'LL PREPARE A ROOM WHERE YOU CAN--
FATHER.
ARE YOU HAPPY...
THAT I'M BACK?
DAMN STRAIGHT, I'M HAPPY.
!
GRIN
YOU'LL BE A STRONG ALLY!
LET'S FIGHT SIDE BY SIDE!!
SMILE

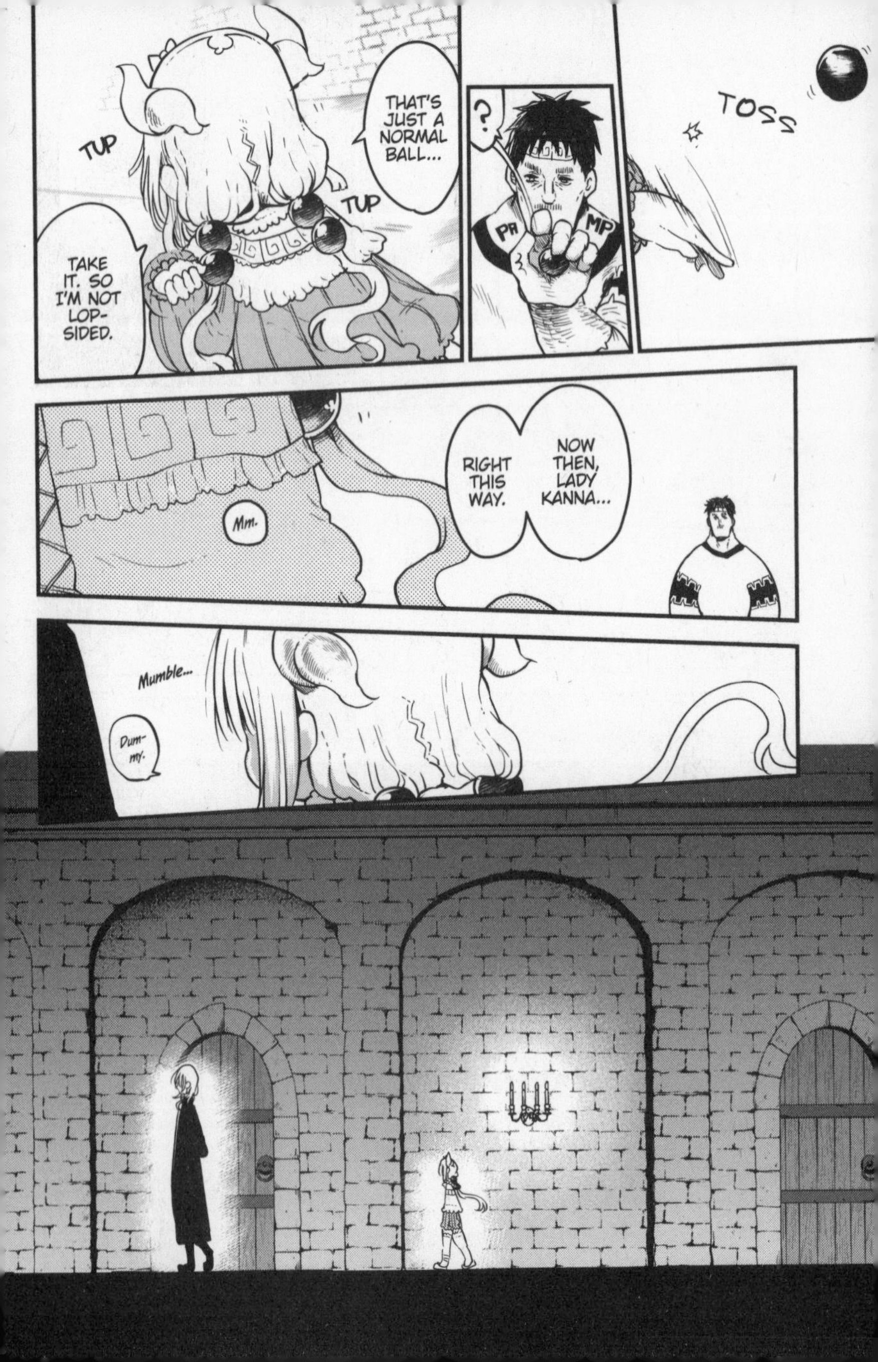
TOSS
?
PAMP
THAT'S JUST A NORMAL BALL...
TUP
TUP
TAKE IT. SO I'M NOT LOP-SIDED.
NOW THEN, LADY KANNA...
RIGHT THIS WAY.
Mm.
Mumble...
Dum-my.

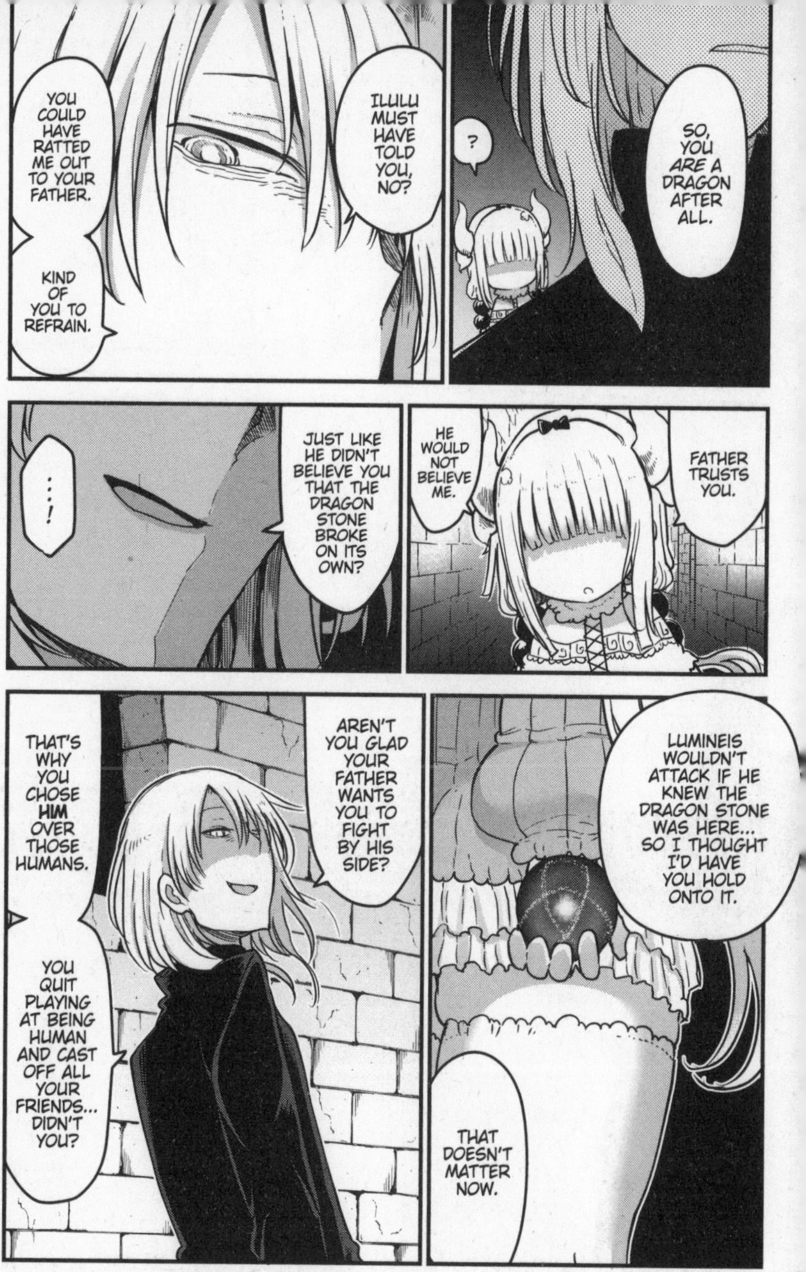
SO, YOU ARE A DRAGON AFTER ALL.
?
ILULU MUST HAVE TOLD YOU, NO?
YOU COULD HAVE RATTED ME OUT TO YOUR FATHER.
KIND OF YOU TO REFRAIN.
FATHER TRUSTS YOU.
HE WOULD NOT BELIEVE ME.
JUST LIKE HE DIDN'T BELIEVE YOU THAT THE DRAGON STONE BROKE ON ITS OWN?
...!
LUMINEIS WOULDN'T ATTACK IF HE KNEW THE DRAGON STONE WAS HERE... SO I THOUGHT I'D HAVE YOU HOLD ONTO IT.
THAT DOESN'T MATTER NOW.
AREN'T YOU GLAD YOUR FATHER WANTS YOU TO FIGHT BY HIS SIDE?
THAT'S WHY YOU CHOSE **HIM** OVER THOSE HUMANS.
YOU QUIT PLAYING AT BEING HUMAN AND CAST OFF ALL YOUR FRIENDS... DIDN'T YOU?

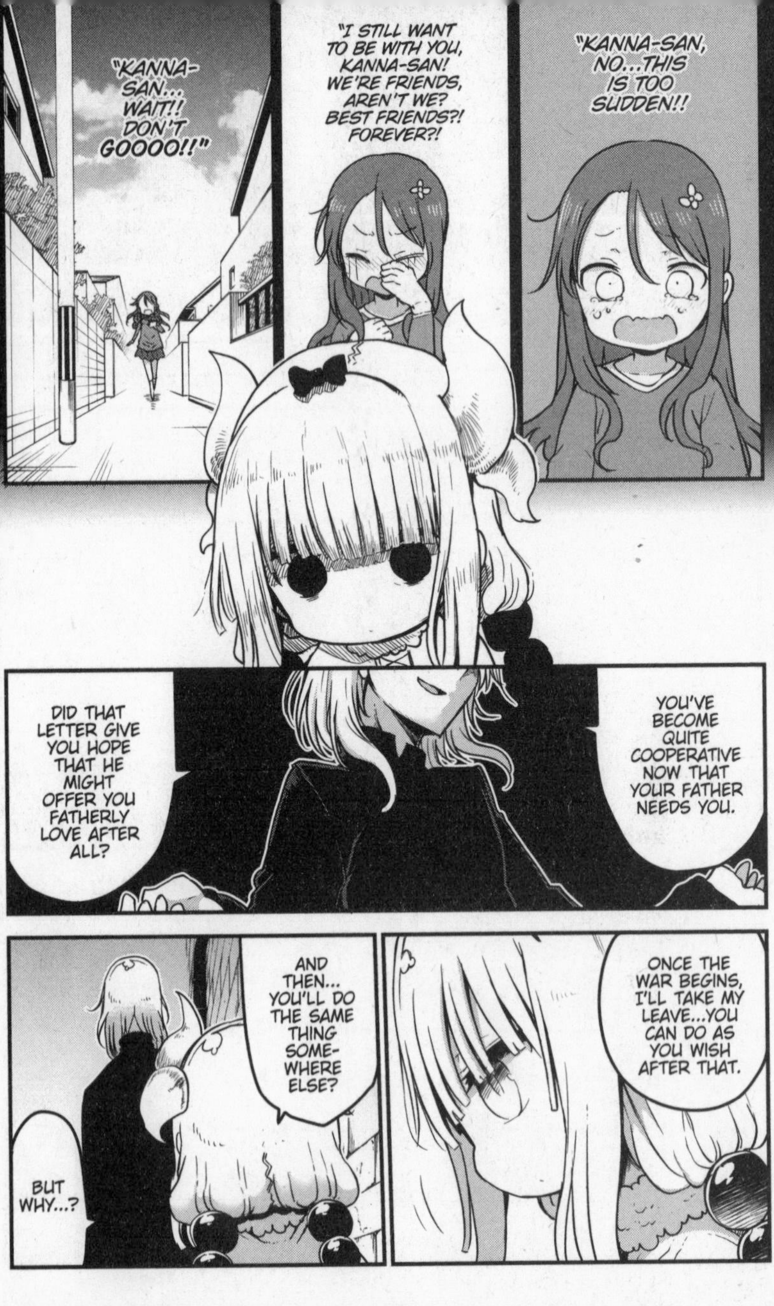
"KANNA-SAN, NO...THIS IS TOO SUDDEN!!
"I STILL WANT TO BE WITH YOU, KANNA-SAN! WE'RE FRIENDS, AREN'T WE? BEST FRIENDS?! FOREVER?!
"KANNA-SAN... WAIT!! DON'T GOOOO!!"
YOU'VE BECOME QUITE COOPERATIVE NOW THAT YOUR FATHER NEEDS YOU.
DID THAT LETTER GIVE YOU HOPE THAT HE MIGHT OFFER YOU FATHERLY LOVE AFTER ALL?
ONCE THE WAR BEGINS, I'LL TAKE MY LEAVE...YOU CAN DO AS YOU WISH AFTER THAT.
AND THEN... YOU'LL DO THE SAME THING SOMEWHERE ELSE?
BUT WHY...?

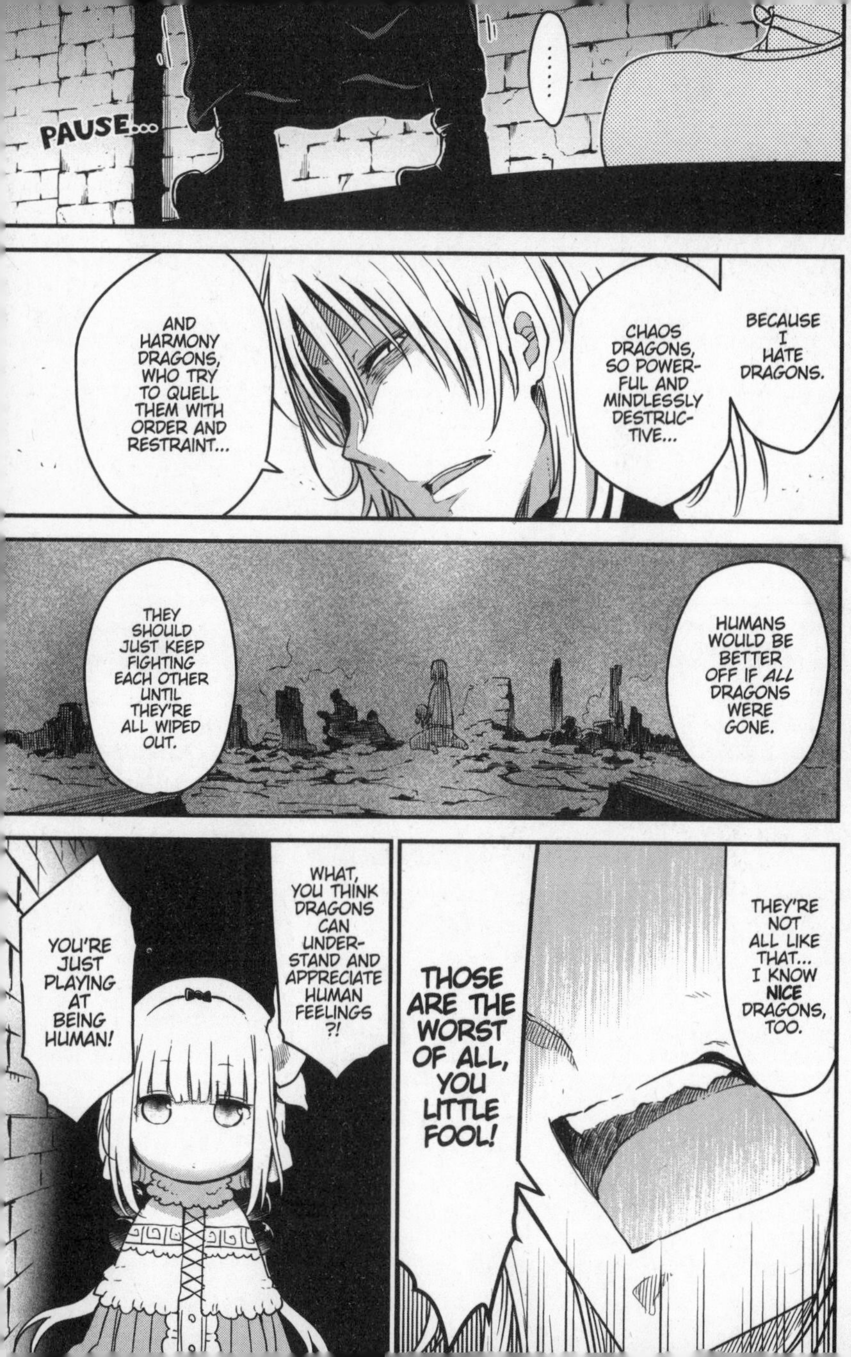
......
PAUSE...
BECAUSE I HATE DRAGONS.
CHAOS DRAGONS, SO POWERFUL AND MINDLESSLY DESTRUCTIVE...
AND HARMONY DRAGONS, WHO TRY TO QUELL THEM WITH ORDER AND RESTRAINT...
HUMANS WOULD BE BETTER OFF IF *ALL* DRAGONS WERE GONE.
THEY SHOULD JUST KEEP FIGHTING EACH OTHER UNTIL THEY'RE ALL WIPED OUT.
THEY'RE NOT ALL LIKE THAT... I KNOW **NICE** DRAGONS, TOO.
THOSE ARE THE WORST OF ALL, YOU LITTLE FOOL!
WHAT, YOU THINK DRAGONS CAN UNDERSTAND AND APPRECIATE HUMAN FEELINGS?!
YOU'RE JUST PLAYING AT BEING HUMAN!

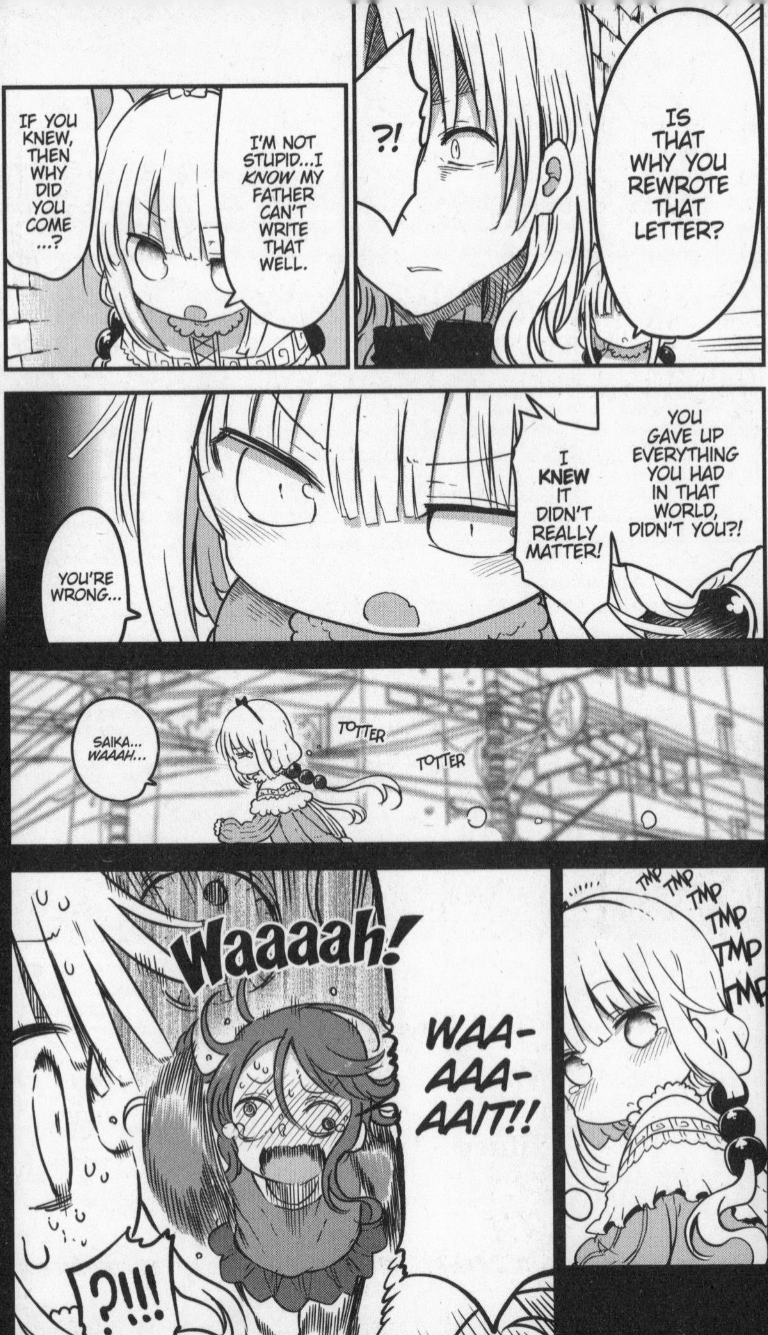
IS THAT WHY YOU REWROTE THAT LETTER?
?!
I'M NOT STUPID...I *KNOW* MY FATHER CAN'T WRITE THAT WELL.
IF YOU KNEW, THEN WHY DID YOU COME ...?
YOU GAVE UP EVERYTHING YOU HAD IN THAT WORLD, DIDN'T YOU?!
I **KNEW** IT DIDN'T REALLY MATTER!
YOU'RE WRONG...
TOTTER
TOTTER
SAIKA... WAAAH...
TMP TMP TMP TMP TMP TMP
...
WAA-AAA-AAIT!!
Waaaah!
?!!!

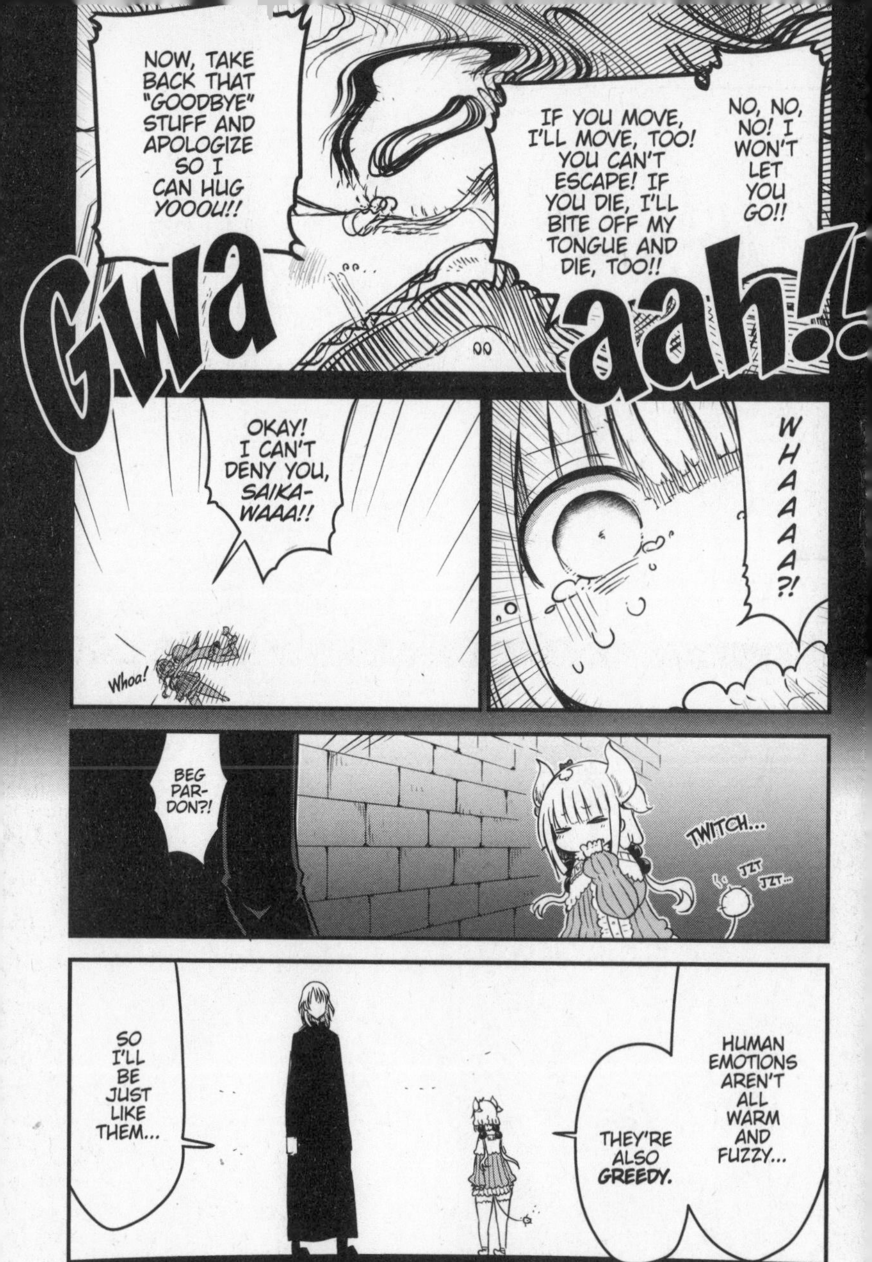
NO, NO, NO! I WON'T LET YOU GO!!
IF YOU MOVE, I'LL MOVE, TOO! YOU CAN'T ESCAPE! IF YOU DIE, I'LL BITE OFF MY TONGUE AND DIE, TOO!!
NOW, TAKE BACK THAT "GOODBYE" STUFF AND APOLOGIZE SO I CAN HUG YOOOU!!
GWA aah!!
WHAAAAA?!
OKAY! I CAN'T DENY YOU, SAIKA-WAAA!!
Whoa!
TWITCH...
JZT JZT...
BEG PAR-DON?!
HUMAN EMOTIONS AREN'T ALL WARM AND FUZZY...
THEY'RE ALSO GREEDY.
SO I'LL BE JUST LIKE THEM...

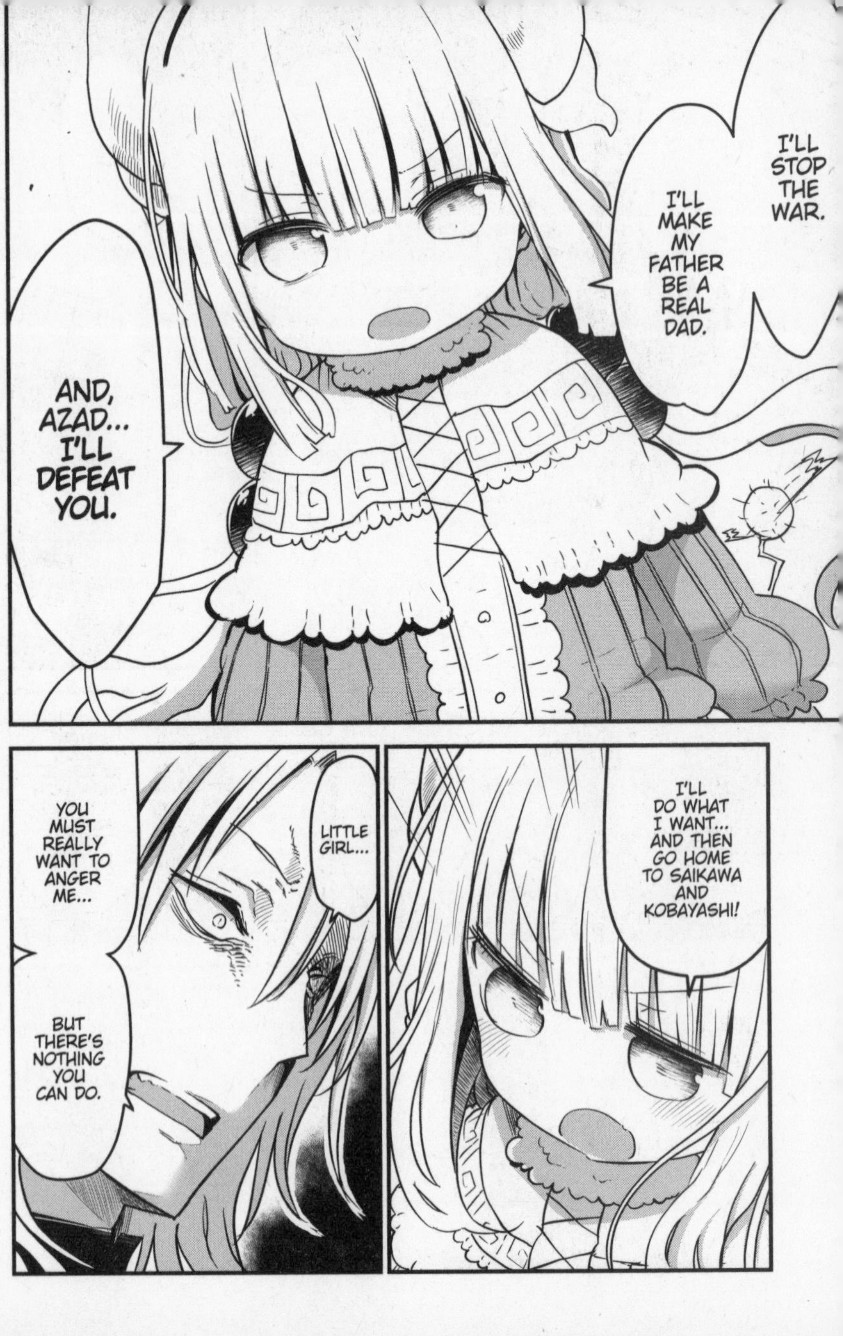
I'LL STOP THE WAR.
I'LL MAKE MY FATHER BE A REAL DAD.
AND, AZAD... I'LL DEFEAT YOU.
I'LL DO WHAT I WANT... AND THEN GO HOME TO SAIKAWA AND KOBAYASHI!
LITTLE GIRL...
YOU MUST REALLY WANT TO ANGER ME...
BUT THERE'S NOTHING YOU CAN DO.

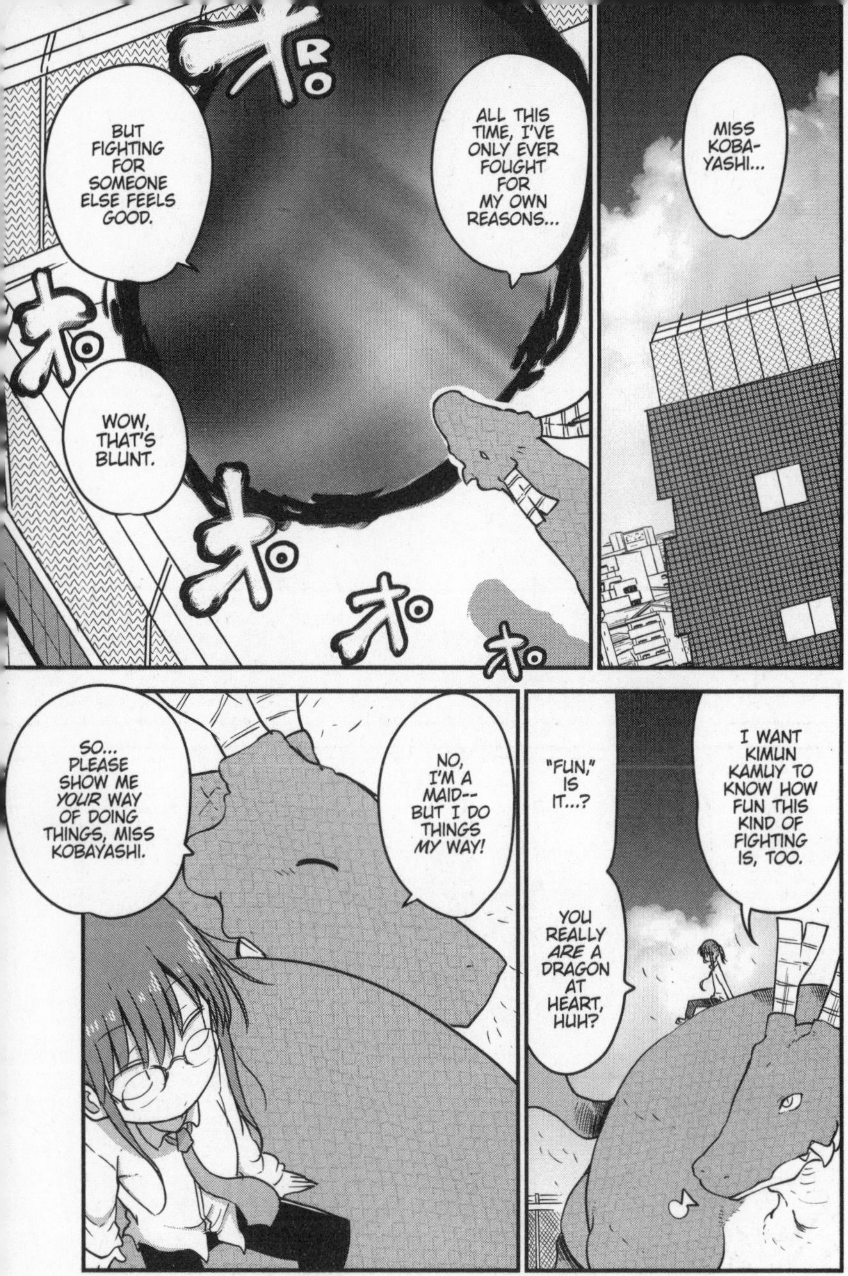
MISS KOBA-YASHI...
RO
ALL THIS TIME, I'VE ONLY EVER FOUGHT FOR MY OWN REASONS...
BUT FIGHTING FOR SOMEONE ELSE FEELS GOOD.
WOW, THAT'S BLUNT.
I WANT KIMUN KAMUY TO KNOW HOW FUN THIS KIND OF FIGHTING IS, TOO.
"FUN," IS IT...?
YOU REALLY *ARE* A DRAGON AT HEART, HUH?
NO, I'M A MAID-- BUT I DO THINGS *MY WAY!*
SO... PLEASE SHOW ME *YOUR* WAY OF DOING THINGS, MISS KOBAYASHI.

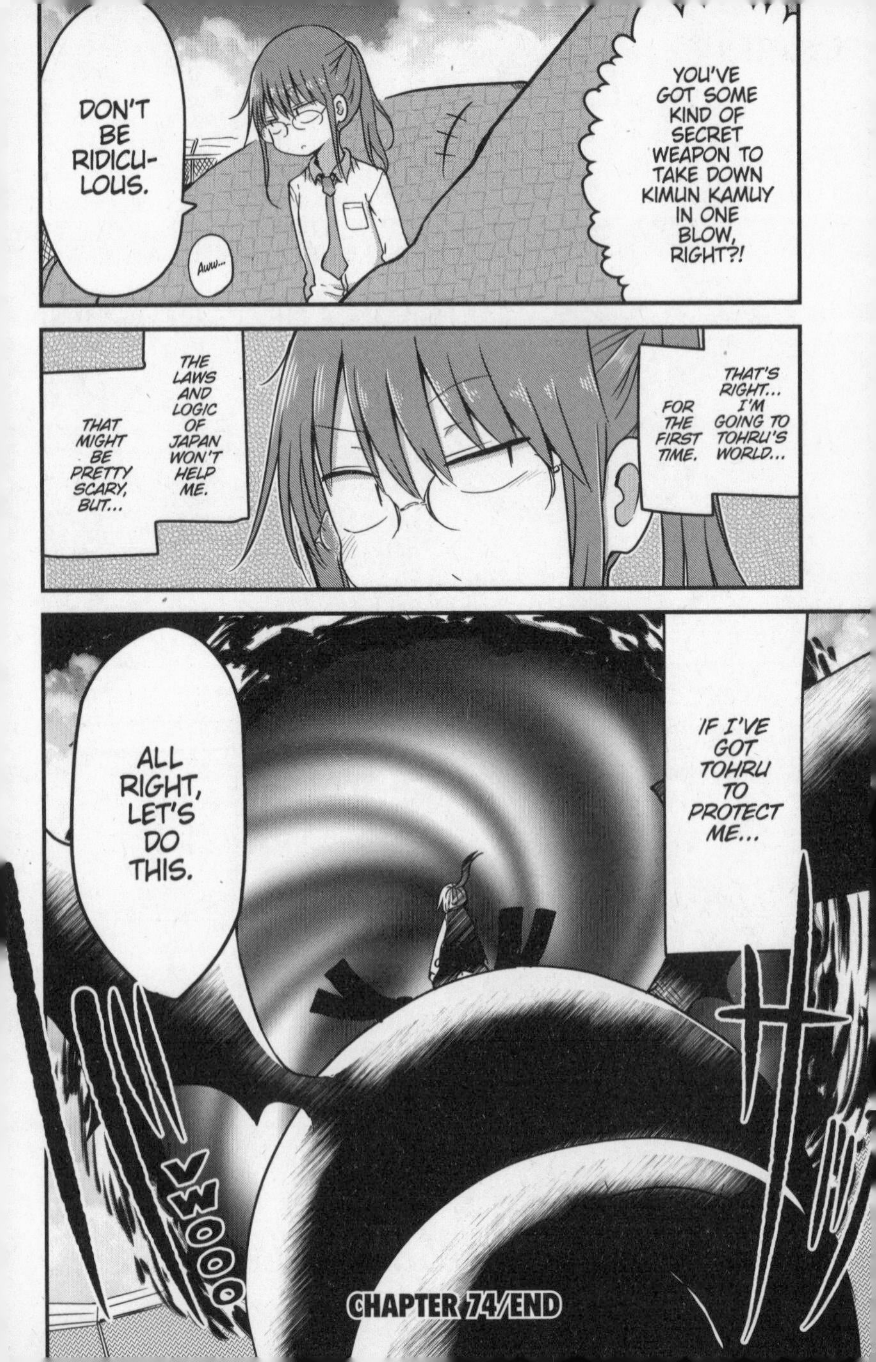

YOU'VE GOT SOME KIND OF SECRET WEAPON TO TAKE DOWN KIMUN KAMUY IN ONE BLOW, RIGHT?!
Aww...
DON'T BE RIDICULOUS.
THAT'S RIGHT... I'M GOING TO TOHRU'S WORLD...
FOR THE FIRST TIME.
THE LAWS AND LOGIC OF JAPAN WON'T HELP ME.
THAT MIGHT BE PRETTY SCARY, BUT...
IF I'VE GOT TOHRU TO PROTECT ME...
ALL RIGHT, LET'S DO THIS.
VWOOO
CHAPTER 74/END

CHAPTER 75

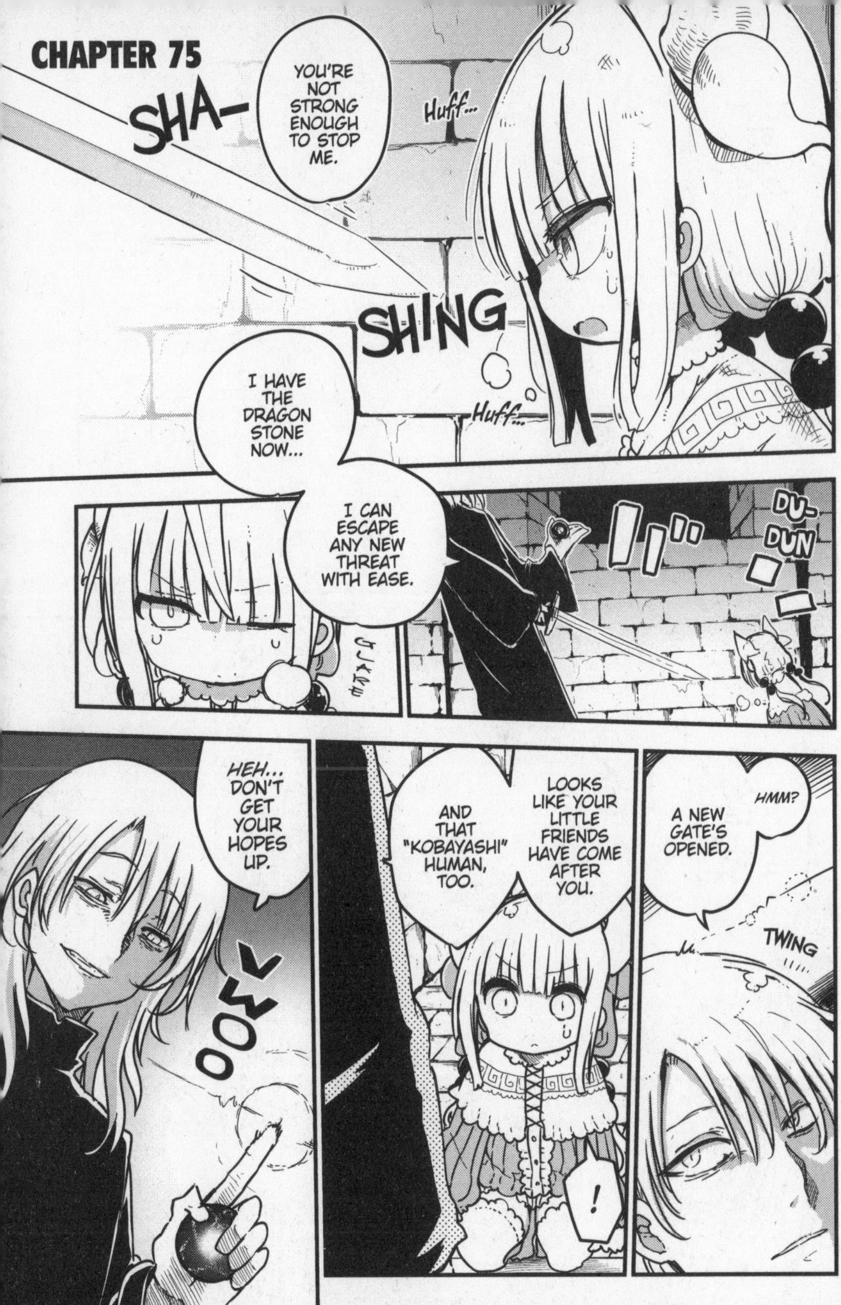
Huff...
YOU'RE NOT STRONG ENOUGH TO STOP ME.
SHA-
SHING
Huff...
I HAVE THE DRAGON STONE NOW...
DU-DUN
I CAN ESCAPE ANY NEW THREAT WITH EASE.
GLARE
HMM?
A NEW GATE'S OPENED.
TWING
LOOKS LIKE YOUR LITTLE FRIENDS HAVE COME AFTER YOU.
AND THAT "KOBAYASHI" HUMAN, TOO.
!
HEH... DON'T GET YOUR HOPES UP.
VWOO

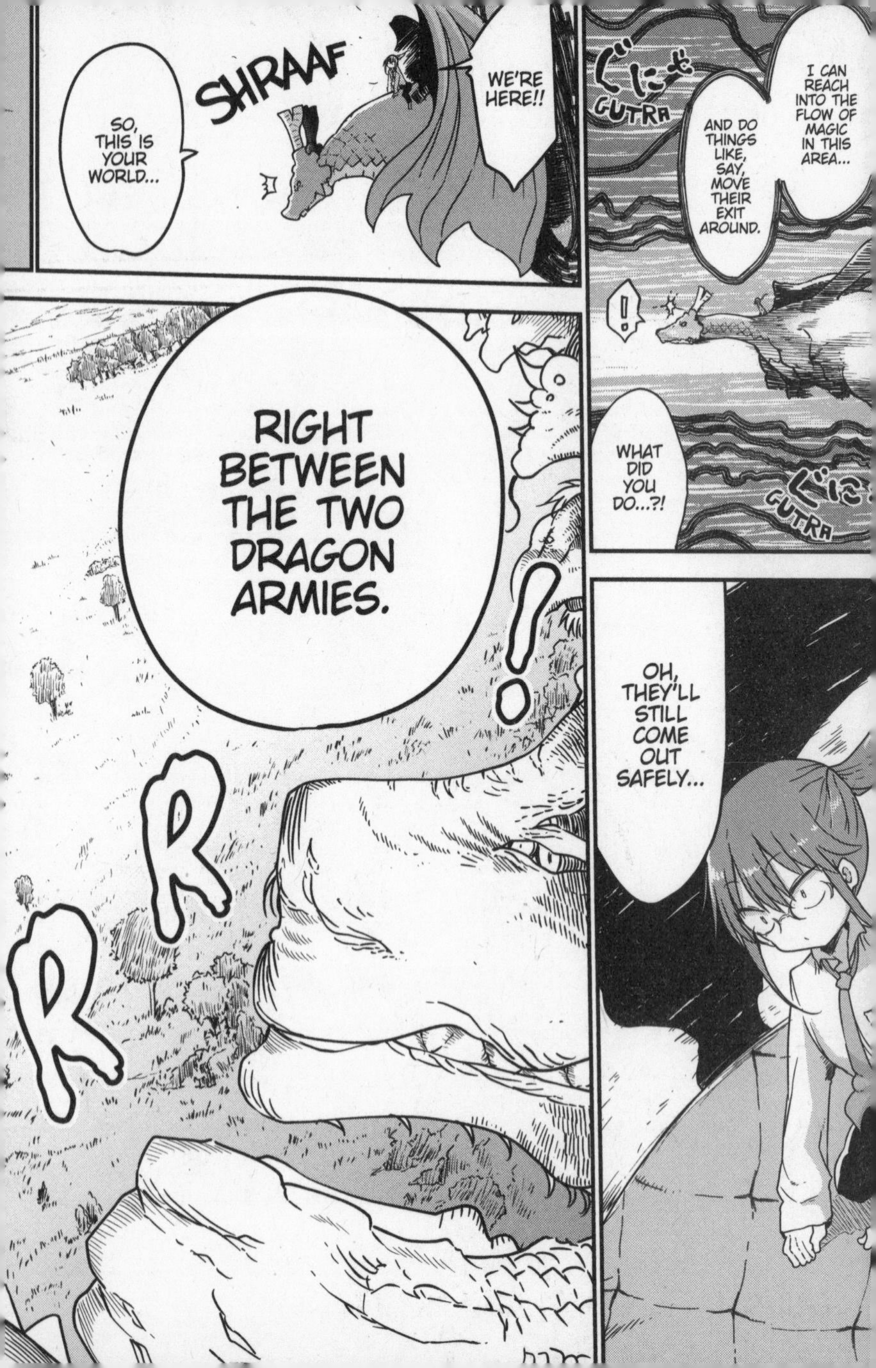
ぐにゃ
GUTRA
I CAN REACH INTO THE FLOW OF MAGIC IN THIS AREA...
AND DO THINGS LIKE, SAY, MOVE THEIR EXIT AROUND.
!
WHAT DID YOU DO...?!
ぐにゃ
GUTRA
OH, THEY'LL STILL COME OUT SAFELY...
WE'RE HERE!!
SHRAAF
SO, THIS IS YOUR WORLD...
RIGHT BETWEEN THE TWO DRAGON ARMIES.
!
RR

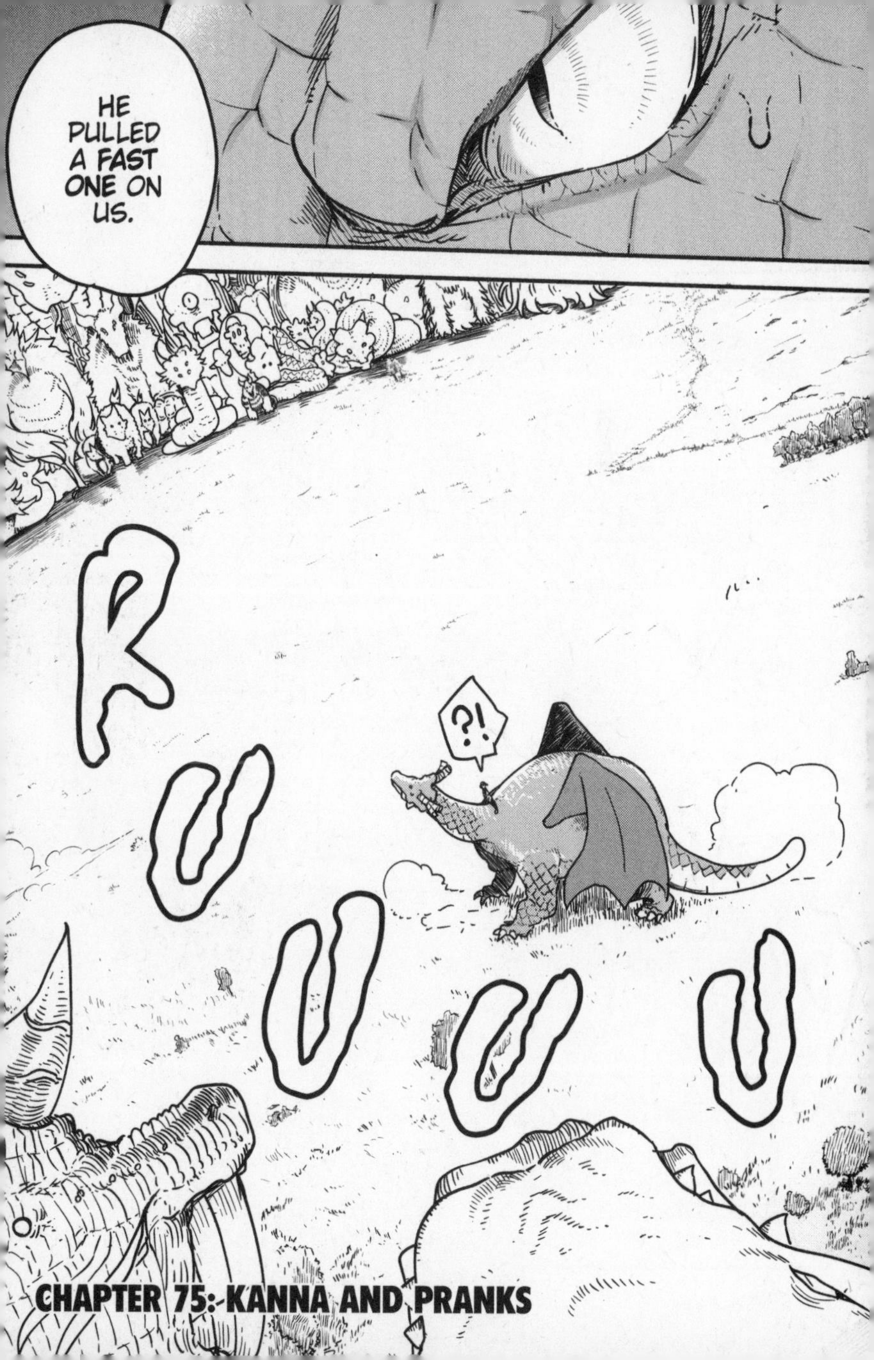
HE PULLED A FAST ONE ON US.
RUUUUU
?!
CHAPTER 75: KANNA AND PRANKS

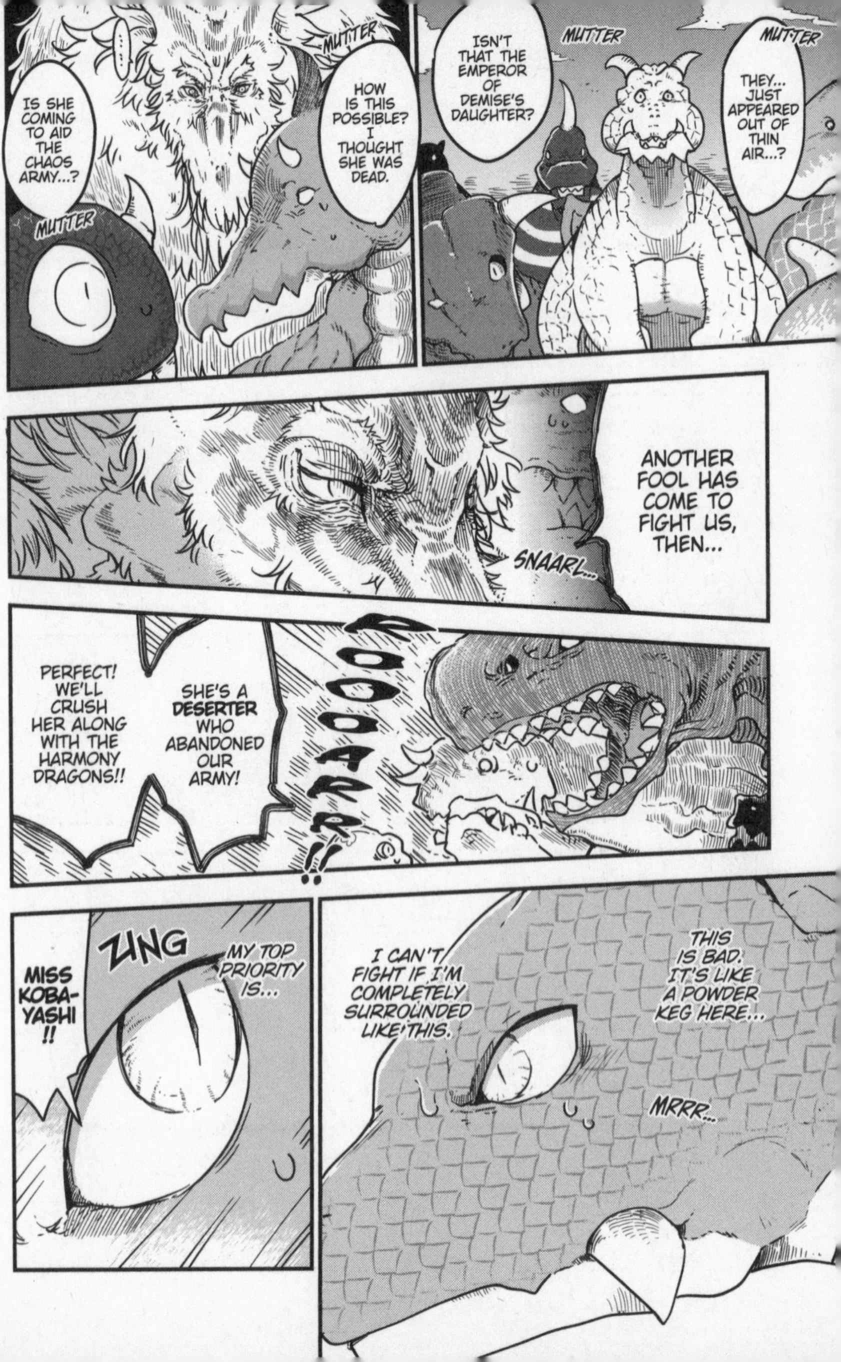
MUTTER
THEY... JUST APPEARED OUT OF THIN AIR...?
MUTTER
ISN'T THAT THE EMPEROR OF DEMISE'S DAUGHTER?
MUTTER
HOW IS THIS POSSIBLE? I THOUGHT SHE WAS DEAD.
...
IS SHE COMING TO AID THE CHAOS ARMY...?
MUTTER
ANOTHER FOOL HAS COME TO FIGHT US, THEN...
SNAARL...
ROOOARR!!
SHE'S A DESERTER WHO ABANDONED OUR ARMY!
PERFECT! WE'LL CRUSH HER ALONG WITH THE HARMONY DRAGONS!!
THIS IS BAD. IT'S LIKE A POWDER KEG HERE...
I CAN'T FIGHT IF I'M COMPLETELY SURROUNDED LIKE THIS.
MRRR...
ZING
MY TOP PRIORITY IS...
MISS KOBAYASHI!!

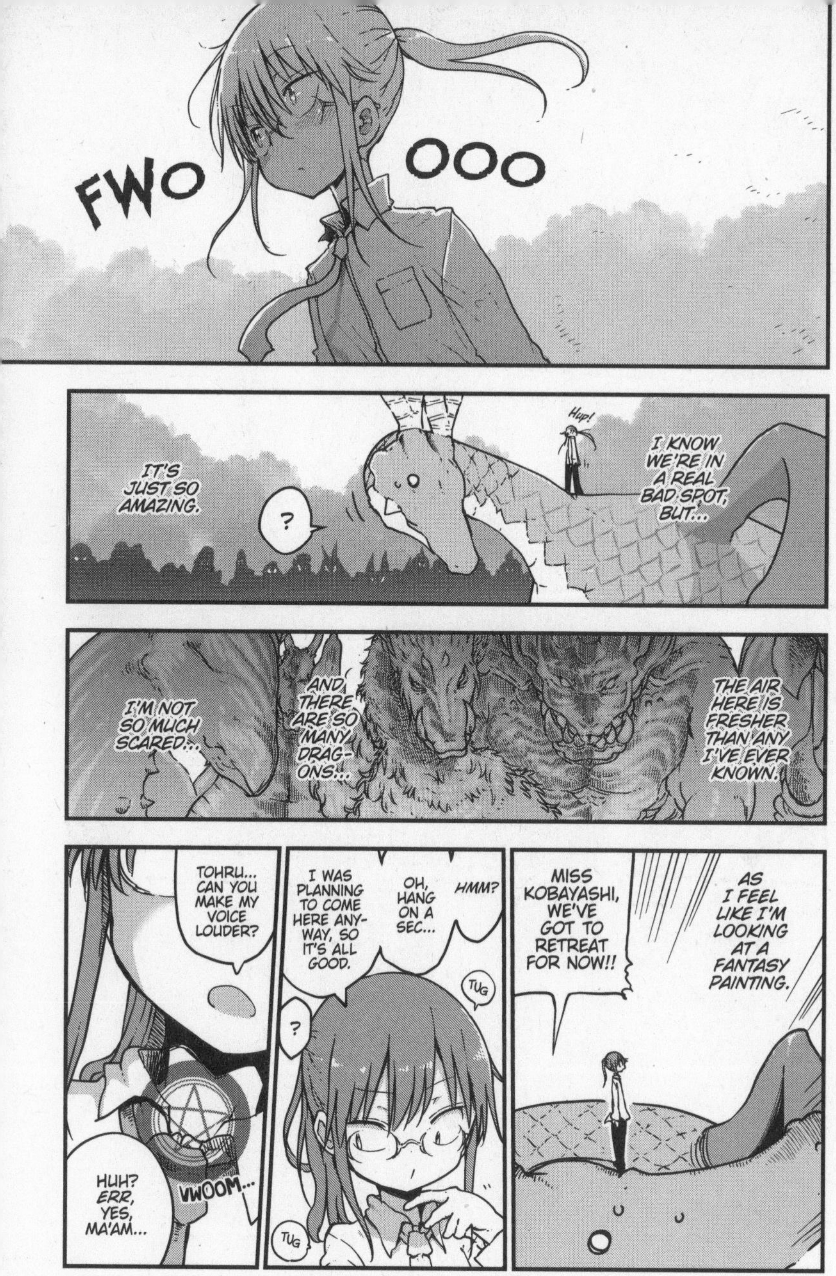
FWO
OOO
I KNOW WE'RE IN A REAL BAD SPOT, BUT...
Hup!
?
IT'S JUST SO AMAZING.
THE AIR HERE IS FRESHER THAN ANY I'VE EVER KNOWN.
AND THERE ARE SO MANY DRAG-ONS...
I'M NOT SO MUCH SCARED...
AS I FEEL LIKE I'M LOOKING AT A FANTASY PAINTING.
MISS KOBAYASHI, WE'VE GOT TO RETREAT FOR NOW!!
HMM?
OH, HANG ON A SEC...
I WAS PLANNING TO COME HERE ANY-WAY, SO IT'S ALL GOOD.
TUG
?
TUG
TOHRU... CAN YOU MAKE MY VOICE LOUDER?
HUH? ERR, YES, MA'AM...
VWOOM...

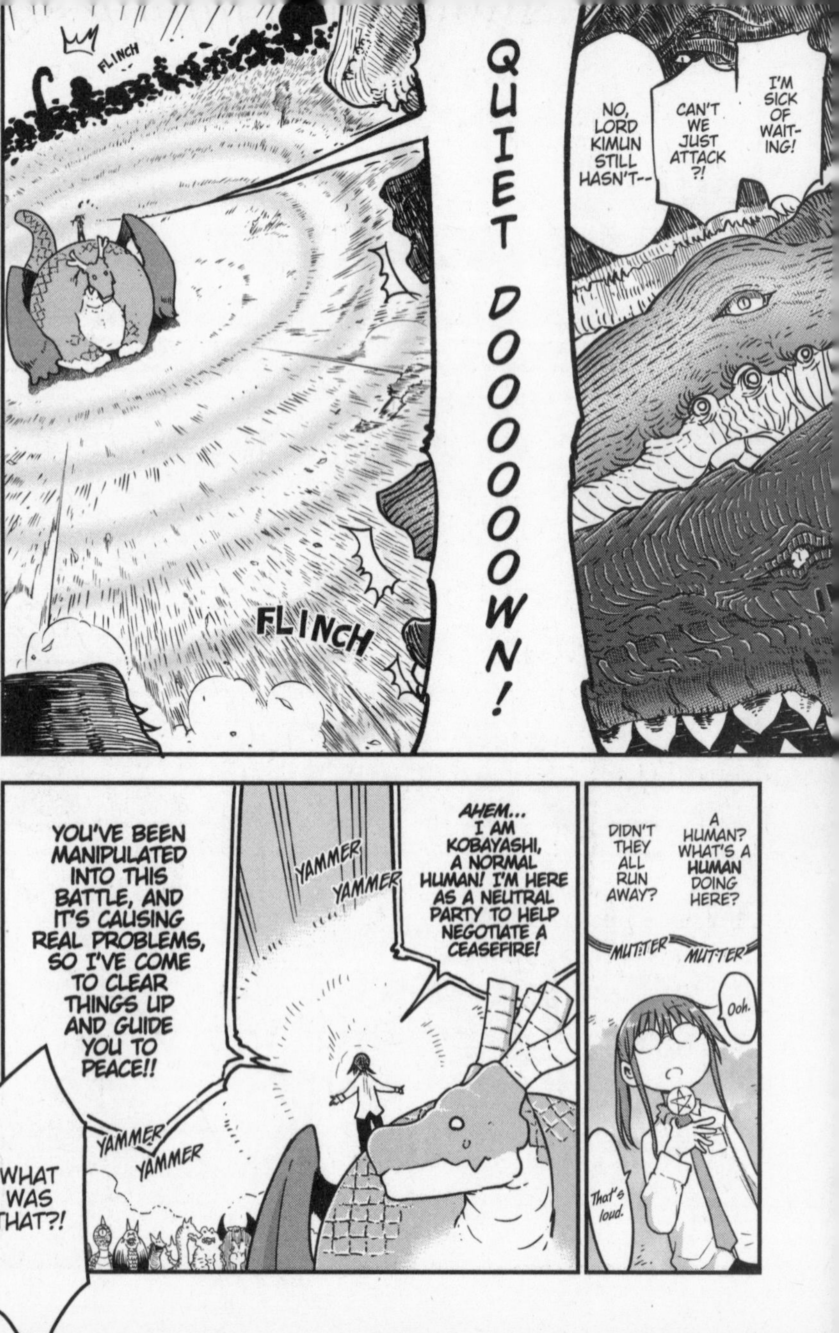
I'M SICK OF WAIT-ING!
CAN'T WE JUST ATTACK?!
NO, LORD KIMUN STILL HASN'T--
QUIET DOOOOOOOWN!
FLINCH
FLINCH
A HUMAN? WHAT'S A HUMAN DOING HERE?
DIDN'T THEY ALL RUN AWAY?
MUTTER MUTTER
Ooh.
That's loud.
AHEM... I AM KOBAYASHI, A NORMAL HUMAN! I'M HERE AS A NEUTRAL PARTY TO HELP NEGOTIATE A CEASEFIRE!
YAMMER YAMMER
YOU'VE BEEN MANIPULATED INTO THIS BATTLE, AND IT'S CAUSING REAL PROBLEMS, SO I'VE COME TO CLEAR THINGS UP AND GUIDE YOU TO PEACE!!
YAMMER YAMMER
WHAT WAS THAT?!

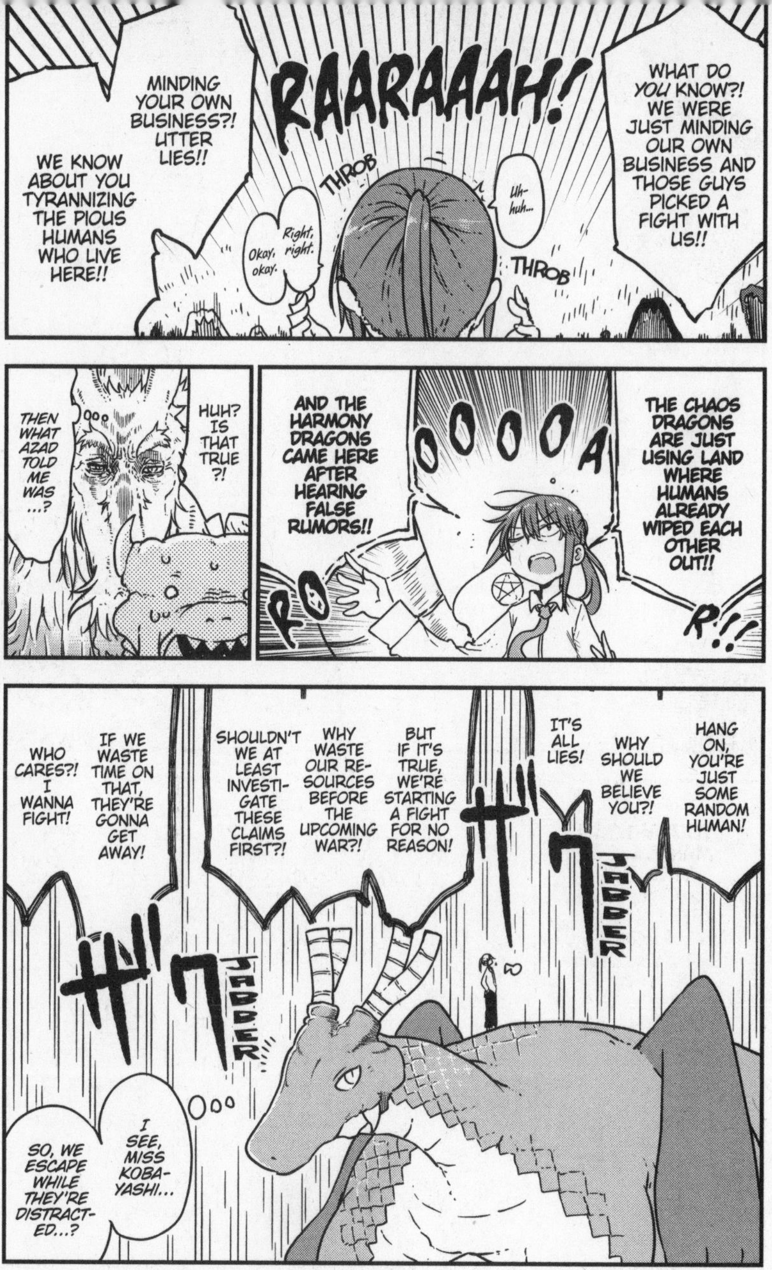
WHAT DO YOU KNOW?! WE WERE JUST MINDING OUR OWN BUSINESS AND THOSE GUYS PICKED A FIGHT WITH US!!
RAARAAAH!
THROB
Uh-huh...
THROB
Right, right.
Okay, okay.
MINDING YOUR OWN BUSINESS?! UTTER LIES!!
WE KNOW ABOUT YOU TYRANNIZING THE PIOUS HUMANS WHO LIVE HERE!!
THE CHAOS DRAGONS ARE JUST USING LAND WHERE HUMANS ALREADY WIPED EACH OTHER OUT!!
R!!!
OOOOA
AND THE HARMONY DRAGONS CAME HERE AFTER HEARING FALSE RUMORS!!
RO
HUH? IS THAT TRUE?!
THEN WHAT AZAD TOLD ME WAS...?
HANG ON, YOU'RE JUST SOME RANDOM HUMAN!
WHY SHOULD WE BELIEVE YOU?!
IT'S ALL LIES!
ザワ
JABBER
BUT IF IT'S TRUE, WE'RE STARTING A FIGHT FOR NO REASON!
WHY WASTE OUR RE-SOURCES BEFORE THE UPCOMING WAR?!
SHOULDN'T WE AT LEAST INVESTI-GATE THESE CLAIMS FIRST?!
IF WE WASTE TIME ON THAT, THEY'RE GONNA GET AWAY!
WHO CARES?! I WANNA FIGHT!
ザワ
JABBER
I SEE, MISS KOBA-YASHI...
SO, WE ESCAPE WHILE THEY'RE DISTRACT-ED...?

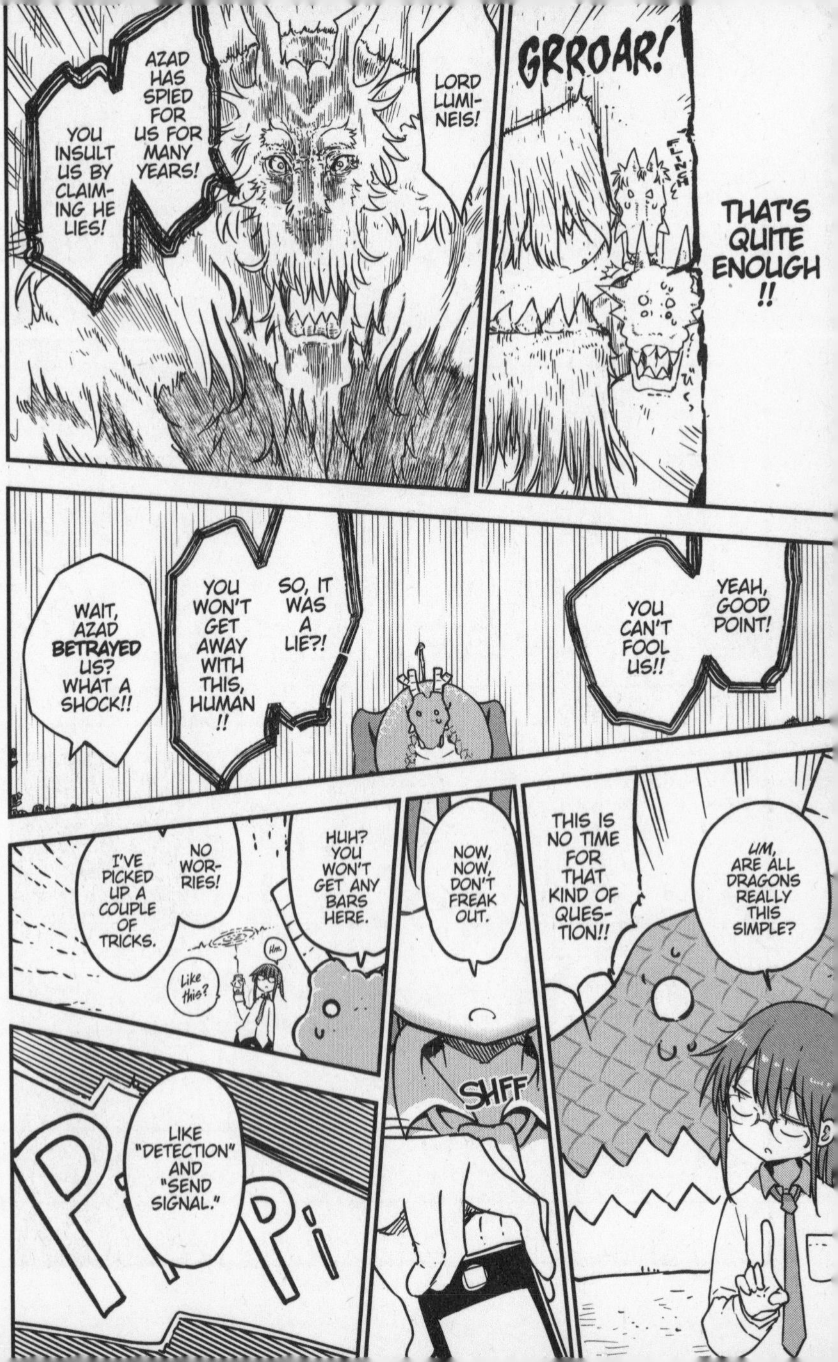
THAT'S QUITE ENOUGH!!
GRROAR!
FLINCH
LORD LUMINEIS!
AZAD HAS SPIED FOR US FOR MANY YEARS!
YOU INSULT US BY CLAIMING HE LIES!
YEAH, GOOD POINT!
YOU CAN'T FOOL US!!
SO, IT WAS A LIE?!
YOU WON'T GET AWAY WITH THIS, HUMAN!!
WAIT, AZAD BETRAYED US? WHAT A SHOCK!!
UM, ARE ALL DRAGONS REALLY THIS SIMPLE?
THIS IS NO TIME FOR THAT KIND OF QUESTION!!
NOW, NOW, DON'T FREAK OUT.
SHFF
HUH? YOU WON'T GET ANY BARS HERE.
NO WORRIES!
I'VE PICKED UP A COUPLE OF TRICKS.
Hm.
Like this?
LIKE "DETECTION" AND "SEND SIGNAL."
PiPi

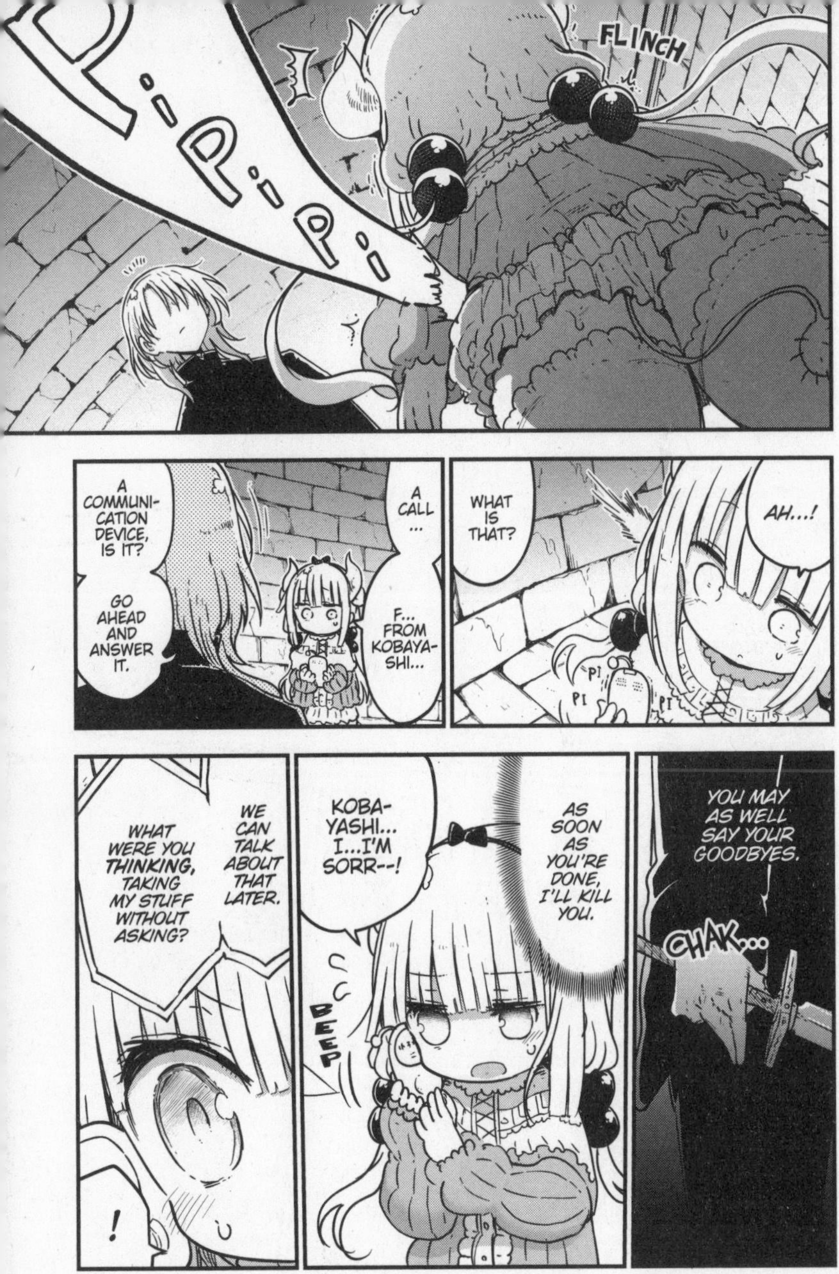
FLINCH
PIPIPI
AH...!
WHAT IS THAT?
PI
PI
PI
A CALL...
F... FROM KOBAYASHI...
A COMMUNICATION DEVICE, IS IT?
GO AHEAD AND ANSWER IT.
YOU MAY AS WELL SAY YOUR GOODBYES.
CHAK...
AS SOON AS YOU'RE DONE, I'LL KILL YOU.
KOBAYASHI... I...I'M SORR--!
BEEP
WE CAN TALK ABOUT THAT LATER.
WHAT WERE YOU THINKING, TAKING MY STUFF WITHOUT ASKING?
!

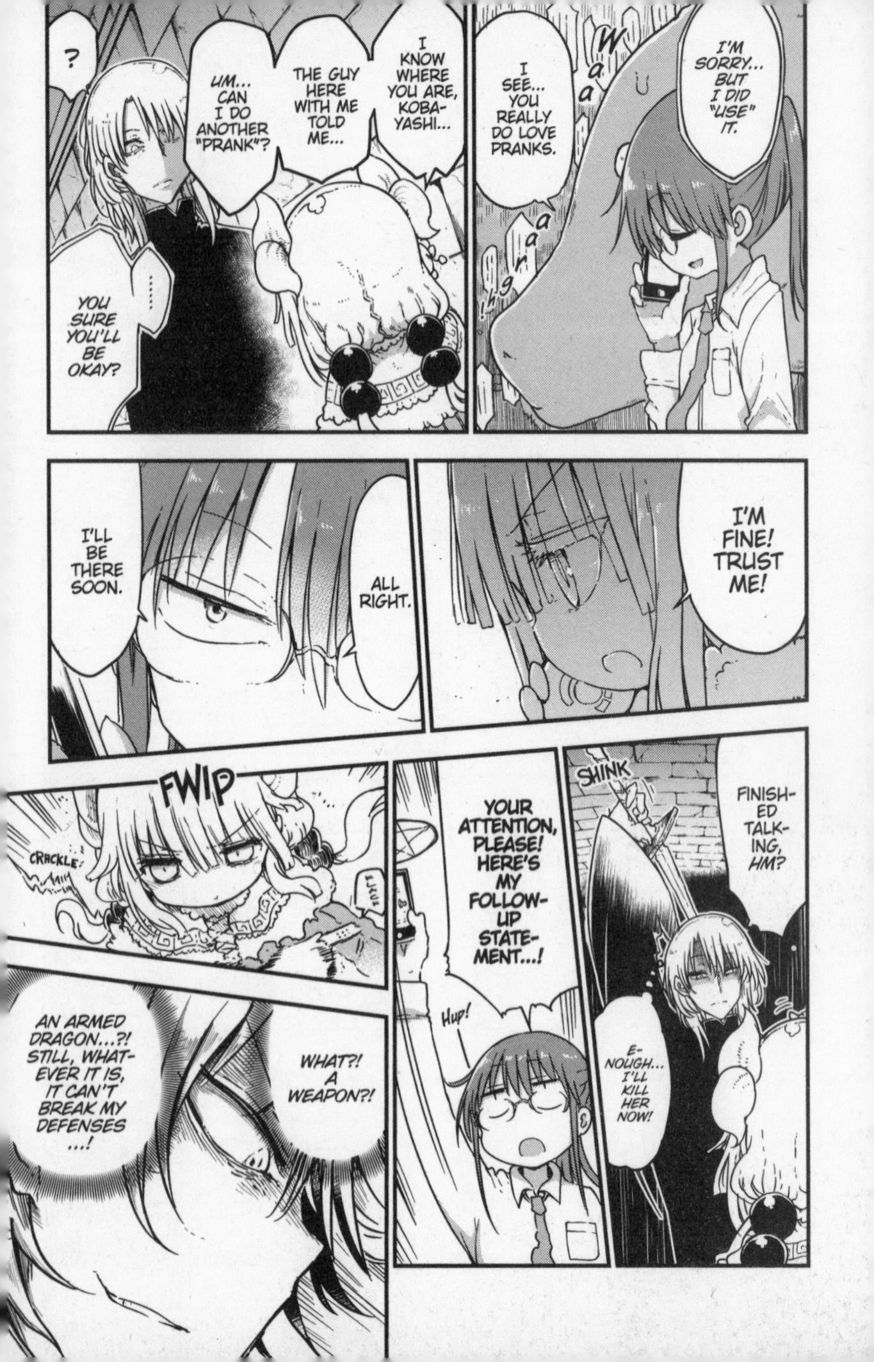
I'M SORRY... BUT I DID "USE" IT.
Waa
I SEE... YOU REALLY DO LOVE PRANKS.
aargh!
I KNOW WHERE YOU ARE, KOBA-YASHI...
THE GUY HERE WITH ME TOLD ME...
UM... CAN I DO ANOTHER "PRANK"?
?
......
YOU SURE YOU'LL BE OKAY?
I'M FINE! TRUST ME!
ALL RIGHT.
I'LL BE THERE SOON.
FINISH-ED TALK-ING, HM?
SHINK
E-NOUGH... I'LL KILL HER NOW!
YOUR ATTENTION, PLEASE! HERE'S MY FOLLOW-UP STATE-MENT...!
Hup!
FWIP
CRACKLE
WHAT?! A WEAPON?!
AN ARMED DRAGON...?! STILL, WHAT-EVER IT IS, IT CAN'T BREAK MY DEFENSES...!

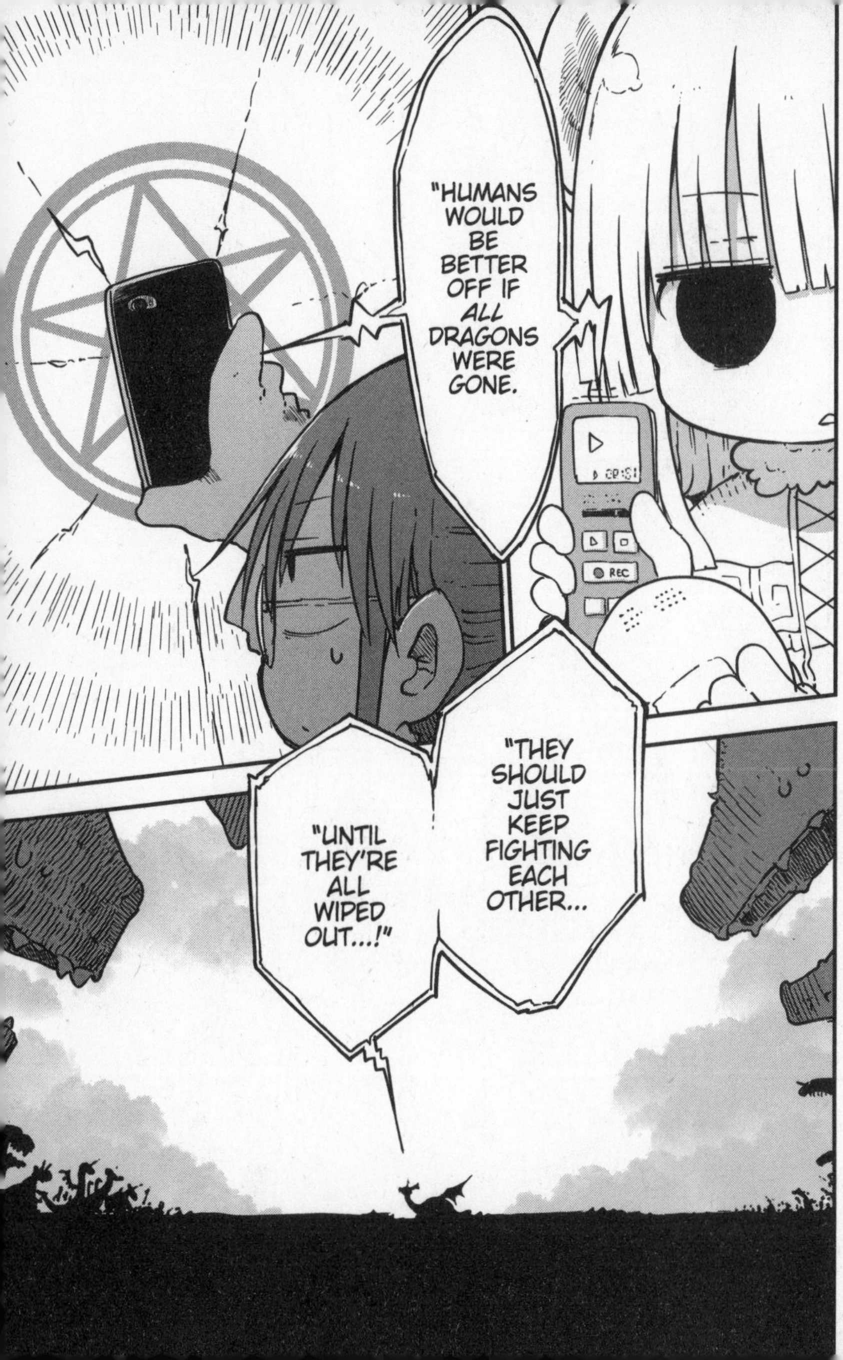
"HUMANS WOULD BE BETTER OFF IF *ALL* DRAGONS WERE GONE.
REC
"THEY SHOULD JUST KEEP FIGHTING EACH OTHER...
"UNTIL THEY'RE ALL WIPED OUT...!"

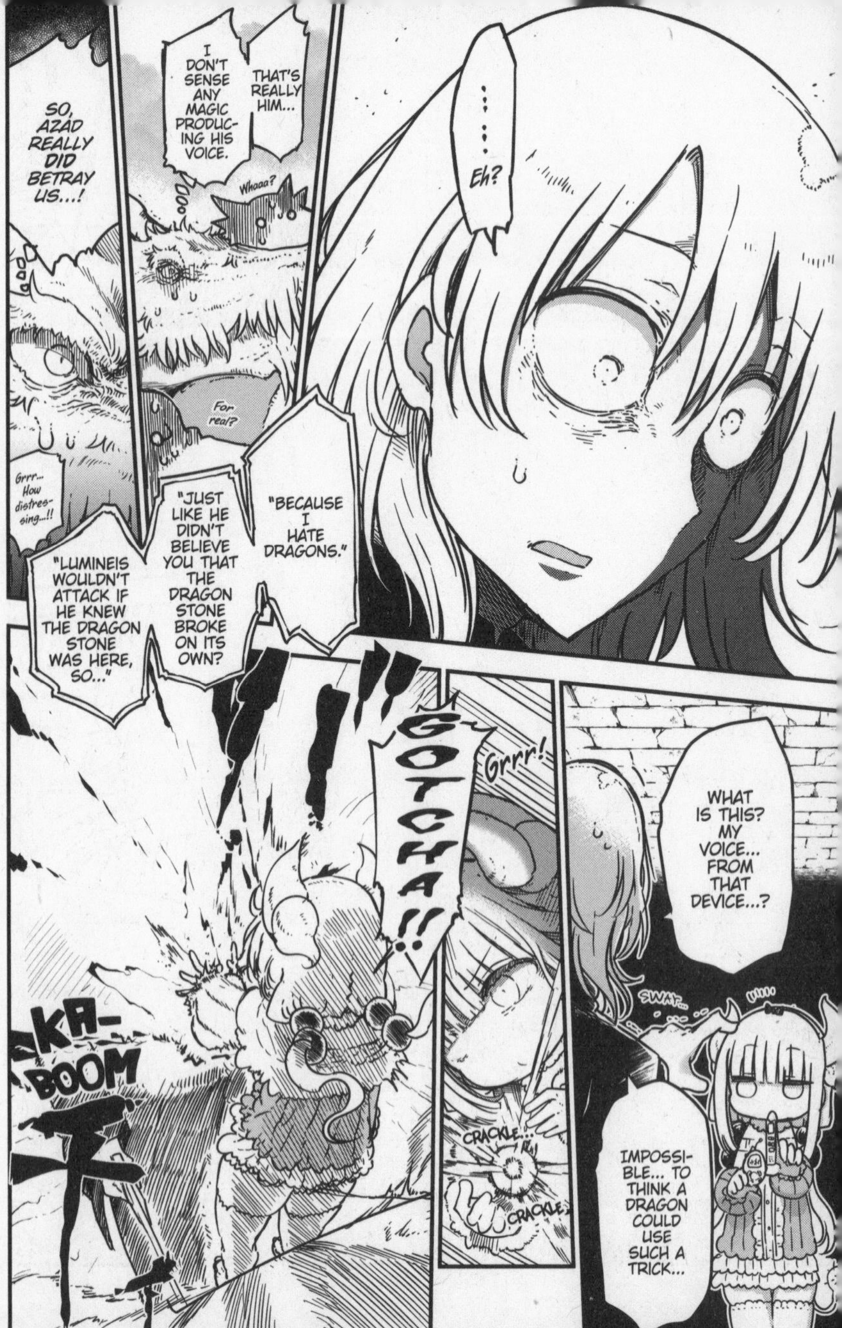
......
Eh?
"BECAUSE I HATE DRAGONS."
"JUST LIKE HE DIDN'T BELIEVE YOU THAT THE DRAGON STONE BROKE ON ITS OWN?
"LUMINEIS WOULDN'T ATTACK IF HE KNEW THE DRAGON STONE WAS HERE, SO..."
THAT'S REALLY HIM...
I DON'T SENSE ANY MAGIC PRODUCING HIS VOICE.
Whaaa?
For real?
SO, AZAD REALLY DID BETRAY US...!
Grrr... How distres-sing...!!
WHAT IS THIS? MY VOICE... FROM THAT DEVICE...?
SWAP...
IMPOSSIBLE... TO THINK A DRAGON COULD USE SUCH A TRICK...
Grrr!
CRACKLE...
CRACKLE
GOTCHA!!
KA-BOOM

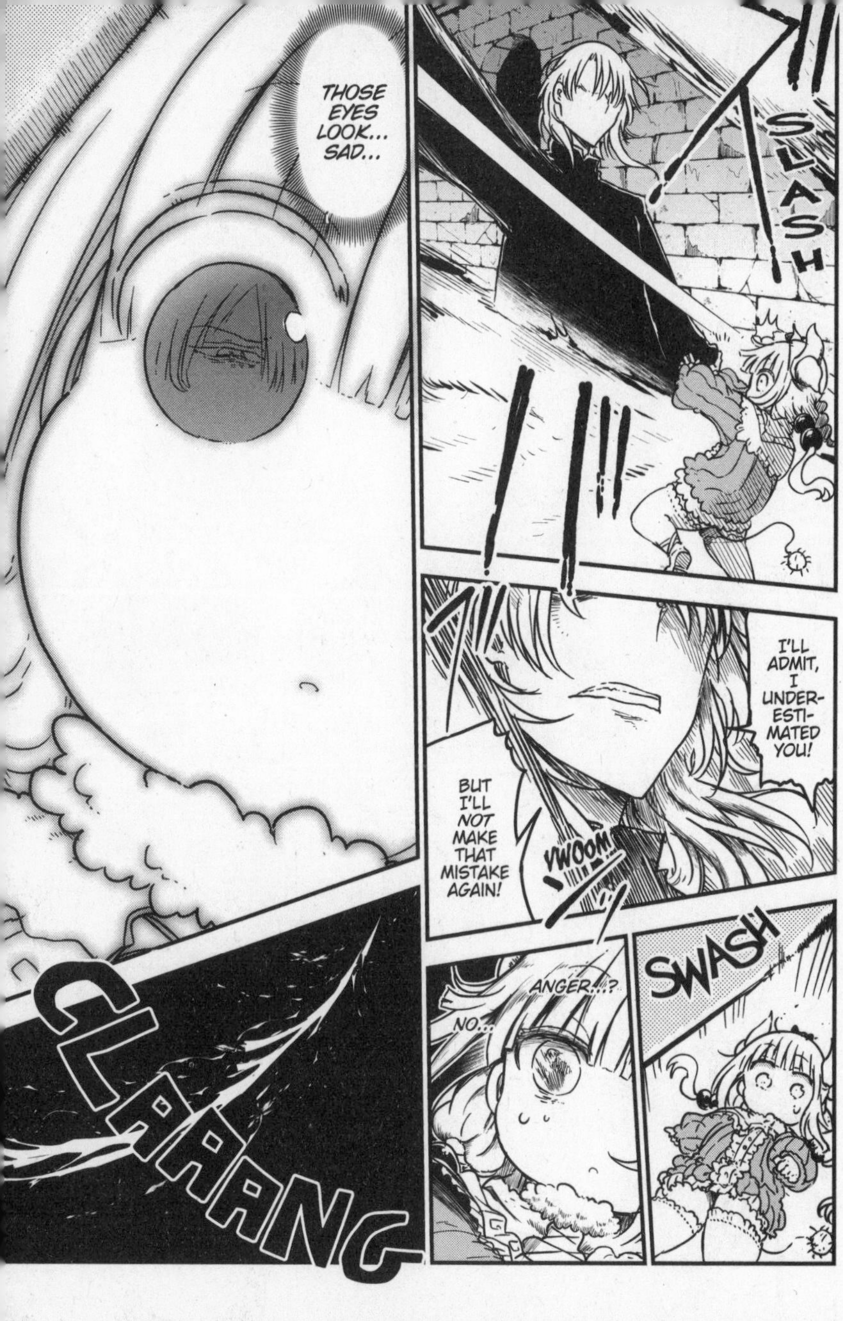
SLASH
I'LL ADMIT, I UNDER-ESTI-MATED YOU!
BUT I'LL *NOT* MAKE THAT MISTAKE AGAIN!
VWOOM!
SWASH
ANGER...?
NO...
THOSE EYES LOOK... SAD...
CLAAANG

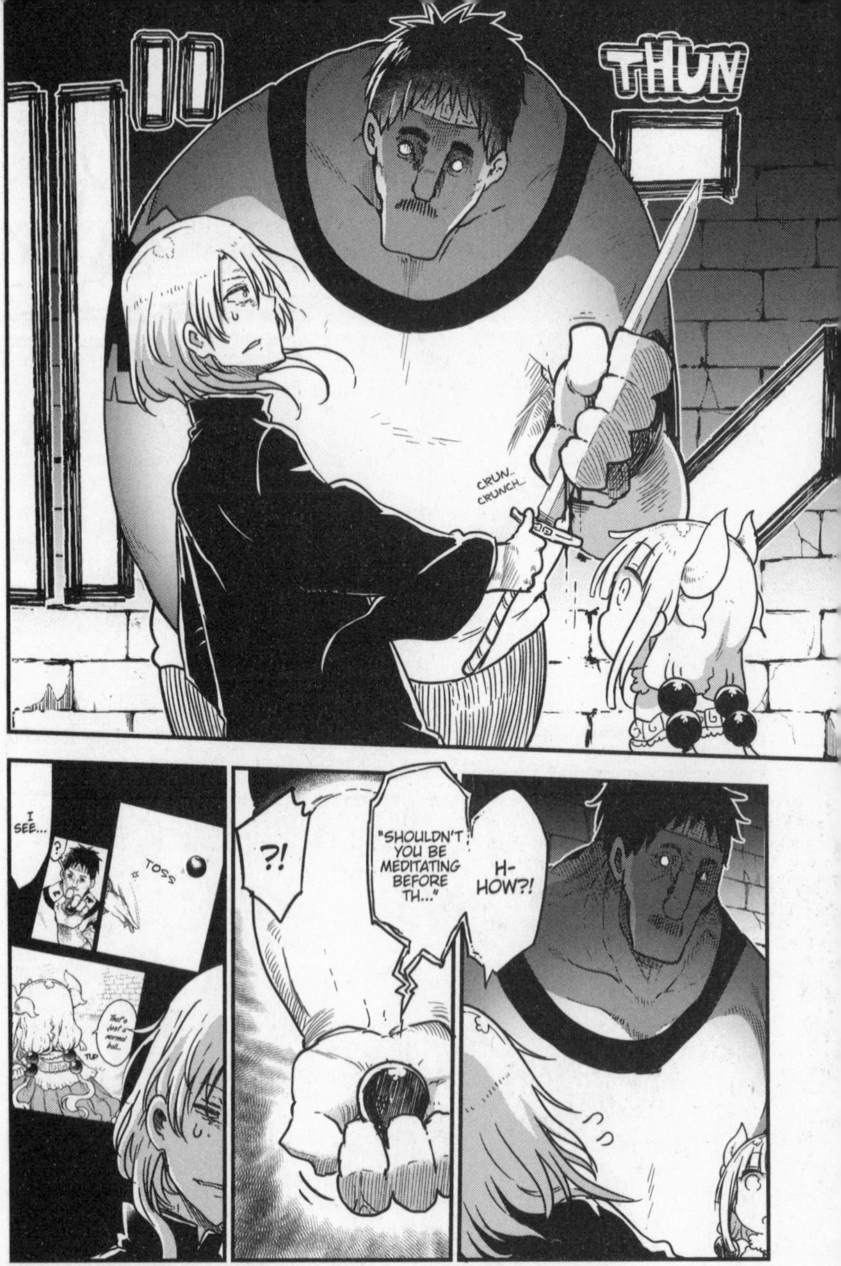
THUN
CRUN.. CRUNCH..
H-HOW?!
"SHOULDN'T YOU BE MEDITATING BEFORE TH..."
?!
I SEE...
?
TOSS
That's just a normal ball...
TUP

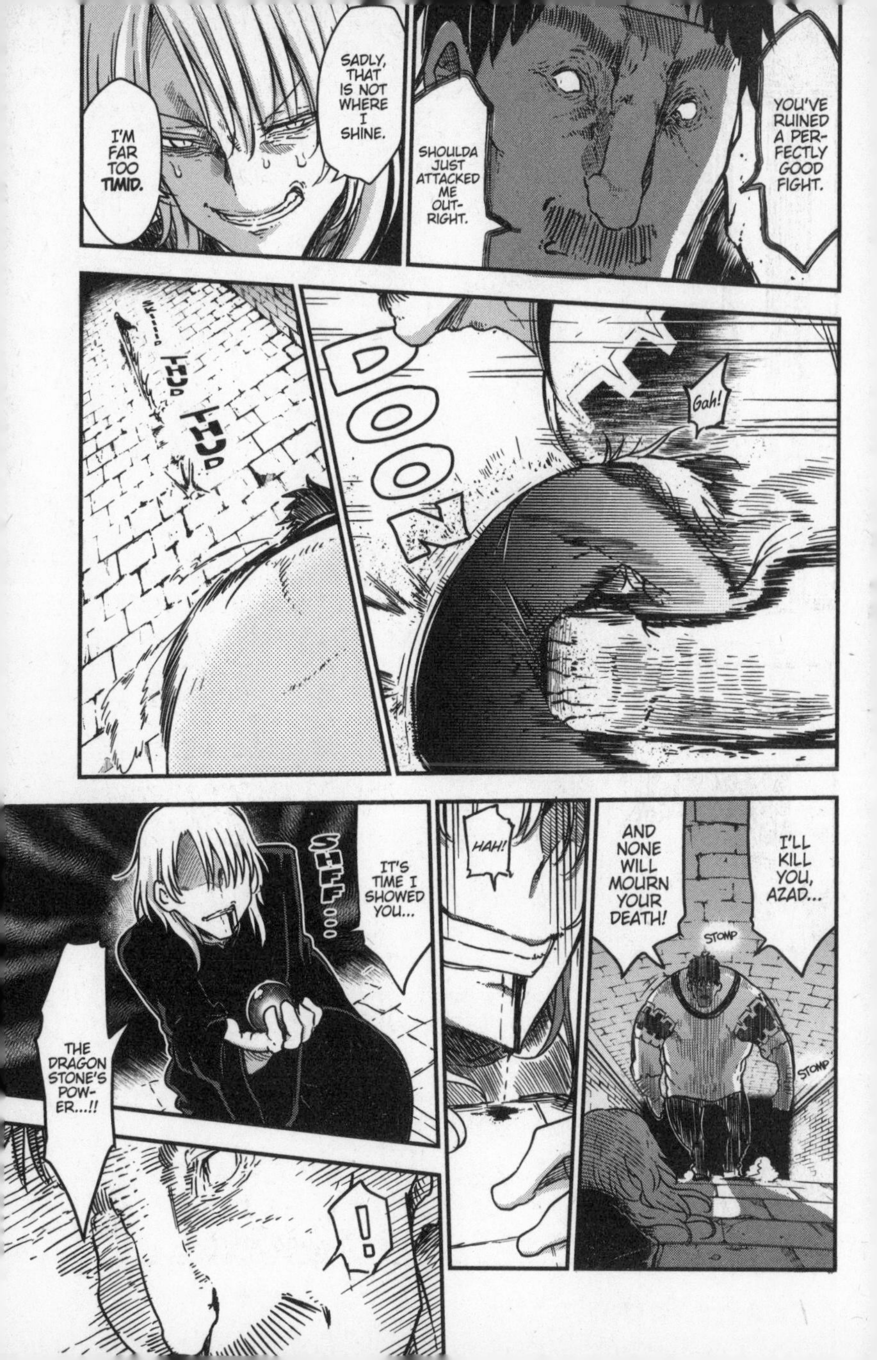
YOU'VE RUINED A PERFECTLY GOOD FIGHT.
SHOULDA JUST ATTACKED ME OUTRIGHT.
SADLY, THAT IS NOT WHERE I SHINE.
I'M FAR TOO TIMID.
DOOON
Gah!
SKIIIID
THUD
THUD
I'LL KILL YOU, AZAD...
AND NONE WILL MOURN YOUR DEATH!
STOMP
STOMP
HAH!
IT'S TIME I SHOWED YOU...
SHFF...
THE DRAGON STONE'S POWER...!!
!

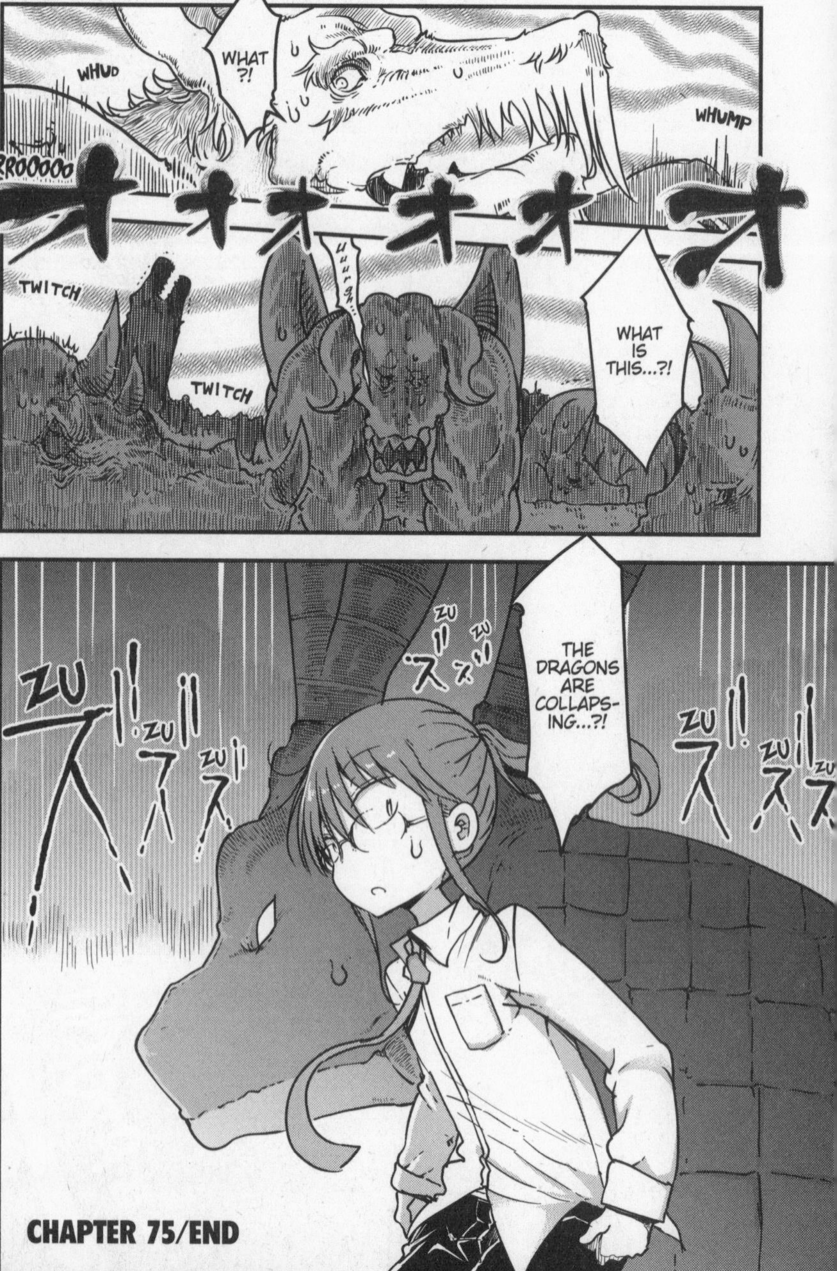
WHAT?!
WHUMP
WHUD
VRROOOOO
オオオオオオ
WHAT IS THIS...?!
TWITCH
TWITCH
THE DRAGONS ARE COLLAPSING...?!
ZU ZU ズズ
ZU ス ZU ス ZU ス
ZU ス ZU ス ZU ス

CHAPTER 75/END

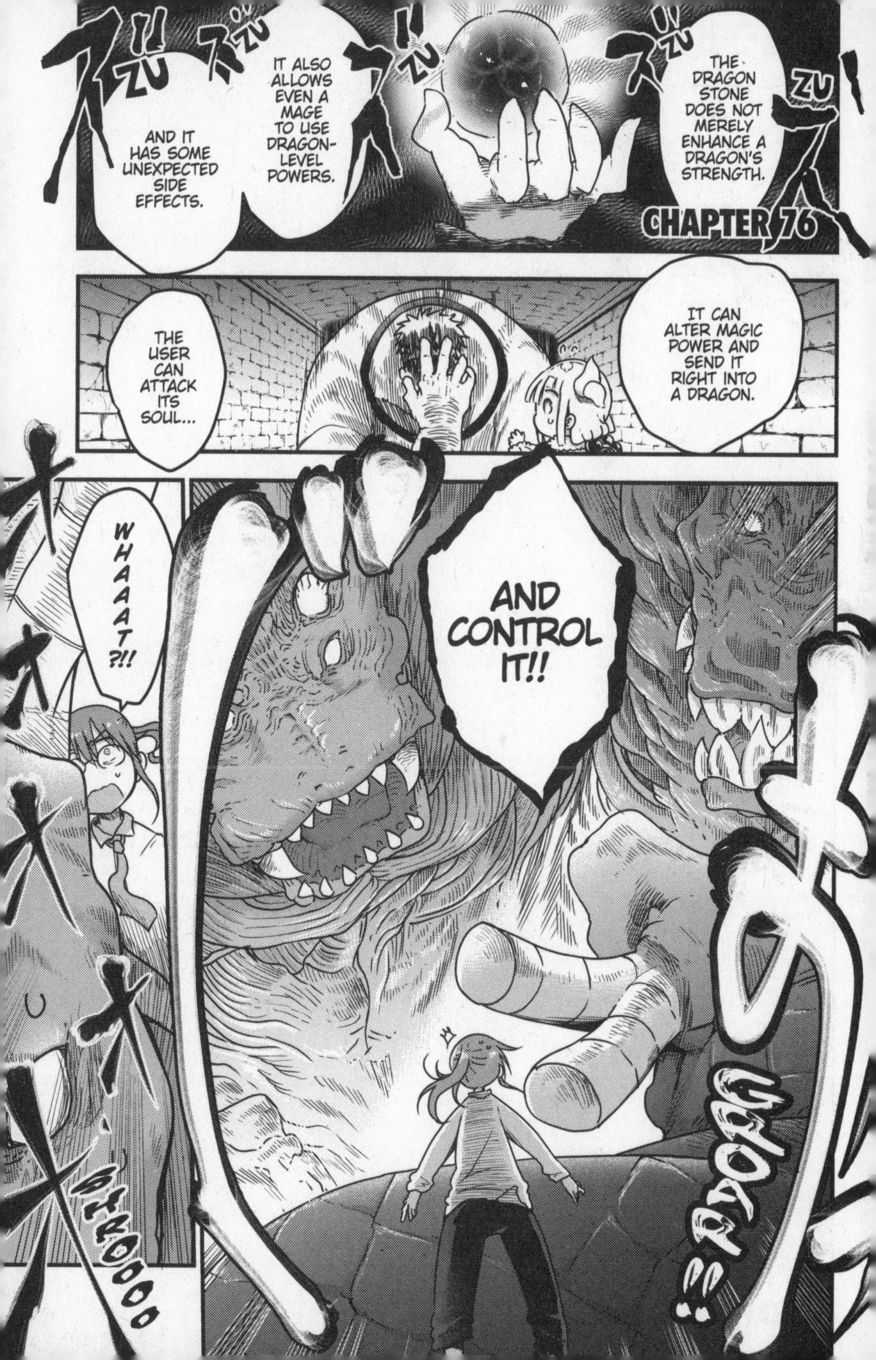
ZU
ZU
THE DRAGON STONE DOES NOT MERELY ENHANCE A DRAGON'S STRENGTH.
CHAPTER 76
ZU
IT ALSO ALLOWS EVEN A MAGE TO USE DRAGON-LEVEL POWERS.
ZU
ZU
AND IT HAS SOME UNEXPECTED SIDE EFFECTS.
IT CAN ALTER MAGIC POWER AND SEND IT RIGHT INTO A DRAGON.
THE USER CAN ATTACK ITS SOUL...
AND CONTROL IT!!
GHOAR!!
WHAAAAT?!!
SHROOOOO

CHAPTER 76: KOBAYASHI AND THE SECRET ART

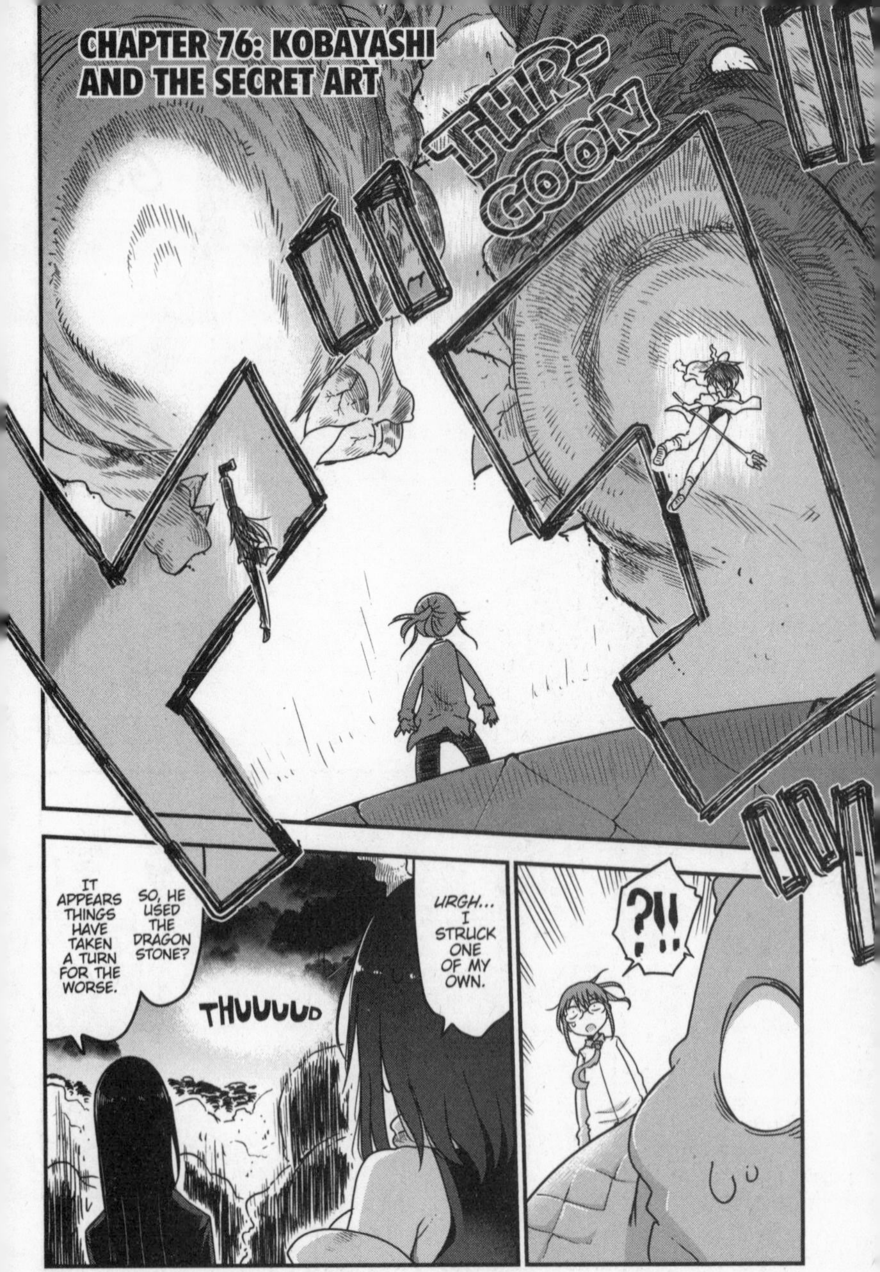
THR-GOON
?!!
URGH... I STRUCK ONE OF MY OWN.
SO, HE USED THE DRAGON STONE?
IT APPEARS THINGS HAVE TAKEN A TURN FOR THE WORSE.
THUUUUD

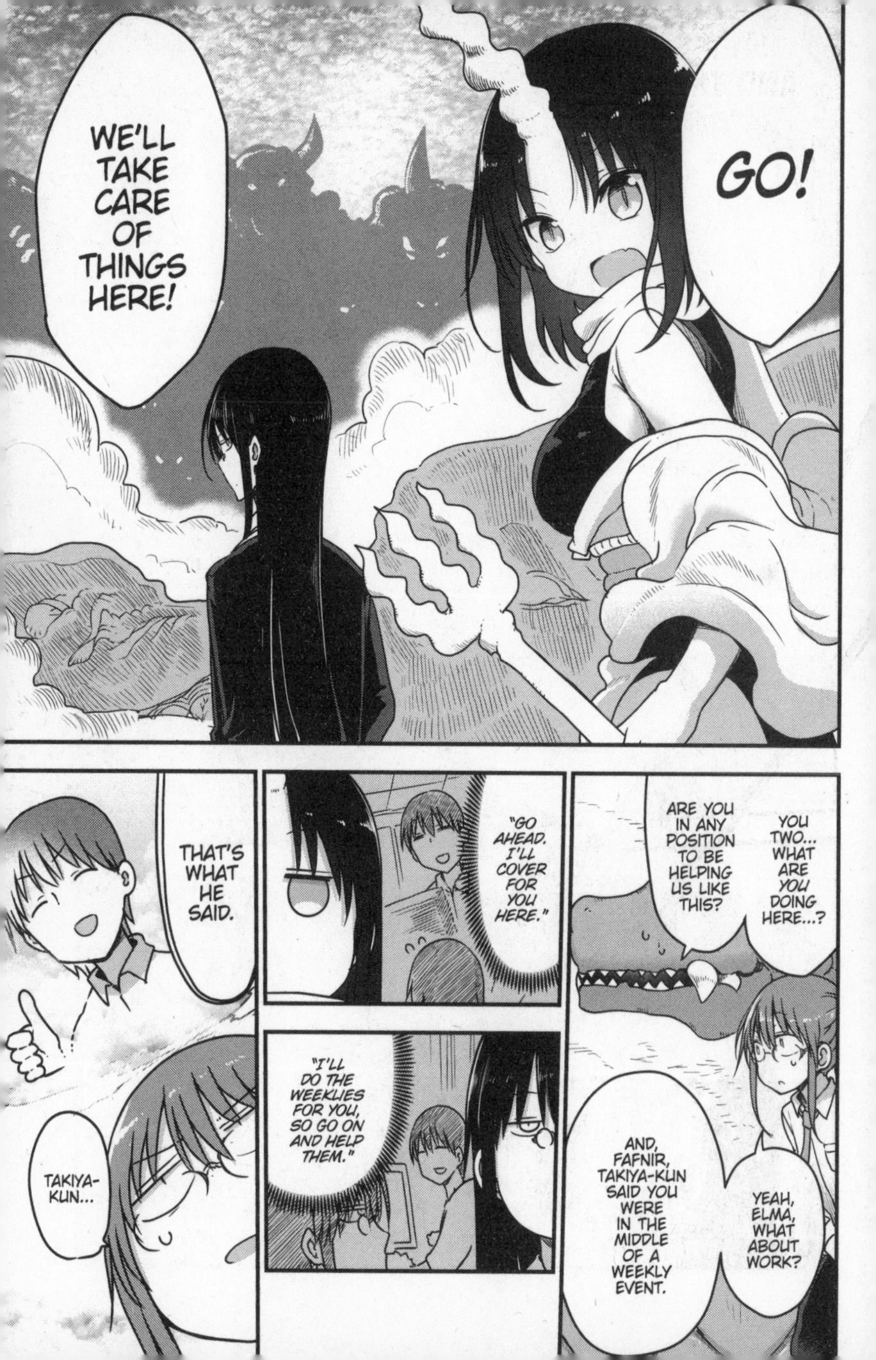
GO!
WE'LL TAKE CARE OF THINGS HERE!
YOU TWO... WHAT ARE YOU DOING HERE...?
ARE YOU IN ANY POSITION TO BE HELPING US LIKE THIS?
YEAH, ELMA, WHAT ABOUT WORK?
AND, FAFNIR, TAKIYA-KUN SAID YOU WERE IN THE MIDDLE OF A WEEKLY EVENT.
"GO AHEAD. I'LL COVER FOR YOU HERE."
"I'LL DO THE WEEKLIES FOR YOU, SO GO ON AND HELP THEM."
THAT'S WHAT HE SAID.
TAKIYA-KUN...

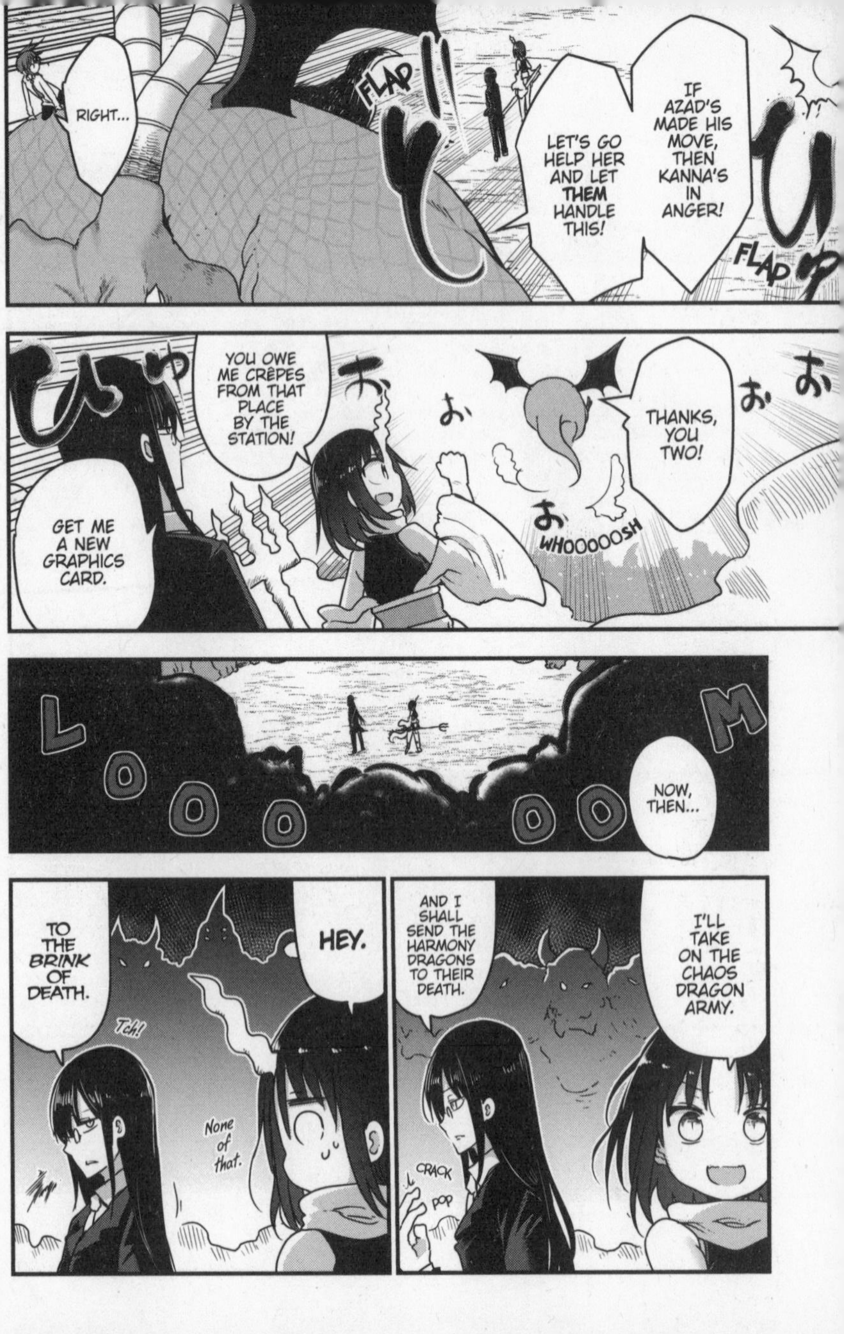
IF AZAD'S MADE HIS MOVE, THEN KANNA'S IN ANGER!
FLAP
LET'S GO HELP HER AND LET **THEM** HANDLE THIS!
FLAP
RIGHT...
THANKS, YOU TWO!
WHOOOOOSH
YOU OWE ME CRÊPES FROM THAT PLACE BY THE STATION!
GET ME A NEW GRAPHICS CARD.
LOOOOOOOM
NOW, THEN...
I'LL TAKE ON THE CHAOS DRAGON ARMY.
AND I SHALL SEND THE HARMONY DRAGONS TO THEIR DEATH.
CRACK
POP
HEY.
None of that.
TO THE *BRINK* OF DEATH.
Tch!

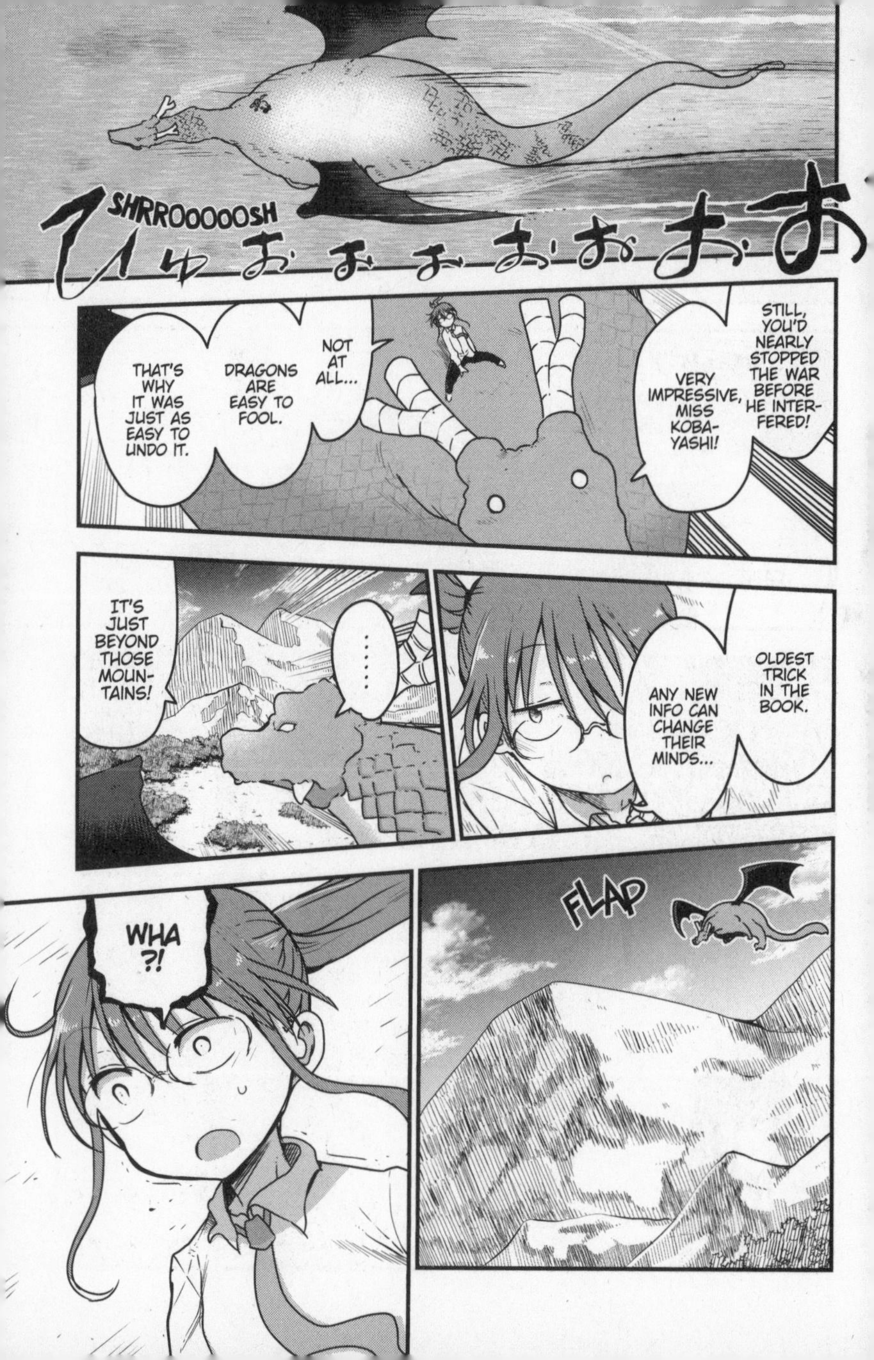
SHRROOOOOSH
STILL, YOU'D NEARLY STOPPED THE WAR BEFORE HE INTERFERED!
VERY IMPRESSIVE, MISS KOBAYASHI!
NOT AT ALL...
DRAGONS ARE EASY TO FOOL.
THAT'S WHY IT WAS JUST AS EASY TO UNDO IT.
OLDEST TRICK IN THE BOOK.
ANY NEW INFO CAN CHANGE THEIR MINDS...
......
IT'S JUST BEYOND THOSE MOUNTAINS!
FLAP
WHA ?!

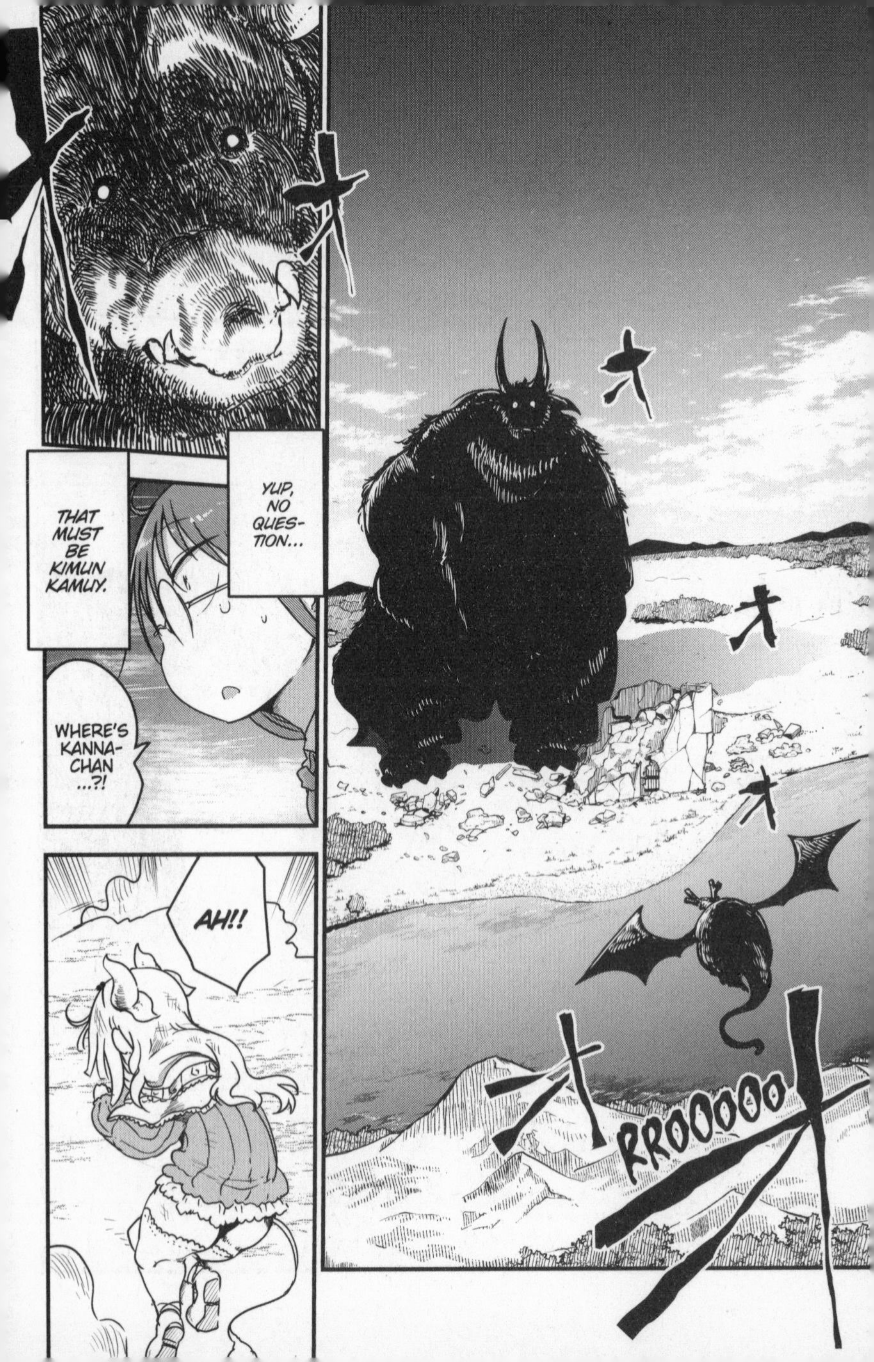
RROOOOO
YUP, NO QUESTION...
THAT MUST BE KIMUN KAMUY.
WHERE'S KANNA-CHAN...?!
AH!!

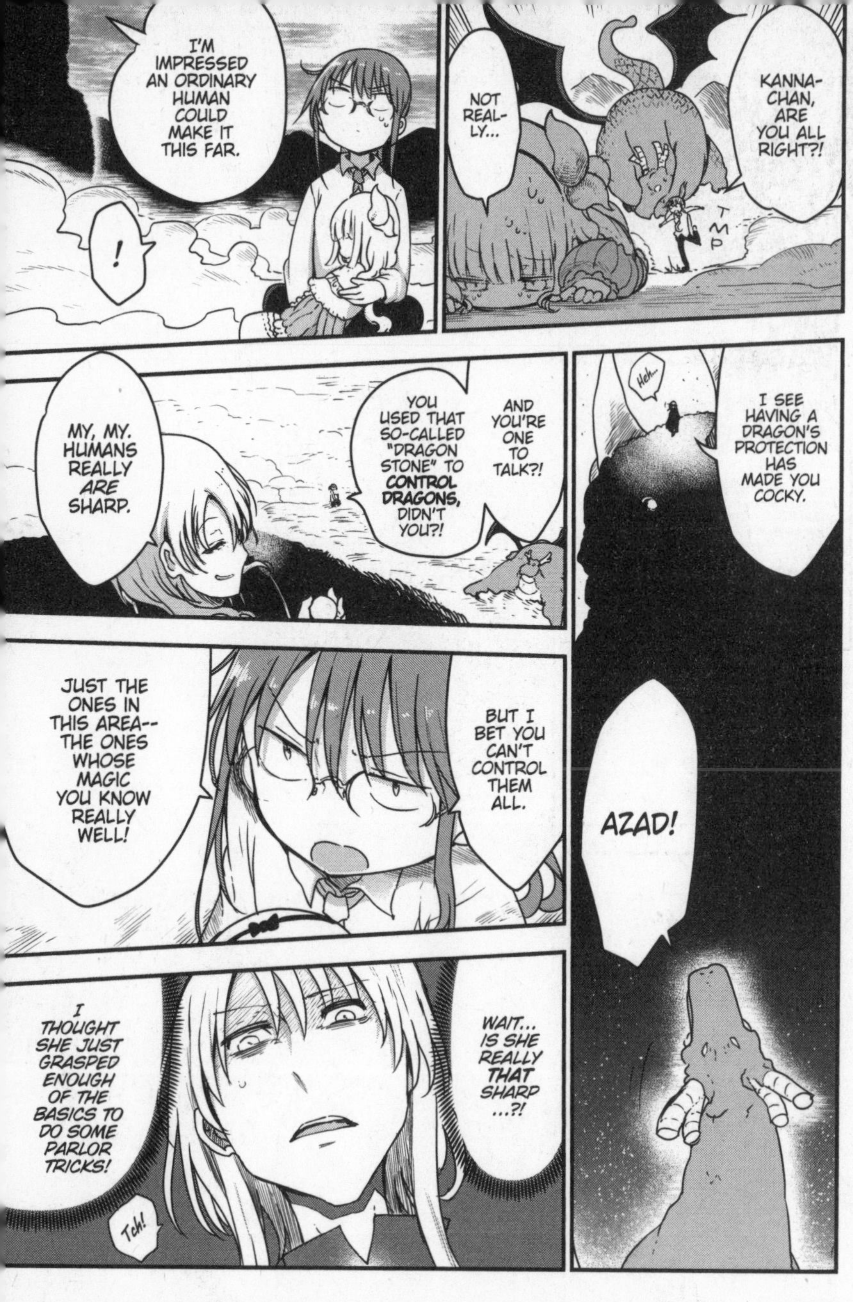
KANNA-CHAN, ARE YOU ALL RIGHT?!
TMP
NOT REALLY...
I'M IMPRESSED AN ORDINARY HUMAN COULD MAKE IT THIS FAR.
!
Heh...
I SEE HAVING A DRAGON'S PROTECTION HAS MADE YOU COCKY.
AZAD!
AND YOU'RE ONE TO TALK?!
YOU USED THAT SO-CALLED "DRAGON STONE" TO CONTROL DRAGONS, DIDN'T YOU?!
MY, MY. HUMANS REALLY ARE SHARP.
BUT I BET YOU CAN'T CONTROL THEM ALL.
JUST THE ONES IN THIS AREA--THE ONES WHOSE MAGIC YOU KNOW REALLY WELL!
WAIT... IS SHE REALLY THAT SHARP...?!
I THOUGHT SHE JUST GRASPED ENOUGH OF THE BASICS TO DO SOME PARLOR TRICKS!
Tch!

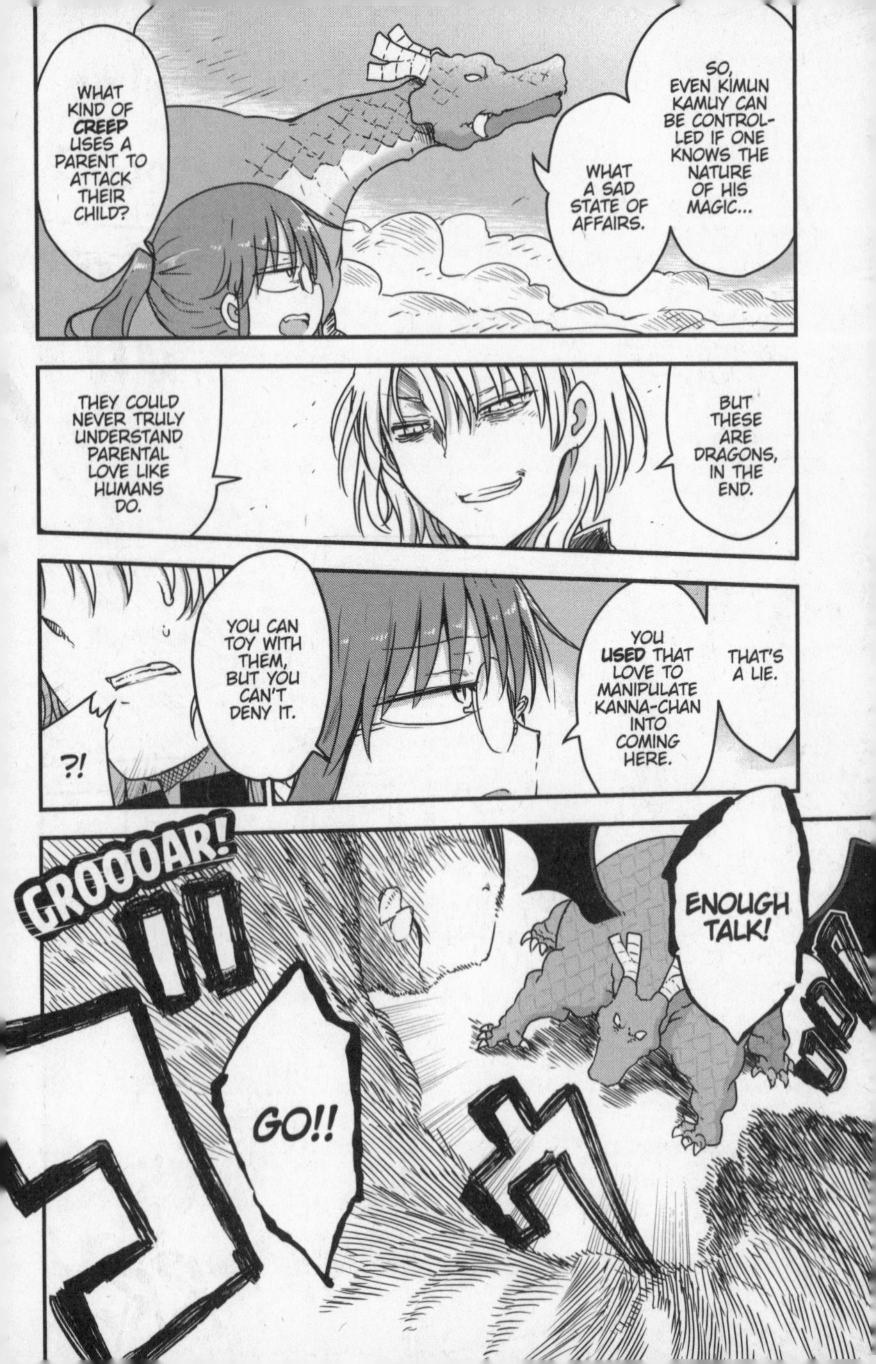
SO, EVEN KIMUN KAMUY CAN BE CONTROLLED IF ONE KNOWS THE NATURE OF HIS MAGIC...
WHAT A SAD STATE OF AFFAIRS.
WHAT KIND OF **CREEP** USES A PARENT TO ATTACK THEIR CHILD?
BUT THESE ARE DRAGONS, IN THE END.
THEY COULD NEVER TRULY UNDERSTAND PARENTAL LOVE LIKE HUMANS DO.
THAT'S A LIE.
YOU **USED** THAT LOVE TO MANIPULATE KANNA-CHAN INTO COMING HERE.
YOU CAN TOY WITH THEM, BUT YOU CAN'T DENY IT.
?!
ENOUGH TALK!
GROOOAR!
GO!!

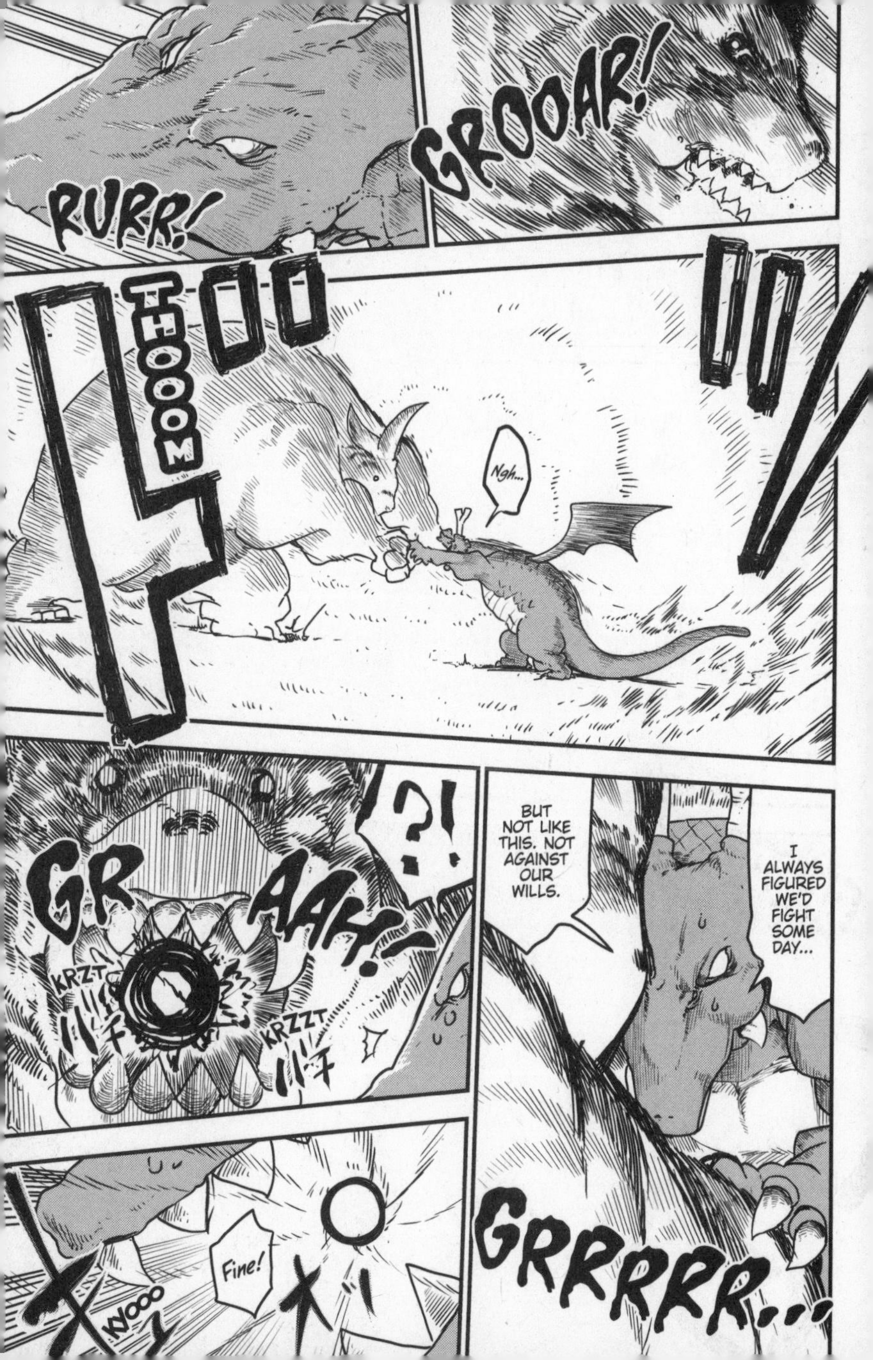
GROOAR!
RURR!
THOOOOM
Ngh...
I ALWAYS FIGURED WE'D FIGHT SOME DAY...
BUT NOT LIKE THIS. NOT AGAINST OUR WILLS.
GRRRRRR...
?!
GRAAH!
KRZT
KRZZT
Fine!
KYOOO

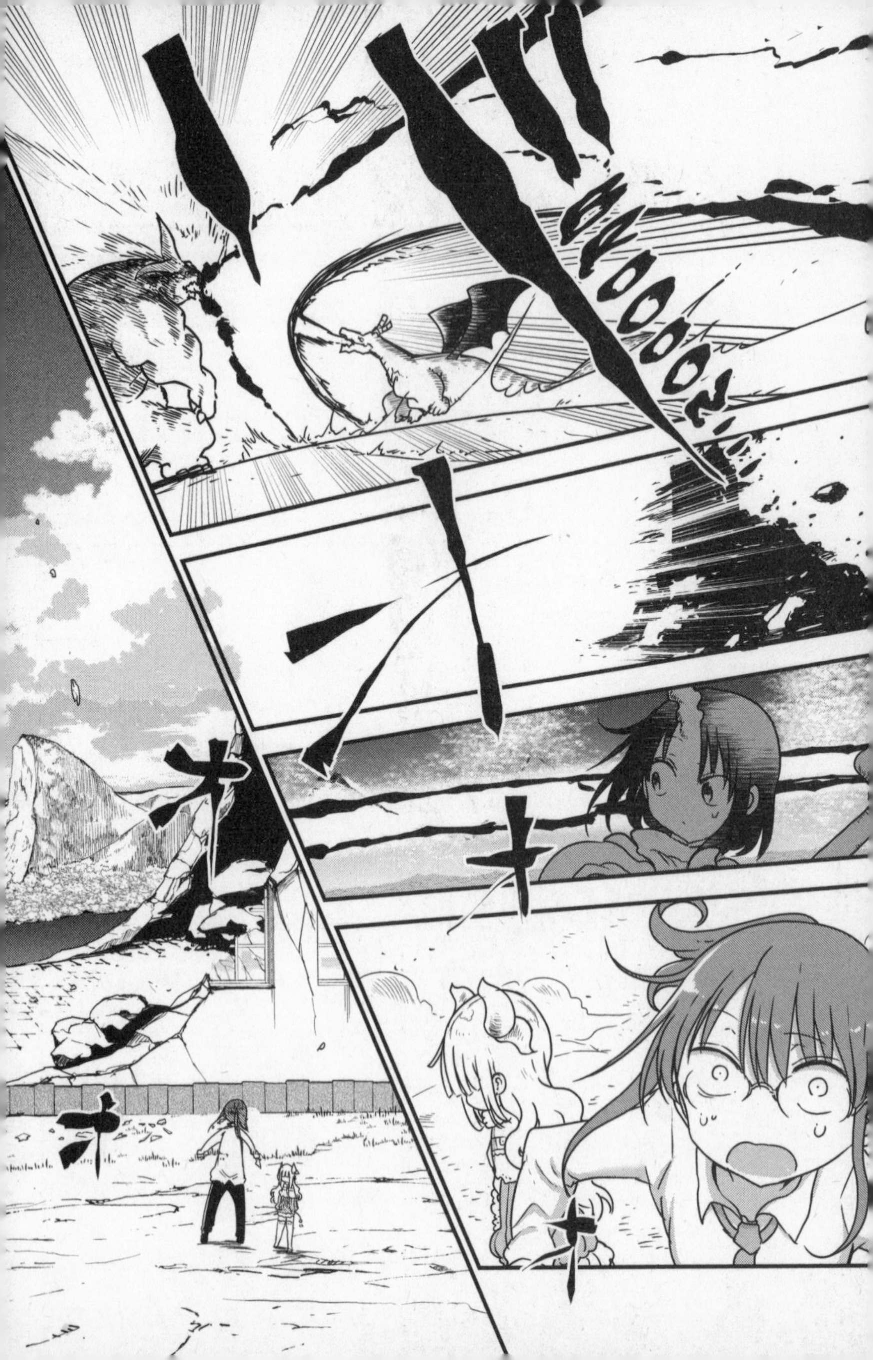
GWOOOON!!!

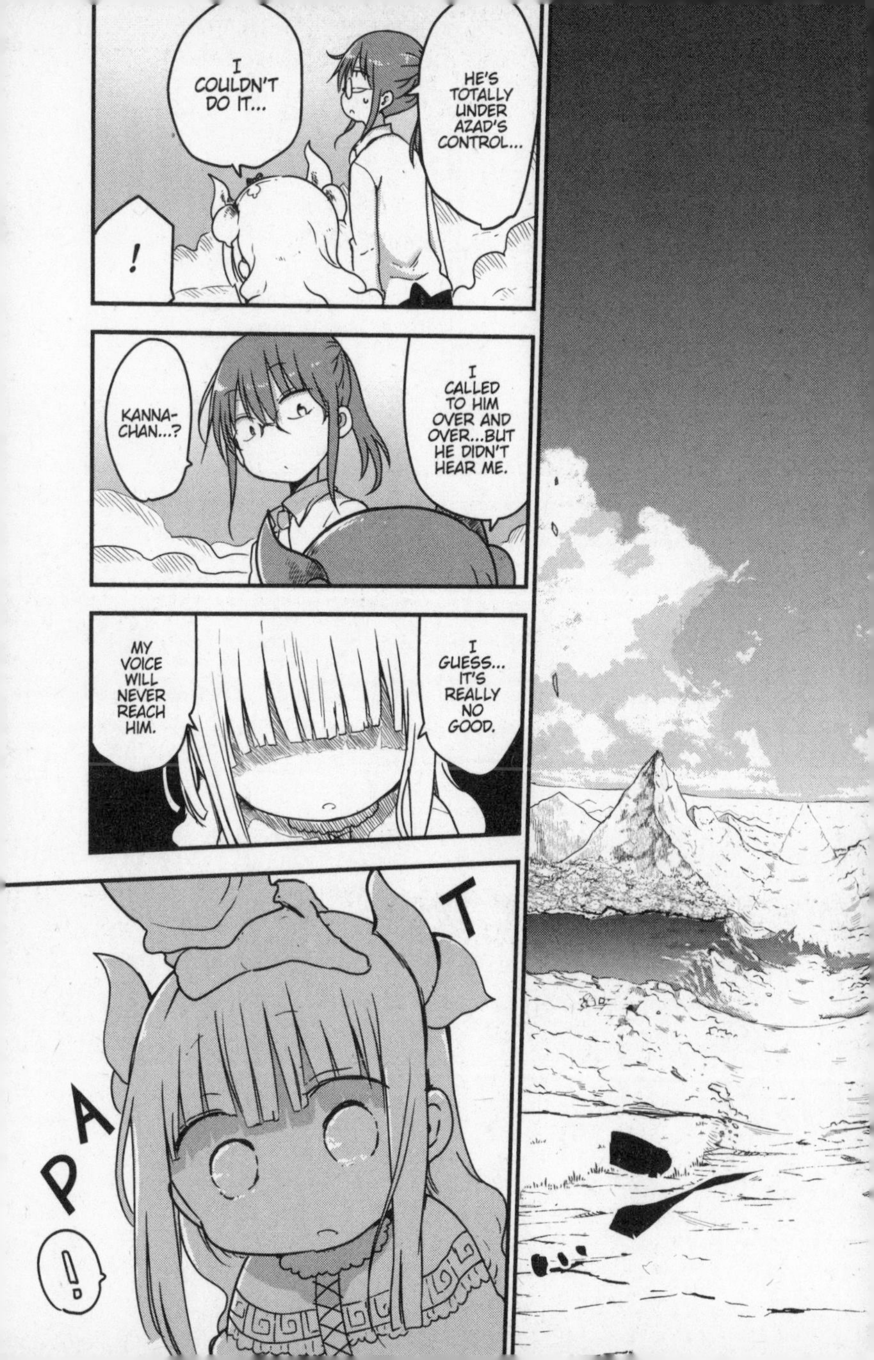
HE'S TOTALLY UNDER AZAD'S CONTROL...
I COULDN'T DO IT...
!
I CALLED TO HIM OVER AND OVER...BUT HE DIDN'T HEAR ME.
KANNA-CHAN...?
I GUESS... IT'S REALLY NO GOOD.
MY VOICE WILL NEVER REACH HIM.
PAT
!

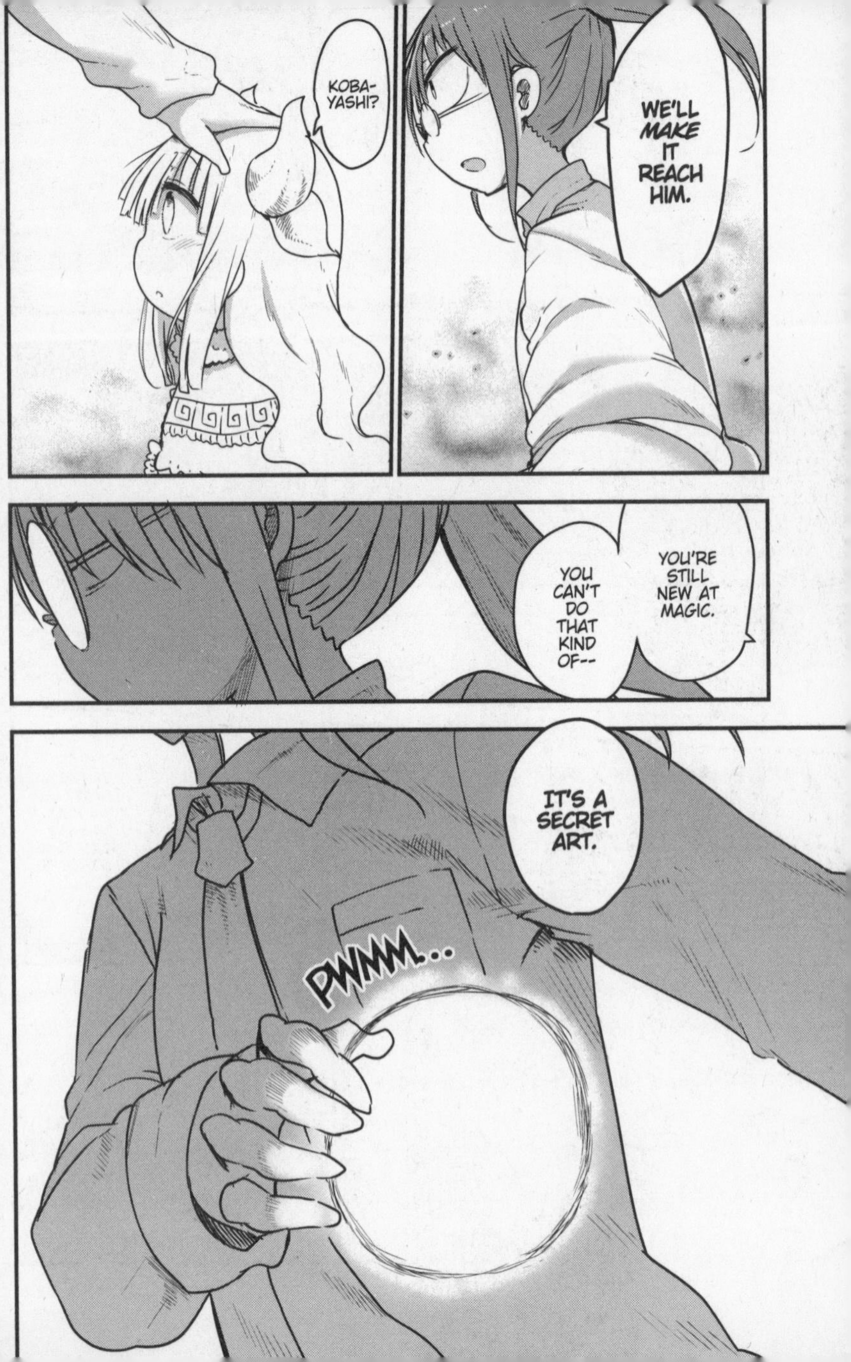
WE'LL MAKE IT REACH HIM.
KOBA-YASHI?
YOU'RE STILL NEW AT MAGIC.
YOU CAN'T DO THAT KIND OF--
IT'S A SECRET ART.
PWMM...

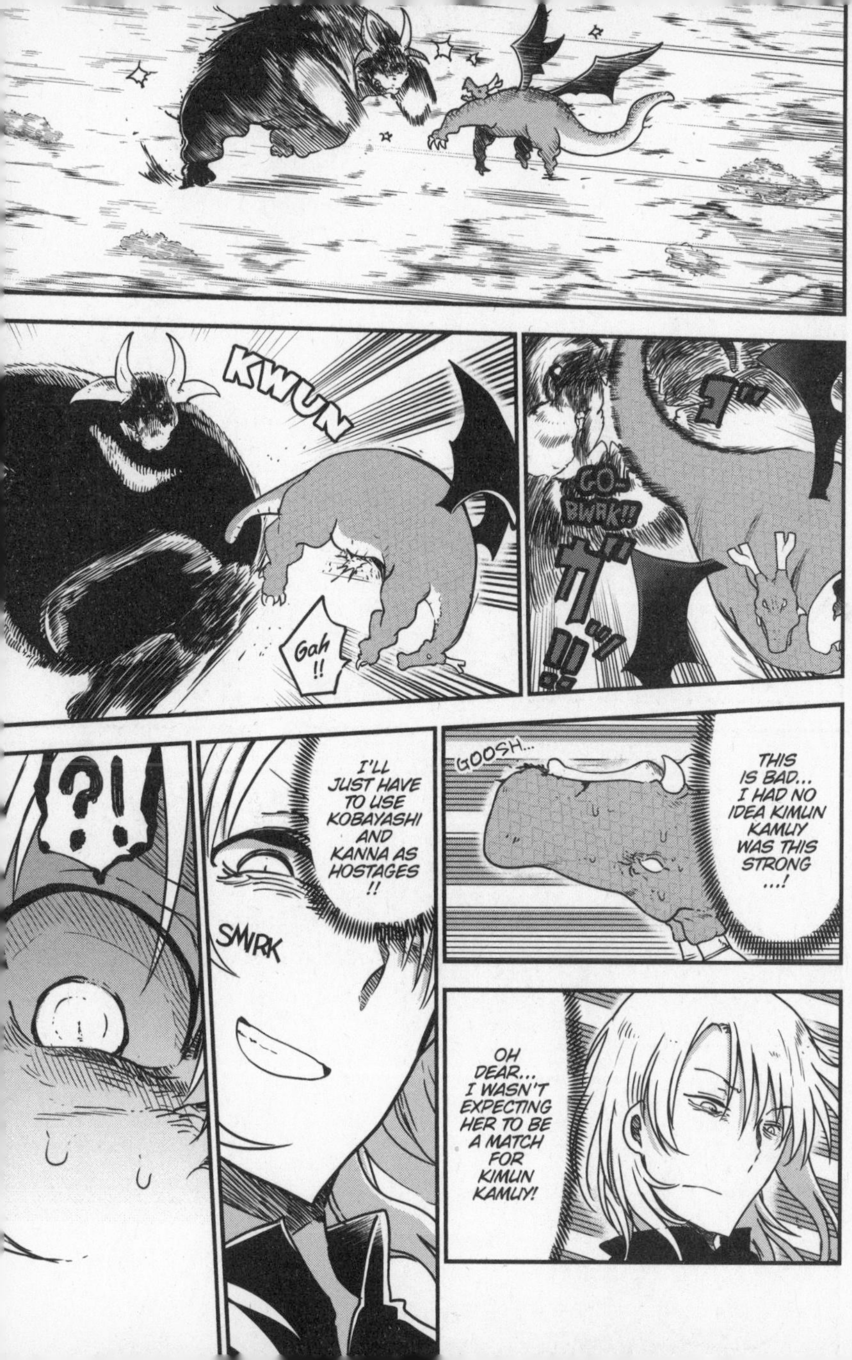
GO-BWAK!!
KWUN
Gah!!
GOOSH...
THIS IS BAD... I HAD NO IDEA KIMUN KAMUY WAS THIS STRONG...!
OH DEAR... I WASN'T EXPECTING HER TO BE A MATCH FOR KIMUN KAMUY!
I'LL JUST HAVE TO USE KOBAYASHI AND KANNA AS HOSTAGES!!
SMIRK
?!

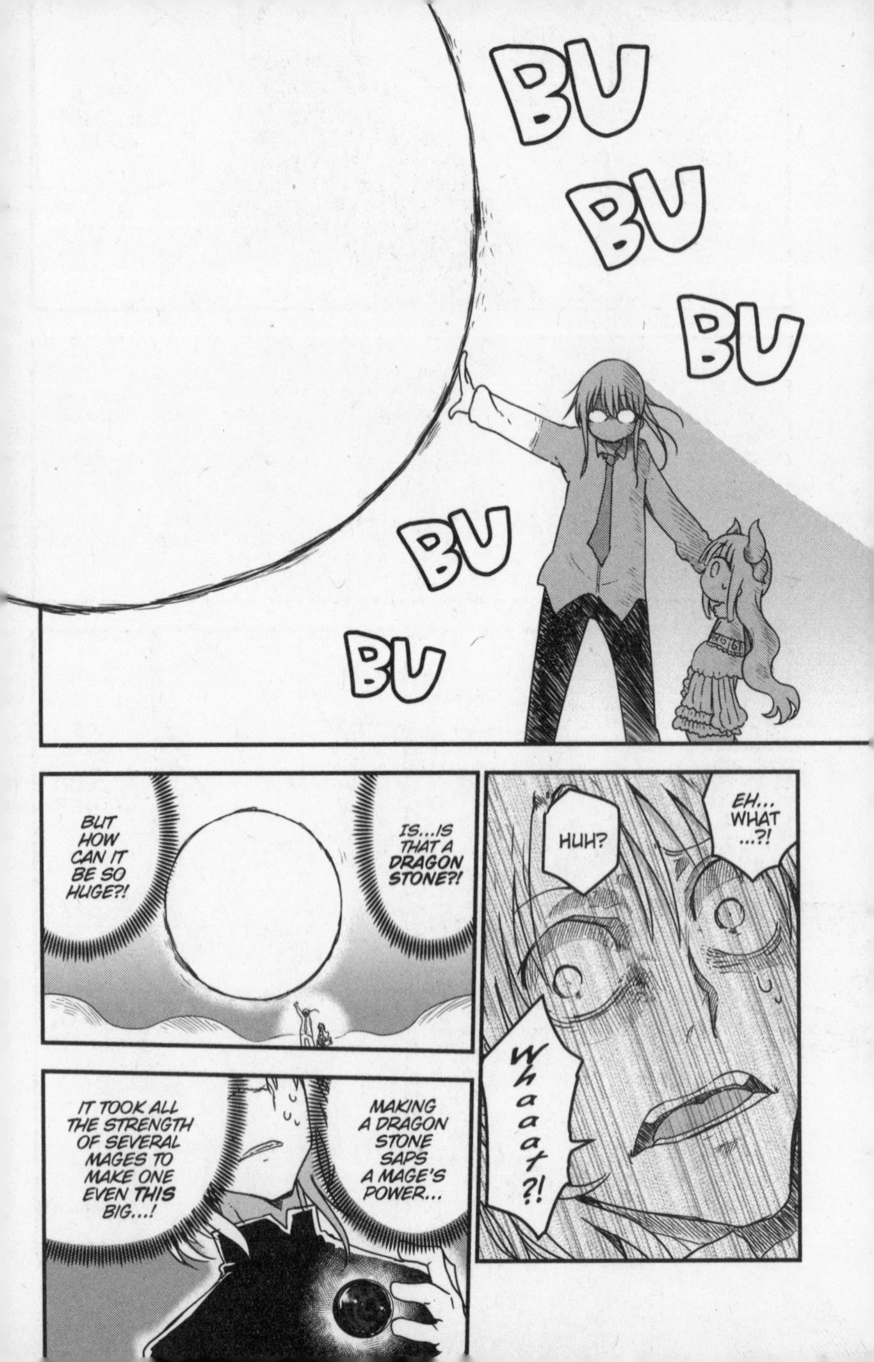
BU
BU
BU
BU
BU
EH... WHAT ...?!
HUH?
Whaaat?!
IS...IS THAT A DRAGON STONE?!
BUT HOW CAN IT BE SO HUGE?!
MAKING A DRAGON STONE SAPS A MAGE'S POWER...
IT TOOK ALL THE STRENGTH OF SEVERAL MAGES TO MAKE ONE EVEN THIS BIG...!

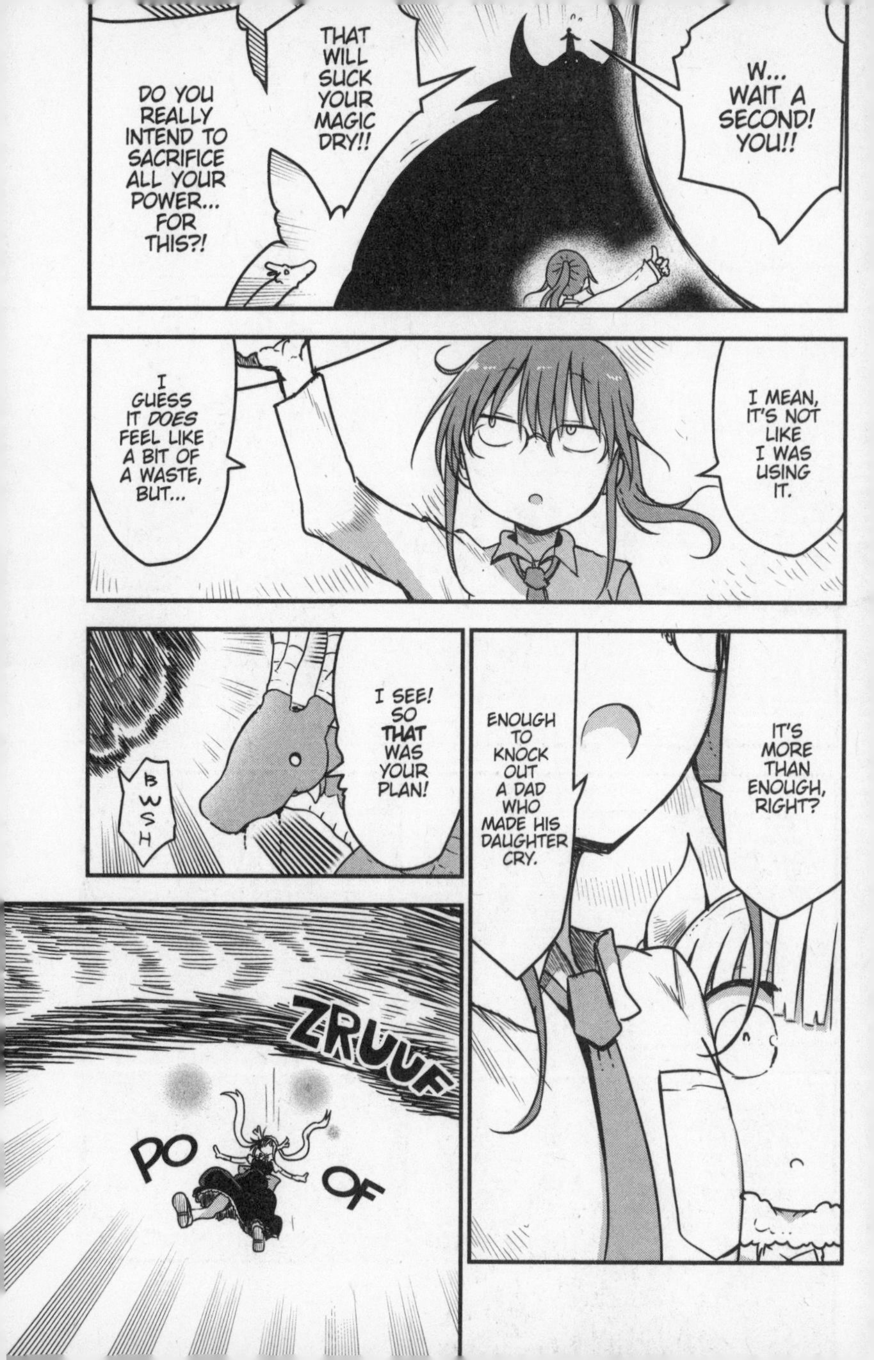
W... WAIT A SECOND! YOU!!
THAT WILL SUCK YOUR MAGIC DRY!!
DO YOU REALLY INTEND TO SACRIFICE ALL YOUR POWER... FOR THIS?!
I MEAN, IT'S NOT LIKE I WAS USING IT.
I GUESS IT *DOES* FEEL LIKE A BIT OF A WASTE, BUT...
IT'S MORE THAN ENOUGH, RIGHT?
ENOUGH TO KNOCK OUT A DAD WHO MADE HIS DAUGHTER CRY.
I SEE! SO **THAT** WAS YOUR PLAN!
BWSH
ZRUUF
POOF

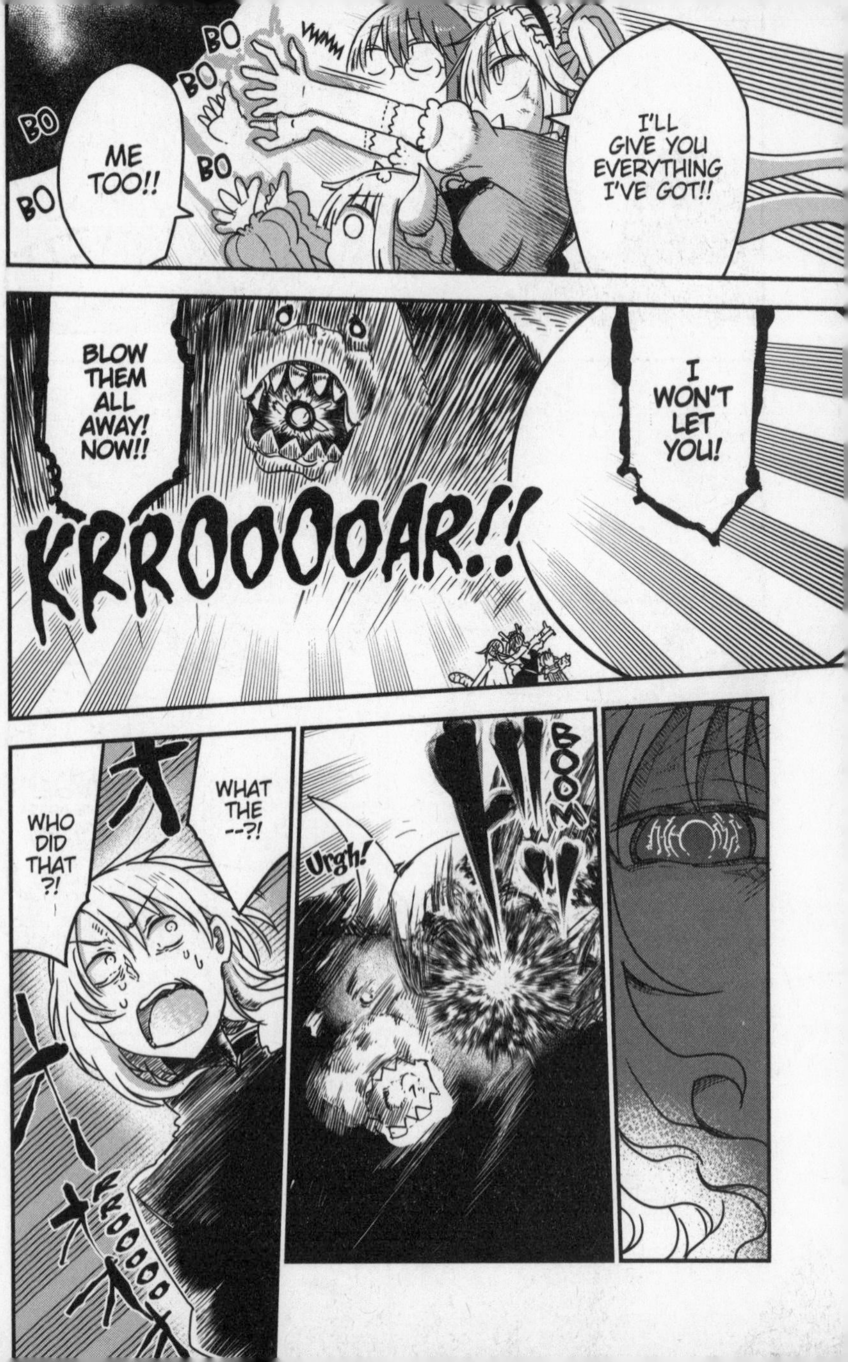
I'LL GIVE YOU EVERYTHING I'VE GOT!!
ME TOO!!
BO BO BO BO BO
I WON'T LET YOU!
BLOW THEM ALL AWAY! NOW!!
KRROOOOAR!!
BOOM
Urgh!
WHAT THE --?!
WHO DID THAT ?!
RROOOOO

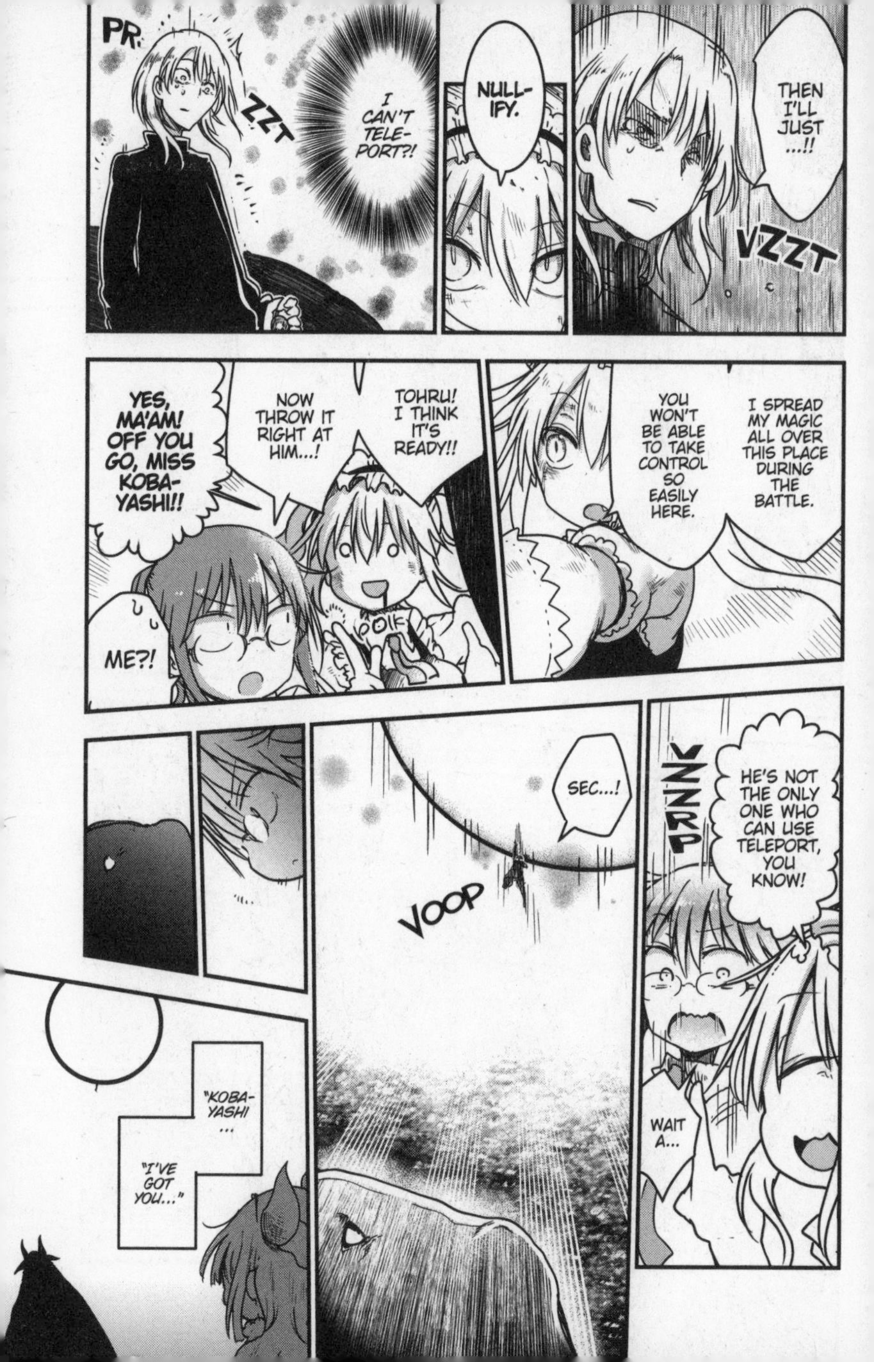
THEN I'LL JUST ...!!
VZZT
NULL-IFY.
I CAN'T TELE-PORT?!
PR
ZZZT
I SPREAD MY MAGIC ALL OVER THIS PLACE DURING THE BATTLE.
YOU WON'T BE ABLE TO TAKE CONTROL SO EASILY HERE.
TOHRU! I THINK IT'S READY!!
NOW THROW IT RIGHT AT HIM...!
YES, MA'AM! OFF YOU GO, MISS KOBA-YASHI!!
POIF
ME?!
VZZRP
HE'S NOT THE ONLY ONE WHO CAN USE TELEPORT, YOU KNOW!
WAIT A...
SEC...!
VOOP
"KOBA-YASHI ...
"I'VE GOT YOU..."

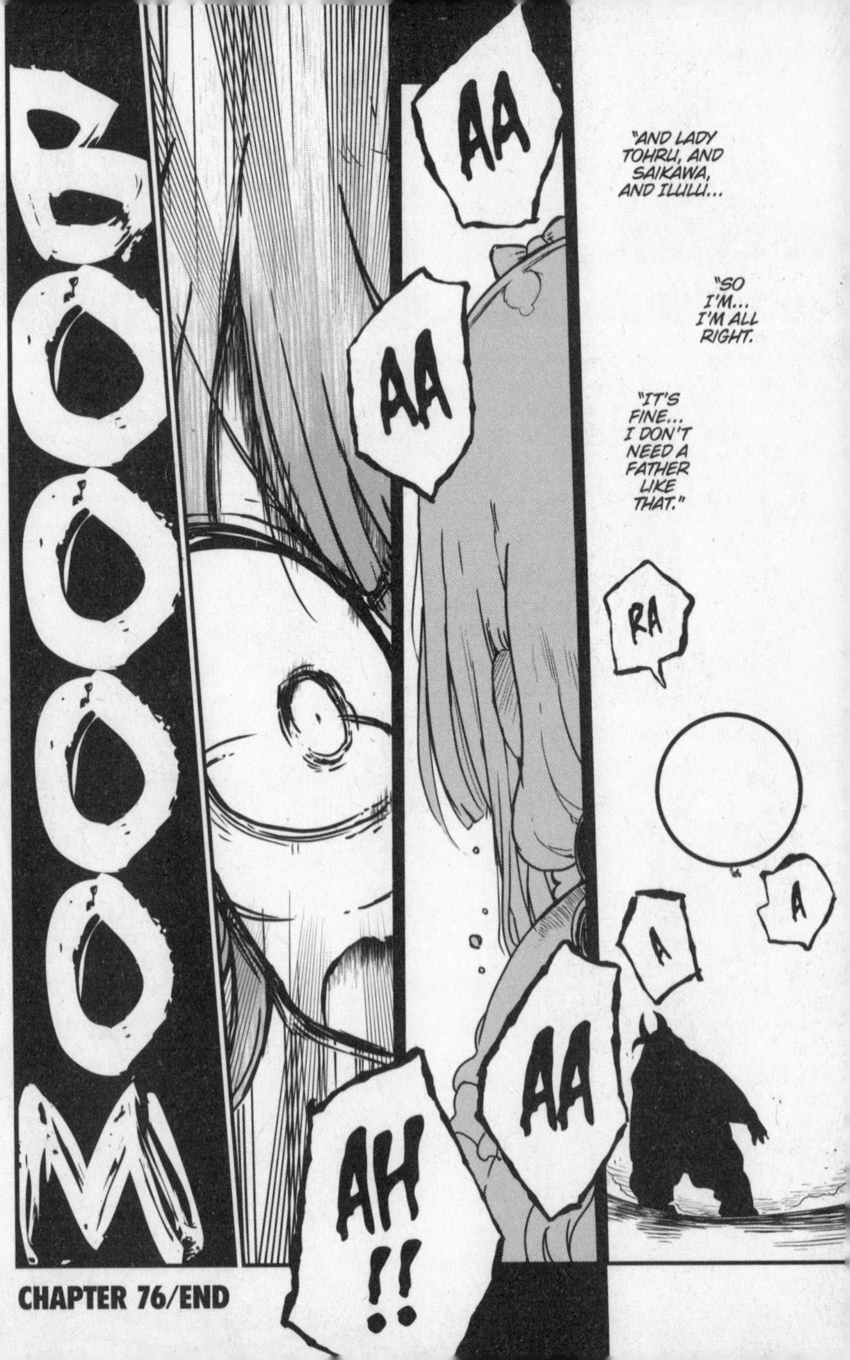
"AND LADY TOHRU, AND SAIKAWA, AND ILULU...
"SO I'M... I'M ALL RIGHT.
"IT'S FINE... I DON'T NEED A FATHER LIKE THAT."
RA
A
A
AA
AH!!
AA
AA
DOOOOM

CHAPTER 76/END

CHAPTER 77

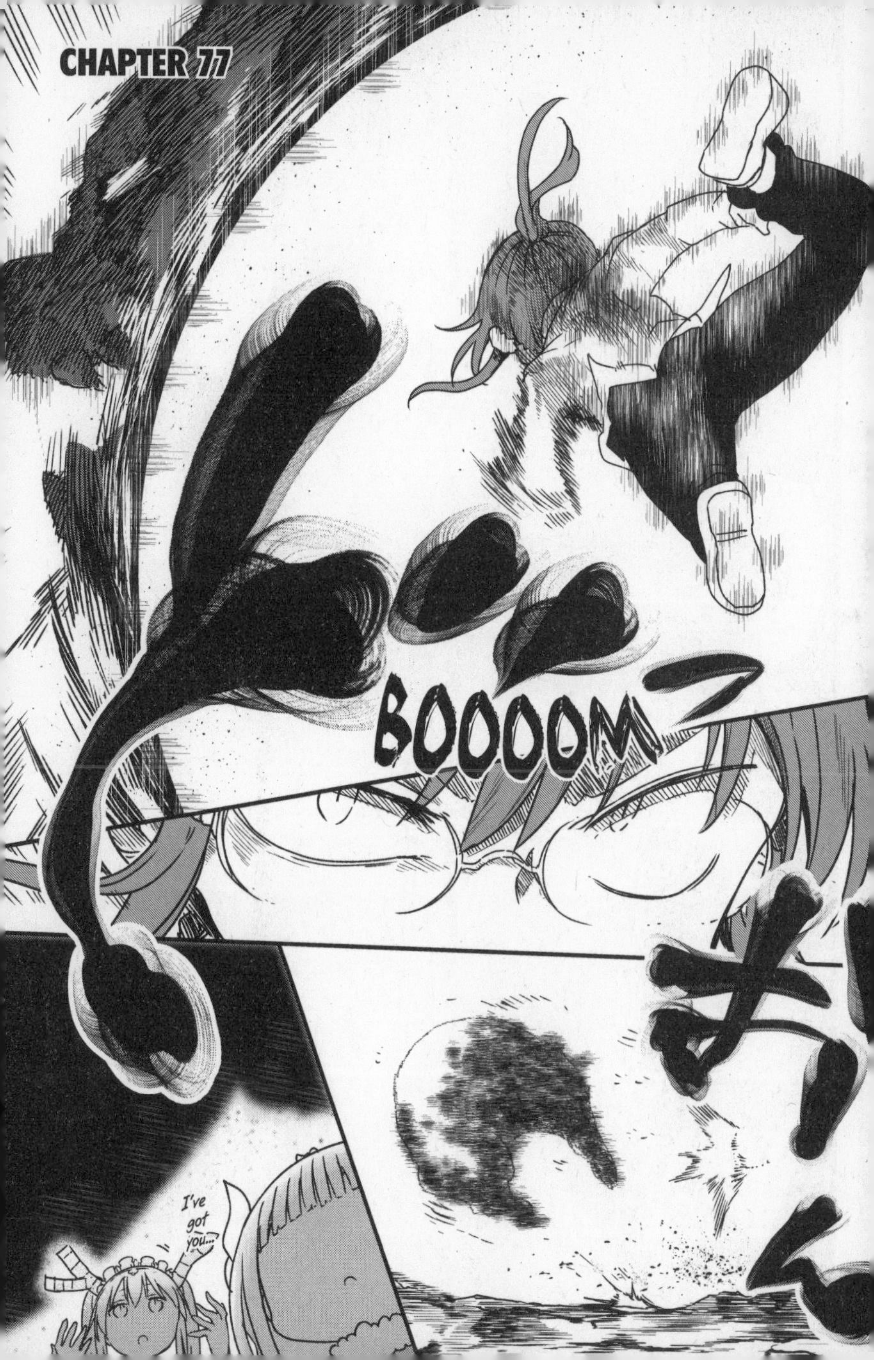
BOOOOM
I've got you...

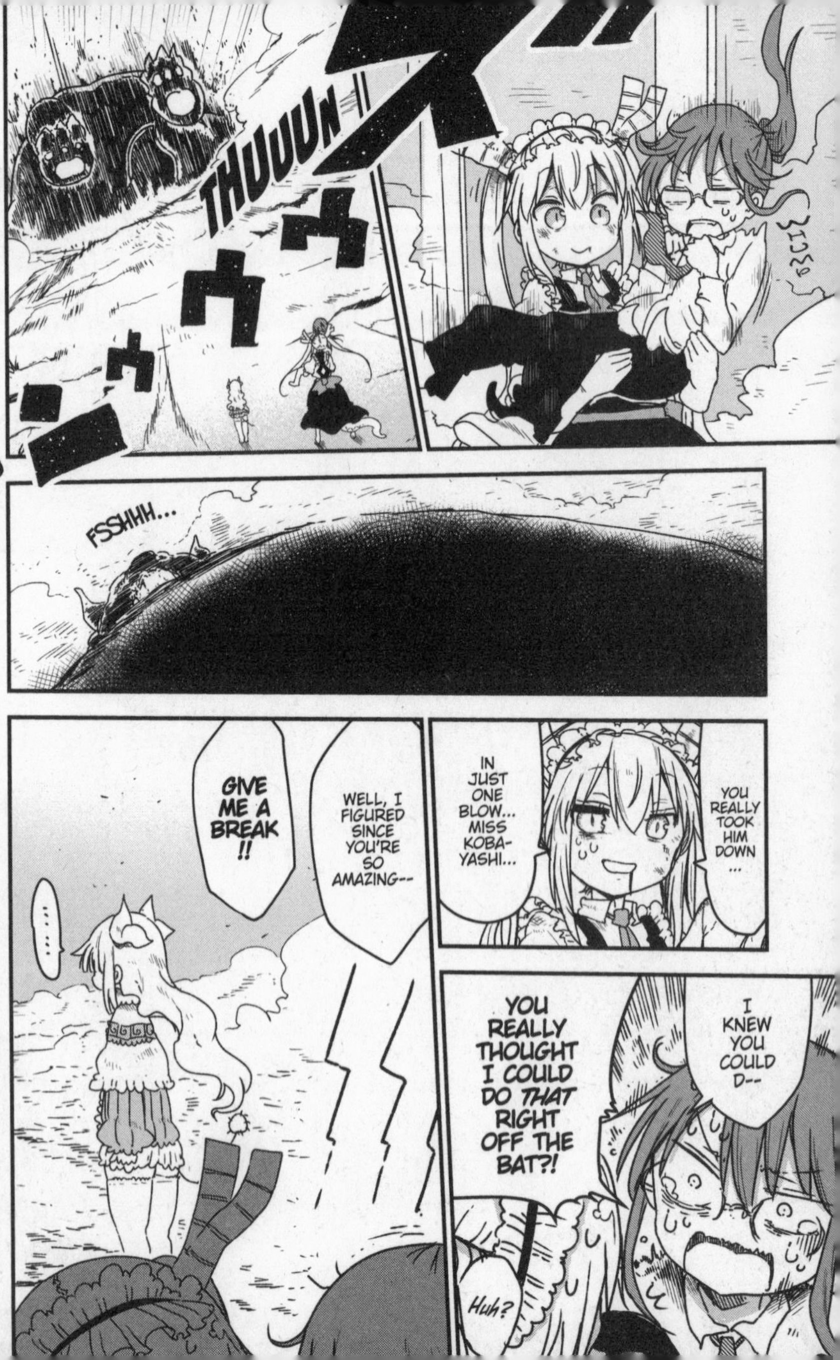
THUUUN!!
FSSHHH...
YOU REALLY TOOK HIM DOWN...
IN JUST ONE BLOW... MISS KOBA-YASHI...
I KNEW YOU COULD D--
YOU REALLY THOUGHT I COULD DO *THAT* RIGHT OFF THE BAT?!
Huh?
WELL, I FIGURED SINCE YOU'RE SO AMAZING--
GIVE ME A BREAK!!
......

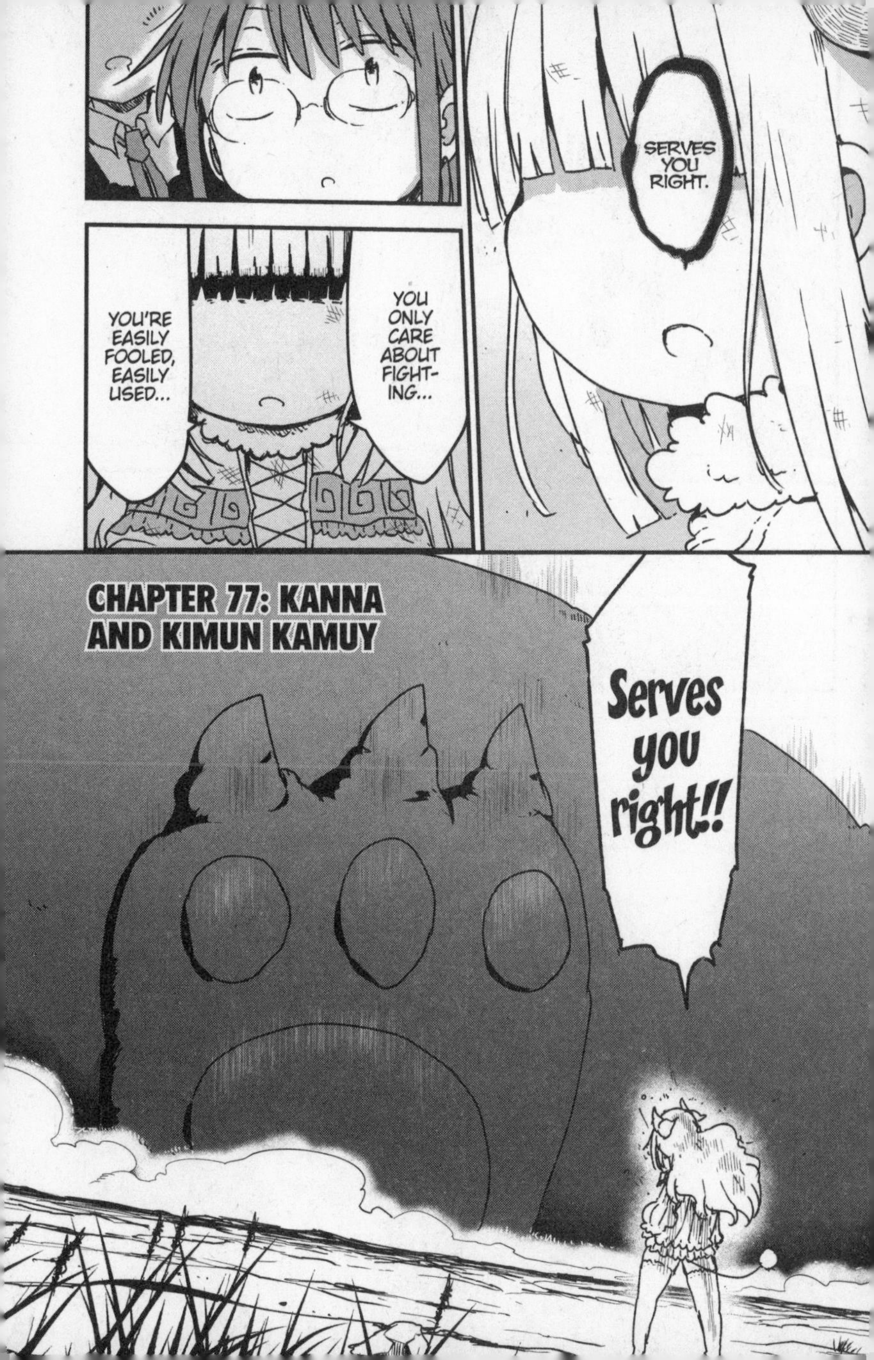
SERVES YOU RIGHT.
YOU ONLY CARE ABOUT FIGHT-ING...
YOU'RE EASILY FOOLED, EASILY USED...
Serves you right!!
CHAPTER 77: KANNA AND KIMUN KAMUY

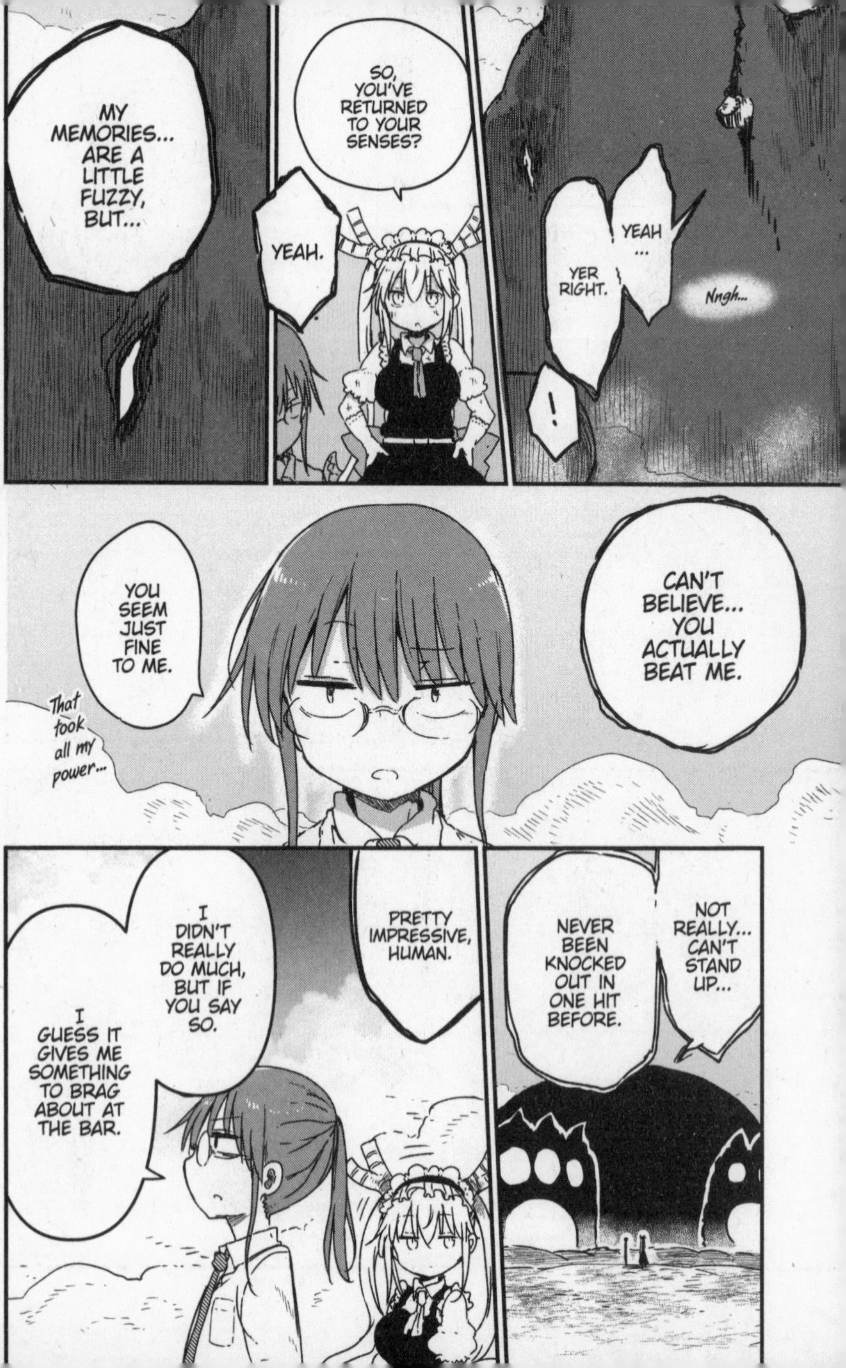
YEAH... YER RIGHT.
Nngh...
!
SO, YOU'VE RETURNED TO YOUR SENSES?
YEAH.
MY MEMORIES... ARE A LITTLE FUZZY, BUT...
CAN'T BELIEVE... YOU ACTUALLY BEAT ME.
YOU SEEM JUST FINE TO ME.
That took all my power...
NOT REALLY... CAN'T STAND UP...
NEVER BEEN KNOCKED OUT IN ONE HIT BEFORE.
PRETTY IMPRESSIVE, HUMAN.
I DIDN'T REALLY DO MUCH, BUT IF YOU SAY SO.
I GUESS IT GIVES ME SOMETHING TO BRAG ABOUT AT THE BAR.

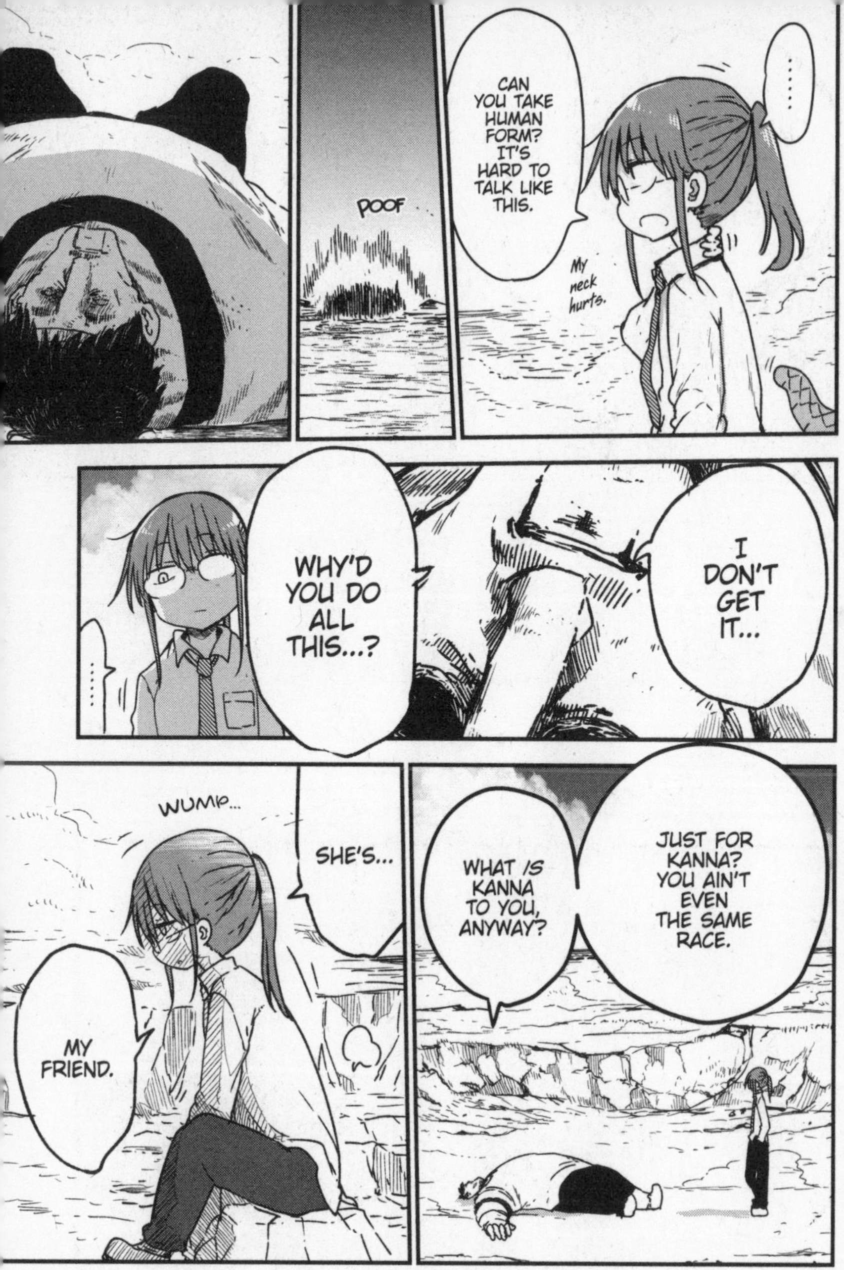
......
CAN YOU TAKE HUMAN FORM? IT'S HARD TO TALK LIKE THIS.
My neck hurts.
POOF
I DON'T GET IT...
WHY'D YOU DO ALL THIS...?
......
JUST FOR KANNA? YOU AIN'T EVEN THE SAME RACE.
WHAT *IS* KANNA TO YOU, ANYWAY?
WUMP...
SHE'S...
MY FRIEND.

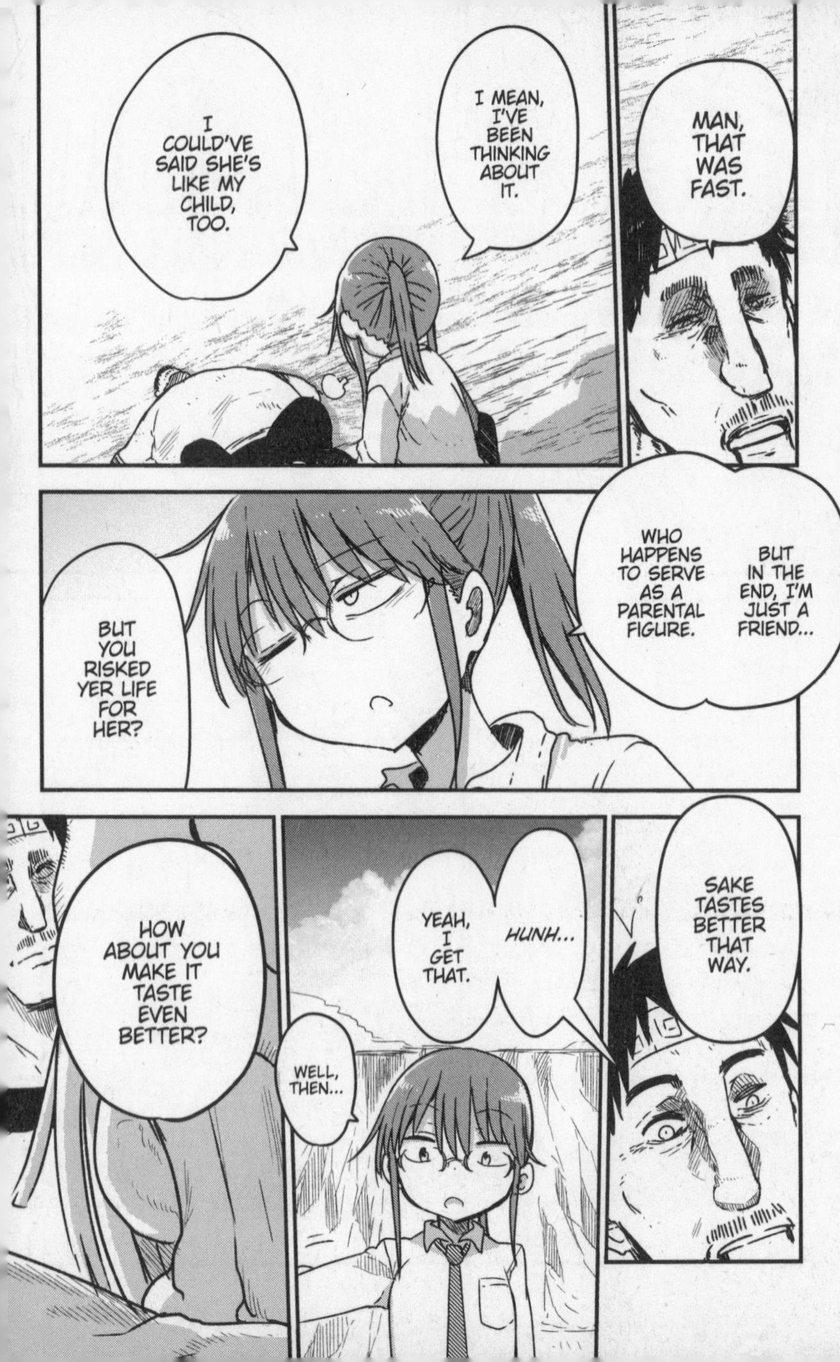
MAN, THAT WAS FAST.
I MEAN, I'VE BEEN THINKING ABOUT IT.
I COULD'VE SAID SHE'S LIKE MY CHILD, TOO.
BUT IN THE END, I'M JUST A FRIEND...
WHO HAPPENS TO SERVE AS A PARENTAL FIGURE.
BUT YOU RISKED YER LIFE FOR HER?
SAKE TASTES BETTER THAT WAY.
HUNH...
YEAH, I GET THAT.
WELL, THEN...
HOW ABOUT YOU MAKE IT TASTE EVEN BETTER?

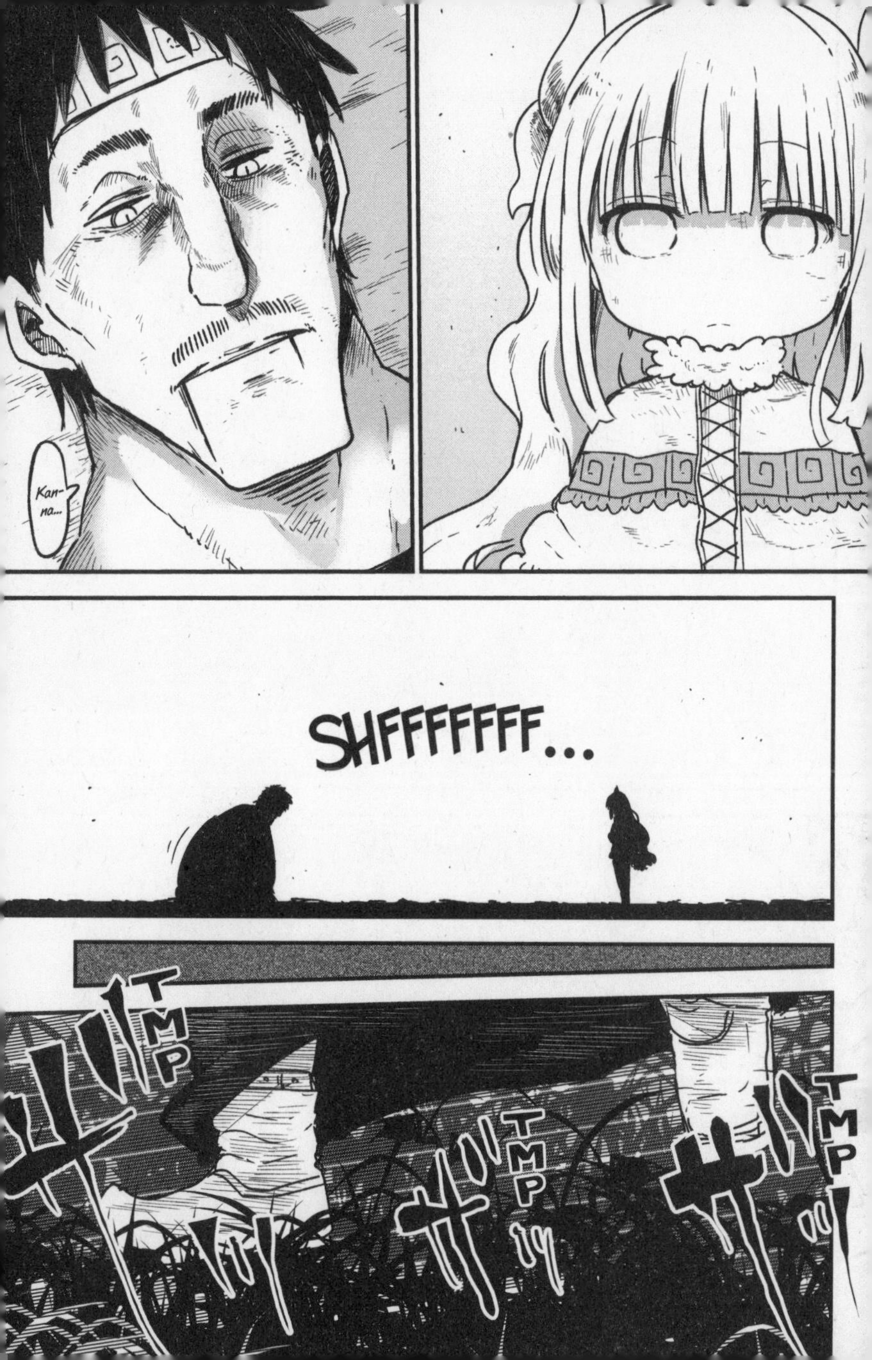
Kan-na...
SHFFFFFFF...
TMP
TMP
TMP

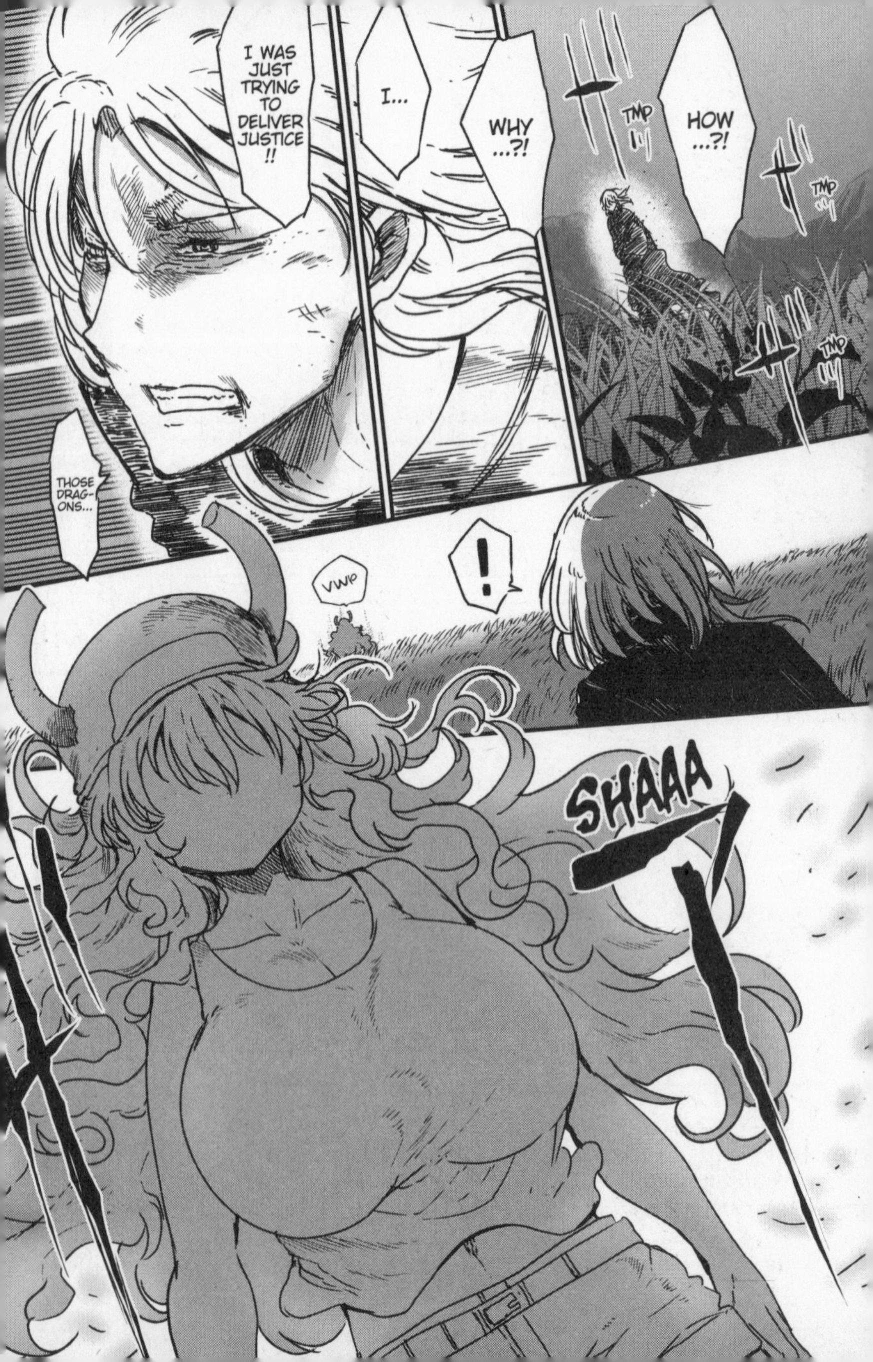
HOW ...?!
TMP
TMP
TMP
WHY ...?!
I...
I WAS JUST TRYING TO DELIVER JUSTICE !!
THOSE DRAG-ONS...
!
VWP
SHAAA

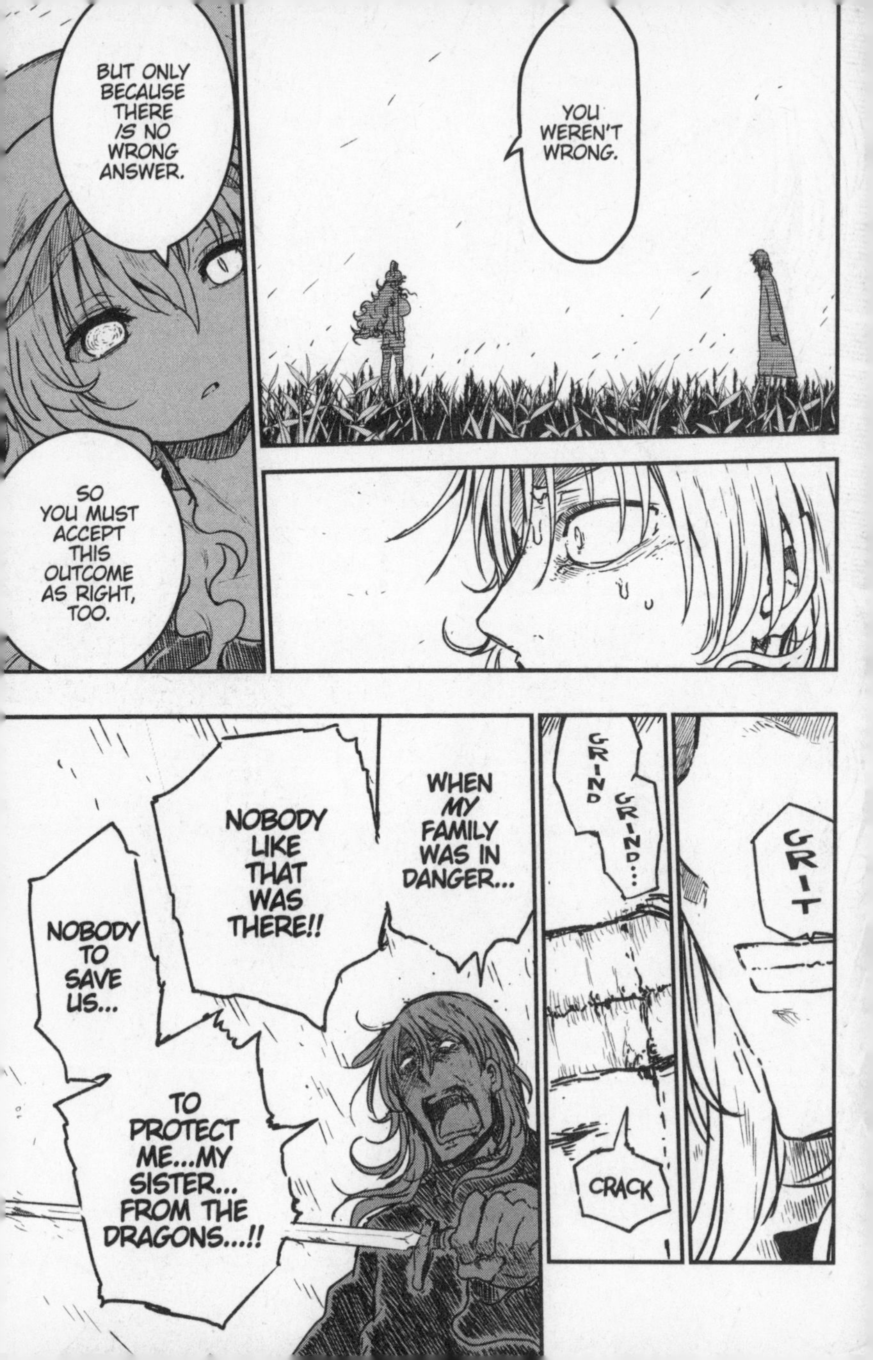
YOU WEREN'T WRONG.
BUT ONLY BECAUSE THERE IS NO WRONG ANSWER.
SO YOU MUST ACCEPT THIS OUTCOME AS RIGHT, TOO.
GRIT
GRIND
GRIND...
CRACK
WHEN MY FAMILY WAS IN DANGER...
NOBODY LIKE THAT WAS THERE!!
NOBODY TO SAVE US...
TO PROTECT ME...MY SISTER... FROM THE DRAGONS...!!

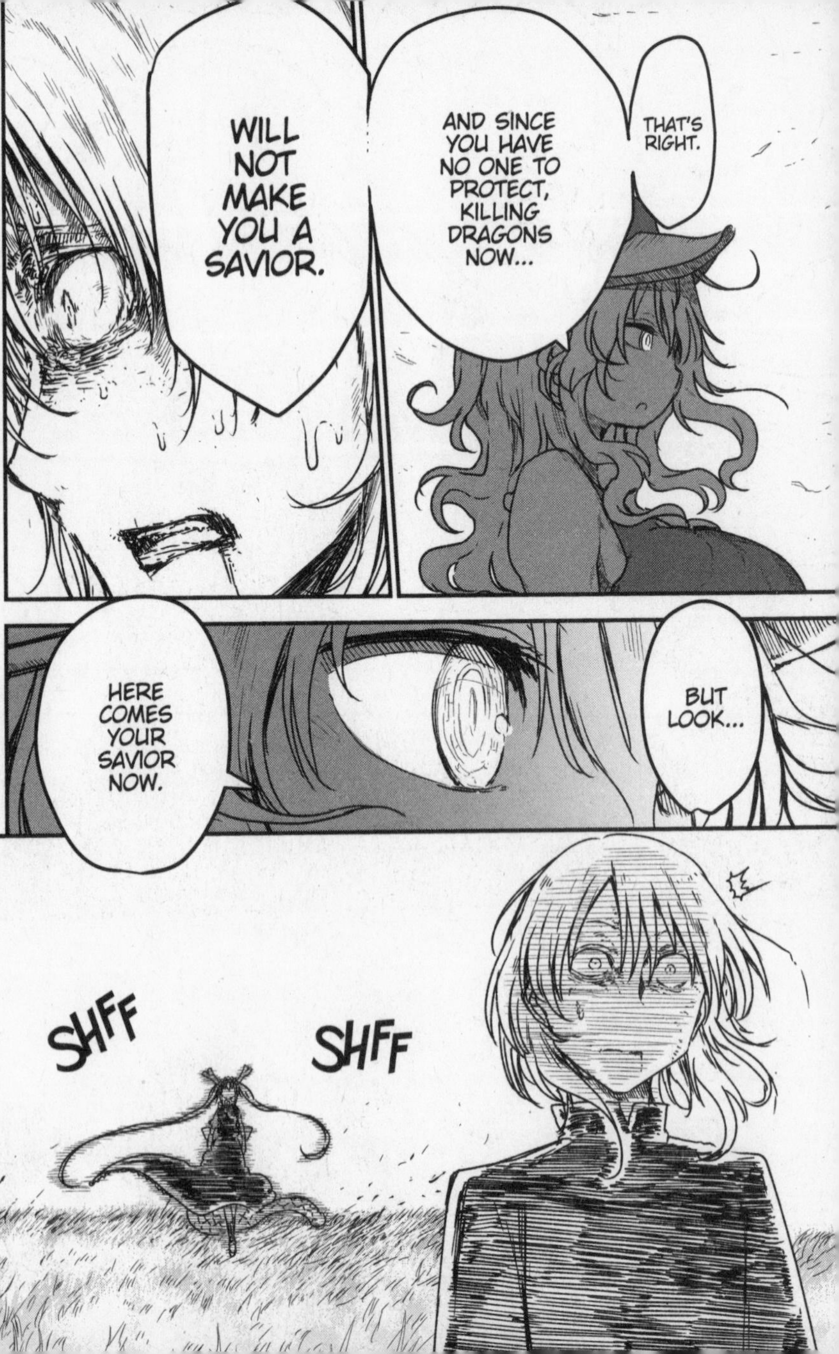
THAT'S RIGHT.
AND SINCE YOU HAVE NO ONE TO PROTECT, KILLING DRAGONS NOW...
WILL NOT MAKE YOU A SAVIOR.
BUT LOOK...
HERE COMES YOUR SAVIOR NOW.
SHFF
SHFF

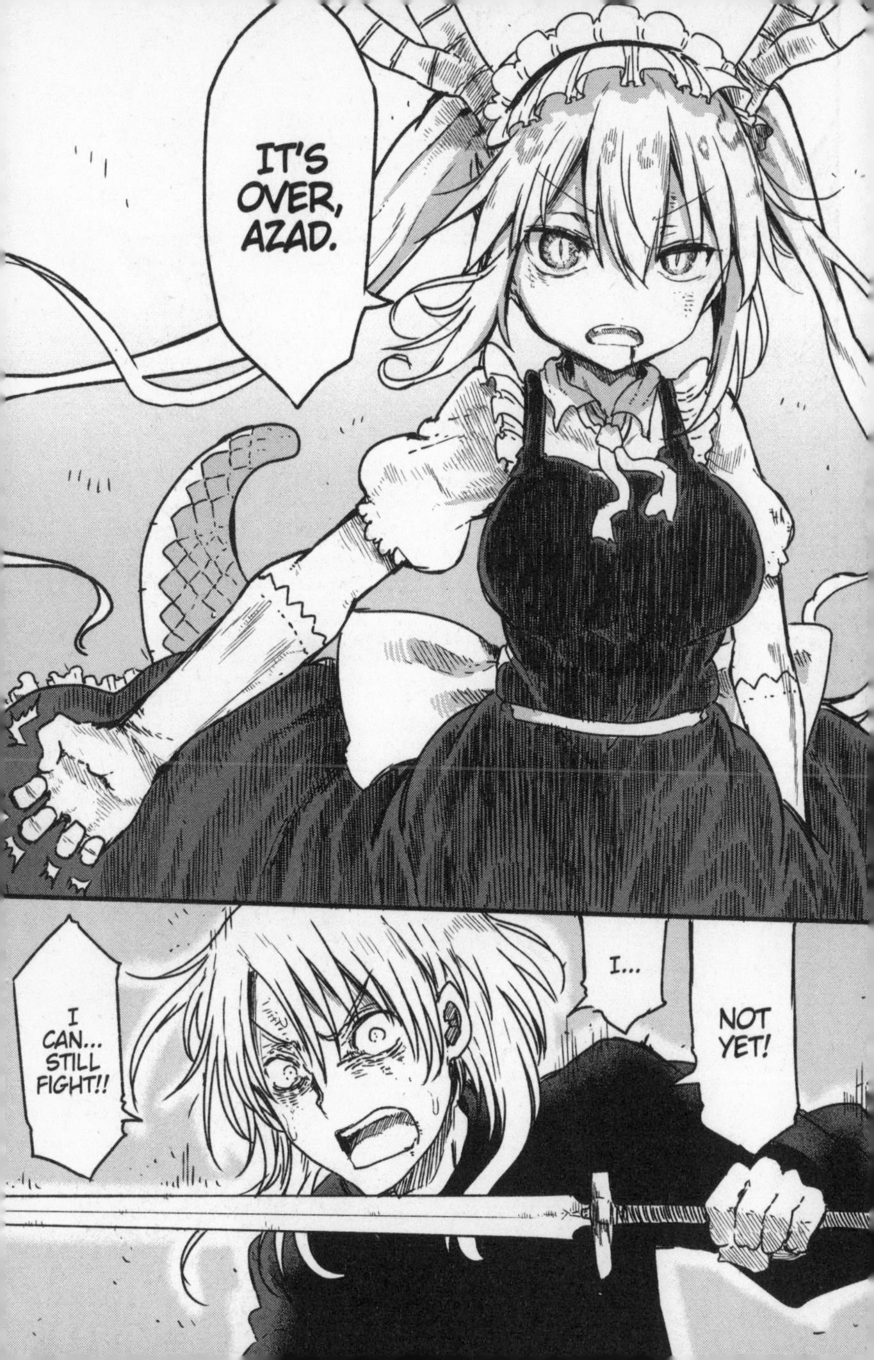
IT'S OVER, AZAD.
I...
NOT YET!
I CAN... STILL FIGHT!!

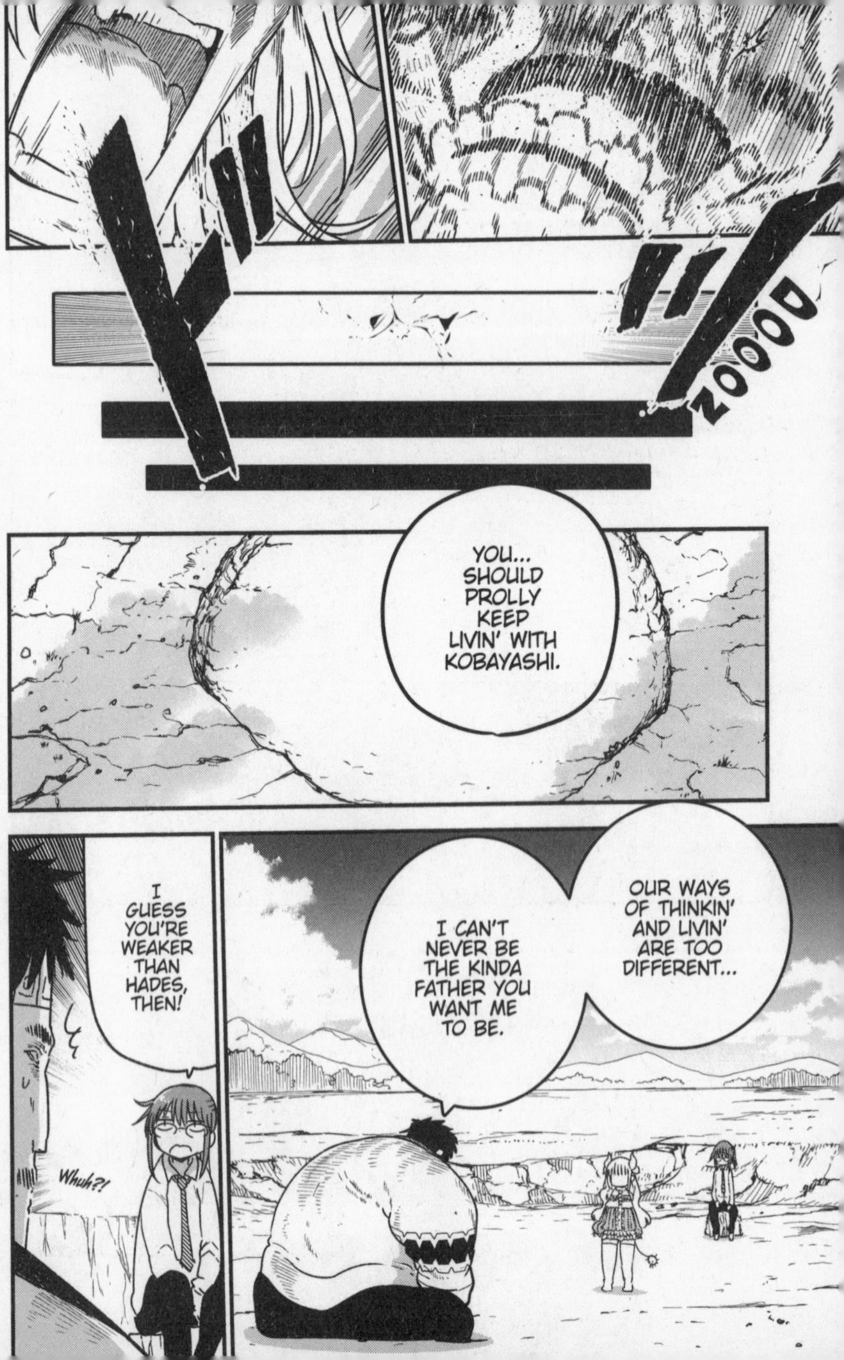
DOOOZ
YOU... SHOULD PROLLY KEEP LIVIN' WITH KOBAYASHI.
OUR WAYS OF THINKIN' AND LIVIN' ARE TOO DIFFERENT...
I CAN'T NEVER BE THE KINDA FATHER YOU WANT ME TO BE.
I GUESS YOU'RE WEAKER THAN HADES, THEN!
Whuh?!

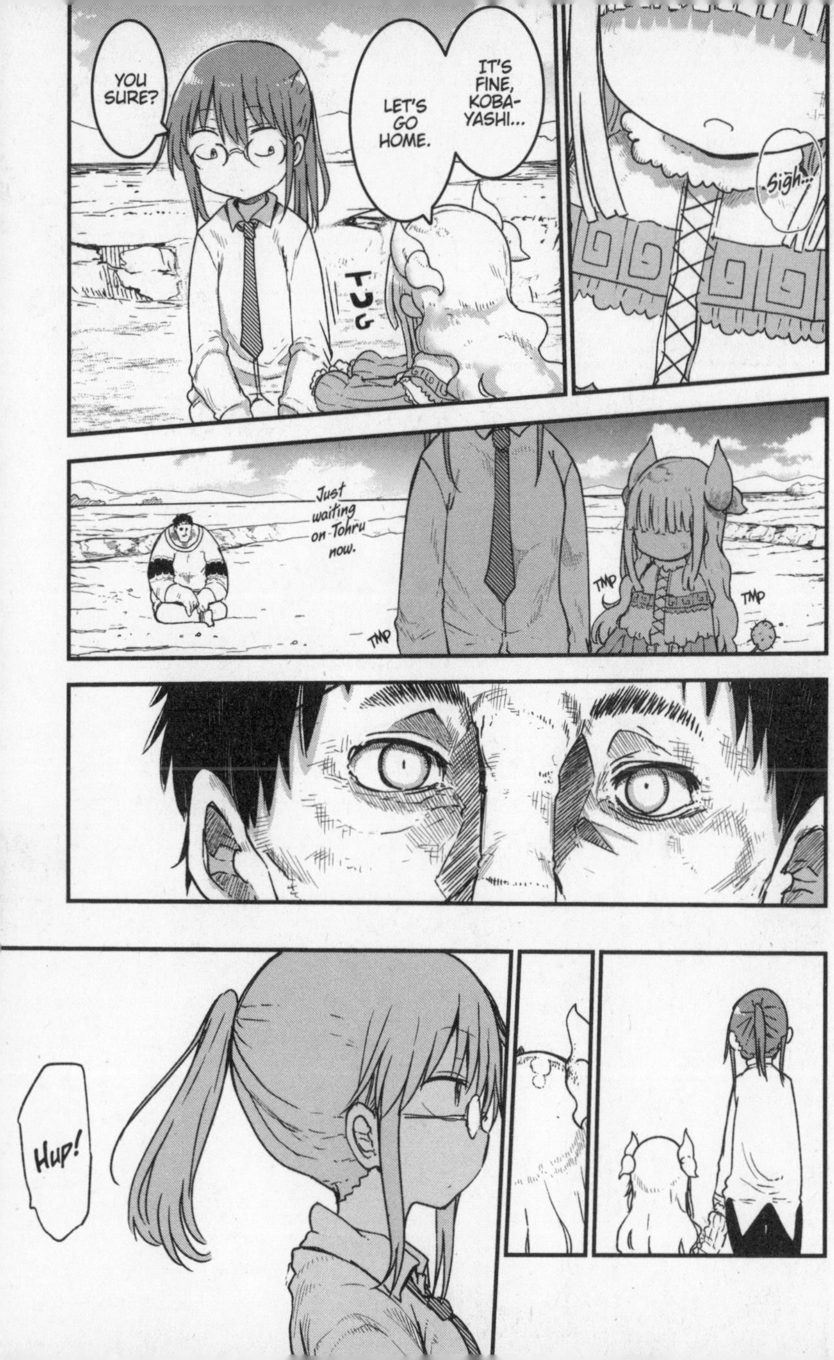
Sigh...
IT'S FINE, KOBA-YASHI...
LET'S GO HOME.
TUG
YOU SURE?
TMP
TMP
Just waiting on Tohru now.
TMP
Hup!

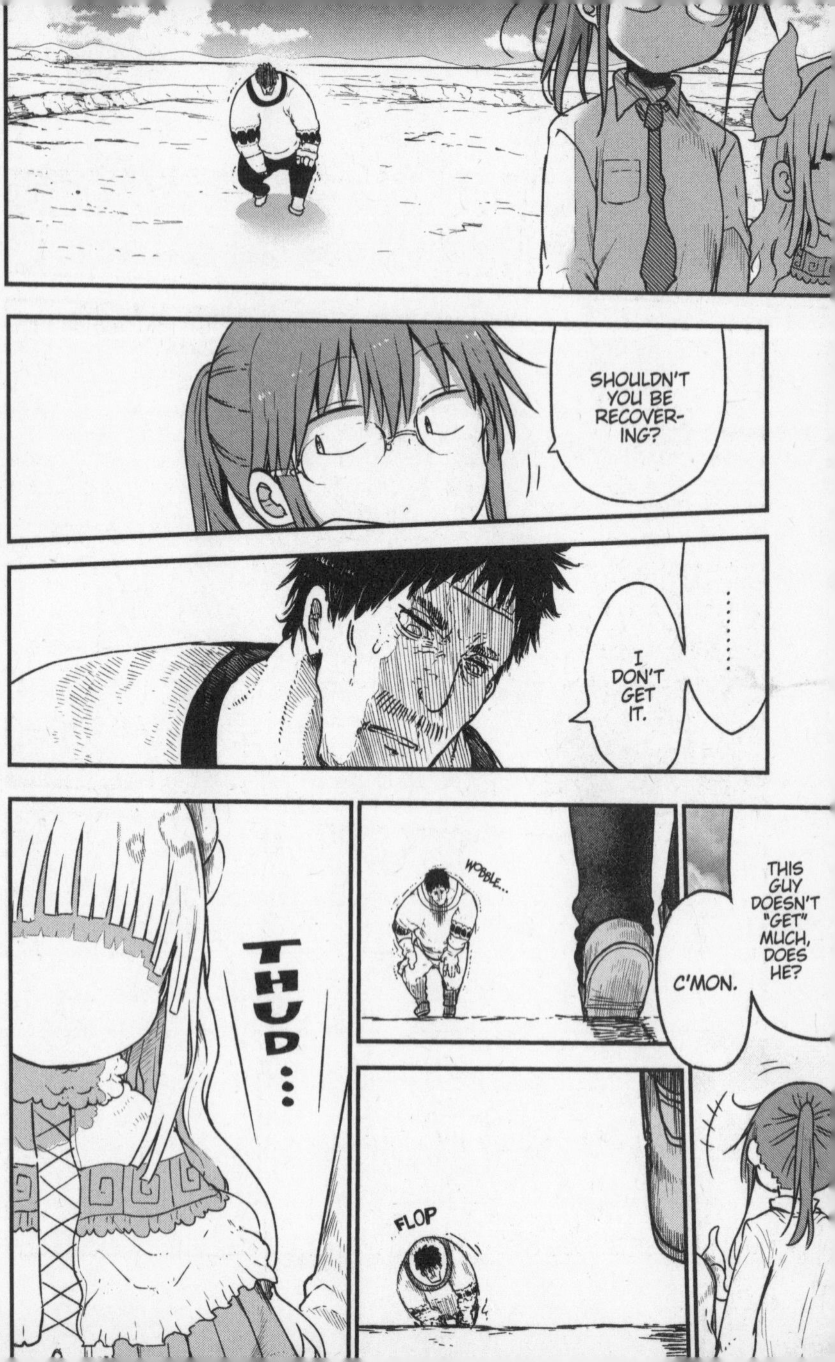
SHOULDN'T YOU BE RECOVER-ING?
......
I DON'T GET IT.
THIS GUY DOESN'T "GET" MUCH, DOES HE?
C'MON.
WOBBLE...
FLOP
THUD...

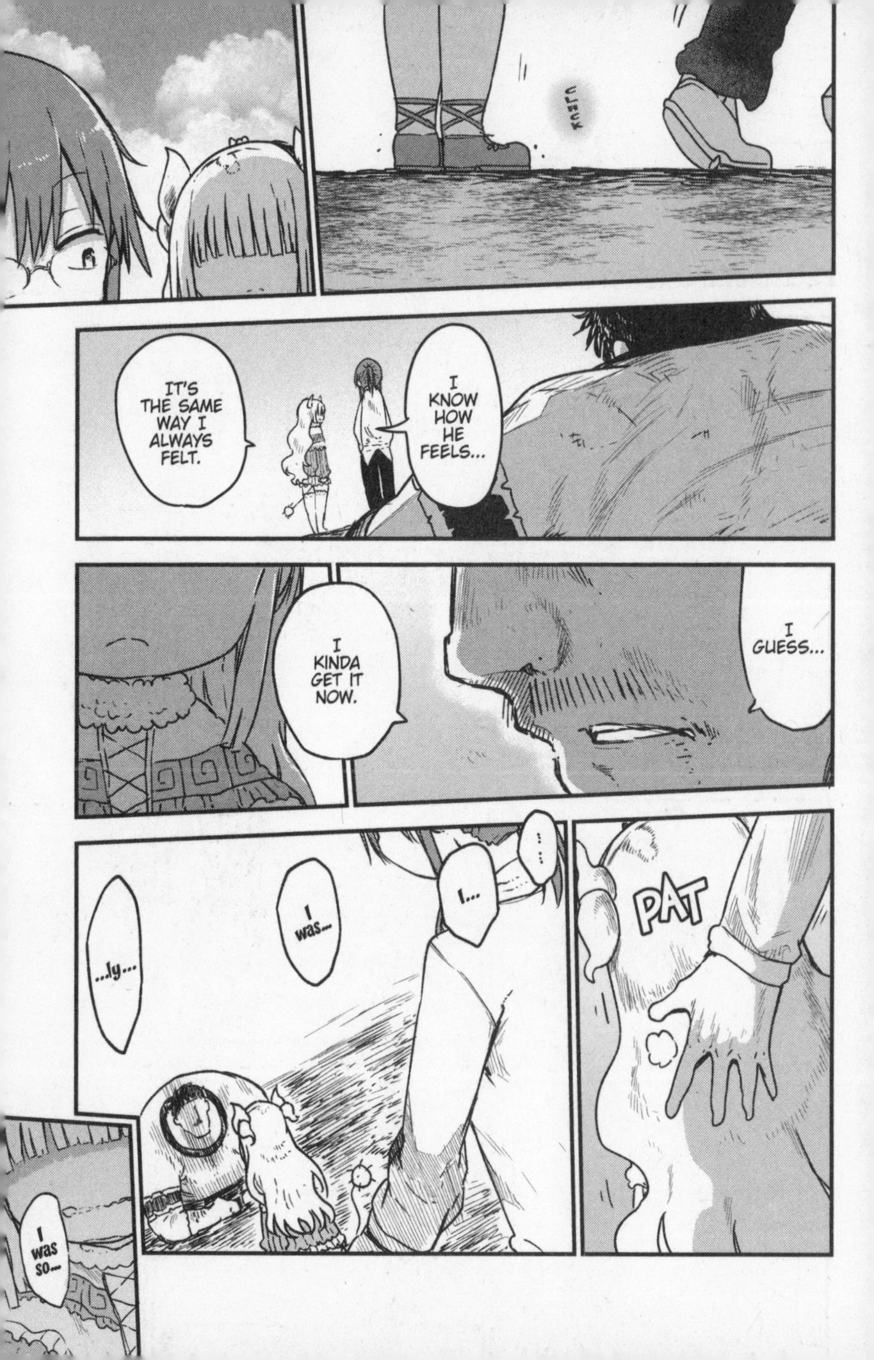
I KNOW HOW HE FEELS...
IT'S THE SAME WAY I ALWAYS FELT.
I GUESS...
I KINDA GET IT NOW.
PAT
...
I...
I was...
...ly...
I was so...

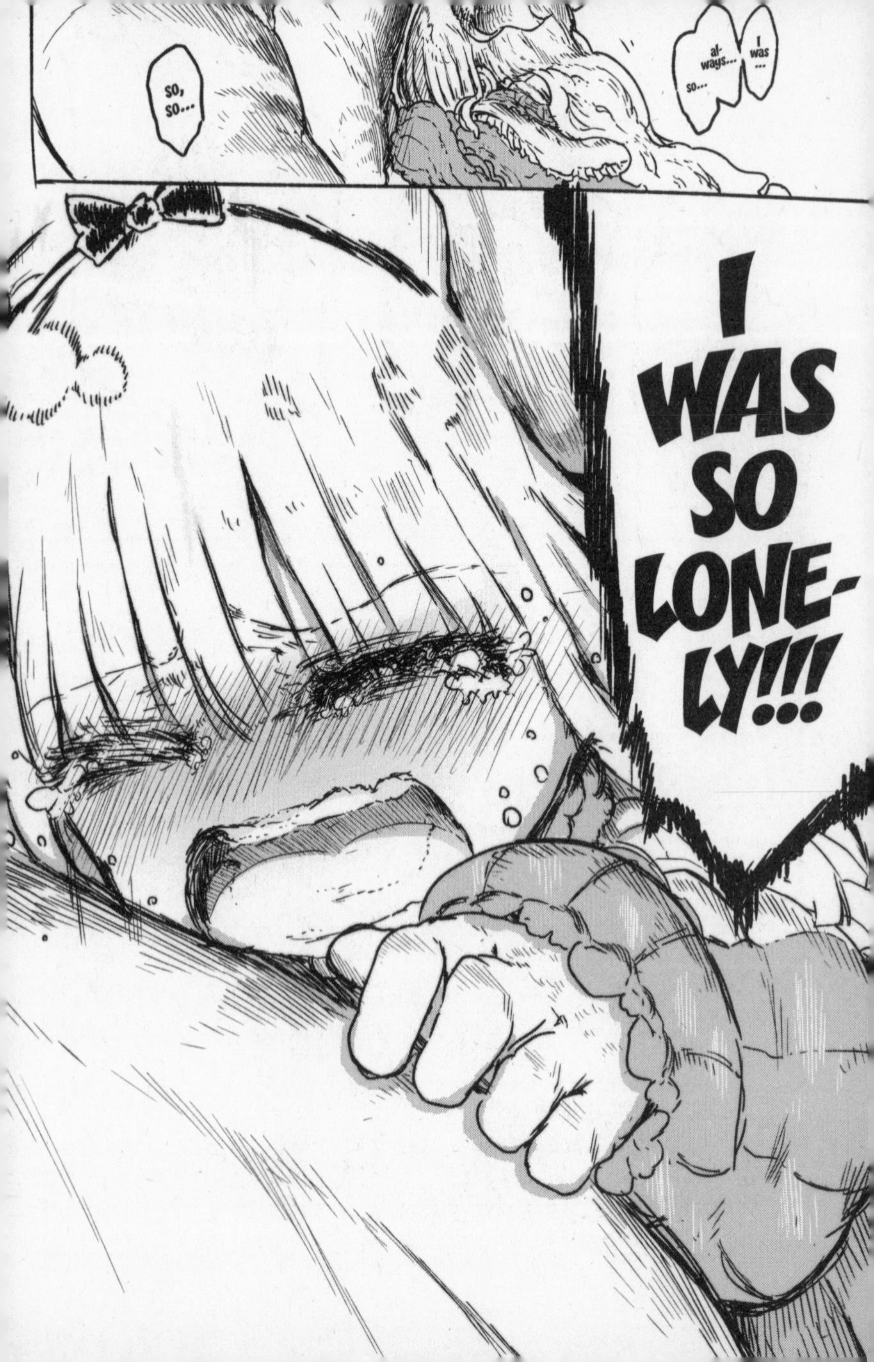
I was ...
al-ways... so...
so, so...
I WAS SO LONE-LY!!!

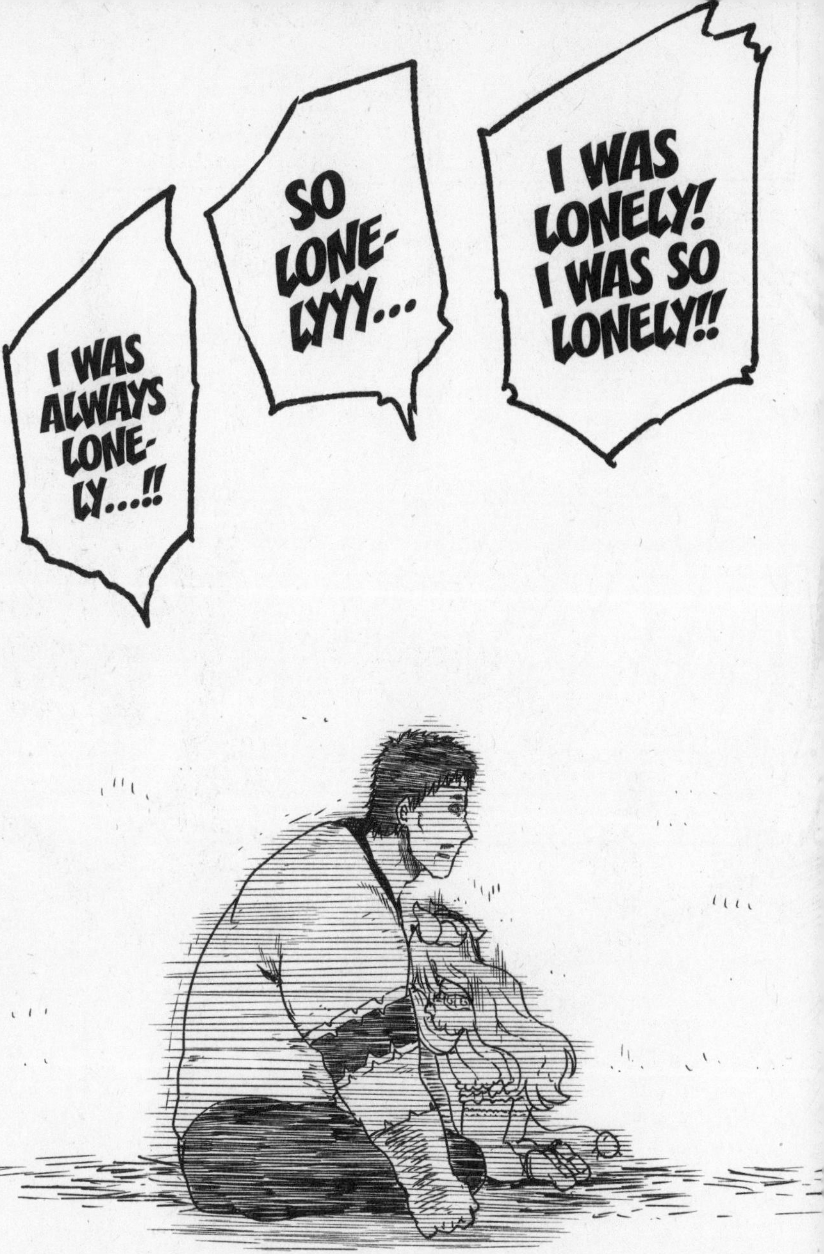
I WAS LONELY! I WAS SO LONELY!!
SO LONE-LYYY...
I WAS ALWAYS LONE-LY....!!

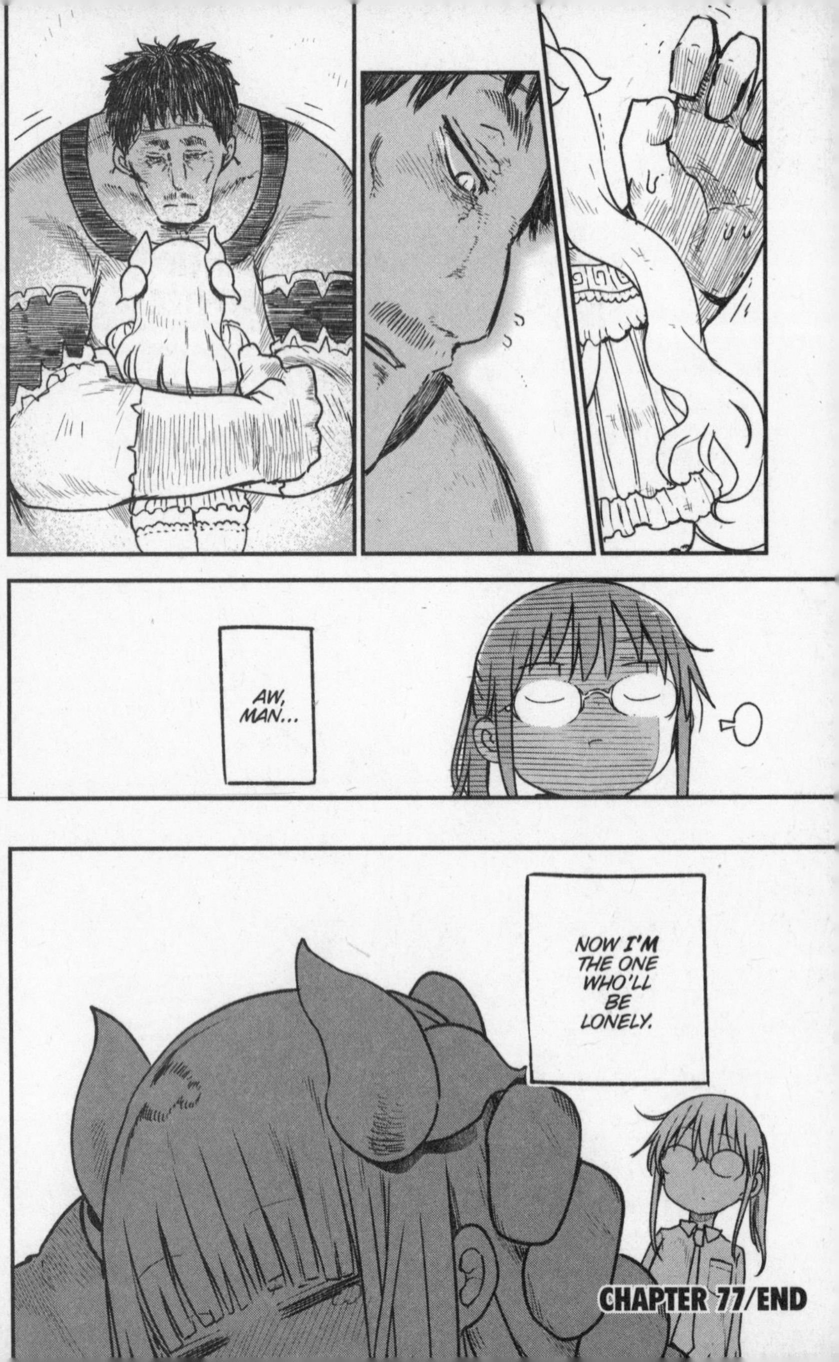
AW, MAN...
NOW I'M THE ONE WHO'LL BE LONELY.
CHAPTER 77/END

CHAPTER 78: KANNA'S FATHER AND KIMUN KAMUY'S DAUGHTER

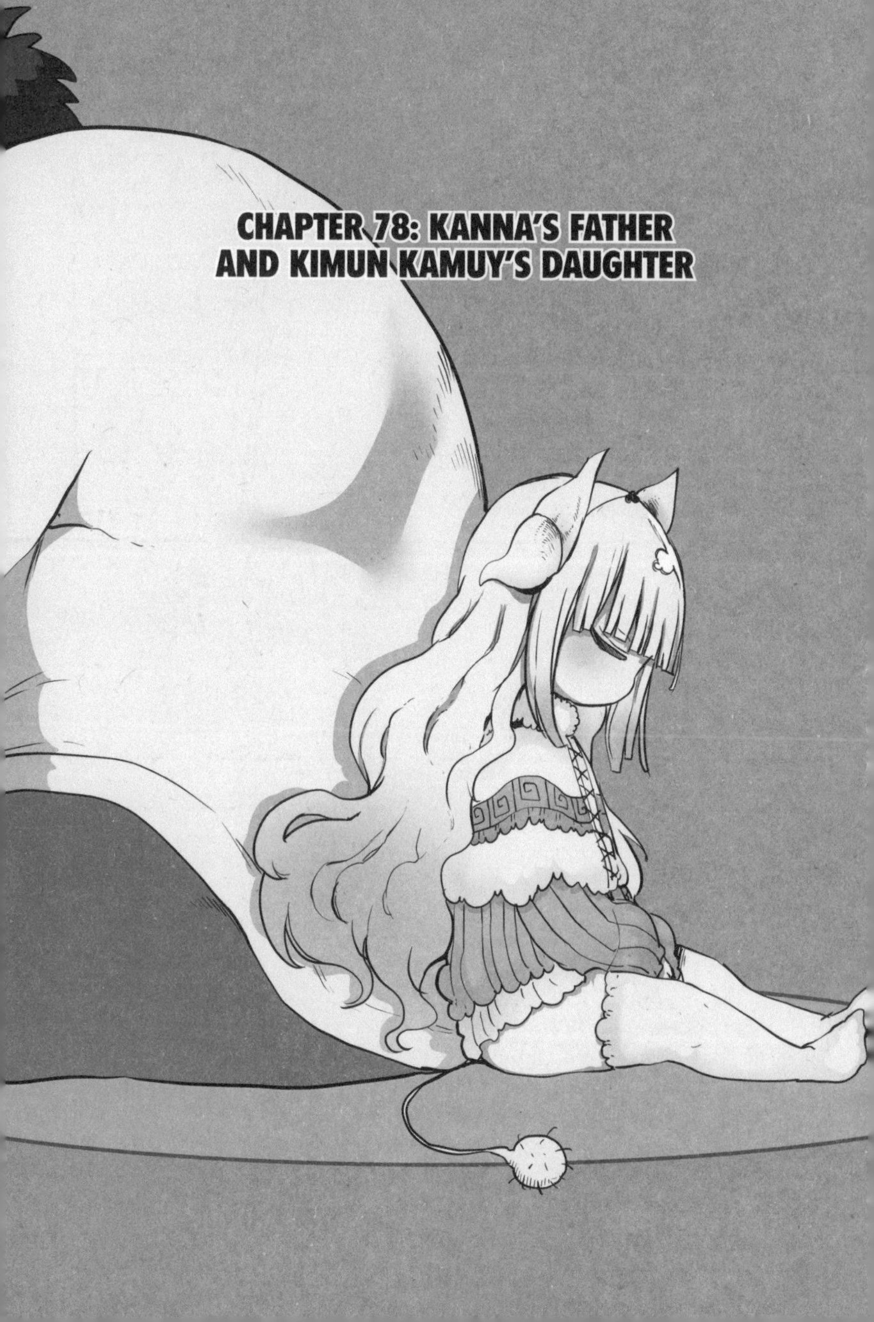

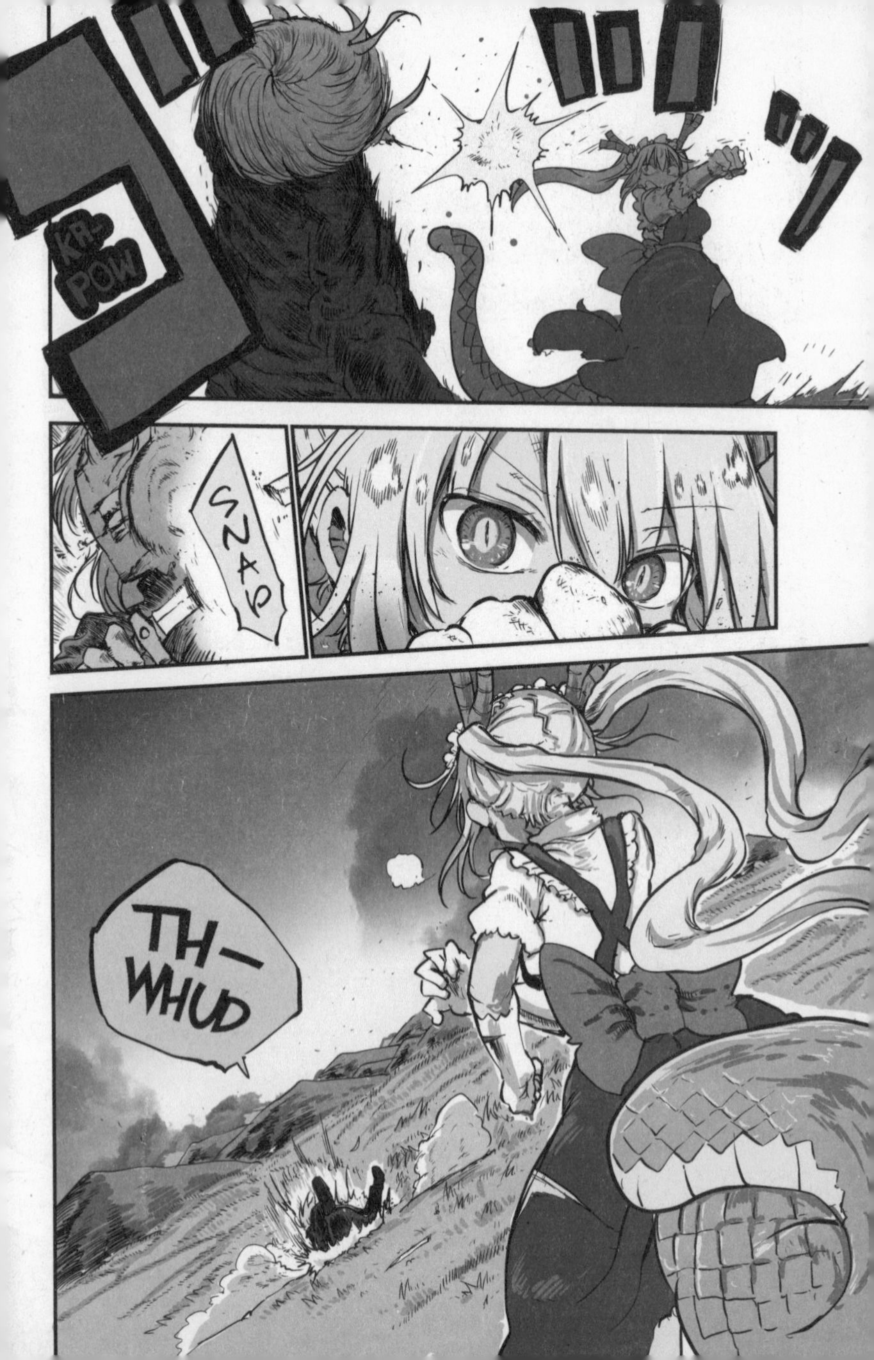
KR-POW
SNAP
TH-WHUD

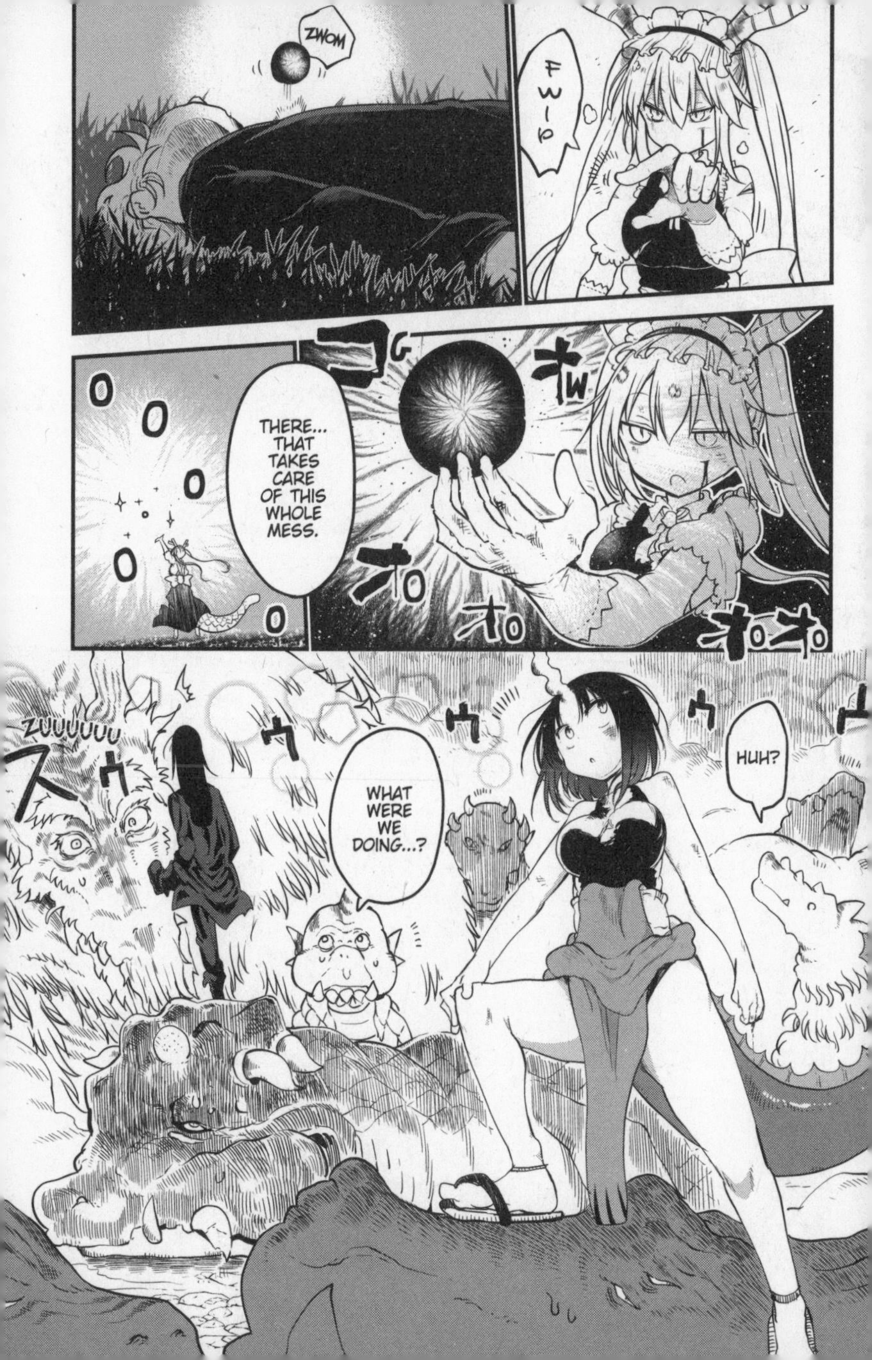
FWIP
ZWOM
THERE... THAT TAKES CARE OF THIS WHOLE MESS.
HUH?
WHAT WERE WE DOING...?
ZUUUUUU

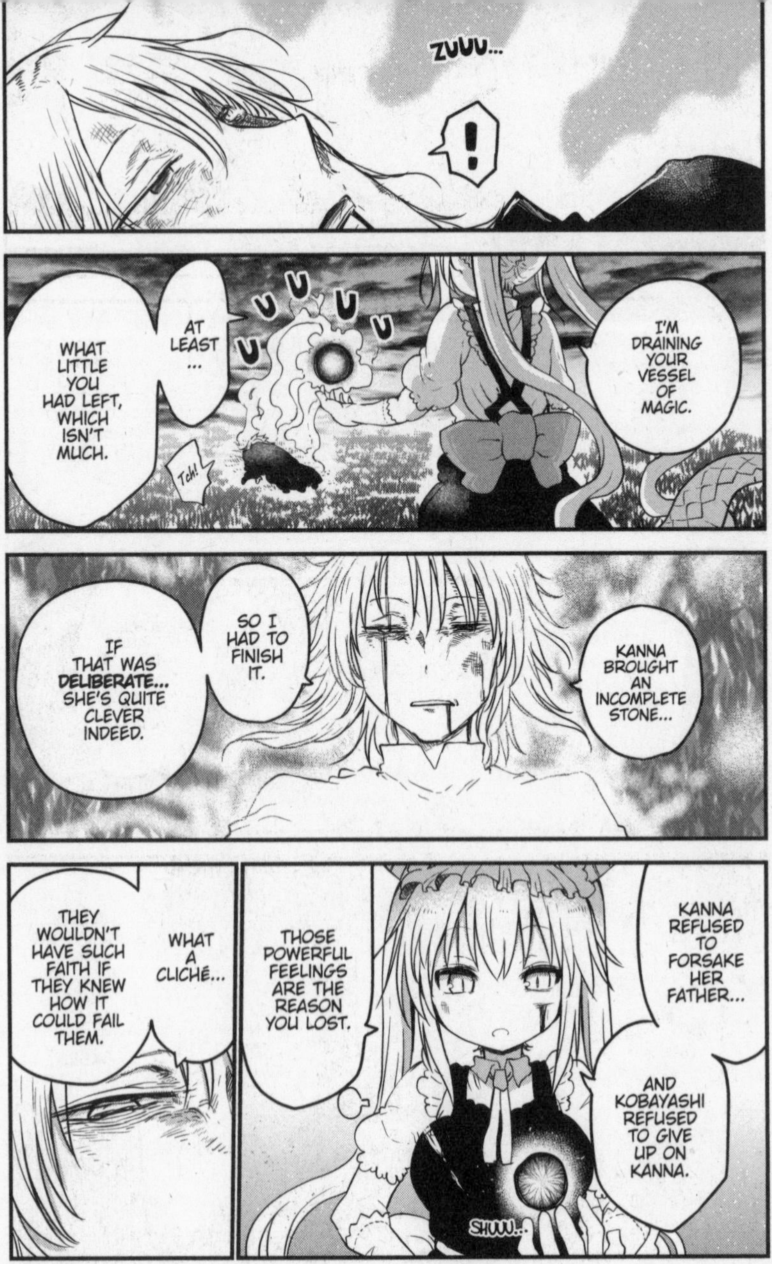
ZUUU...
!
I'M DRAINING YOUR VESSEL OF MAGIC.
UUUUUU
AT LEAST...
WHAT LITTLE YOU HAD LEFT, WHICH ISN'T MUCH.
Tch!
KANNA BROUGHT AN INCOMPLETE STONE...
SO I HAD TO FINISH IT.
IF THAT WAS DELIBERATE... SHE'S QUITE CLEVER INDEED.
KANNA REFUSED TO FORSAKE HER FATHER...
AND KOBAYASHI REFUSED TO GIVE UP ON KANNA.
THOSE POWERFUL FEELINGS ARE THE REASON YOU LOST.
SHUUU...
WHAT A CLICHÉ...
THEY WOULDN'T HAVE SUCH FAITH IF THEY KNEW HOW IT COULD FAIL THEM.

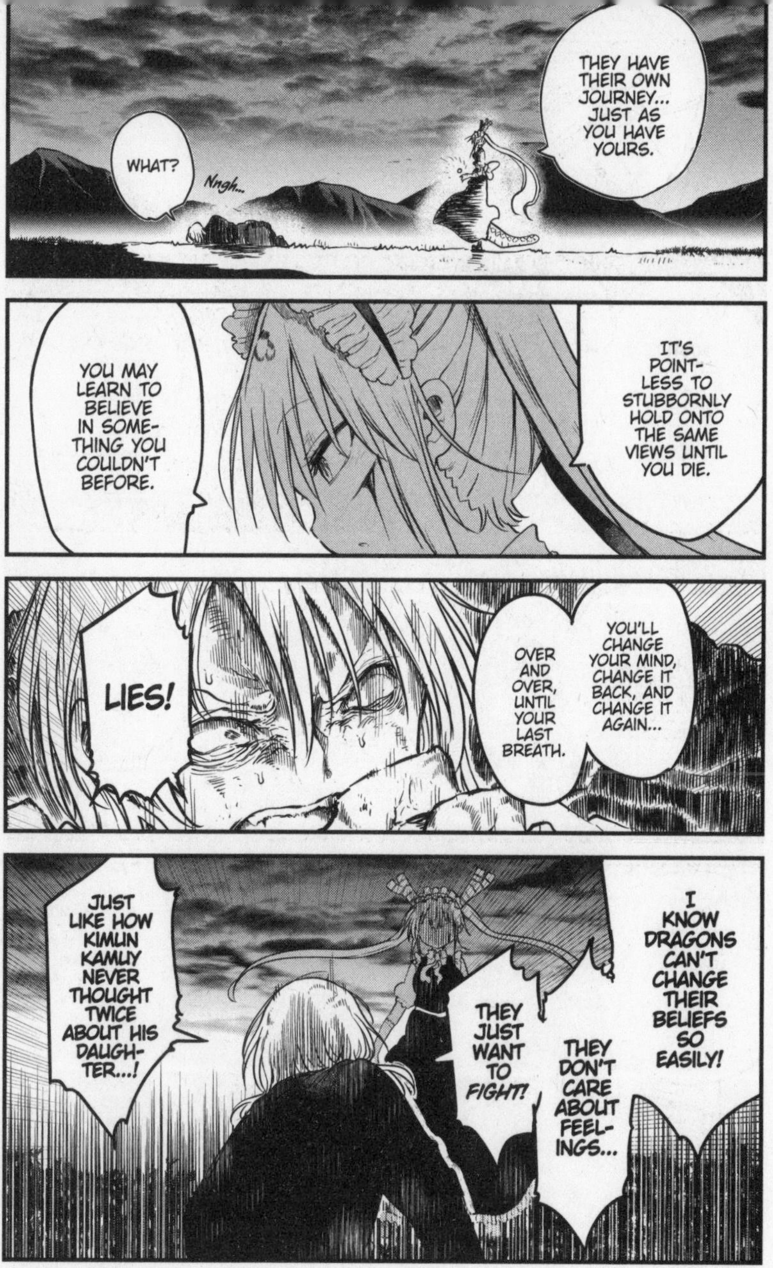
THEY HAVE THEIR OWN JOURNEY... JUST AS YOU HAVE YOURS.
Nngh...
WHAT?
IT'S POINTLESS TO STUBBORNLY HOLD ONTO THE SAME VIEWS UNTIL YOU DIE.
YOU MAY LEARN TO BELIEVE IN SOMETHING YOU COULDN'T BEFORE.
YOU'LL CHANGE YOUR MIND, CHANGE IT BACK, AND CHANGE IT AGAIN...
OVER AND OVER, UNTIL YOUR LAST BREATH.
LIES!
I KNOW DRAGONS CAN'T CHANGE THEIR BELIEFS SO EASILY!
THEY DON'T CARE ABOUT FEELINGS...
THEY JUST WANT TO *FIGHT!*
JUST LIKE HOW KIMUN KAMUY NEVER THOUGHT TWICE ABOUT HIS DAUGHTER...!

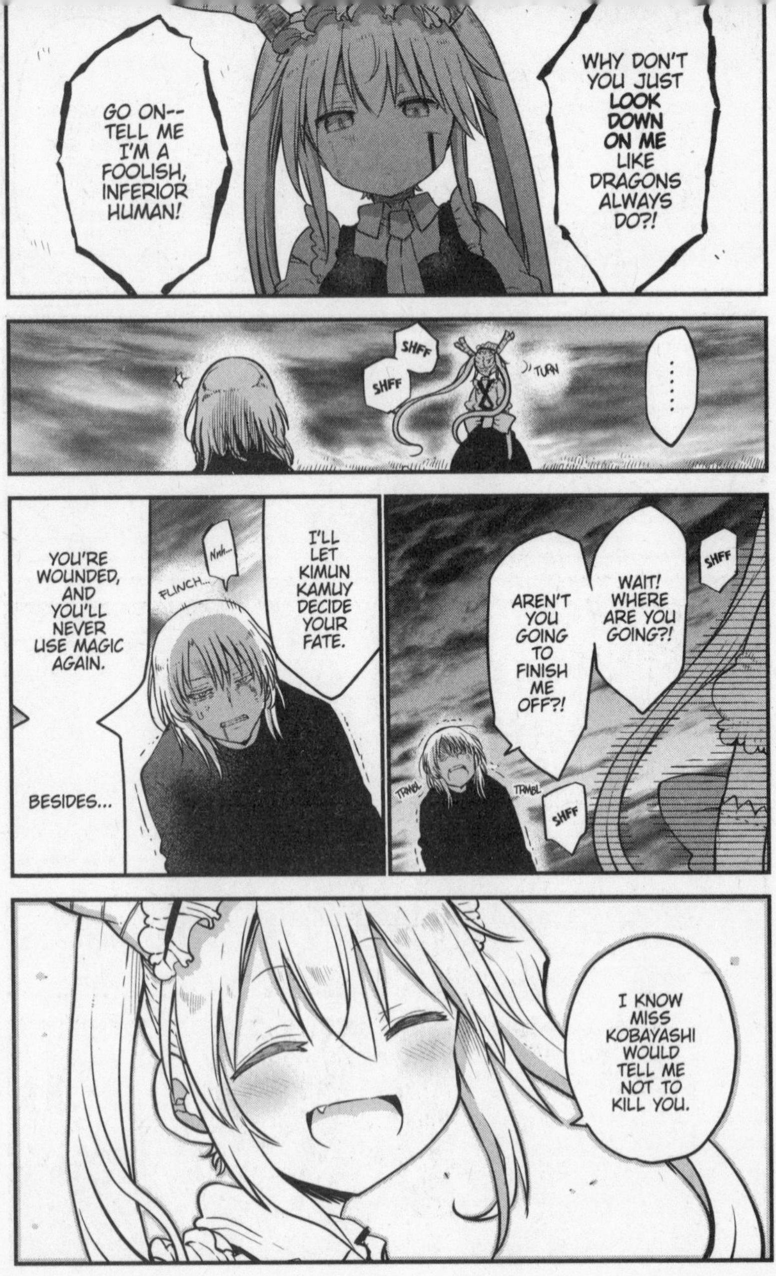
WHY DON'T YOU JUST **LOOK DOWN ON ME** LIKE DRAGONS ALWAYS DO?!
GO ON--TELL ME I'M A FOOLISH, INFERIOR HUMAN!
......
TURN
SHFF
SHFF
SHFF
WAIT! WHERE ARE YOU GOING?!
AREN'T YOU GOING TO FINISH ME OFF?!
TRMBL
TRMBL
SHFF
I'LL LET KIMUN KAMUY DECIDE YOUR FATE.
Nnh...
FLINCH...
YOU'RE WOUNDED, AND YOU'LL NEVER USE MAGIC AGAIN.
BESIDES...
I KNOW MISS KOBAYASHI WOULD TELL ME NOT TO KILL YOU.

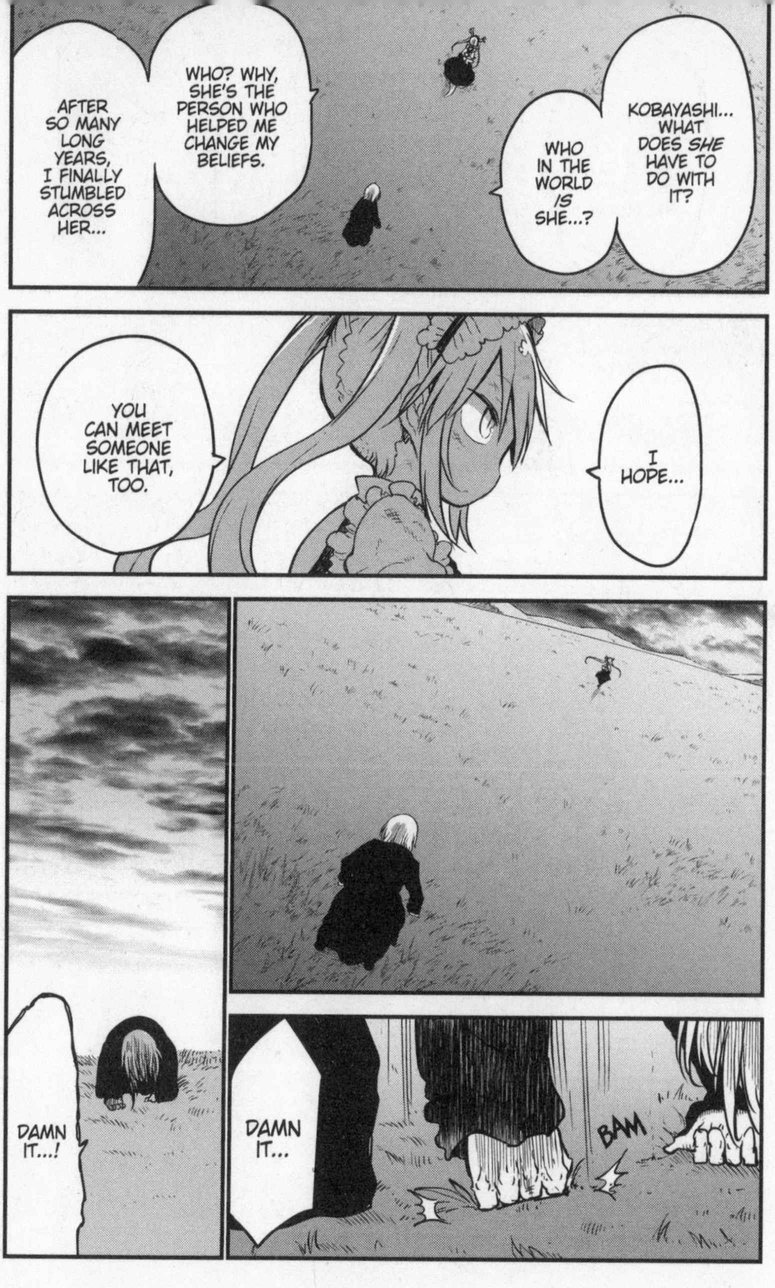
KOBAYASHI... WHAT DOES *SHE* HAVE TO DO WITH IT?
WHO IN THE WORLD *IS* SHE...?
WHO? WHY, SHE'S THE PERSON WHO HELPED ME CHANGE MY BELIEFS.
AFTER SO MANY LONG YEARS, I FINALLY STUMBLED ACROSS HER...
I HOPE...
YOU CAN MEET SOMEONE LIKE THAT, TOO.
BAM
DAMN IT...
DAMN IT...!

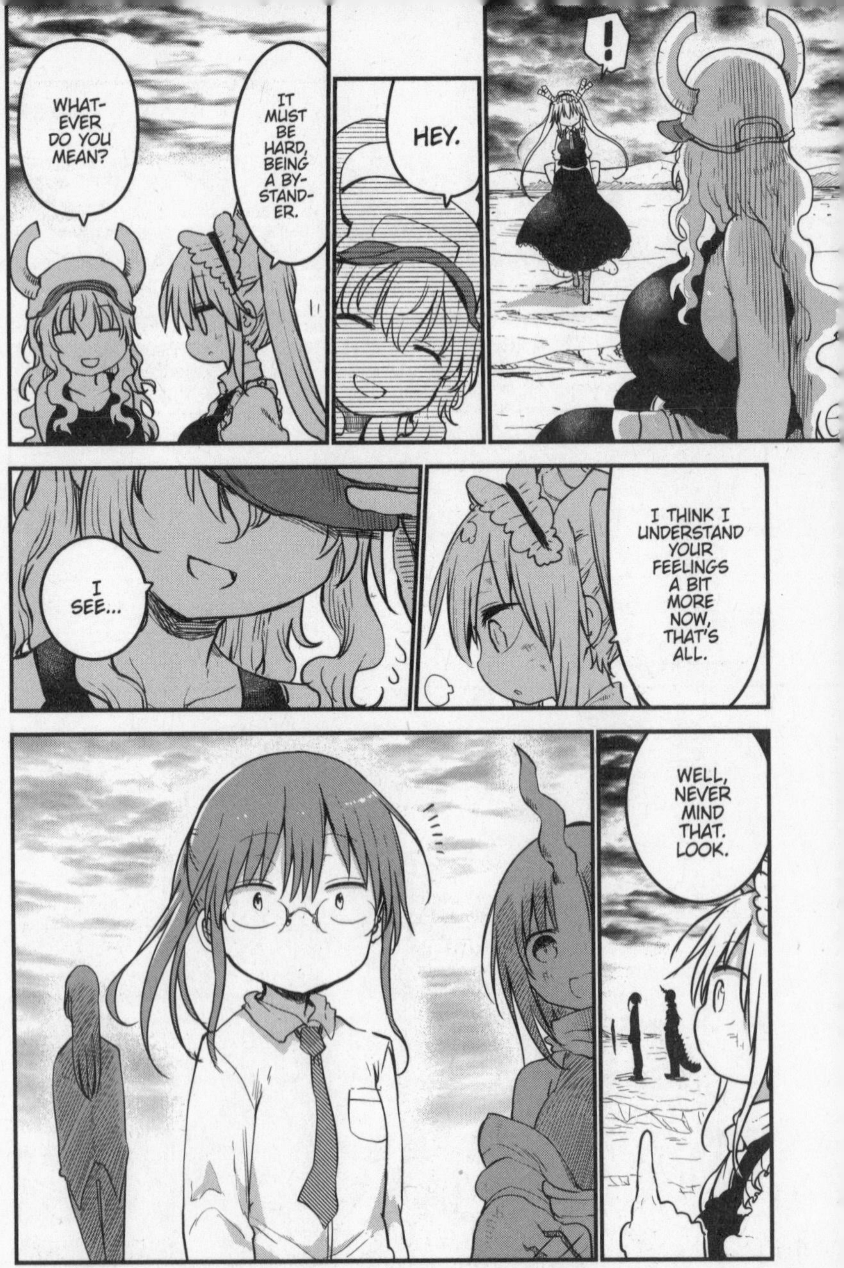
!
HEY.
IT MUST BE HARD, BEING A BY-STANDER.
WHAT-EVER DO YOU MEAN?
I THINK I UNDERSTAND YOUR FEELINGS A BIT MORE NOW, THAT'S ALL.
I SEE...
WELL, NEVER MIND THAT. LOOK.

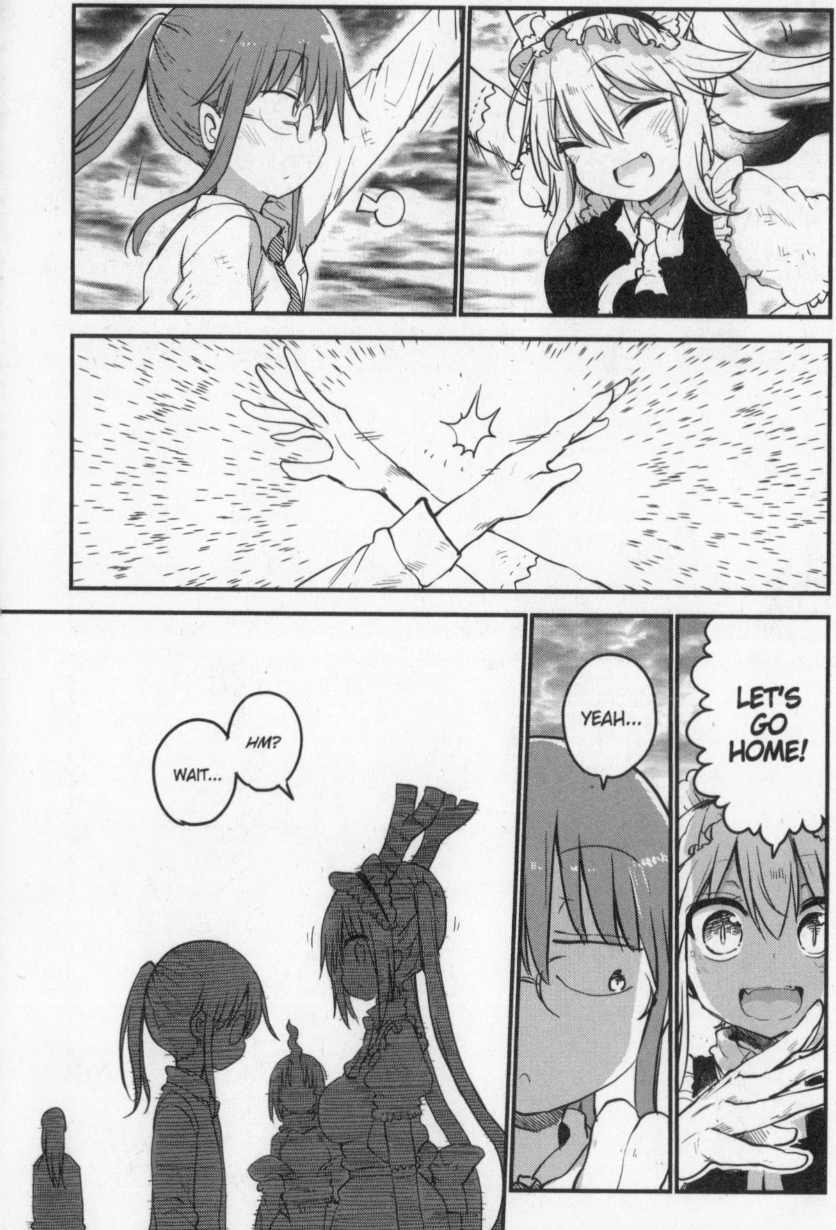
LET'S GO HOME!
YEAH...
HM?
WAIT...

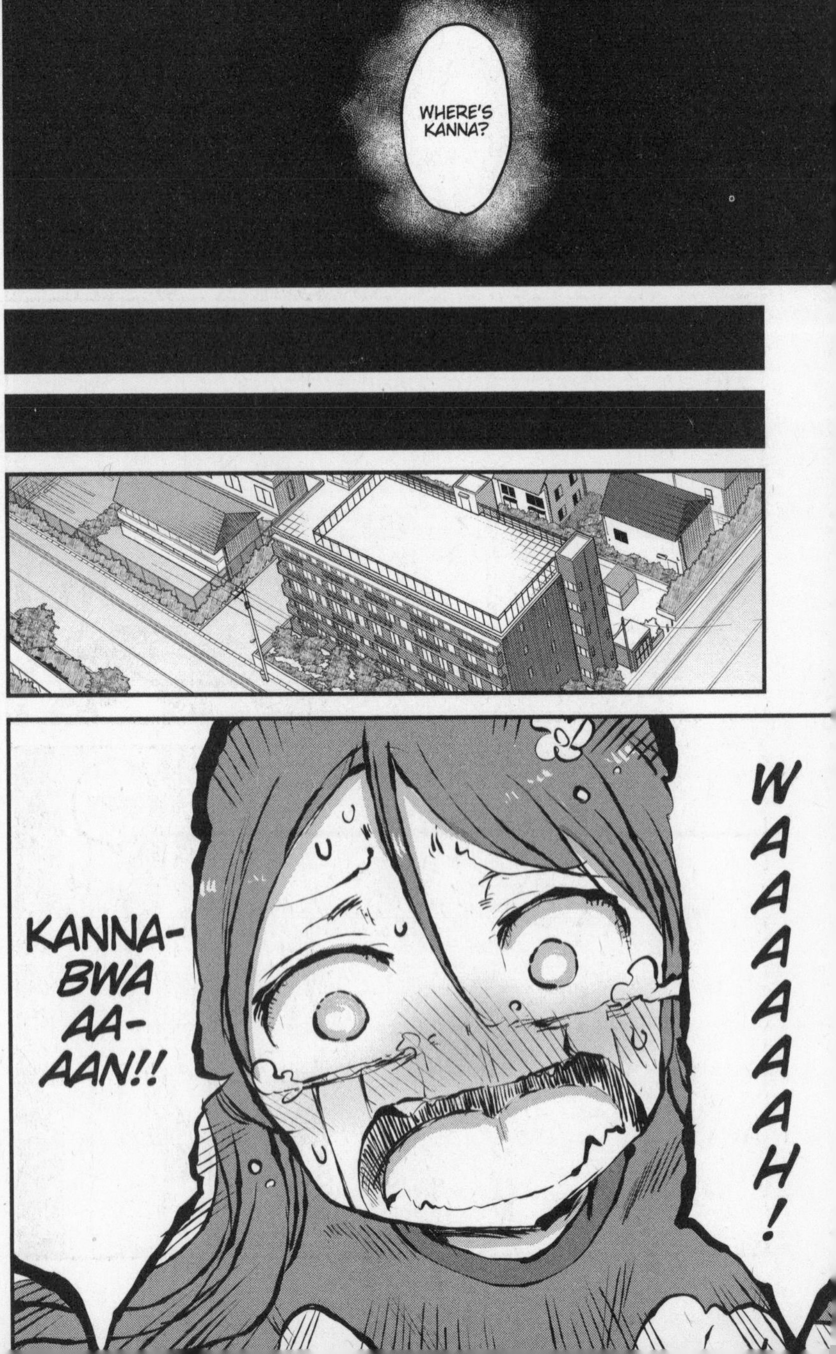
WHERE'S KANNA?
WAAAAAAAH!
KANNA-BWAAA-AAN!!

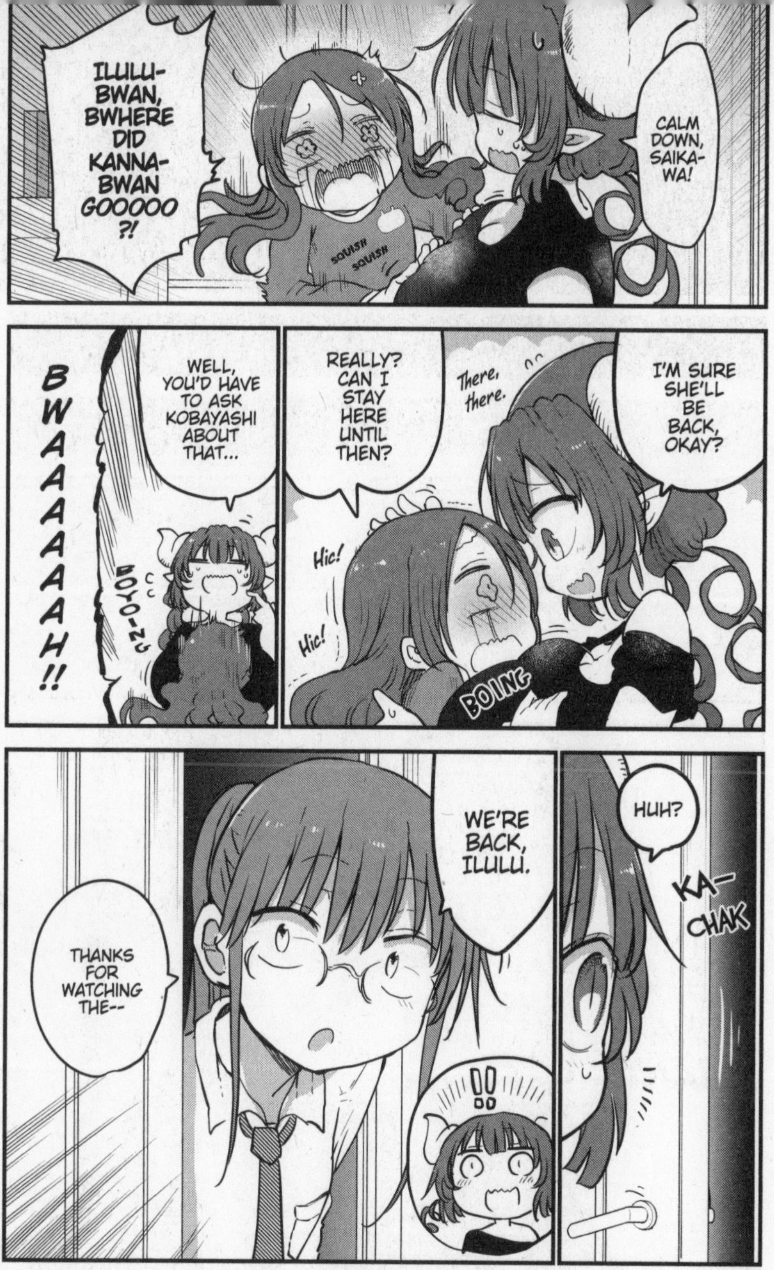
CALM DOWN, SAIKAWA!
ILULU-BWAN, BWHERE DID KANNA-BWAN GOOOOO?!
SQUISH SQUISH
I'M SURE SHE'LL BE BACK, OKAY?
There, there.
REALLY? CAN I STAY HERE UNTIL THEN?
Hic!
Hic!
BOING
WELL, YOU'D HAVE TO ASK KOBAYASHI ABOUT THAT...
BOYO-ING
BWAAAAAAAAAH!!
HUH?
KA-CHAK
WE'RE BACK, ILULU.
THANKS FOR WATCHING THE--

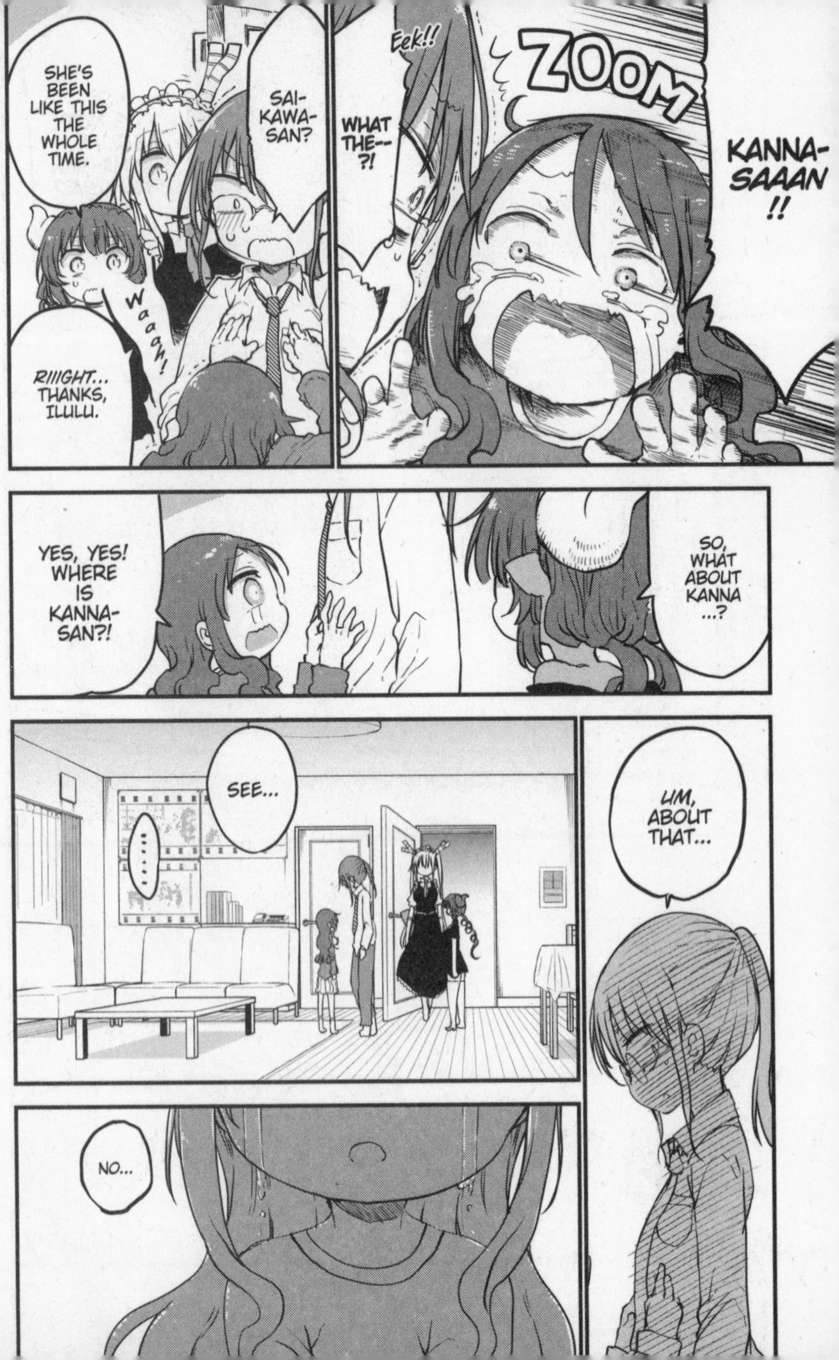
KANNA-SAAAN!!
ZOOM
Eek!!
WHAT THE--?!
SAI-KAWA-SAN?
SHE'S BEEN LIKE THIS THE WHOLE TIME.
Waaah!
RIIIGHT... THANKS, ILULU.
SO, WHAT ABOUT KANNA...?
YES, YES! WHERE IS KANNA-SAN?!
UM, ABOUT THAT...
SEE...
......
NO...

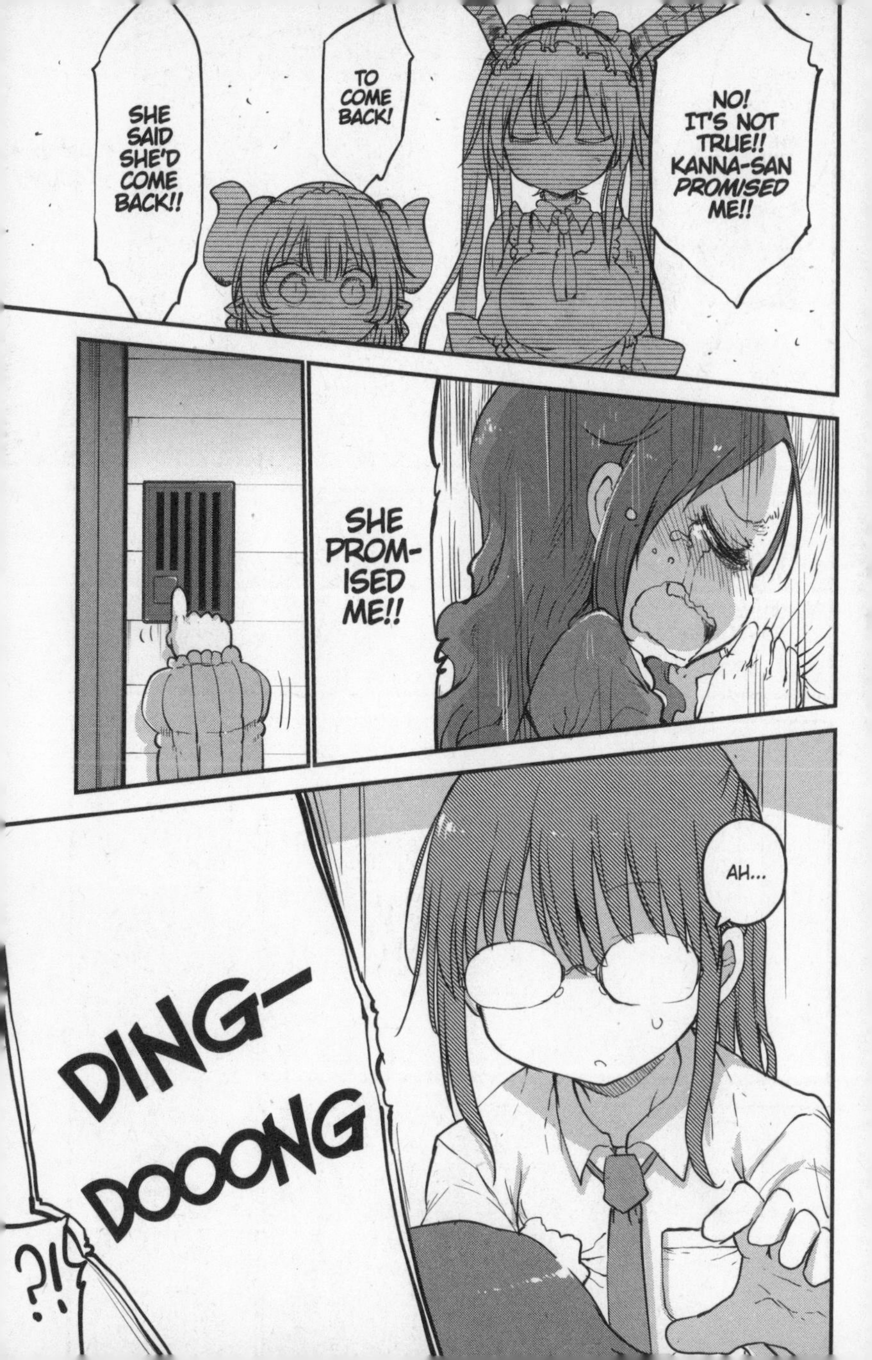
NO! IT'S NOT TRUE!! KANNA-SAN PROMISED ME!!
TO COME BACK!
SHE SAID SHE'D COME BACK!!
SHE PROM-ISED ME!!
AH...
DING-DOOOONG
?!

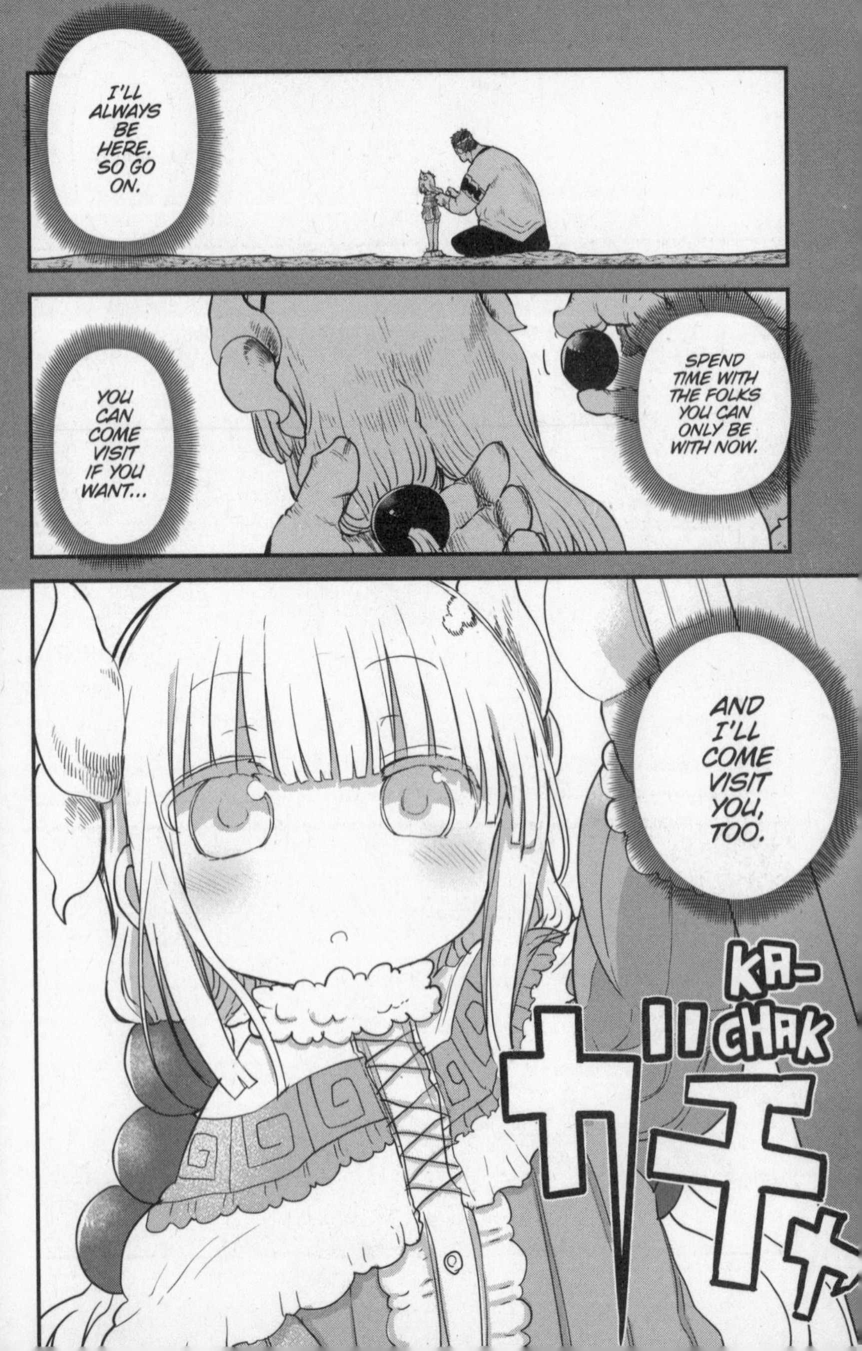
I'LL ALWAYS BE HERE. SO GO ON.
SPEND TIME WITH THE FOLKS YOU CAN ONLY BE WITH NOW.
YOU CAN COME VISIT IF YOU WANT...
AND I'LL COME VISIT YOU, TOO.
KA-CHAK

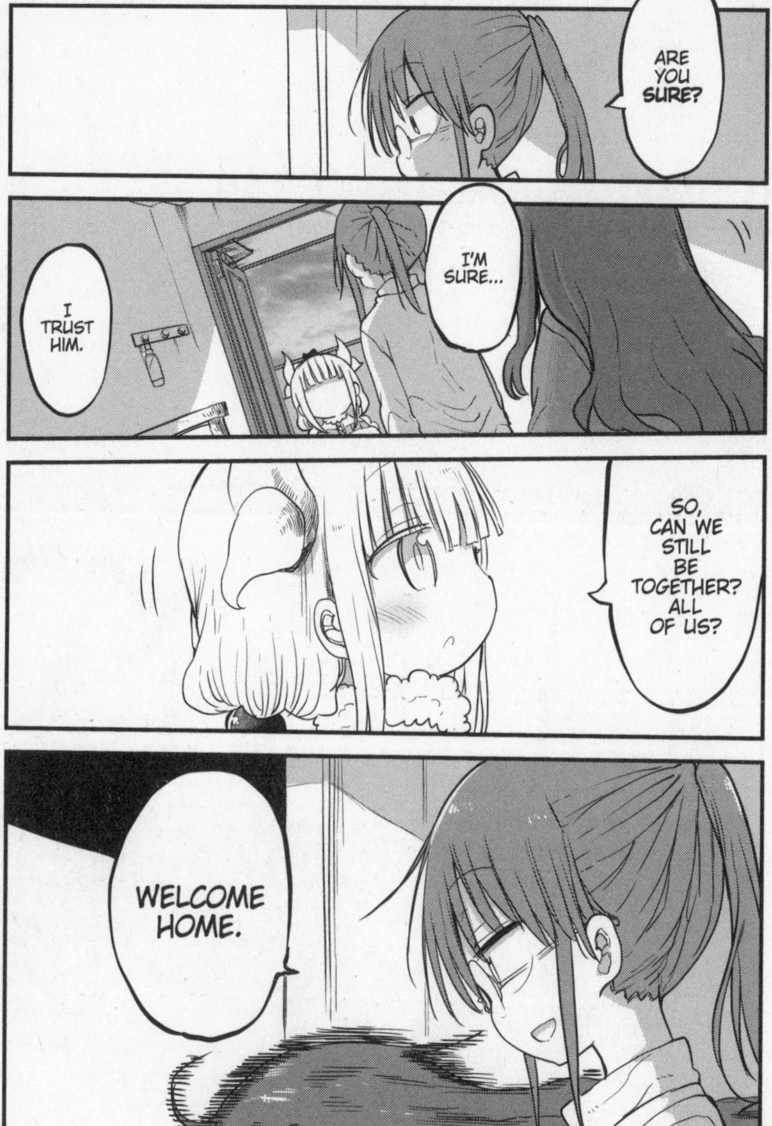
ARE YOU SURE?
I'M SURE...
I TRUST HIM.
SO, CAN WE STILL BE TOGETHER? ALL OF US?
WELCOME HOME.

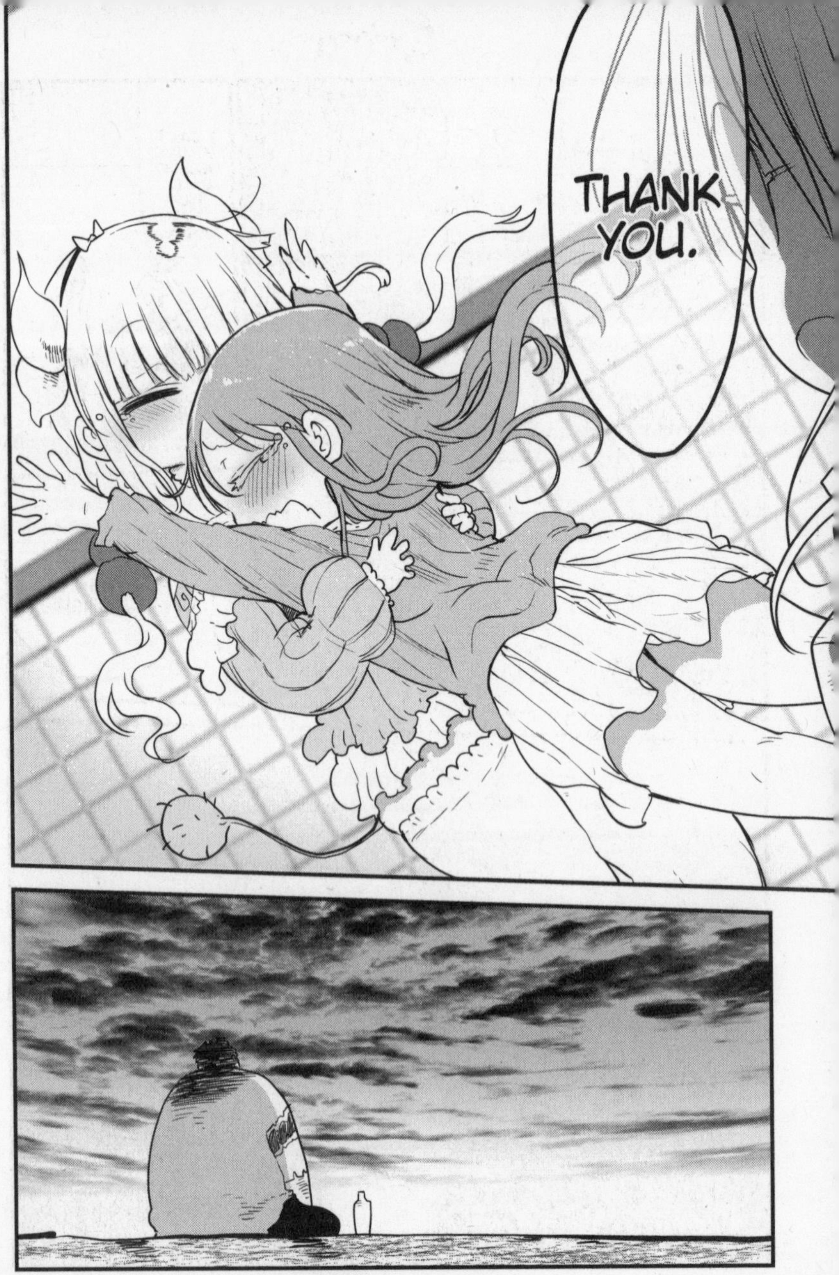
THANK YOU.

CHAPTER 78/END

Extra

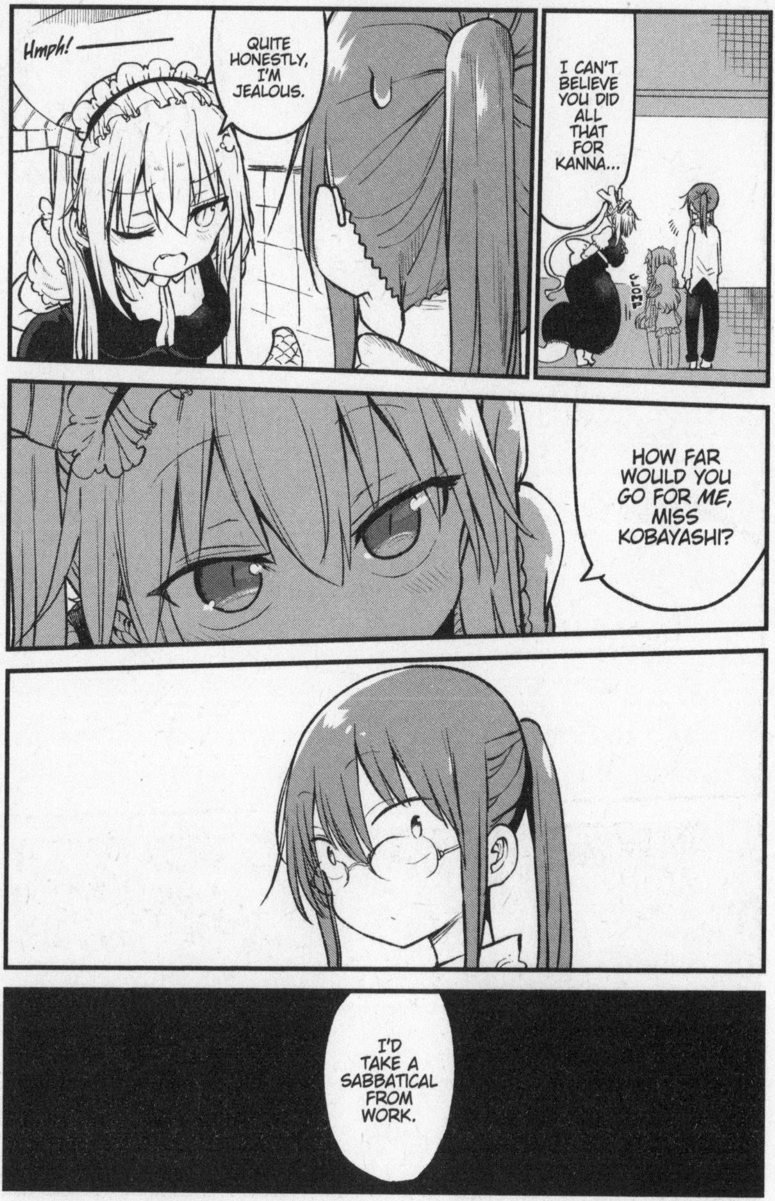
I CAN'T BELIEVE YOU DID ALL THAT FOR KANNA...
CLOMP
QUITE HONESTLY, I'M JEALOUS.
Hmph!
HOW FAR WOULD YOU GO FOR ME, MISS KOBAYASHI?
I'D TAKE A SABBATICAL FROM WORK.

Miss Kobayashi's Dragon Maid

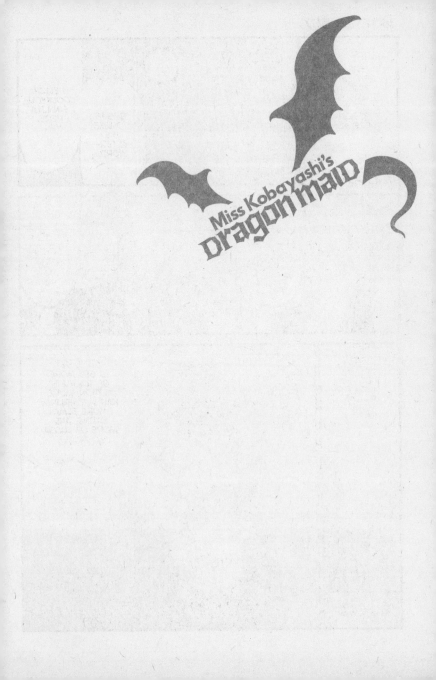

AFTERWORD

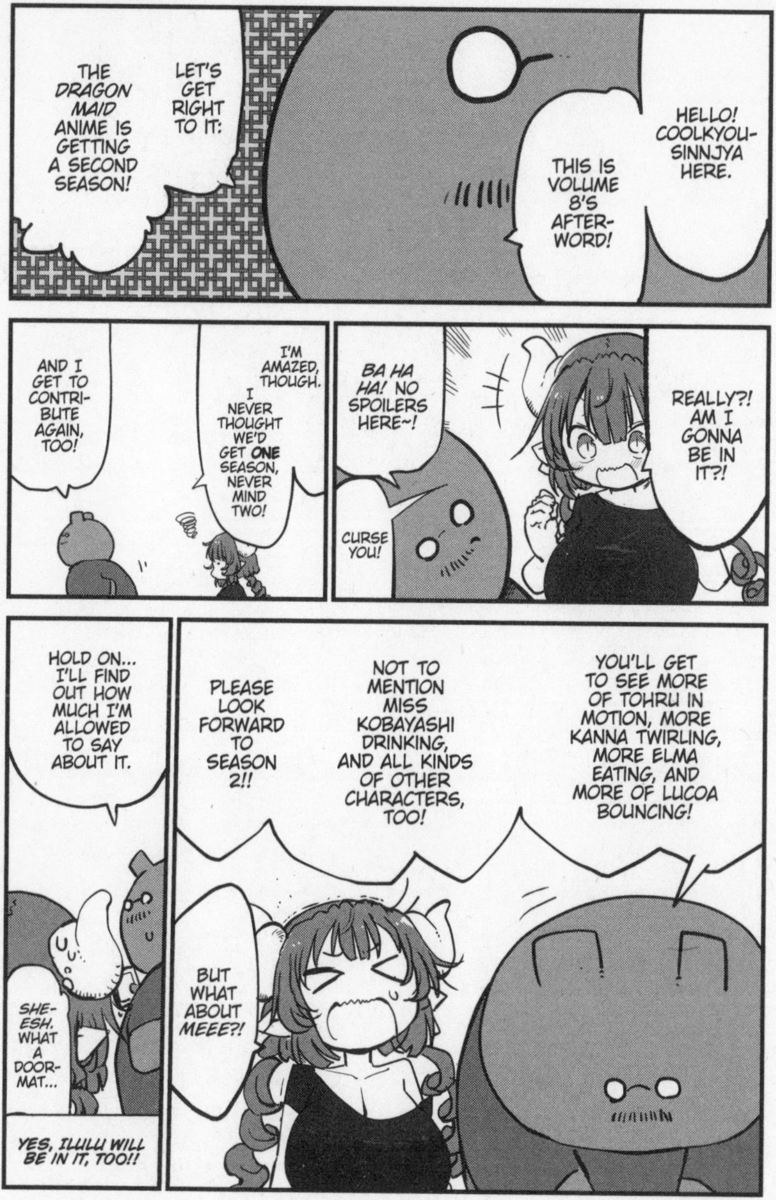
HELLO! COOLKYOU-SINNJYA HERE.
THIS IS VOLUME 8'S AFTER-WORD!
LET'S GET RIGHT TO IT:
THE DRAGON MAID ANIME IS GETTING A SECOND SEASON!
REALLY?! AM I GONNA BE IN IT?!
BA HA HA! NO SPOILERS HERE~!
CURSE YOU!
I'M AMAZED, THOUGH.
I NEVER THOUGHT WE'D GET ONE SEASON, NEVER MIND TWO!
AND I GET TO CONTRIBUTE AGAIN, TOO!
YOU'LL GET TO SEE MORE OF TOHRU IN MOTION, MORE KANNA TWIRLING, MORE ELMA EATING, AND MORE OF LUCOA BOUNCING!
NOT TO MENTION MISS KOBAYASHI DRINKING, AND ALL KINDS OF OTHER CHARACTERS, TOO!
PLEASE LOOK FORWARD TO SEASON 2!!
BUT WHAT ABOUT MEEE?!
HOLD ON... I'LL FIND OUT HOW MUCH I'M ALLOWED TO SAY ABOUT IT.
SHEESH. WHAT A DOORMAT...
YES, ILULU WILL BE IN IT, TOO!!

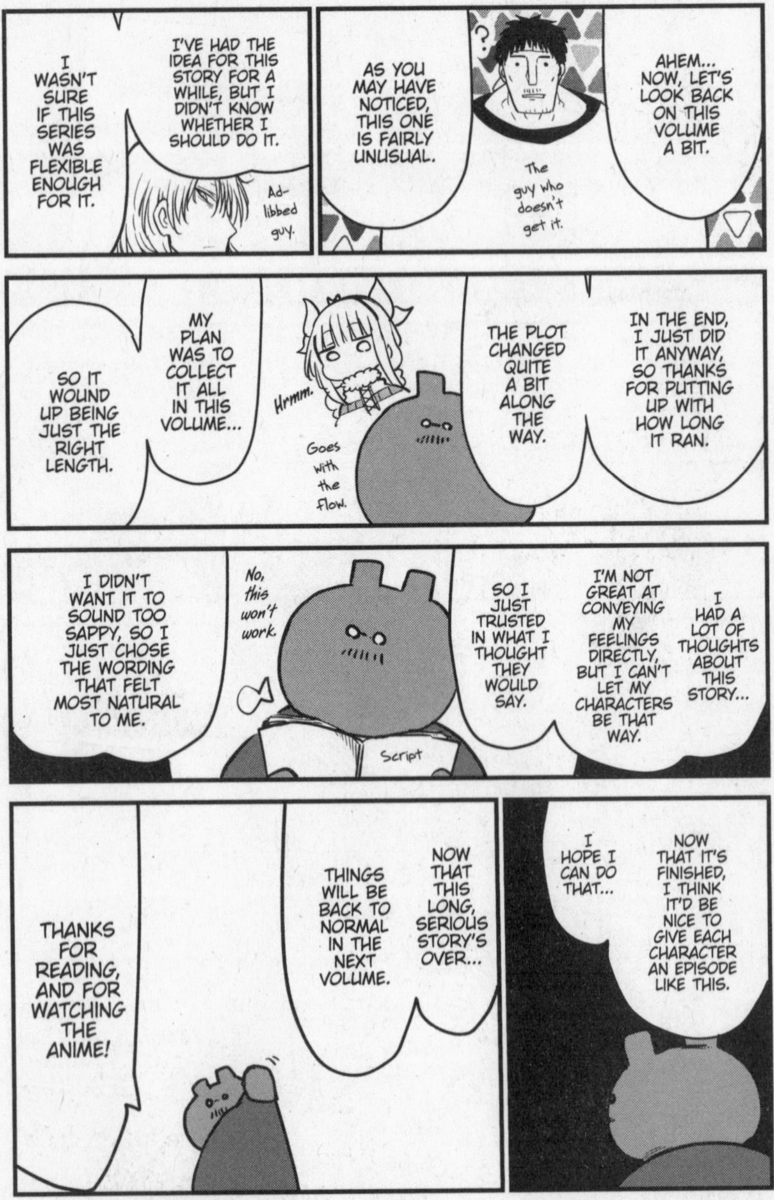
AHEM... NOW, LET'S LOOK BACK ON THIS VOLUME A BIT.
AS YOU MAY HAVE NOTICED, THIS ONE IS FAIRLY UNUSUAL.
The guy who doesn't get it.
I'VE HAD THE IDEA FOR THIS STORY FOR A WHILE, BUT I DIDN'T KNOW WHETHER I SHOULD DO IT.
I WASN'T SURE IF THIS SERIES WAS FLEXIBLE ENOUGH FOR IT.
Ad-libbed guy.
IN THE END, I JUST DID IT ANYWAY, SO THANKS FOR PUTTING UP WITH HOW LONG IT RAN.
THE PLOT CHANGED QUITE A BIT ALONG THE WAY.
MY PLAN WAS TO COLLECT IT ALL IN THIS VOLUME...
Hrmm.
Goes with the flow.
SO IT WOUND UP BEING JUST THE RIGHT LENGTH.
I HAD A LOT OF THOUGHTS ABOUT THIS STORY...
I'M NOT GREAT AT CONVEYING MY FEELINGS DIRECTLY, BUT I CAN'T LET MY CHARACTERS BE THAT WAY.
SO I JUST TRUSTED IN WHAT I THOUGHT THEY WOULD SAY.
Script
No, this won't work.
I DIDN'T WANT IT TO SOUND TOO SAPPY, SO I JUST CHOSE THE WORDING THAT FELT MOST NATURAL TO ME.
NOW THAT IT'S FINISHED, I THINK IT'D BE NICE TO GIVE EACH CHARACTER AN EPISODE LIKE THIS.
I HOPE I CAN DO THAT...
NOW THAT THIS LONG, SERIOUS STORY'S OVER...
THINGS WILL BE BACK TO NORMAL IN THE NEXT VOLUME.
THANKS FOR READING, AND FOR WATCHING THE ANIME!

Assistants: "Ogasu-sama" "Giovanni Works-sama"